Dark History, Bright Future
Anthem of Evolution

Thurston's Thoughts

Thurston K. Atlas
Creating a Buzz

Creating a Buzz Developement and
Distribution, LLC

Further Extent Productions, LLC

Dark History, Bright Future
Anthem of Evolution

Thurston's Thoughts

ISBN 979-8-9884-8601-5
First printing 2023.

Publishing

www.whenplaytimeisover.com

Dark History, Bright Future
Anthem of Evolution

Thurston's Thoughts

This book is dedicated to:

My ancestors and loved ones who prepared the way before me and shaped my earthly and spiritual being. I acknowledge and appreciate their sacrifices yielding the balance of their time and wisdom that forged mine. Special thanks to G.L.P., the mighty oak and beacon, and C.A.S., the oracle whisper and healer, for their diligence and patience when almost all others had forsaken me.

Special thanks to B.D.H., the pathfinder, who has never left my side. Her fortitude and love transcend time and space, propelling me forward for her glory and lighting my path. Also hopes and aspirations for the future of Jayden "Green Acres" Swader and La'kayla Rose to evolve into Phoenixes rising exploring the stratosphere of their dreams and potential.

Preface

Dark History, Bright Future
Anthem of Evolution

Thurston's Thoughts

Thurston K. Atlas started a blog entitled "When Playtime is Over" to express his point of view on relevant topics and present an alternative voice. Thurston K. Atlas's diverse life experiences and challenges provide a basis for his perspective he felt compelled to express. The author hopes that the perspectives and ideologies offered are used for motivation, contemplation, and progression. Thurston K. Atlas' primary objective is to generate introspective thought, facilitate candid conversation, and arouse free-thinking perspectives.

This book is presented in a series of observations and commentary of perspectives intended to editorialize and illustrate the surface ramifications of underlying racial principles and ideologies. It further explores and challenges some long-accepted fundamental socializations and the consequences of adhering to these thoughts, beliefs, and behaviors. The goal is conveying a deeper understanding. Part A is the conventional or historical perspective, while Part B is a companion article offering a more specific interpretation applying causation and intent, hopefully leading to awareness and solutions.

The articles in Part A illustrate factual experiences, while Part B stirs the sediment of its implementation and impact. The psychological and sociological dynamics causing and promoting racial discrimination also produce many other biases affecting various socially marginalized subgroups targeted by discriminatory treatment. These dynamics transcend racism and geography, but many of the solutions are similar since many of the root causes are comparable.

The primary goal is for you to include these ideas and considerations in your family and subgroup discussions, making the exchange a philosophical family affair. Finally, part C is a series of questions intended to encourage conversation to preemptively ad-

Preface

dress issues clarifying possible actions, responses, and perspectives applied to real-world situations. Whatever your perspective, it should be factually and logically defensible but certainly withstand debate.

The discussion within the Black family is crucial as a rite of passage, survival, and recognition to avoid the distractions and traps that deplete our aspirations and progression. We must place the narrative in our hands, emancipated from the residue of slavery and focused on future prosperity. It is only a generation away if the proper approaches are applied. Applying enhanced knowledge, altered perception, and practical actions for those sufficiently determined and disciplined are the treasures that will summon fortune, astutely changing the Black condition.

The advantages of aggressive pursuit are undeniable, while the complacency of the past is inadequate. The absence of change prolongs assured damages, while the sluggishness of progress stalls optimism and is insufficient to execute solutions. We are all familiar with the old methods the same old results. Time to change the channel to visually, emotionally, and intellectually recalibrate our psychology, sociology, and methodology.

Hopefully, we will reconsider what we validate and from what we seek validation. We must visualize our objectives directing our actions toward achieving them. So, welcome to when playtime is over, where our goal is to stimulate thought and conversation, not to convert your perspective. Any persuasion is solely at your discretion and deliberation. So, let the discussions and transformations begin.

Table of Content

Dark History, Bright Future
Anthem of Evolution

Thurston's Thoughts

Introduction to Thurston's Thoughts

Every so often, there is a seismic shift in circumstances brought about by a demand for change. Those who benefit most from change position themselves to capitalize upon that change. They then endeavor to maintain their advantage to sustain their benefit. But, the same is even more true for those adhering to the existing circumstances anticipating changes unfavorable to their concerns. It is the short-sighted cycle of selfish accumulation and consolidation without considering long-term implications or progress.

In an ironic twist, this hedonistic short-sightedness, selfish exploitation, and immediate gratification usually initiate the resulting demand for change. Figuratively milking the cow dry. The cycle feeds upon itself, continuing to circulate cleverly disguised with different variances of the same dynamic and sequence of results benefiting the usual suspects. Therefore, we must change the operational dynamics to alter the cycle and change the outcome.

The current process is constructed whereby there is no scenario where we, as Black people, collectively win. The odds are partly because our effort to shape the dynamic lacks definition and unity while facing staunch opposition. Speaking to power is vastly different from having authority. Speaking to power is more or less a formal complaint, while authority only exists to the extent it is recognized or exercised.

The objective is well defined in these terms on what shapes the narrative or dynamic. It is having power and speaking with authority. We need our power recognized to configure methods asserting authority to regulate our desired outcome. Primarily, the plight of our race is what is understood must not only be spoken but, to a more significant degree, demonstrated. The demonstration is not in organized protest or rioting but psychology and sociology. Let us systematically break down our constraints with brutal honesty, good, bad, or indifferent.

We must navigate a progressive path to acknowledge our power despite the history of slavery and any arising inferiority insinuations. The historical narrative has predominately focused on the dredges of slavery while ignoring or embezzling Black people's achievements and contributions before, during, and after slavery. That narrative propagates inferiority to fill the void created by deception furthering the ignorance of white superiority and their insistence on Black subservience.

We should take an analytical approach to detect, identify, isolate, infiltrate, and dismantle our challenges regarding racism. So before any other considerations, it must first be determined what is the objective. Next, what are the strengths and vulnerabilities of the challenge? Then, how can the challenge be divided and overcome? Followed by what portion of the challenge must be prioritized and focused upon for maximum or strategic neutralization? Then finally, what will be installed in its place, and how will it be implemented to further achieve our objective?

The process will then come full circle, returning to the initial intent and evaluating it from its beginning to the acquisition of our objective. The subsequent actions are the steps needed to create any power-wielding authority or influence quantified by practical results. So, the starting point is to build power they cannot ignore. The goal in building it is a strong horizontal foundation. That is the strategic phase, but there is also the practical logistics of having the unity, personnel, and preparedness to accomplish the task.

Any movement starts in silence and thought, building a presence where the efforts cannot be snuffed out in its development or execution. Consequently, preparation creates resistance to collapse, countering an anticipated condition or a predictable response based on contingency and method of implementation. A lesser power can withstand a more significant power when properly positioned to diminish the options and possibilities of opposition. Any concepts deployed must be applied using psychology and translated into sociological, political, and economic strategies.

Force and confrontation are not a part of the equation unless required, in which event self-defense is not unreasonable. Unnecessary confrontation should be discouraged and avoided because of the net loss of being drawn into an engagement of little benefit. However, persuasion and representation are the weapons of choice. Either way requires being about it, not just asking or hoping for it. The fork in the road is divided by permission and pleading versus declaring and demanding.

Power permits while all else can only be a request at best and begging at worst. It demonstrates the balance of power, either not having it forced to yield and capitulate or in possession, granting and dictating favor and concession. Ultimately, any action taken must be taken from a position of strength to influence the dynamic as a recognition of our power. Power is not to be confused with violence or force but with achievement.

Violence and force are revelations of emotions and usually lack self-control. I am not a proponent of non-violence because I hit back. But, I am also not a proponent of expressing disapproval in the form of violence or emotional outburst. Violence and force are reserved options recognized as self-defense when reason is not possible to resolve a physical threat. Systems provide a different threat and must be dealt with by dismantling that system's operational code.

Destroying the operational code involves neutralizing the system's philosophical function. Only destroying the equipment replaces it with better equipment, leaving the code intact, contrary to the objective of neutralizing it. So with a strategic plan and practical coordination, calculating the implementation of a timetable is the final critical point of action to secure the objective. Finally, we must realize that only the objective matters, not personal accolades or emotions. In this regard, an unselfish mindset of resilient effort propels the common goal more efficiently.

The objective's challenges are social injustice, systemic racism, economic disparity, and inequalities of our humanity. When examining these conditions, the root denominator of ideological commonality reveals beliefs and psychologies based on perverse morality and distorted history. History cannot be changed, while stubborn morality is well entrenched religiously and societally. Still, they can be altered, especially within us. That leaves the perverse underlying psychology to be changed as the overriding common denominator.

As we get closer to the core, we must determine if efforts to change others or outside influences are the best courses of action instead of changing ourselves. To further demonstrate the answer, we have spent over four hundred years, knees bent and back sore, trying to change others but still waiting. Just as beauty is in the eye of the beholder, so is reality. Reality is subjective to the purveyor, so we must change our reality or the widespread misrepresentations of us.

Undeniably, current times dictate that we reevaluate our understanding, reactions, and expectations of the traumas carried by time and history. Not to forget or necessarily forgive but to progress beyond. The first law of power is knowing and managing what is in your control, while the following law of power is the first law is not optional. Self-knowledge, inventory of capabilities and resources, along with conviction of action facilitate us accumulating power.

Any thoughts or perspectives of inferiority cannot penetrate a resolute mind forged in the power of self. It otherwise requires our acceptance and complicity agreeing to be weakened. Therein lays the simple answer to resist conforming to the principles of psychological trauma regurgitated from slavery. The best way to honor our ancestors is to shake the shackles of slavery and throw away the crutches tethering our minds to the subjugating deceptions.

The goal of these articles is to acknowledge many facts and sentiments to convey that I fully recognize the enormity of the perspective I am compelled to share. Even if others deny it, we know what happened, but do we really need anyone's tearful confession of history for us to progress? Harping on wrongs helps prolong our pain and delays our healing. Overcoming them accelerates our healing and progress.

So it seems the only guaranteed course of action that matters is in our hands to accelerate our healing as a people and promote our well-being through adjusting our psychology. Not surprisingly, this assessment brings us back to the common denominator of the problem, ours, not theirs. Back to our beliefs, psychologies, and sociologies contrived in control mechanisms and racial bigotry with us readily susceptible to the lingering effects.

Changing our psychology and perspective is not simple and requires time, at least a generation. Yet, we are already over four hundred years into this, so a generation requires less patience than we have already exhausted. The heavy lifting comes in two parts. One is our willingness to change, and the other is our willingness to divert from conventional indoctrinations inviting self-inflicting harm. Unfortunately, we have been lured into a trap whereby the cycle repeats itself replicating a variation of the previous version.

In addition, to this extent, we have been complicit without sufficient accountability for our actions and perspectives that harm our progression. The mighty lion is easily caught by complicity, being deceptively lured to its demise. Any attempt to capture the lion will cause it to fight or flee, but the lion must be lured to be trapped. The lion can only then succumb to a power lesser then its own by harnessing its power against itself by the element of deception and thereby neutralizing its resistance, instincts, and intellect.

Although not for delicate ears due to profanity, Dolomite's Signifying Monkey depicts emotional manipulation at its finest. Rage and hopelessness are the psychologies used to ensnare people, diminishing intellect and willpower while encouraging an impulsive reaction of anger or despair. Composure creates or negates advantages, but lack of composure reduces faculties. However, voluntary compliance by deception is the most effective and diplomatic enticement to incentivize conformity or otherwise become unknowingly complicit.

It is an observation of nature that the most effective way to teach the young is by conditioning the old to demonstrate an impulsive reaction as a code of conduct. The old will set the standard by which the young will learn unfiltered by logic and faithfully entrenched by nurture because of their blind trust. It is essentially programming and dictating behavior superseding logic, suspending resistance, and culminating in continuity with the indoctrination.

The programming is implanted perspectives incorporated as normalcy to accept dysfunctional behavior as routine. The dysfunction is mistaken as cultural identity or stereotypical behavior when it is actually socially engineered to deceptively lure us into a conforming expectation and projection of inferiority. It is voluntary compliance to a manufactured image of stereotypes so engrained that rejects the origins and purpose of the portrayals, thereby supporting the images. Make no mistake about it. It is designed to damage our image in our eyes and other's.

The perpetuating influence of slavery and racism gets it staying power by our permission when we capitulate by our perspectives and actions. We can no longer concede our power contrary to our efforts or benefit. We must realize our continued trauma of expectations hoping to retrieve historically earned reparations, may not be paid simply because we are owed. We cannot continue to check the social mailbox waiting for the check that's been in the mail for over four hundred years but has yet to arrive. It is time we pay ourselves first by first grabbing the wheel and steering a new course.

Determination will be required but mostly patience. Not blind patience to wait, but patience to mature. Expecting others to champion recourse for our historical challenges places the power outside our control. We must produce an alternative to erase the stagnation holding us in place. Each A-article illustrates a spectrum of events, anger, ideology, methodology, and sociology pervasive throughout history and the effectiveness of some countermeasures. But mainly show the enduring social and economic hardships that had to or must now be overcome.

However, their motivation and inspiration should not be overlooked as incentive and is not just for us to assign condemnation. Condemnation has not achieved our objective, and if it were to be effective, it would have occurred long before now. It is an emotional and inefficient use of our efforts and expectations, lacking sustainability and focus when demonstrated as rage or guilt. Remorse cannot be forced upon those who refuse to admit wrongdoing, but it is not needed for our objective to succeed.

The underlying principles of each B-article present suggestions and implications to reveal a tentative blueprint forward with adaptive allowances for practical nuances and realities that may arise. The chapter's fundamental examination isolates foundational perceptions and vulnerabilities, proposing clarity and a tactical application of history, sociology, and psychology. The primary intention is to navigate a path forward, discarding past grievances that detract from future progression.

The focus should be on a proper perspective and quantifiable advances, not retroactive outrage or redress. Redress will be a consequence of advancement. We need permission and cooperation for redress, but our perspective and progression require our actions, not their approval. I intend to honestly explore the subject matter while not concealing my perspective beyond what is actually written. My perspective focuses on us while eliminating all other considerations because, ultimately that is what we are left with, just us from an accountability standpoint.

It is time to strip the names and judge the deeds. If it is our deed, it is our correction, regardless of the reason. Brutal accountability will break it down to be built better and stronger regarding our psyche and perspective. With that said, after revisiting history through my lens, let's expand beyond that assessment, focusing on calculated ascension and generational opportunity explored from a wider angle.

Whether real, imagined, or psychological, determined people don't use metaphorical crutches or legitimate excuses. Neither can be allowed, as these indulgences have shackled us for far too long. Unpopular perspectives will be presented in the articles, followed by evaluating the prevailing ideology or methodology to achieve, support, or dismiss them. Finally, I will offer pertinent questions to expand on during your discussions with others.

Hopefully, discussing this information with younger family members, relatives, and friends will nurture a new understanding and approach to racial identity and contortions of our self-worth. The probing thoughts will explore and circulate knowledge, stimulate debate, and modify perspectives to prepare for or counteract current circumstances. Time is our collaborator, beginning a generational shift compounded by time and knowledge, producing progress. Time is the currency but our accomplishments are the receipts.

The spirit sees beyond the mind while the mind sees what the eyes cannot. Time is immortal, soul is eternal, and spirit is infinite but none is observable despite their perpetual presence. Manifestation evolves according to actions precipitated by thoughts or circumstances to produce transformation. The portal is revealed by the observable manifestation of this focused metamorphosis of our energy by change and expansion.

We must think globally with the world's shrinking and demographic shifts encouraging interactions of unprecedented diversity linked by business, social media, music, sports, fashion, and many more connectors. We do not live in a vacuum but are connected by humanity. Race and all the other distinctions or isms of society are being challenged and reshaped, rejecting the limitations and binary definitions of past conformities, abuses, and biases.

Due to expanding perspectives, the knowledge and skills required for new opportunities, services, resources, and products level the social and economic playing field as never before. Qualifications are influenced less by race, gender, or lifestyle as time takes its place and changes emerge. Blockchain, cryptocurrency, and solitary or binary rejections are prime examples of the changes occurring to shake the foundation of the temple gatekeepers. We must parlay our fight for racial equality by participating in the new world economic ascension and benefits.

A diametrical shift in humanity and technology occurs every sixty or seventy years and lasts about the same period. That time is upon us now to anticipate future developments and the preparation needed to benefit from them. Instead of a continuation, we can separate from the past by converting our focus to the future. Growing pains leading to maturity come with some discomfort. Our mental and spiritual recalibration is what redefines our perspective, altering the future and celebrating our freedom from the past by shedding its restrictions.

The past was primarily conditions not of our choosing but coerced. We are shadows of yesterday and silhouettes for tomorrow. Yesterday is a shadow of memories with the past as a receipt, and tomorrow an imaginary silhouette with the future unscripted. But, the present tethers both. However, can we continue to be tethered in the present by a past that was forced upon us? Better yet, a past that is a delusional manipulation of racial inferiority and exploitation.

Still, we have normalized it as ours because that was how it was presented or always has been. Mainly as our reaction to their action. Freedom and choice are the cause, not the effect. They are the action, not the reaction brought about by some other occurrence. We should scrutinize the action and reaction for autonomy and selection. By default, we must compare any assessments made to the source or intent seeking to clarify whatever may be their original calculated impact. We must create our self-identity by self-determination without being influenced by indoctrination or historical atrocities.

We must refuse to any longer be culturally perceived by what occurred, what was permitted, or the many detrimental concessions we made. Today's circumstances are not yesterday's oppression. Increased knowledge and skills elevate the intellect making the mind the method of labor and weapon of choice. It is a thinking person's game with our mind as our tool and weapon to create prosperity. Preparation for prosperity is a necessity and mindset to excel. Prosperity is a mindset applied, not an ornament worn or opulent display which is a byproduct of vanity and seeking validation.

Prosperity is a producer mentality as opposed to a consumer dependency. The root word of flashy is flash, meaning quick flicker, where you flash bright but fade quickly. Survival and sustainability are the beacons that signals time has yielded favor upon us by our fortitude and diligence. We must play the long game to enjoy and multiply the fruits of our endeavors. Progress is the goal, thinking now in terms of generational building blocks, not survival.

We can replicate an expanding foundation of cultural growth and prosperity to ensure our equity and equality. The social vortex of equality demanding recognition governing many different social issues is joined by the commonality of others' struggle to ours, namely equity and impartiality. Synchronicity and circumstances have converged to form evolving perspectives, realizations, and socializations now conducive to economic and social equity. Our demands for equality to carry maximum credibility must include three-sixty impartiality even if subjectively viewed.

Any examination of our coping mechanisms, their necessity, and the origins for their purposes must be therapeutically honest regarding their assessment in order to implement solutions. The overall societal shift must include recognition and consideration for our unobstructed equal and equitable representation and opportunity. The current assault on our humanity has extended beyond just race to include other subgroups' social and economic interests. Many are also jeopardized by these intrusions of colonialist conservatism infringing and violating rights to force "moral" conformity while preaching puritan freedom.

The authoritarian insistence on control and conformity by all who disagree with the conservative religious self-righteous endangers many social gains thought to be secure. While it makes the social structure unstable, it also presents opportunities for us to exploit vulnerabilities and consolidate coalitions. These coalitions would support our shared objective instead of forfeiting theirs. These conditions of authoritarian imposition promote change and resistance that we can benefit from as a participating demographic for social justice.

Playtime is over! We must conduct serious business not to squander the current atmosphere, which has never been more conducive to change beneficial to our interests. Complaints and complacency are the beggar's tools. Strategic action rewards the bold. The vehicle for a bold evolution of the Black reality is here. We just have to drive it. The obligation and business at hand are ours and others' to resist racist zealots bent on a homogenized society under their sociological control. So, if you want to talk serious business, let's talk business, but check your feelings at the door because they may get hurt.

Now let's get down to the business of clarity.

Theory of Critical Race
Does the past matter for the future?

If history suddenly doesn't matter now being deemed irrelevant, why would telling it accurately and truthfully matter? Why is it so increasingly crucial to conceal or sugarcoat it? Critical race theory has been a contentious issue of late. It is not because it is divisive or misunderstood but probably because it is factually liberating and objectively accusatory by history's revelations. It is freedom from lies and critical of alterations of the truth. The cry of divisiveness from those who would deny its occurrence, effect, or privilege is deafening.

As it has been asked many times, what does your record says you are? Racism may no longer be a barrier to success. Still, it is a burden of success by the subjective suppositions, connotations, and expectations of overcoming biased standards to which others are not subjected. Discrimination is when a unilateral standard is not applied, not whether you overcome it or not. It is like running a race with extra distance only for us, the same contest applying a separate set of rules.

The remarkable perseverance needed to compensate for society's diminished impartiality and selective morality is not burdensome unless it is you who must compensate for its discriminatory biases. It may not prevent us from being what we can be, but it does dictate what it takes and if we will get an unbiased opportunity. So factually, CRT does not promote Black victimization or white condemnation. Racism does. CRT merely reflects history.

Systemic obstructions are often a reflection of structural intent and the bigoted sentiment of individuals in executing their duties. As extensions and reflections of the perspectives and biases of the people who comprise them, these personal discriminatory sentiments express themselves in systems built to ignore, deny, or accommodate them. In addition, these systems are consequently calibrated as inducements of prejudice despite the stated letter of the law regarding fairness and equality.

Theory of Critical Race
Does the past matter for the future?

21

This inducement is regarded as white privilege, and it is conceivable that some whites are oblivious to its benefit or existence. However, most are not clueless and expect it as a regular dispensation. Despite the scope of its impact and expectations, a discretionary or selective element is applied biasedly, creating preferential or prejudicial treatment. But certainly, Black people are painfully aware of its duality and existence. Black people call it racism and discrimination, while white people call it normal.

So systemic racism and discrimination are a byproduct of the routine practices of the individuals within the system to restrict or deny fair and equal considerations contrary to legal expectations, thereby creating disparity. It is technically irrelevant if we overcome it because we should not have to when others don't. The persistent reason for this condition is rooted in historical perspectives that covertly avoid detection and are offered many protections of plausible deniability.

It then becomes accepted and commonplace to not be viewed as a violation that, in fact, normalizes it. Once normalized, it becomes invisible to all it does not adversely affect. Time magnifies its impact, expanding the divergence of conciliation. Here are ten perplexing queries regarding critical race theory that may clarify any misconceptions about its necessity or intent. First, it is not to assign oppressed or oppressor status to anyone. Still, it is to either accurately tell the history or discontinue the deceptions regarding the historically known facts causing today's systematic injustices.

One. Who has more to gain or lose from the truth being exposed? Is it the Black or Native American casualties of the racial atrocities who exclusively experienced the worst crimes against humanity in America? Maybe, by exposure the Caucasian/British Colonial Anglo-Saxon European transgressor's modern-day descendant's image would be at risk? After what was done for centuries, what is there now for them to gain which has not already been achieved?

Theory of Critical Race
Does the past matter for the future?

22

Could it be the transgressors stand to lose their societal masquerade as superior, privileged, religious, honorable, moral, or civilized? Can this be the real reason to oppose the truth of critical race theory teachings as irrelevant to history and reality? Would that not make all history irrelevant, unteachable, and universally littered with racism including religion? If the facts are irrelevant, how could manipulating them passed as the truth be more acceptable when we know it to be a lie? Would that be lying about the lie or selectively lying about the truth?

Two. Supposing the Confederate heritage is so great and endearing, why not reveal in totality for all to see its infinitely appalling and brutal deeds? Could we still arrive at the point where it is today portrayed as the proud apex of conservative values and southern morality? The conflict of morality inconsistent with reality has been selectively applied to alter the integrity of history and justify atrocities as in their past, yet their Confederate pride is current. Why would there be opposition and division associated with the actual unadulterated history of America or the experiences of any race here in America, including whites?

For those who wish to honor their southern Christian Confederate patriotic conservative roots proudly, would not CRT be the best way to do so as a testament? So wouldn't teaching CRT actually glorify the Confederate heritage just as the monuments and names praised today as testimonies to their treason, exploitation, and brutality? After the civil war, the Military Reconstruction Act of 1867 banned the Confederacy but allowed the treasonous states back into the Union.

Sure enough, they eventually rebelled against the stipulations dragging their symbols, names, and contempt with them, never essentially abandoning their advocacy for discrimination. The government has ever since given tacit approval by plastering the Confederate heritage on government entities honoring their racism. It sure was not in opposition as the so-called civil war to abolish their ideology of slavery would have suggested.

Three. How much longer can these original sins be concealed from white children as the truth is being vomited forth, revealing the degree of depravity that this country and your ancestors committed? Since it is not your crimes, actions, brutality, or inhumanity committed long ago, why hide it now if it is unassociated with you? Does it not become yours by extension when you embrace, conceal, or support its heritage and continuation by deceit, commission, and privilege today? How can you claim the benefit but deny how it was acquired?

Is it not more devastating for white children to learn that the truth is being withheld from them, that they were purposely deceived by the ones they trust the most, you? It will be disturbing to discover that their self-image is a lie that everyone knows except for them. It would seem the truth would discourage them from similar evil beliefs and behavior while the lies expose them to believing in delusional fabrications and bigotry.

Four. Why would some protest CRT as indoctrinating their children with the truthful history of America? How can you oppose the truth, claiming it as indoctrination instead of factual revelation? After all, the truth is the Christian thing to do, but where is the concern for historically and criminally brainwashing other races and nationalities' children with lies about America? Where is the outrage for that? Then what you complain about would be the very thing that you have committed against others and refuse to acknowledge or discontinue.

Yet, you resist subjecting your children to the truth while promoting lies to others. Is there no shame in indoctrinating other's children with historical lies? What nonsense is readily taught in schools today while concealing or manipulating the truth? Should we start with the genocidal thief Christopher Columbus or the first President of the United States of America, the slave owner and friend of slavery George Washington?

How about Andrew Jackson, another President who did more than anyone in the United States' history to exterminate the Native Americans? So, should that also be put on the twenty-dollar bill to honor his accomplishments? Did the Declaration of Independence, Freedom, Inalienable Rights, Bill of Rights, and born equal forget about Black people or just remembered to exclude us?

Five. Supposing these actions were not divisive and destructive. How can any revelations be divisive or detrimental to the self-image of yourself or your children? Why would any shame be attached to them if they were noble in cause or actions? Could it be that preserving your self-image is not as critical to us as us improving ours?

Could your shamefulness now be a reminder and formal accusation of your ancestor's callousness lacking decency and humanity? Where were their Christian values then? Where are yours now as you distance yourself by word but not actions from America's original sin? Could CRT be to promote the truth and a factual depiction of America and not a commentary on blame, inferiority, or superiority but ignorance?

Six. Do we need to look any further as evidence that factual and cultural brainwashing is real even among adults when a former daytime talk show host proudly stated that everyone knows Jesus and Santa Claus are white. Is this blasphemous against Christ, comparing him to an exaggerated commercialized character, Santa Claus? Is this blasphemous against the Bible to depict Jesus in any likeness, especially where the rest of his body is a separate color than his bronze feet, as stated in the Bible?

What's the purpose of a blue-eyed, blond-haired white Jesus with a halo, if not propaganda and the instigation of a lie? Is this a blatant example of using religion to subliminally insinuate white likeness as holy and superior? Isn't it a stark contradiction to your demonstrated depravity during slavery as the farthest depiction from that fallacy? Does the hatred of Black people expose insecurities that make you fearful of your inadequacies, or does it simply serve as justification for exploitation?

Is it both or possibly pure ignorance searching for validation to be absolved of crimes against humanity? Racism and narcissism are personality disorders. Both are mental health illnesses characterized partly by feelings of insecurity. These insecurities make people more likely to hold racist beliefs or engage in racist behaviors. Denial of these syndromes is expected since the sufferer embraces them as normal, thus making them invisible to themselves.

It is a complete consumption of the mind projecting a perspective removed from awareness or acknowledgment outside their perspective. Rationalized justifications validate and conceal these self-defeating characteristics by projecting deficiencies on others while aggrandizing oneself as superior or confident. Also, they are often morally and religiously condescending weaponizing religion as obedience to religious guidance.

By the way, the Bible also says to love thy neighbor as thy love thy self and that man shall dominate woman. So, is it obedience or selective enforcement? Better yet, how about contortion of biblical scripture? How could teaching CRT violate religion, truth, or the Bible? So, would teaching CRT break your sacred moral or religious covenant to persecute, exploit, and exterminate races you deem inferior using the Bible as justification?

Would CRT prove these races not to have been inferior but instead exploited and deprived of opportunity making you devoid of superiority? How many casual deceptions are passed as perverted truths which are known to be false? This nonsense is the danger of grow-

Theory of Critical Race
Does the past matter for the future?

26

ing old and being blinded to the truth and guided by the lie. Why lie when the truth would be sufficient, or would it?

Seven. Are there any accomplishments in this country that Black people were not present for or participated in achieving? Beginning with Crispus Attucks, who was the first to die in the liberation of this country from British rule, or the Industrial Revolution and the Cotton Gin, whose idea was a slave's idea. Automation is what really so-called "ended slavery" and gave America a competitive economic edge better than slave labor. However, indentured servitude and exploitation were still needed, contrary to granting the slaves freedom.

Our participation has been critical to winning every war this country has ever fought. Black people were often receiving the most hazardous missions as a privilege to participate, such as members of the Rough Riders and The Tuskegee Airmen's contribution! Our people accomplishments extended beyond slavery but were either discredited or destroyed by white racist's revisionism and malicious dishonor. For centuries Black people ingenuity and prosperity were seized, defrauded, or destroyed while despising us for our resiliency. Can there be any denying that our most significant accomplishment has been our survival of you?

Eight. Every perceived measure of negative human behavior in America reflects the image attributed to or associated with our people from lack of intelligence, poverty, a natural tendency for criminal conduct, drug addiction, violent aggression, scattered family tree, and many other negative stereotypes. Conversely, every positive human behavior and shining example of humanity is attributed to white people, despite their multitude of barbaric atrocities committed against us while claiming white wholesomeness.

We can't mention that part because you look and feel bad, yet you still espouse your superior virtues. Imagine how bad we feel and look being on the receiving end. I bet you wouldn't trade feelings

Theory of Critical Race
Does the past matter for the future?

27

and switch histories, would you? So everyone's record is their record except for yours? Assuming the past should not be levied against you, how do you levy against those whose crimes and atrocities are less than the inhumanities you committed? Shall we now indiscriminately do away with your accountability but not others?

If we cannot tell your history, are we also forbidden to tell ours? Is it not a shared history of actual experiences and occurrences? Can American history be told without mention of racism and slavery by its various incarnations against not only Black people but as an ongoing matter of American imperial practice? How can the Confederate Heritage be a source of pride but the Confederate deed a source of shame? What separates them from being the same?

Is not slavery the defining element of contention for the Confederate resistance? Should the truth of slave atrocities be ignored but the stain of the Confederacy tolerated or celebrated? If you are so proud of the Confederacy, surely your children cannot be ashamed of its brutal history, can they? Why not stand in the distinction of the brutality that affords your white privilege? But maybe you could or should renounce it? But, nah you wouldn't dare. Would you?

Nine. Why deny CRT claiming its teaching is more harmful than the practice on which it rested? Is it currently necessary to further stroke fear and deceit by claiming its exposure divisive? In the annals of history and the recesses of your mind, it can't be concealed without history shamefully betraying the pervasive truth. The truth is racism is more divisive. Is it your obsession with race, pursuit of history's accuracy, or fabrication of superiority that you fear? Is the factual pursuit of history racist by the documented racist accusing others of being racist by exposing them as racist?

Well, whose history involve racism, discrimination, and practicing slavery in America? Maybe, that is who we should be addressing. But again, that would be you. You should want to correct your accusers by identifying the actual practitioners of racism in America if

it was not you. By telling the truth of history it exposes these imposters sullying your race, if that is the case that history supports.
But it isn't. So, either way, it is truthfully told.

Unless history was racist at its core and the immoral practice typi-
cal, what could there be to deny by whoever practiced racism assuming it was not you? Consequently, would not CRT represent a
reliable ledger of racial atrocities from the volumes of history? Denial is not a river in Egypt. It's what you tell yourself to feel better.
So, since racial advantages and disadvantages still exist, can there
be parity while you still enjoy concessions reserved for whites.
Ones that no one else enjoys but you.

Would that not amount to continued willful discrimination and exclusion by you? Ironically, the Confederacy and its heroes represent
the very definition of CRT. That questions whether that, too, should
be banned from being mentioned in schools. By the definition of no
mentioning of racism, much of your history would be banned from
teaching, including the Confederacy, Civil War, and America's
founding. Now we must tell the truth or stop telling lies, teach it all
or teach none of it still ends at the same destination, discontinuing
the lies.

Ten. Why do your American dream and your core conservative values have to be a discriminatory nightmare for so many? As your
demographic advantage shrinks by self-identification, not replacement theory, it would seem wise to denounce any racist ideology.
Notwithstanding your immorality's historical blemishes, establishing an impartial social equilibrium invites the normalcy of inclusion.

If racism were a significant part of building this country, it would
make sense that it has to be a substantial part of what was built. It
must be deconstructed with the structural and systematic remnants
of racism identified and addressed. While the oppression of racism
has diminished in quantity, it still is a significant reality in sub-

stance. The obstacles are not insurmountable, but they do exist. CRT is an understanding of why and how, hopefully offering solutions. That is only if you are seeking solutions, which is highly questionable.

When denials of racism dismiss lingering resentment while it is still being perpetrated, it only fosters its continuation. Therefore, it remains an issue that should have been put to rest long ago. Denying the deed will not make the pain or damage go away. Since you will not feel others' pain, do you not see it can only bring more, maybe even yours? No longer do all others have to beg and submit themselves to your graces and permission or denounce their identity to assimilate with you. So, the grasp of your grip is slipping while losing control to exploit or convert others with fear, lies, and manipulations.

Has the curtain finally been pulled back too far? The gig is undoubtedly up! Still, you have nothing to fear but yourself as your most significant threat to yourself by insisting on an ancestral ideology and Nazi slogan to make America great again. Hitler was able to rise by using make Germany great again propaganda. America has origins from the same doctrine of morality, nationalism, and racial superiority regarding slavery and racism, but that is partially where Hitler got it.

As a sidebar of further discovery, research the heritages and origins of Anglo-Saxons and continue from the population of that destination repeatedly and observe the intersection. More revealing is the ideologies applied to the same metric. By ideology, observation, and history America, Europe, and Nazi Germany specifically practiced the same superiority ideology based on bloodlines. Likewise, they have common lineage and ideology in Germanic origins.

So coming full circle past slavery to discrimination Africans are not of that Germanic bloodline. However, Germanic is of African bloodline upon deeper observation. Notwithstanding, Nazi and

Theory of Critical Race
Does the past matter for the future?

30

American ideology was identical in perspective but different in "execution." The remnants of Nazism was then exported to America's infrastructure as surplus superiority manifesting to fortify racism. The ongoing racist sentiment is rooted in the lineage of superiority and ideology self-defined and widely identified as Neo-Nazi and white supremist as being synonymous.

Consequently, the adaptation of racism is infused with bloodlines and Nazism as a ruling class distinction designated as white privilege. The rhetoric, methods, and concealment spans from the subtle to the blatant preservation of that privilege. The deception is in the deflection of the similarities openly displayed but regulated as a trickle of progress. The formula is compounded by time. Consider the racial progress from 1665, 1765, 1865, and 1965 to imagine 2065 and 2165 to observe the trickle. This is the obvious incentive for acceleration by our own actions and volition as a tidal wave of perspective washing our minds. Until then, it is an uninterrupted cycle.

Not so coincidentally, a modern former President of the eighties and trickle-down economics and racism also frequently espoused the dog whistle of making America great again. We all know well his feeble mental state and devastating policies for minorities and discrimination under his vision. It seems his best acting role was as an incompetent leader although his worst acting was not to reveal his racism. America rejected the Nazi evil propagation and the ensuing holocaust while continuing to practice an elitist economic extermination of wealth redistribution and oppression.

Still, America has continued to embrace the same defective ideology rooted in so-called conservatism and patriotism. Variations of this ideology smear a fragile national image exposing a moral inferiority insistent upon hiding the truth and pursuing a fallacy. This concept, at its core, eliminates not only certain races but religious freedoms and economic viabilities, marginalizing everyone except the white prototypes. Denial and refusal to deal with historical truth

through CRT or any other substantial means of truth only exacerbate the problem and prolong its relevance.

It further restricts America's democratic greatness and social
progress. If you want us to put slavery behind us, why don't you put
it behind you? Believe me we want to more than you do, if you will
only let us. If we should get over having it done to us, how much
easier should it be for you to get over having done it to us? Feelings
and self-images cannot take precedence over truth. What damage
could the facts do to your history that it has not done to ours?

So let's be reasonable and forthright that we need education and
correction to make for a sustainable society, not continued concealment and oblivious posturing. Society cannot live in the past,
resistant to progress. However, a discriminatory past should not
thrive in the present or future. Therefore, it is unreasonable and unwise to reject viable solutions when projecting the harmful effects
of your continued opposition moving forward. As the lie festers, the
damage expands, and so do the consequences.

The first step is admitting historical facts and seeking remedies for
these actions. They are too enormous simply to forget or cover up.
Secondly, solutions are problematic when you deny the truth and
promote the mentality of injustice as fairness. Thirdly, it is not so
much denial as the entitled mentality and protection of the justifications without remorse or accountability. Finally, it is the utter impunity with which it is done. When will it be time to teach the historical accuracy of the truth?

Silence and pretending will no longer cover this deeply gashing national wound. Racism is an ideological wound that infects all directly or indirectly globally. Has the time come, to tell the truth as a
reflection of history, not race, guilt, or blame but fact? Contaminated soil can only produce a poison tree. The foundation of truth and
education changes the mentality on all sides, re-aligning the future.

Theory of Critical Race
Does the past matter for the future?

32

Critical race theory is incidental to race but essential to history yet to be made moving forward.

More important than the race factor is the historical manipulation, minimization, and ignoring of the intentional occurrences that formed this country. Race only matters in identifying the victims and perpetrators because the facts speak for themselves, just as the identity of any group's participation. Also, you prefer to pretend that color doesn't matter when it exposes you and heap contempt on your actions. But color is, in fact, the only thing that matters regarding your practice of racial discrimination. Can you seriously claim victimhood or accuse others of it?

Why doesn't your unconditional love for America include its blemishes? If history and heritage are so important, shouldn't it be essential to contain their factual imperfections? Otherwise, how can it show progress except by comparison? The past should contrast any current improvements made over time. Otherwise, the albatross continues hanging from the indignity of this country's racist neck.

With humanity seemingly on the brink of another evolution through science, technology, biology, quantum physics, medicine, space exploration, and yes, maybe self-destruction, can we afford to adhere to politics and policies which are antiquated or detrimental to the expansion of our societal evolution? We can surmise that change, nature, science, and universal forces do not care or respond to what we think or want but instead to their assigned circadian rhythm according to physics and evolution without our consent.

Time will only move forward even if we remain stagnant or resist. The linear future is tethered to the sequential past. Change is inevitable, and the needed social change is just a matter of time as a function of human evolution. The past always matters as a lesson for adaptation and evolution for future survival. We already know there are powers beyond our denial or resistance, such as time, history, and change. We cannot change history or avoid change, but we can affect the future because society will be broken without the flexibility to bend. Those who forget the past are condemned to repeat it.

The theoretical mission statement and tenants of this country's founding, need to finally ring true from sea to shining sea for all who occupy it, or collapse will follow. It is the same insanity of those who refuse to change but seek a different result using the same method when the current condition is unsustainable. Are we all so naïve to believe that the white race or any other race on this earth is superior to any other? How about the entirety of all universes and dimensions that exist?

Or, for that matter, is any race on this earth inferior, or have opportunities been denied? Are we to sacrifice the future by living a historical lie that breeds disregard for the equity and equality of humanity? History is not a condemnation of anyone or their children, be it factual of the oppressed or oppressor. Still, the liberation from the ignorance of its past over time absolves all of its control. Facing the truth of the past rids us of our collective shame, but only if we veer from the same mistakes in the future.

The division, shame, and injustices blamed or sought to be avoided by concealment is no affirmation against the truth. The racist historic skin tone distinctions have made it a problem and a disparity. You cannot condemn complaints of racism while still practicing racism. That would effectively promote its silent furtherance preserving a racist fallacy instead of correcting it. Opposition to CRT, then, by default, would not be condemning racism. It would be condemning the exposure of it.

If knowing about racial atrocities and injustices might damage your children, what effect will being subjected to them have on our children? If not learning would make your children love themselves, the Flag, and America, what does knowing make our children love, certainly not discrimination? If your children are not taught the evil of racism, how can they know it is evil or not perpetuate it? Is it not your obligation to not lead them astray but deliver them from evil?

If expecting Black people to demonstrate love for symbols of oppression, does your behavior yet demonstrate condemnation of oppression and racism? How does the doer of wrong not be attributed the shame of that wrong? Repentance and remorse belong to the wrongdoer. Restitution, anger, or forgiveness belong to those who have been wronged. Is not the criminal justice system built on punishing the doer of crime and not the victim of such crimes?

As a matter of law, evidence is entered, witnesses can testify, records presented, and accusers have an obligation to confront defendants. Why not here unless it is extremely prejudicial? What is not good for the goose cannot be good for the gander. So how do the ones wronged become vilified for acts committed against them becoming known? It only makes sense if the wrongdoer wants to continue the wrong.

Should you continue preserving your image and injustices at our expense? How can we allow it? It will not just magically go away. The iniquities of your forefathers descend upon their descendants like the curse of Ham upon Canaan. Subjectively and summarily ignoring redress accumulates a higher toll of injustice by attempting to maintain a racist benefit and concealment. That is where the shame lies for your children and you to continue racism by the iniquity on your watch.

Your children will learn what is shown and taught to them. Changing both would solve both of our racial problems moving forward. The past always instructs the future if lessons learned are applied wisely. Otherwise, it is just a sprint, a senseless race to the finish line of implosion. Now, how is that for a critical race theory or the theory of a critical race against history? But, it is not a theory. It is a fact and has been a proven fact evidenced by history despite all denials.

Thurston's Thoughts
Distorted History

There are two sides to a coin and truth is the limitation of knowledge extended to our limits of understanding. Known history has no such duality being a fact of occurrence. The truth and history rest on its foundation only obscured by deceit or concealment. Therefore, once known they reverberate on their own validity or rationality. Informed minds will converge on the truth but only when awakening to the deception, concealment, and intentional manipulation used to sustain ignorance.

Forbidden from the fountain of knowledge restricts information and understanding encapsulating the mind, dooming it to a perpetuity of oblivion and regulation. Learning is silent, knowledge whispers, wisdom listens, ignorance yells, truth persuades, and history reveals. So, our concern should not be about Critical Race Theory or the intense debate regarding the history of slavery in America being taught in schools. It can be taught outside the structured school system, and that problem is solved.

When we consider only our interest, we need to be educated about CRT and its psychological extenuations with minor concern for teaching CRT in schools for other's children to learn. We need to know it and they will eventually learn it. Of greater concern is what they ARE teaching in schools. Our primary concern should be the harmful essence of miseducation, concocted projections and distortions of our self-image, and intentional misrepresentation of facts and truth.

Truth reflects knowledge which affects beliefs, which don't always equate to facts, especially historical facts. Self-image is an acquired simulation of impressions composing an identity, again not always factually based. Education is repetitive teaching and the most impressionable images form at an early age. But, education and self-image are susceptible to manipulation, so let us not be distracted by the symptoms. Instead, let us focus on the cause and intent, which is susceptibility and manipulation as the causality of the resulting interpretations and portrayals.

Intent frames the substance that influences or fills the void, builds the identity, and corresponds to our subgroup's practices and principals. This substance creates societal norms and expectations. The distinctions usually start before any conscious intellectual ability to evaluate and accept or reject them. Thus, they shape the belief system by circumventing any logical foundation for evaluation. This circumvention is where we must focus on this gestational cultivation before it is implanted and would require removal.

Once the desired character traits are inculcated, they are inoculated by education and repetition as certainty of fact. Inculcation is to train and is the basis for education. Education is not to dispense knowledge but to train obedience and conformity as standardized responses. Knowledge is learning the truth, while education is the tool of conditioned training. So, knowledge can be education, but education is not necessarily knowledge. Education is the method by which things are conducted for anticipated outcomes.

Knowledge discovers the truth, but education tells you what the truth is according to a particular disposition or presumption. When knowledge is suppressed, the promotion of analytical thinking is reactionary and intolerant of facts instead of proactively seeking information and solutions. So, critical race theory reveals presumptions exposing a system where all parts perform a specific purpose in its manipulation. Historically, these presumptions establish and further justify the racially social imbalances and psychological propaganda used to maintain their advantages.

Conversely, it exploits and denies equal opportunity to the disadvantaged group based on these presumptions. The vacuum created is the distractive chaos concealing the harmonious humming of the real agenda. The real agenda is controlled subjugation by class and educational credentials, with race as the most visible distinction.

Many other distinctions, such as gender, religion, caste, and so forth, keep us too busy in-fighting to notice.

Racially obsessed fractions are preoccupied with distracting elements emotionally consumed, ignoring obvious projections of destructive repercussions and implications that make the quarrel as damaging as the dispute. Essentially a cycle, making it futile in its pursuit, becoming an irrational revolving conflict. Racial distinctions fall into this category of psychological shenanigans that stroke emotions on a rollercoaster, ride after cyclical ride.

The thrill is to have someone to blame for your condition or, by comparison, feel superior to or morally affirmed, transforming and creating a hierarchy without impartial substantiation. Some white people have become convinced that any opportunity for others diminishes theirs instead of realizing what is factually affecting their reality. This dynamic is not exclusive to white people or racist but results from comparisons and contempt. As a prism of comparisons, the caste system has contracted to feed on its own, where greed knows no color, not even white. Meanwhile, contempt knows no rational restrictions.

However, both generate rage and exclusion. It creates pretentious rituals instigating a struggle regarding image, equity, and disproportionate treatment. The system stimulates or suppresses for the system's benefit, not the individual's. The individual is crucial to the system, but individuality is discouraged although incidentally allowed. Education teaches the indoctrination and perpetuation of conformity to sustain its ideology of maintaining the status quo.

Race can then be used as a potential agitator and regulator in the sense of allocations enjoyed comparative to those produced. But economics and delusional biased confirmations are the actual regulators. The dispute is a fractional byproduct while the exploitation is universal, no matter what side of the racial conflict you find yourself aligned. This situation gives breath to the systemic institution of conflict and exploitation, producing predictable outcomes disguised as reasons.

To topple the system that produces conflict among people, we must identify the cause. We instead engage in mutual conflict with both sides unwittingly pawns in the game. Hence, identifying the cause leads to dismantling and suffocating the creation, outlet, and expression of these dysfunctional alignments that sustain racism. At its source is education and socialization. Acknowledging racism and providing sincere remedies will not destroy the white psyche.

Still, it will expose the deceptions of which they, too, are a victim. The first step to any affliction is its recognition and admission. Your head in the sand leaves your rear end exposed. To insist on this absurd denial reflects malicious ignorance or detached reality. The detachment is from the Black experience and contrary to nearly every aspect of the racist purported belief system, including lawful, moral, and religious claims. This severing from reality is also demanded of others to maintain the masquerade they cling to, requiring that others do as well.

As a matter of knowledge, color as a visionary image is the degree of reflection or absorbance of light. As a matter of race, color is an adaptation to weather extremes, and the level of melanin is created and activated to establish skin tone protecting the skin. All races have variances in skin tone for this reason, environmental adaptations through DNA. Consequently, all the nonsense surrounding racial discrimination is ignorance of genetics, the biology of melanin, or a purposeful lie. Racism based on color is contrary to the tale of evolution.

Genetics is a physical expression of time, the memory of evolution, and spectrum of existence before our experiences. It is passed generationally as physical characteristics just as poverty is passed as a psychological limitation. Melanin is the memory of ecological adaptations. Since this information is not new and resists claims of widespread ignorance, racial distinctions must be for deceptive purposes.

These misleading purposes are only held by the portion of racist zealots holding out against all reason and logical thinking. If racists were sincere, sun tanning would not be as profitable or desirable for aesthetic purposes or vanity. The dissonance is irrational. The human anatomy is universally the same. Only the coverings and sizes are different. It is the social indoctrination that causes the distinctions leading to prejudice.

For example, fish breathing underwater is an environmental benefit in the water but a detriment out of the water, i.e., its element of survival. Shaping survival adaptations are circumstantial differences causing genetic and biological variances for a species' survival under specific circumstances. So it is also with humans and skin tone. Consequently, species adaptations are determined by its environment contributing to its genetic code. Skin tone when used as a measure of social relevance also disregards mating patterns and DNA merging.

For these reasons projected forward skin tone will have less significance in the future as bi-racial is a dominate expanding reality. The detection and exposure of normalized beliefs and behaviors must be scrutinized for relevancy. The obscuring of biology, genetics, science, rationale, and religion contribute to many misconceptions. These falsely long-held indoctrinations protected by reverence that are not to be questioned or exposed harbor ignorance and primitive superstitions.

Society's progress requires updating knowledge and practices when improvements are known, factually debunking previous habitual conformities. The attack on books, history, and knowledge replicates the Garden of Eden symbolic of the apple representing forbidden knowledge. However, they are not God and why selectively restrict knowledge if not to promote ignorance? Restricting knowledge and discarding advancements essentially rejects progress promoting the psychological and sociological stagnation of society. There is a movie that checks the temperature of intellectual tolerance that depicts the rejection of books and knowledge favoring control and conformity by programed ignorance.

All must examine the why, but for Black folks, our focus must be on the what. The accusatory why keeps our vision in the rearview mirror, but by our self-determination, the practical resolution of what, must focus on the road ahead. What and how we overcome it must be our future concentration of mind and effort. We change others by handling our business, changing the enduring impact of slavery to plot a new course. Liberated from the triggering subjugation and memories of racism incentivized by disassociation from the emotions, beliefs, and umbrella of steppin and fetchin oppression.

This new course should only deal with remedies for our condition, not retentions of trauma. Our concerns are more significant than what others are or are not taught in school. Our problem is what we are taught in schools, at home, and by societal rituals that reinforce subconscious self-deception. This temple of deception crumbles under the scrutiny of us changing our ideological directives. Our reminders of societal, cultural, economic, and religious misconceptions not rigorously vetted for present and future application are riddled with past manipulation.

We must know our history beyond slavery. Slavery is not the complete history of our existence or the condition that defines us. Our ancient African heritage before colonialism, imperialism, or repatriation was for a longer period with great accomplishments. We did not originate with slavery in America. We survived it, but slavery is the psychological crutch promoted to sustain our hopelessness and confusion.

These deceptions are all constructs of the past that contain manipulations that must not persist. Discontinuing these deceptions requires rejecting labels that shatter our collective identity, individual assertion, and singular humanity. Our impact on the whole has defined the whole. As primary components of American history, there is no way of removing our part within it. We have been and are integral components in the spectrum of society.

Therefore, society must redefine its narrative to transform the ignorance of racism rectifying its indoctrinations. Our indoctrination has been just as profound as others by us submitting to "innocent" rituals and socializations. These indoctrinations on both accounts viciously obstruct our progress. We must identify and reject any long-held falsehoods originating from our survival mechanisms resulting from oppression. Our power has always been there but has been used to survive.

Discrimination has diverted our power which should now be used for our progress, no longer focused on survival from oppression. Moving forward, the destination must justify the journey, especially with the hardships already overcome. We must travel by sight guided by vision completing the ancestral circle with deliberate navigation to arrive at our destiny. If our journey has been scripted, then so has our destiny. It is dependent on our determination to move forward beyond the limitations of the past as we have done repeatedly.

Likewise, it is dependent on discarding self-inflicted obstructions and rejecting propaganda designed to suppress us. We have traveled on faith and goodwill far too long, blinded by hope and hopelessness, seeking validation and being invalidated. The positive will encourage, while the negative has obstructed. Release the harm by releasing the pain, becoming twice as good, not for half the chance but twice the gain.

Resilience and survival are hereditary in our DNA, inherited from hardship and transformed into our super-power. The climb has been challenging and hazardous, but the summit is within sight. Its vision reinvigorating the spirit to thrive, no longer consumed just to endure. Our knowledge, resolve, representation, and resources are considerable if focused, realizing that our long awaited destiny is solely in our control.

So while critical race theory may educate whites about the horrors of slavery and their past, it does little for us without their consent. Then again, let us not pretend that there are multitudes of white folks running around with no clue, only needing to be made aware. Their imposed exposure to CRT will probably satisfy an emotional craving for Black folks, but it probably will not move the needle much. Besides, we should be well past settling for emotional gestures instead of practical progress.

Remember how we have been "given" freedom, equal protection under the law, and voting rights many times over again. We even have a couple of holidays, but we still have the same struggles despite that. Our undeniable irrevocable freedom and prosperity must be granted to us by us. There is no other way, no other guarantee, and no other choice. We have work to do, time for a hard hat and a lunch pail, and overtime will definitely be required.

So now we find ourselves tested by fate to see if we really want it by sacrifice and determination, not request. We have operated long enough off our emotional longing, not utilizing or maximizing our ingenuity and determination. We often conform to systems designed to discourage and marginalize us into complacency when throwing us an occasional bone. Our sociology and psychology should primarily concern us, not the teaching of CRT in schools, supposedly for others' benefit.

We already know the absence of CRT is not the problem. It is the presence of bias and propaganda in educational, religious, economic, legal, and societal constructs. Consequently, global CRT is more representative of the authoritative systems globally reflected and demonstrated by the volume of racially oppressed people worldwide. It is a universal social construct of control and separation tarnishing truth, justice, and humanity. Steadfastly, these autocracies of racism promote greed, control, and exploitation.

Racism is global in one form or another, with many experiencing its evil effects with only the names, geography, and circumstances changed but the method constant. The cause is usually greed and exploitation behind a veneer of control and superiority by race, religion, politics, or caste. Meanwhile, constantly condescending towards those they deprive of the same opportunity or fairness they enjoy. Nationalism and patriotism are two prominent "isms" often used to proclaim justification of atrocities and mayhem for the benefit of the subjective loyalist.

The global influx of racism compounds its mentality and practice as long as it is against an excluded group. Wherever you globally find racism, there is a story of CRT or a history of abuses based on racial fabrications. Seemingly the solution would be to tackle the underlying causes globally instead of escaping to the same form or practice of racism in a different land. The only solace is the varying degree of racism may be less but its presence is assured. The racially marginalized are doubly bludgeon by poverty accompanied by the trifecta of exploitation.

The three are interchangeable as the primary affliction but usually come as a trio seasoned with social relegation. The same can be applied to immigration since it is seemingly governed by racism. Immigrants would have no need to leave if their conditions were not hopeless or undesirable usually by some standard of oppression. It is the prospect of opportunity and improvement which motivates the dream despite the obstacles. They are compelled by the survival instincts of the human organism to gravitate towards ideal conditions.

It reveals the intentional inhumanity of custodial greed supported by the established systems of imperial ideologies, even in postures of pseudo-democracies. Furthermore, to condemn global inequalities and inhumanity but condone it domestically is ridiculous and hypocritical. Cleaning your house as an example by deed, not word, would be a greater influence. Besides, demonstrating compassion for those outside of Europe would dispel the traditional biases which gave rise to racism.

A notion of sincerity would be for those holding jurisdictions or sovereignty over a land to also be financially responsible for their sustenance. Something like child support as a managerial responsibility. Maybe we should ask the United Nations or some international tribune why are they a poor nation while their overseer is a wealthy nation? However, history notwithstanding, it does not dictate the future but motivates it and defines our objective.

History is written in stone, but the future is still unscripted. So we must prepare and cultivate ourselves intellectually, psychologically, economically, and emotionally. We must be ready to participate in the global ideological shift and upcoming transfer of wealth. We need to drench ourselves in emerging technologies, financial developments, and sociological understandings. Doing so will illuminate our future undefined by the past, thereby initiating generational prosperity.

The other component is to detect and reject perspectives that project discrimination and oppressive systems upon us and others. In our prosperity, we must not create humanitarian disgrace by becoming sponsors of the cycle which we despise as abominations. Often blame by association is caused by condoning the actions committed, not always by participating in committing them. Continuation of associative ideologies sequences a global network of interchangeable segregationist. So racism appears to be the global immovable object obstructing cultural identity and social inclusion.

Repeatedly it is a tool used just as surely as education, economics, religion, and ignorance. Racism lacks the moral integrity or factual basis to be an evaluator of humanity. It operates under a mask of pretense, projecting glorified dysfunction and hateful influences sustained by fear, deception, or greed. The ghastly behaviors needed to disguise, defend, and promote racism cannot persist as an exercise of power without destructive consequences. Thus, as an expression of our liberated resistance, we can no longer be confined by obedience or seeking permission.

Accordingly, the evils of the past cannot be allowed to participate in our future. The past cannot be yesterday and tomorrow if tomorrow has expectations of shedding the extensions and desensitized acceptance of bigotry. Race is divisive by definition by creating a distinction of difference, thereby creating conflict by classification. It depends on the subgroup's sample size by comparison and circumstances assigned further context such as Black, American, human, or earthling. Whereas by an inverted classification, earthling or simply human is inclusive with no further delineation needed.

A later reference will address the distinction and determination of race to further illustrate its deceptive and illogical inconsistencies. When we know, everyone who we need to know knows. Still there is more we should know to elevate our understanding. To further elaborate on CRT at its essence it must be traced back to its roots in history, religion, and etymology but not necessarily racism for a contextual understanding. Viewing America is a microscopic view while the totality of history is an expanded universal observation. Our inculcation is a contorted western storytelling spell of revisionism and concealment viewed through a peephole.

Slavery and its justifications, biblical or otherwise, explored at its origins leads to Mesopotamia, Alexander the Great. Egypt, the word niger, Mizraim, and Noah's descendants most notably Ham and his other children. Further context and clarity is revealed by The Tower of Babel, Nimrod, Tama-Reye Egyptians, Nubians, Moors, Khazarian, Turkic and Hun history, Paleolithic and Neolithic periods, Canaanites and their culture, Phoenicians, the Bronze Age, Byzantine Empire, Arab Peninsula, Iran, Babylon, Persia, and the land of Canaan. They all provide fascinating insight into history, slavery, and religion.

The model for slavery in America resembles the principles rationalizing the enslavement of people in many lands accept theirs was

generally not racially based. Exploit their labor, suppress their reproduction, and divide their interest devoid of hope but a surplus of
converted faith was the model. Modern civilization can be surmised
as the reincarnation of Rome influenced by Greek culture and structure. CRT is a narrow view of the past and disregards a pragmatic
future not based on race. GRT, global race theory, resolves many of
the questions, deceptions, and confusion.

Much is learned from researching history to discover the fabrication
of skin tone distinctions as a method of control and altering heritages and genealogy. History reveals the genealogy many would
seek now to deny by skin tone distinctions assigning inferiority and
disadvantage. Certifiably, there is a converging of shared lineage
where a departure based on race occurred to strong arm cultural and
ideological dominance. Nations, populations, cultures, and millen-
nia have operated under misconceptions and deceptions either ignorant of or refusing to honestly acknowledge history.

History in many ways shape the future but if history is any indication it also changes the trajectory of events which steer a new
course for thousands of years to come. Our history extended forward depends on our knowledge of real estate, investments, economic responsibility, ownership, and unfiltered education. They offer farther reaching benefits and reverberations than CRT focused
on America's past. That is America's past but not our history, just
some of it in America.

So, CRT has its value but also distracts from history still to be
made. Check your six but focus on your twelve. History's lessons
begin with world history not American history. To understand our
history it must be viewed in the context of its origins and the religious, political, and conquest that occurred in antiquity. We surrender our history distracted with America and CRT without the unity
and continuity of a global connectivity to the tribes of the transatlantic slave trade.

This human trafficking from the Sub-Saharan region by France, Spain, and Portugal goes unnoticed. The population of the Caribbean, South America, and many populations now marginalized originated from the same slave ships and geography as ours. We are relatives living in different neighborhoods whose history returns to the same home and ancestors, Sub-Saharan Africa. Those of African descent scattered across the globe must now have the courage to claim our history and autonomy as equal citizens of the universe.

The nationalism of our captivity incorrectly separates our commonality and identity localizing it from global. We are one but lack the unity and vision that a GRT perspective would reveal. This global perspective would also unravel the shallow narratives before they were perpetuated. When we see a tree, we know it grew from a seed over time. Its life will also span some measure of time and circumstances. Racism origins, impact, and evolution has mutated over time but its illogical ideology remains severely flawed from its seed.

It is time GRT (global race theory) reveal who, what, why, when, where, and how. It is about time the roots of global racism are viewed in a comprehensive way which allowed its structural expansion. Since we are the targets of racism globally, we are required and obligated to know and practice its antidote. They are not required or obligated, and by some accounts not even morally compelled.

There is much more to be told of the immoral story beyond America when considering our Sub-Saharan relatives scattered globally, especially in the western hemisphere. Same scam different location, same transatlantic slave routes but different destination. For that matter, the Native Americans have a CRT history of atrocities they could tell. So does the Caribbean and South America. They end differently but the origins are the same, oppression and exploitation.

Surrender comes in many forms when the will is broken.

Erasing identity is the tool to decimate the will.

Remembering who we are makes our connectivity unbreakable.

We transcend the vastness of time, history, and knowledge.

We span the globe and its origins as its original seed.

<u>Let me ask you a Question</u>

1. When race is objectively considered by historical, genetic, and empirical analysis, how can it not be a fabricated referendum of illogical classifications? What is racism about when origins, geography, biblical curses, eugenics, and genetics are debunked? Could it be exploitation, ignorance, or faulty dissemination of history and religion? Did you know many millions in South America, 90 percent Native Americans, and millions more Blacks where lost to imperialism or its ramifications such as disease and abuse?2. Is the more significant revelation of CRT not slavery but the more pervasive concealments such as religion that was used to support it? What is the purpose of the concealment? Why must we forfeit our history in America but are forced to accept their interpretation of theirs?

3. Is the educational system the camouflage used to program the concepts that CRT would expose? What horse and buggy ideologies are still taught? What is the benefit of limiting knowledge or facts about history? Is that the height of censorship? Doesn't Christmas and Easter violate the same supposed principles that CRT do?

4. Is the dispute of CRT in schools the best use of our energy and is it a battle not essential to winning the war? Would Dr. Claude Anderson's philosophy implemented in our lives, homes, communities, economics, and politics garner greater benefits? What about addressing the psychological and economic captivity we still feel as the sting of the whip? Should Alex Haley's Roots be shown every Black history month or on Juneteenth?

5. What does opposition to CRT reveal when the political actions and ideologies espoused today are not more divisive than history's account of a similar ideology? Why is CRT denounced as divisive but not the current agitation of racism by national politicians and certain governors?

Absolute Certainty
No Doubt

According to Google, crimes against humanity are defined as purposeful acts systematically committed against an individual civilian or an identifiable part of a civilian population. These crimes are specified as extermination, murder, enslavement, torture, imprisonment, rape, forced abortion, and other sexual violence. In addition, they also include persecution on political, religious, racial or gender grounds, the forcible transfer of populations, the enforced disappearance of persons, and the inhumane act of knowingly inflicting any of these atrocities.

If such crimes are first to be proven, let us not use the highest burden of proof used in a criminal trial which is guilt beyond a reasonable doubt. Yet, even beyond a reasonable doubt, let us apply absolute certainty without any doubt. History bears witness to the overwhelming evidence that has been left littered throughout time for over four hundred years just in America. There is no doubt about the elements of these savagely immoral crimes, their vicious intent, or their subsequently devastating impact.

Even today, the identity of these perpetrators and their oppressed victims are apparent, and the resulting damages are astronomical. The implementation, commission, and racist repercussions can be factually demonstrated and traced back to even the highest levels of society and government as their customary practice. These actions and pervasive patterns have attempted to be disguised and minimized by time, and history itself has been altered to conceal and protect the guilty.

Still, the evidence remains obvious and cannot be justified, denied, or erased. These crimes committed were widespread in national and global magnitude. Furthermore, these crimes were arbitrarily executed while deliberately and methodically enforced by brutally inhumane acts of violence and murder. America and Britain became gorged on their insatiable appetite for greed and thirst for slavery. Is it not pompous and sarcastic that these two countries would hold themselves above reproach and of the highest moral character, etiquette, and civility?

Yet, they savagely were the primary vendors of slave atrocities in America. Even beyond the grasp of slavery, America exterminated prosperous and aspiring groups of Black people and their opportunities, ensuring generational poverty and educational inadequacies. Murder, lynching, intimidation, miseducation, and systemic discrimination sanctioned by law served this purpose well. Public hangings were occasions for a picnic, to dispense fear, and elicit submission.

Interestingly, lynching has a biblical origin similar to hanging on a cross. The cross loosely symbolizes a tree, and the bible reference hanging from a tree as a curse from God if left there overnight and not buried the same day. However, the hanged person resolves every one of their sins by absorbing the curse and bestowing redemption upon them. So theoretically, by hanging Black people, they curse the Black body before God. But by leaving it there, desecrated God's law but redeem themselves from the act, with the hanged person paying for the hangers' sins.

It cleansed the perpetrators granting them forgiveness but eternally condemned the hanged. It is symbolic of the murder of Jesus on the cross to pay for man's sins. It was specific, just as burning at the stakes was purifying by fire. So, I guess lynching was a religious ceremony of sorts. Jesus was hung from wood, the cross, to mock and humiliate him as King of the Jews to promote compliance. Black people were hung from wood, tree lynching, to defile and eternally condemn their soul and spirit to promote fear.

Consequently, there are veiled messages to the rationale and methods used, then and now. Another favorite pastime was "coon" hunting, where Black men were chased by dogs and killed for sport. This activity was akin to whites casually hunting raccoons or some modern-day traffic stops. These were twisted forms of summary judgment, entertainment, and validation for racist whites. Public whippings and "buck breaking" were activities leisurely implemented as deterrents to defiance and to extinguish hope.

For good measure they also had the old tar and feather at their disposal for more deprived occasions. Our people were to be kept in a place of despair through violence despite racist's claim as firm believers of Christianity but devoid of civilized compassions. The forced exclusion from protections and opportunities effectively eliminated us from the possibility of prosperity. Instead, the prosperity created was solely for the economic exploitation of us to contribute to whites' societal benefit and wealth accumulation.

Acts of murder, genocide, massacre, and summary executions were indiscriminately and brutally applied to reinforce white superiority and maximize our compliance. Therefore, ensuring a free labor force that they could literally work to death for the slave owner's benefit. Working conditions or workers' rights were not considerations, and complaints were not well received and ill-advised. This enslavement, exclusion, and exploitation of life and liberty were at the sole discretion of the slave master because the law considered Black people property and not humanity.

Psychological conditioning and physical abuse mainly achieved and maintained this position of dominance. Escape seemed pointless, and routinely as a reminder, public torture was used to deter other slaves from any hope of escape other than death. The slaves' imprisonment and hopelessness were compounded by geographical captivity, considering where they would run and in which direction being so far from home. Also, how far would they get trying to escape before their dark skin tone alone would raise suspicion and eventual capture.

Still, today escaping racism is elusive. Black people are weary avoiding summary judgments, disproportionate imprisonments, discriminatory housing, economic suppression, and poverty. We are haunted by the looming prospect of law enforcement roadside injustices which are still today a sad and incredibly disproportionate reality for us. More modern refinements are through wealth depletion, societal and criminal justice systems, and discrimination by unequally applied standards.

For example, the bail bond system is economically and socially prejudiced. Healthcare, rehab, and diversion programs are biased. Jail sentencing is abnormal, and law enforcement is supposedly in perpetual fear and predisposed to resort to racial profiling and excessive force. Still, these abuses, disparities, and indifference to our lives continue. They are established, vindicated, and institutionalized by law almost as much as before.

This modern twist perfectly suits denial with claims of progressive changes that seek plausible deniability, ethnic adjudication, and qualified immunity. Yet, given the extent of its intrinsic foundation, persistent continuation, and frequent occurrences, are we to be duped into believing racism is no longer practiced? The harsh reality of selective enforcement of laws and disqualifying stipulations against our people are systematically designed to reject us in every facet of society.

Limited access and opportunity regulate the number of us who can enjoy what is taken for granted by others as their entitlement and expected pursuit of wealth accumulation. In addition, our exposure to lingering subtleties from psychological damage, intentional miseducation, and racial reprisals are constant obstacles. A Black person is unqualified, while a white person is a candidate for training or internship. In addition, a Black person is a drug addict by choice. By contrast, a white person has a disease and is addicted by medical predisposition or social exemption.

Suspiciously, a Black person commits a crime while a white person makes a mistake for the same offense. Therefore, a Black person must be locked away to protect society. Still, a white person is a prime candidate for rehabilitation and second chances while often given the benefit of the doubt. Perception is reality, and the historical fact has been that there is no act too horrendous against us when committed by a white person.

Refer to the George Floyd or Ahmaud Aubrey case that sparked outrage just as much for the injustice as the attempt to justify it. Even sexual crimes against our women by white slave owners were just how business was done, notwithstanding the degenerate slave master's predatory nature. Often the unmentionable acts of rape, forced pregnancy, and what amounts to gorilla pimping have been historically used to defile the Black woman. It was supposedly rationalized by her insatiable appetite and animalistic desire for sex.

These sexual assaults were legalized because Black women was just property and the virtuous white woman was above exposure to white men's despicably degenerate sexual desires. Their despicable acts against our women didn't stop there. It was inconceivable to them that the bond between mother and child could not be so casually severed by the sale and forced separation of families.

Except, considering the lack of humanity of the white perpetrators without regard for the pain either mother or child suffered. They were viewed as less than human, only property. As property they had no feelings or bonds which needed to be respected when severing family attachments. The Black males' detachment from the family unit was reinforced by the forcible transfer of children, siblings, and spouses without a moment's notice. The emasculation of the Black male was mandatory. It still is a sinister objective to sever the head from the family body.

We were by legal decree a commodity to be sold or dealt without regard except for value as free labor and breeding. No race in America has been treated as gruesomely for as long as the Black race. No race has had a society built upon their backs like our race without significant participation in the benefits. No race has had the law of the land orchestrated against their existence and humanity as brutally and blatantly as our race has. The suffering has been long and harsh, with the effects still fully observable today in most aspects of society.

The hateful and righteous indoctrination of discrimination has been such a long term insidious force in America's DNA. Ironically, those who have benefited the most and practiced it vigorously pretend not to recognize or acknowledge the advantages provided them due to slavery and racism. They refuse to accept the generational impairment and destruction it continues to have on our lives, in addition to their continued expectations of white privilege.

No other race of people who have been the victim of such extreme oppression is expected to exhibit Stockholm Syndrome. No allegiance is expected to their oppressors' doctrines, symbols, and traditions after supposedly being freed from them. The beloved American Flag, the Star-Spangled Banner, and the very moral blueprint known as the United States Constitution are things that Black people fought for, died for, and were expressly excluded from its benefits and protections.

So likewise, after the Nazi Regime fell, there was no expectation of forgiveness and devotion to the Third Reich by the Jewish population, who were so barbarically tortured and massacred. Appropriately there is no time or distance, which is too great for the accountability of Nazi war criminals for their crimes against humanity. They rightfully cannot go unpunished. America has expressed no limit to the outrages committed in other countries. At the same time, America remains oblivious to America's deeds where we are concerned.

However, after the carnage we have endured at the hands of America, there is still an expectation that we should honor these instruments of oppression without reservation. The Holocaust has no time limit but the repercussions of slavery has supposedly expired. Both are still felt but are expected to be absorbed differently. Honestly, it is our responsibility to hold others accountable for insults and offenses to our history, dignity, and abuses of our humanity. We must handle ours as others have handled theirs without wondering why they are not equally offended by violations against us.

The continuous occurrences happens partly because they are allowed without immediate and sustained corrective consequences. In essence, WE allow it and then complain that others do nothing. Their reply is why don't we do something ourselves and they are right. We embrace too many submissions that cause us to allow our foul treatment, so it is done. They only treat us as bad as we let them and we let them where other nationalities don't. They are not beholding to any disrespect of their humanity where we are.

Why are we equally beholding as the obedience to our oppressors would have us believe? America's history and the Confederate Flag oppose the very humanity and freedom of the Black race. Still, today, we are expected to honor or tolerate these as if they had beneficially applied to us. None less than the United States Constitution quantified a Black person by LAW as three-fifths of a human being. It has also continued with the theory of eugenics.

By extension, it propagated that a Black man was deemed not smart enough to quarterback a football team or suitable for a college education during many of our lifetimes. The founding principles of equality, freedom, and opportunity were never meant to include or apply to us. Nor was the U.S. Constitution, Pledge of Allegiance, equal protection under the law, economic prosperity, or social respectability afforded to us. But our allegiance to and defense of them are required, expected, and proven.

Still, unfortunately, our life, liberty, and the pursuit of happiness have yet to be delivered unabated by racism and brutality. Love it or leave it is the cliché, but the love for us is not equivalent to the love we have given. The forced elimination of our roots and culture makes leaving problematic. Especially, considering we were here before the influx of many European immigrants. We have contributed more to America's wealth than those who would send us back to where we come from while refusing their return to their origins.

Those who would claim these entitlements lack sweat equity or seniority in this country compared to us. But, what place of origin do whites belong to or can return? They claim many lands but only by conquest, migration, immigration, or assimilation but not indigenous origins. White's nomadic tendencies and conquest history are concealed by their claim to superiority otherwise not born out. Whites are opportunistic Nomads while we are Africans.

We were forced to this land, but whites chose this land for the vast wealth and opportunities Black people directly or indirectly provided. We are defined by our origins but whites by their composite integration. They are emulsified to create a majority and exploitation of others. White ownership of everything imaginable and their way of life has been subsidized by exploiting us and others. Subsidized in a twisted, demented form of highjacked affirmative action minus the required experience of discrimination or suffering.

Still, the extent, benefits, and longevity of white privilege have not proven to be sufficient. With such a massive coerced subsidy, they still dare to expect those oppressed not to seek equitable treatment and opportunities, not to mention an end to systemic racism. The fruits and benefits from racism are comparable to the grandest of larcenies of receiving stolen property ever committed. Black people should be reimbursed equal to what was taken or the stolen value returned.

The actions of these murderous thieves have been historically identified for the record but not yet held accountable by legal or financial decree. From the introduction of our people to this land, there has been political persecution, dismissive human rights, and omission from the voting system. There have been biased restrictions in the governing elements of society, wealth suppression, and derogatory stereotypical perceptions and misrepresentations. Injustices are still prevalent today, with obstacles and disparities in the voting, wealth, and social processes.

The moral corruption of white privilege combined with the absolute obsession with greed and control has created a moral justification anointed by religion and allegedly granted by God. Disguising their greed by an alleged religious zeal and conservative values supposedly vindicates their actions. Yet, it significantly contributed to their clear conscience, allowing for some of the most heinous crimes ever committed against humanity anywhere or anytime. The resulting righteous immorality stands in opposition to the self-proclaimed white virtue of God-fearing worshippers.

It instead exposes their money-worshipping and blood-thirsty tendencies cloaked in religion. Religious assimilation and indoctrination have been intentionally used as psychological tools to placate and control our people. Forced adaptation and embracing of docile perspectives serve to contort our minds with obedience, hope, tolerance. We are left seeking salvation that has eluded us but enriched and emboldened racist expectations of privilege and superiority. Religious symbolism and inclinations have perpetuated white supremacy and Black inferiority.

Strangely enough, largely due to the presentation and acceptance of these written and visual perversions and manipulations as holy. Moreover, these influences have been thoroughly effective. Once again by contaminating the hearts, minds, and beliefs of those who have committed racial oppression or have been victims of this oppression. The world's wealth-generating commodity globally has been Black slave labor, whereby many countries' and organizations' wealth can be attributed to Black suffering.

The damage from legally sanctioned racial discrimination and suppression of education, along with the lack of quality of that education, can never be understated, exaggerated, or casually dismissed. It was illegal for us to learn to read, which maintained the uneducated heathen narrative and our disadvantage. Although oddly enough, the first book most we read back in the day was the Bible. It was our hope of relief or salvation. It was required reading as their critical race theory to ensure our submission.

A deviously structured social depravity has now replaced mutilation, murder, and brutality. It is reflected in the lack of fair economic considerations, lack of educational integrity, law enforcement abuses, prejudicial incarceration rates and sentencing, and discriminatory housing. On the financial front by usurious bank loans, higher insurance rates, excessive unemployment rates, minimal Black business investments or empowerment, and generational poverty. Also in areas of health care inadequacies and food deserts.

The above-documented history and methods of crimes against the humanity of our people can no longer be justified, ignored, denied, or minimized. Those whites, assimilating immigrants who self-identify as white, and even some of us, must now educate themselves on the crimes, thefts, robberies, appropriations, seizures, and deceptions committed. Then, with an honest and comprehensive examination of the facts, what conclusions can be drawn, and what reflection has it on the treatment of us in America?

Suppose you cannot envision it from our perspective. What would you or your identifying subgroup think, do, or tolerate without protest or resistance if this were your history in America? If it was white's history in America? Consider the Capitol was stormed over far less. Some from other nationalities that have come here have also assumed the white supremacy discriminatory perspective of racist America. They have assimilated and subjugated their own cultures while compounding the racial problems for us.

Can those who champion America's proud history include a time when racism wasn't always present? Their memory has faded, but the stain endures. The future cannot co-exist in the past. With a history like America's, what manner of person would want to return to when only white males were of any consequence and racial savagery overflowed? Imagine yourself, white America, yielding to such nonsense without protest or a call for change. After all, the founding fathers never experienced this kind of vicious oppression but still revolted.

They were indeed spreaders of much greater than they ever suffered. Unjust treatment and coerced economics are why there was a revolt called the American Revolution, which led to the founding of this country. Or in other words, America reneged on payment terms to Britain, it was not taxation without representation. It was freedom from payment, commonly known as creditor avoidance or default. By principle, America's government was charged with ensuring a Bill of Rights and that these slavery atrocities were not permitted.

Instead, they institutionalized them for monetary gain to our detriment. However, they were not alone in promoting these atrocities, accompanied by most long-tenured businesses and institutions in this country. They, too, are responsible for the ravages and should be financially brought to account for the resolution of their actions and participation. The Bill of Rights regarding the protection of individual liberties did not extend to Black people in America, nor do international tribunes.

It was most certainly not fairly applied when it did, specifically Constitutional Amendment IV to be secure in person and place. Not Amendment V due process of law or Amendment VIII freedom from cruel and unusual punishment. Arguably Amendment XIV in earnest regarding equal rights as naturalized citizens. The United Nations, under its basic principles and guidelines on claims for a remedy, sanctions the right to reparations for victims from the offending party for crimes against humanity. America, by slavery, has violated the majority of the infractions but did so before the establishment of the United Nations governing body.

America has indemnified itself from the United Nations authority, essentially having immunity grandfathered for its crimes against Black humanity. However, the crimes against humanity perpetrated against slaves necessitate compensatory and punitive damages acknowledging restitution as a restorative material obligation of redress. Admittedly, reparations insinuate a more jovial delay of payments owed. Still, they should include judicial, societal, and institutional resolution of the abuses and violations committed. Either way, it would seem that redress and compensation are well overdue. Of that, we can all be absolutely certain beyond a reasonable doubt.

Clarification: This is not to claim that simply being white automatically allege participation in slavery or racism. However, traditionally whites but more specifically racist, by demographic distinction, have been the predominant sponsors who participated, brutalized, and oppressed Black people in America. It is not a comprehensive indictment, just an overwhelming observation of a historical fact.

Many did participate, but many more benefited by skin overtones as an extension of white privilege. Not all, but many did, and some still do. There have also always been white allies, abolitionists, and freedom fighters opposed to racism and not afraid to stand against its evil. Their solidarity always was and is appreciated just as others has or will be. Nevertheless, the facts of history reveals what it reveals. It is less than flattering or sparkling and mostly incriminating but true.

Thurston's Thoughts
Most Certainly Did

One thing for certain, and two things for sure, there is an absolute certainty that we are unbreakable and indestructible. We have been indoctrinated with falsehoods, deprived of self-identity, subjected to atrocities, and tyrannically oppressed. We have been psychologically subdued, economically suppressed, demonized, dehumanized, endured legislative biases, and otherwise systematically relegated. We have suffered murder, lynching, rape, family separations, arson, the whip's lash, kidnapping, and bondage.

We have been subjected to religious brainwashing, medical experimentation, nutritional and healthcare disparities, purposeful drug addiction, and disproportionate incarceration. If it can be detrimentally done, it has been viciously done to us without reservation. Yet, here we are in defiance of all odds and hardship. History has proven our resiliency. Superman had kryptonite, and Achilles had his heel as their only vulnerability to attack.

Our only vulnerability has proven to be the self-propagating psychology of captivity. One of our most illustrious Black scholar in his famous book called it psychological bondage. He recognized bondage to the past and the demons of the atrocities committed against us still makes us reluctant to self-define our identity. To finally define our autonomy which is not shaped by assimilation, trauma, or propaganda. The chains have long been dissolved, but the psyche persists. This psyche is a struggle against us and within us.

In the recesses of our minds, we must dismiss the unworthy eye of our oppression and stop seeking validation from the oppressor to belong or be accepted. Essentially to recognize there is no need to prove ourselves worthy by their designation. We are because we choose to be. This dynamic of unworthiness psychologically establishes that the subgroup we belong to is inferior to the subgroup into which we seek inclusion. The fabrication of an inferior subgroup promotes a mentality that it is important to be worthy or qualify for the exclusivity of the superior group.

It is an evaluation of self-worth by someone else's standard. Humanity's primary and primitive need is to be internally swayed for prestige and hierarchy. It is especially effective when fueled by the painful emotion of proving you are good enough to be included. The main benefit of membership is excluding others deemed unworthy, confirming you are better than them. The ambition or satisfaction, by comparison, is the association of either exclusive or celebrity status that the separation defines. It carries a sense of elite identity attached to that separation.

A big-shot syndrome of prestige elevates you above those excluded. Still, if by definition the criteria exclude you, by that criteria if race is the determinate, then you can never qualify except by exception, not inclusion. Even though both are classified as produce, an apple can never be an orange. Likewise, as humans these distinctions of race are traits, not qualities. By strict measurement of an arbitrary prerequisite such as money, the ensuing prestige or status is judged by that primary requirement of money.

The requirement exceeds the boundaries of other selective criteria, such as secondary considerations like race or gender. Consider what separates a millionaire from a billionaire, strictly their inclusion by the threshold of money as the exclusion, not race. It has no race, color, or gender for inclusion, just money as the primary standard. The flaw in racial inequality is the classification by subjective distinction not being of relative and objective criteria. The price of inclusion is the primary distinction that separates the group.

Whether it is money, intelligence, ability, beauty, athletics, possessions, hall of fame, or otherwise, as long as it is specific to the subgroup's projection of exclusivity. The comfort, prestige, and security of others' exclusion are just as alluring as belonging. However, combined it ignites an insatiable obsession to belong at great sacrifice, determination, or pathological peril. This pathology triggers a psychological dysfunction of inferiority by the exclusion of not measuring up or possessing the cachet to qualify.

Understanding this pathology and methodology leads to who, what, and why racial criteria were implemented. It was to distort and fabricate societal assessments for racial exclusion. This distortion is at the crux of racism and the foundation of America's political, economic, and legal structure. The falsification and misrepresentation by racial measurement are so deeply embedded and concealed that denial rest with its inconspicuous acceptance. Dependent on the system's foundational identity, otherwise known as societal norms, tradition, and nationalism.

Crimes against humanity would also depend on who is classified as humanity and possess the inalienable rights to life, liberty, and the pursuit of happiness. The crimes against Black humanity regarding reparations would depend on who is now qualified as Black. The one-drop rule was flawed from the outset by official definition. Black people, by designated exclusion from humanity, were as three-fifths of a human being not eligible for rights or protection and thus far certainly not reparations either.

Immunity from these bully tactics, gorilla pimping, and human trafficking was written into the law and repeatedly upheld under religious and judicial review. The same trust and obedience that granted impunity to law and government require the same submission and delay of redress from the same arbitrators of racism. Good luck with that. Furthermore, immunity secured over time indemnifies crimes committed on American soil by the American government as not subject to international sanctions as crimes against humanity. The victims are well established, and the culprits with their atrocious deeds are identified but the sanctions must be voluntarily self-imposed.

Still, the remedy remains voluntary outside any measure of international law recognizing the global stain of slavery or racism requiring accountability or restitution to Black people around the world. This exemption is a catastrophe of global proportions, with America just being our neighborhood of residential genocide and exploitation. The devaluation of Black people is indeed institutionalized into America's DNA and globally sanctioned, thus normalized by consistent practice. There was never a time when it was not internationally practiced or condoned.

It has also been summarily ignored concerning reparations, redress of exploitation, or rectifying conditions of inhumanity suffered. By contrast, others' plight past and present has been compassionately championed. Childhood trauma is universally recognized as formative to behavior, damaging to development, and a barrier to trust. The same is true with nationalities and ethnic groups subjected to trauma and atrocities. Still, regarding race, some summarily dismiss it and brush it off as the past.

Nevertheless, if it did not exist any longer, there would be nothing to expose. However, it is still a problem. In America, the expectation of Black people loving the way you hate me is a paradigm of mental illness concerning the flag, constitution, and America's societal degradation of us. In other countries Black people history is unique to their country but no less dreadful, sharing many similarities with America's atrocities and abuses. In short, deprivation of human rights, economic exploitation, and violent suppression based on ethnicity are supported by distorted nationalism. It demands our indoctrinated loyalty coercing integration or submission.

Missionaries were always the front line of peaceful conquest, sort of scouts to survey the terrain and temperament of the natives. They are usually the advance team before conquest. They come in peace and love but later occupy by force and deceit. The same blueprint has been repeated across the globe infiltrating nations by religion and pretenses of goodwill. It is the global blueprint of submission to chase equality and inclusion while faithfully enduring the intolerable. The blueprint provides hope and a minor consideration as a token starter kit offering salvation.

Once faithful and pacified, we supply and sustain wealth or benefits that elude us, basically the old wiener for the ham scam. Then, when any benefits finally extend to us, the actual victims of the robbery and extortion, they are chided as subsidies and us as dependent. Religion is often the pacifier initiating the robbery and extortion, promising the sweet by and by for our patience and prayer. The Christian religious indoctrination was mandatory for the subdual of the so-called heathens and savages. It rejected, corrupted our existing spirituality, and replaced it with the docile doctrine of obedience and suffering, the Theseus Paradox of replacement parts.

This swap was perpetuated significantly by the spokesperson of the religious oppression. They are commonly known as the priest, pastor, clergy, or minister, preaching the go-along or die doctrine with heaven as our reward. Over time, we have wholeheartedly embraced this, praying for a savior while enduring a savage. Christianity is prevalent everywhere slavery has been, often predating it or strong-armed into acceptance as a tool of compliance. The same religion shared by slave and slave masters allowed for their brutality towards us and our endurance of it.

Yet, how can it not be subjectively a binding component of our exploitation by which we are still psychologically immobilized? The Roman Catholic Church promotes the Christian faith, with the Pope as God on earth. There is only a minor distinction between Christianity and Catholicism. It appears to glorify Rome's ideological structure. Still, they are passed on as a tribute to Rome disguised as a testament to Christ and God. Are the principles of Rome or the doctrine of Christ worshipped by the expectations and actions associated with the religion?

Has it been the primary justification, tool of oppression, and cause of war for centuries for the betterment of humanity or the continuation of the glory of Rome? The acceptance of our economic condition is justified by the similarity to Jesus' vow of poverty and forsaking earthly goods. Furthermore, we must also embrace suffering. If this is Christ-like, why aren't whites following suit? Why has every reason for national outrage dating back before the American Revolution not justify our dissatisfaction or disillusionment?

Yet, we cling to hope and equality bolstered by faith. We are told we must, and we have kept the faith. But is it faith or foolishness? Determining our future requires reckoning with our past from our perspective. Once we examine our devotion to systems of suppression, can we still be guided by systems of relegation and religious capitulation that subjugate us? I can assure you that this is not an attack on religion in general or Christianity in particular. It is an attempt to illustrate the weaponization of faith to pacify our demographic and conceal an agenda.

An agenda of sustaining Black inferiority by compliance, endurance, and hopelessness waiting on salvation or the granting of dignity, equality, and inclusion. Hopefully, we don't have to wait until we make it to heaven. The escalating standards for inclusion are constantly shifting, provoking more patience from us while promising the same things yet to be delivered. The mind is a microscope and actions are magnifications of thoughts. We are grasping for methods confined by the boundaries of our beliefs blinded by hope, the spell of deceit, and assumptions.

Religion and dangling possibilities fill the void ignoring the improbabilities. We are inflated with faith by our desires, desperation, and pleadings instead of practicalities. Once the so-called heathens are domesticated, they are convinced it is uncivilized to aggressively pursue their humanity. Consequently, expected not to carve an identity undefined by the prescribed social template. If you are offended by the mere insinuation, then perhaps you are opposed to critical analysis, hopelessly indoctrinated, or faithfully convinced forfeiting your right to inquire by your certainty.

We must do our own research, determined to detect and adequately analyze the deceptions randomly accepted as narratives of history, society, and religion. The taboo of questioning these pillars of belief must be cast aside to verify their origins and validity. Remember, beware of false prophets bearing false witness. By not evaluating what we hold true simply from conditioning and not applying logical scrutiny ensures our intellectual and spiritual captivity. Our intellectual captivity has lasted beyond the physical confinement and is guaranteed to continue unless we replace it.

Without exploring society's faulty suppositions embedded in our beliefs and programmed into our psychology, we will not shake them. Examine fluctuating motives and possibly manipulative beliefs scrutinized for intent, purpose, and validity can only either strengthen or dispel them. Our responsibility is to develop our own inquisitive conclusions free from the detrimental depictions and promotions of history's intentional fabrications. Any acceptance postdates our belief system and identity to accept current contrived glorifications, structures, and deities adopted after our captivity.

Our responsibility for our fate and destiny are not removed by the mechanisms and pathologies of racist influences that continue to poison our perception and possibilities. Our hands will remain out as beggars as long as our minds remain shackled and unbroken from a chronic, self-defeating belief system of conditioned behavior. By not doing so, it further distance us from finally being free. What price is freedom? Freedom on our terms is beyond any reparations sought, reparations that still leave us fractured.

The purpose of reparations and restitution is to make the situation or victim whole, but that is not the method to make us whole. Reparations should be measured by our criteria to be made whole again as a people and individuals. But, only we can restore ourselves to a time beyond the damage. We can get the rest if we provide ourselves with the psychological freedom gained from eradicating the grips of imposed racist ideologies. Rejecting these traditional symbols of deceptions used to control us, exploit us, or require complicity from us.

We change others' behavior and opinion by amending our own. Modifications that don't diminish our integrity, image, or intelligence. Not for others' purposes but because it is necessary to our objective. It is essential that we maintain a level of composure, dignity, and character of our noble choosing. No longer bent to other's depictions and definition of us. We must identify, isolate, and eliminate the cycles of mental captivity which reinforce subliminal pillars of racism residing in the recesses of our psyche, hindering our identity and prosperity.

The shifting global paradigm is shedding the carcass of primitive distinctions, rituals, and inhumanities. These inclinations strangle compassion for personal expression, economic prosperity, and psychological freedom from socially engineered indoctrinations of control. Preserving outdated coping mechanisms and rituals are symptoms of lingering mind control.

Therefore, begging for equality is the mentality of a hostage thoroughly broken seeking integration. Seeking relief for survival, even at the expense of our identity or dignity. This is no longer the case for our survival, so it no longer has to be the practice. Time to break the mold. It is over four hundred years old. It is about time for a new mold and the courage to forge it.

Courage is how you are cut when pressure is the tester.

Will you resist, submit, or withdraw?

Progress requires participation.

The battle wages whether we join, hide, or run away.

Slavery was an occurrence, not a choice, but this is a choice.

Let me ask you a Question

1. What are the psychological, sociological, and religious effects of thousands of years of manipulated history, doctrines, and beliefs on us? What about on others? Can we just be dismissive of its effects? What is the connectivity of these purposes, ideologies, and manipulations? Is our programming so pervasive to prevent escaping the matrix?

2. Did our ancestors overcome much more than we now easily succumb? Have we gone all the way soft? Are we tricks to our fears and challenges? How about our habits, desires, or impulses? How about history's revelations and evaluations beyond America's microcosm or the limitations of our beliefs? Is this a squid game for exploitation, control or, worst, amusement?

3. Has religion saved us, condemned us, or both? Why is religion the one sacred indoctrination we refuse to consider as a tool of racism and slavery? Why are we so entrenched in religion without a working knowledge of its history and evolution? Are we aware of Enoch, Josephus, Titus, the Flavian Dynasty, Tertullian, Lilith, The Council of Nicaea, the many resurrections or virgin births, or the origins of some religious symbolism? Does it matter to know or if we knew?

4. Can we be saved when we reject that which would save us? Is turning a blind eye and hypersensitivity the answer to our problems and some of our beliefs? Is our stagnation a legacy inherited from poverty, a scarcity mind set, societal and government injustices, or personal responsibility?What controls us, externally or internally and did we choose it or was it chosen for us?

5. Are we too wounded, hiding behind our denial to rise above our circumstances? Have our resolved sank to maximizing the hurt and damages from slavery to our psyche? Are we in a state of depression from racism eroding our ambitions? What distractions do we allow to weaken us?

To Tell the Truth
Naming Names

The culprits of atrocities can be recognized by name, face, deed, nationality, or government as history speaks loudly regarding their identification. Everything has an origin or beginning, just as there cannot be a lie unless there is a liar to tell it. The lie starts with its telling, not its conception. The conception reveals the unspoken intent. It is always the act, which is damaging, but the thought gives breath and motivation to the deceitful act. The deceit and causes of racism can generally be attributed to religion, nationalism, greed, and misrepresentation translated into slavery, discrimination, and fear.

Britain introduced these crimes against humanity into America as a model of an aristocratic utopia for white Anglo-Saxon protestants of etiquette. It was primarily instituted by Britain and King James, yes the same sponsor of the King James Version of the Holy Bible, aided by other European countries and monarchs to enrich themselves. Greed and wealth-building were the overwhelming factors. Murder, kidnapping, and brutality were the methods. Exploitation, remorse, or humanity was not as much as an afterthought.

These conditions and aspirations set forth a calamity that is still prevalent four- hundred plus years later. By the way, so is their wealth accumulation. We cannot separate the names and intent identified by history from the resulting atrocities. They are interwoven with religion in general and Christianity in particular. Christianity was used as the moral justification and mitigating reason for slavery. The self-pardoning of their animalistic sensibilities for committing such diabolical acts of butchery. Just as their deceit, greed, and disgrace knew no limits, nor did their racist depravity.

Google any King James Bible verse about slavery and ponder how the Bible has been systematically used to justify slavery sanctioned as the word of God. Scriptures were interpreted and manipulated specifically to promote white superiority. The intent was worshipping whites as God-like and designating others as servants and heathens beneath them. Whiteness alone was seen as the apex of the human species characterizing superiority. As such, whiteness was ordained to exploit and dismiss the Black race primarily as servants.

Black people were considered beneath animals and equal to property. The deception is that Noah cursed Canaan, who was Black, to be a servant and a slave. Supposedly because Canaan's father, Ham, saw Noah's drunken nakedness, had knowledge of Noah's wife, or sexually violated Noah as Noah slept. Logically speaking, if the cursed Canaan was Black, then his father Ham was also Black. Likewise, so were Ham's brothers being Noah's pure seed, which would have made Noah Black. Therefore, the theoretical analysis of the story implies Noah, Ham, and Ham's brothers all had to be Black.

Accordingly, Noah and Ham's brothers of the same mother and pure seed of Noah, were more likely made white to support the deception. This deceptive twist designated and justified Black people as slaves condemned to servitude. The racial disparity and distinctions between pure seeds do not accommodate separate races among Noah's pure sons. Instead, it bolsters the deceptive entitlements for slavery of Black people.

Conversely, if Ham were Black, why did his color differ from Noah's lineage of the same seed, supposedly white? Would they also have to be Black too, or was Ham's white color conveniently manipulated to justify Black servitude? Noah displayed no such power until the day he cursed a single offspring of Ham, Canaan, because Noah got liquored up and was seen naked. Ham had other offspring not cursed.

It leaves a lot for the knowledgeable faithful to gullibly assume, especially if Ham's grave sin changed Ham's or Canaan's skin color. If Ham had been white, Canaan's skin tone would have changed because he had already been born supposedly white. Inconsistencies emerge from the interpretation and accuracy of the events and circumstances where racism first seeks its justification. To illustrate the concocted narratives relied on today and to dismiss the concept of color based race, race is a relatively modern concept.

Race in the context of color did not exist in the time of Noah or antiquity. Black and White is not a genetic description, it is a contrived classification of visual convenience and separation. Africa and Africans were referred to as Cush in biblical lore. Speaking strictly of lineage, Canaan's lineage could have evolved to what is classified as Black today, but not exclusively. Speaking strictly of genetics, other nationalities are of Canaan's descent besides Black people.

Canaan's lineage would be Canaanites of Southern Levant region who were driven from the land by Joshua that was promised to Abraham and Moses. This region was also known as Canaan. Furthermore, a lineage, Canaan, which was cursed by Noah would curiously have the land promised to Abraham and Moses named after him. It seems someone has an ironic sense of humor but obviously not the Canaanites.

Canaanites were declared evil and idolatrous to be conquered as penalty for a "dark" culture and evil practices. This was further justification for animosity towards Canaan's descendants. We all remember the old spiritual of Joshua beating the Battle of Jericho and the walls come tumbling down. Nothing that breathes was left alive in the conquest as God commissioned Joshua to destroy the Canaanites. So, racism can be seen as God's destruction of Canaanites which substituted others as the instrument to achieve it. But if Joshua exterminated the Canaanites, how could Black people now be the lineage of that curse or of Canaan destined for servitude?

How could the descendants of Canaan be distinguished from the descendants of Cush, Misraim, or Put by color when there was a spectrum of colors or skin tones among all races? How, especially with their close common genetics and geography? Is there any evidence Noah curse the brothers of Canaan from Ham's lineage? If the Canaanites were destroyed, the remaining Black people, Africans, or whatever designation assigned them had to be free of Noah's curse. The curse was specific to Canaan's lineage and not Ham's.

These musical chair interpretations and classifications morphed over time leaves Black people without a chair when the music stopped, the chair is pulled from under us, or the deceit is justified. In the columns of history, Africans curiously just magically appeared without context in a land where much of these occurrences actually happened, in Africa. Consider that Egypt is considered a Middle Eastern country although it is located in Africa. This classification adds to why Africans are considered as Sub-Saharan, but why? Are we designated as Africans according to the continent, our color, or by geo-political global exploitation?

Further factors in history's narratives are the exodus from captivity involving Kemet or Egypt and Moses. The farther back in time, the commonality of nationalities would have to have been less separated but somehow the resulting narratives are now more complex. Many complexities precede the common knowledge concerning everything we believe. The Epic of Gilgamesh has a strikingly similar context preceding Noah. But, we pick up the trail after the great flood when Noah's family repopulated the earth.

So the lineages of Noah's descendants doesn't allow for any mating between the lineages or interracial mingling by strict interpretation of who was designated as what tribe. However, would they still not share more genetic similarities to their other relatives? With others sharing genetic traits and geography the curse could not have been on skin tone but some other considerations but still not geography. So, the curse of Black people through Canaan's curse lacks continuity in the totality of biblical, geographical, ethnic, and genetic application. The curse would be on lineage and not color or race as we know it today.

But lineage was murky at best so it is likely that it evolved into skin tone which was in fact substituted as a compilation much as white is today. Besides, if humans evolved from apes and cross mating of species, wouldn't Caucasians and others evolve according to their genetics and geographical region of origin? In that context, Caucasians are labeled as white but their genetic lineage would have to come from what was before their evolution. Could it be ape, African, or Black? Wouldn't we all be ape, neanderthal, or African descent if we travel back far enough? Wouldn't Noah be our common ancestor?

I think we all know the answer despite modern classifications. Named after their region of origin, the Caucasus Mountain, whites according to origins cannot now be classified geographically as the majority of the world. Using the same standard, labeling Black people according to a specific region while whites are labeled by migration would seem more than a bit contrived. Africa and the Caucasus Mountains existed in the same period. So, why is there a difference in delineation regarding classifications according to origins?

Caucasian is largely not used while we are classified as African. Why is this, has the Caucasus Mountains now somehow ceased to exist? Even if it did, what would that change as far as historic origins? If we accept the biblical curse of Noah over four thousand years ago, yes four thousand, what other occurrences do we accept or reject since that time? It appears someone has been picking and choosing, but for what purpose? The usual suspects are mind control, exploitation, social hierarchy, greed, religious justification, and an inexhaustible list of possibilities.

Remember Jesus came after Noah, Abraham, and Moses so are we to believe when he absolved sin he left out Ham's sin which Canaan nonexistent descendants now suffer. So, does religion support racism or is racism using religion as justification? It is highly speculative since God curses, and Jesus does not exclude Black people from his blessings and salvation. Does he? Presumably, even Canaan's descendants should have received deliverance from Jesus after Noah's curse. Are we to believe that Noah was elevated to God-like status to curse generations, and after the fact, his curse extended beyond Jesus' salvation and teachings?

The excuse is supposedly it is Mosaic Law and Ham's blessing from God prevented him from being cursed but Canaan's curse is eternal. But, how can a curse on the son not be a curse on the father especially if the father's deed brought it about? So theoretically, since God is never recorded to have reversed it, Black people cannot escape slavery or its mandate. To do so is in opposition to God. But God is never attributed as giving it to anyone as Mosaic Law or backing Noah's play. Seems quite convenient except this interpretation would render all those opposed to slavery blasphemous.

It would also assign to God something attributed to Noah. So, the lineages were assigned their fate and as such eternally subject to its relegation by Noah? Curiously, God did not curse Ham Noah did prior to Moses receiving the Commandments which absently omitted Noah's disdain. So, is Noah's curse the Mosaic Law which was given to Moses much later in which Jesus himself said he is the fulfillment of the law given to Moses, not given to Noah. Would the debt not be paid when all sins were included in Jesus salvation and resurrection?

Romans 6:14 says we are no longer under the old law. We are under grace. Galatians 3:13 state we are also no longer under the obsolete requirements of the Old Testament. Mosaic Law was given to the people of Israel. So, is Noah's curse in rebellion of God? Why does Galatians 5:1 refer to the freedom by Christ setting "us" free never to submit to the yoke of slavery again. Either way, this was done two thousand years after Noah and long before colonialism. Strangely, there are those who would disregard the New Testament as misguided or incorrect. Makes one wonder, how far are some willing to go to justify slavery?

However, history shows us how far. I think we all know by now we have a better chance at guessing someone's weight at the carnival than deciphering this circus of lies. The Bible states to be a servant of God and Jesus, not man. Only man says be a servant to man. Could this be the same God or religion? The rationalizations get to be more ridiculous as the cloak of deceit falls away including it will all get straightened around in heaven. Meanwhile, we should grin and bear it or just bear it as the Christian thing to do. But, how much harder would it have been for others to bear brotherly love or forgiveness? They are obligated to tell us but we are not obligated to listen to evil disguised by evil doers as the voice of God.

Do we submit to the word of man or the word of God? How can we be sure? If God wanted us to know, God would have told us directly. Therefore, were slave masters then explicitly elevated to Noah-like status to be worshipped and obeyed as if they were below God or just above Christ? Was this blasphemy run amok to further justify slavery yet adhere to Christian principles that allowed such savage atrocities under Jesus's salvation? By Christian principles, Black people who believe in the bible must also believe in Noah's curse of servitude and as such still submit to slavery or servitude now as a Christian ideology of obedience.

A subservient psychology of submission to God, Jesus, Noah's curse, and white people is explicitly stated and sanctimoniously implied uncontested by our embrace of the Christian faith. It is in the book. If all Christians believe in the Bible, how can they not believe in the curse or oppose Black servitude? So, it seems Black people are a little pregnant with the ideology which justified slavery or must scrutinize an imposed faith which marginalize our humanity. But, don't worry, we have company because women face a similar dilemma regarding their belief in the Bible and their marginalization. It is also in the good book.

So, it becomes very confusing or a flat out sinister falsehood perpetuated by unconditional cursed inferiority or a twisted racial deception. Black and white are expressions of racism and oppression, not lineage or genetics. Biologically, genetically, and dismissing external features there are trivial difference between humans including blood types, bone structure, or any other superficial classification. Even complexion or hue of skin is not a definitive distinction. The shallow differences rolled back in time was then a similarity. Racism is used as a moral judgement and instrument of ignorance.

This ignorance spans history, society, government, education, and religious dogma. It makes one wonder if Heaven is segregated or reserves a sign stating whites only. Can racists be admitted to Heaven? They think so. For that matter, can racists go to hell? No, really, can they? At least they think probably not. Jesus is attributed as preaching to love thy neighbor as thyself. Still, the enslavement and oppression of other humans are not included in that concept among some so-called Christians even to this day.

Maybe that was why it was essential to spread Christianity worldwide to "lost sheep." To effectively enslave their minds so thoroughly that even now, the misrepresentations and contamination persist beyond logical reasoning. The lie has become the doctrine, and the doctrine has been embraced without scrutiny or analytical rationale. A brief history of Christianity is in order to identify shifts in its progression. Not to disparage Christianity origins or infancy but to contextualize the machinations of evolution influencing today's observation, practices, and racism.

Christians were persecuted until Emperor Constantine I made it the official religion of Rome. During that period religious conversions were forced even by death. As Christianity spread throughout the world, it also expanded the Roman structure of government, social construct, and ideology with it. Most governments today are replicas of the Roman Republic with minor tweaks whether an aristocracy, pseudo-democracy, or autocracy. These replicas are ruled by select groups with an emperor figure at the helm but different or no limitations of powers.

Constantine I and Theodosius commissioned Christianity by their Roman authority and at times brutally forced conversion. These two are most responsible for the spread of Christianity from a religious and political perspective. Under Emperor Constantine I a consortium of Christianity was held for consensus establishing religious doctrine. This consensus provided clarity for the Church and not for Christianity. It was the Nicaea Council of 325AD that set the template for Christianity still followed today. It also had racial overtures and altered beliefs, doctrines, and practices.

There were other subsequent councils to further define the beliefs and practices of Christianity. Another Nicaea Council, Council of Hippo, and Carthage Council altered the books in the bible to their discretion. Even the name of God allegedly was removed from the bible during the Second Temple period so that it cannot be spoken. There are many books that were excluded or removed from the Bible. Probably, the most notable is The Book of Enoch, who was said to have walked with God. Why do we only know of The Ten Commandments and not the other commandments?

There was even some contention as to whether God dictated the bible to Moses or whether various writers composed it. The world by biblical context is roughly 6,000 years old but the Paleolithic and Neolithic Periods far predate the bible's world creation by 2.5 million years. Even still, before Genesis there was a preexisting society in heaven with Adam having a first wife named Lilith. But, was Adam ever in heaven or is that his earthly identity after his fall? It is also believed that there are seven heavens and one above them were God resides.

Coincidently, there are eight planets in this solar system orbiting the sun. Even the father, son, and holy spirit as a three part deity was debated and finally the interpretation settled upon. Furthermore, the holy trinity of three equal parts concept was popularized by the assertion and interpretation of Tertullian. Many consider Tertullian the father of western theology but the holy trinity is not a stated concept of the bible. The bible has scripture that can be very liberally interpreted as a trinity but does not state a trinity.

God said I am, not we are, God is singular, definitive, and infinitely the only ONE. Nonetheless, the trinity and even the divinity of Jesus was debated until it was settled in the 5th century. Many tenets of our beliefs were adopted hundreds of years later and retroactively applied. They were then projected and purported forward to justify future occurrences and past narratives. Likewise, The Doctrine of Discovery ordained by the Church was used to justify slavery and repatriation of any land Europeans invaded under the cloak of religion and civility.

Consequently, the historical truth often depends on how far the verification, etymology, or interpretation goes back but not far enough back to the seminal origins. The Roman Scepter, British Crown, Papal Ferula (Staff), and the America's Presidential seal all directly sanctioned slavery and racism as a means of power or wealth. The temple of racism slithers back to the African Diaspora and Sub-Saharan delineation to the Doctrine of Discovery. The Doctrine of Discovery served as a manual of operations stating finders keepers or take it and it's yours.

This decree was the basis for colonialism, imperialism, slavery, and racism across the globe by Europeans. The Portuguese, Spanish, Dutch, and subsequent marauders primary region of slave trafficking occurred in Sub-Saharan and the west coast of Africa. There we find the reason the Census Bureau do not classify northern African descendants as African American for purposes of race because they know where they committed their atrocities. To this day we are governed by religious doctrine despite separation of church and state.

America is erroneously by baseless speculative default a Christian nation where everything extends from that basis. God Bless America is spoken every time the President officially speaks. Roe v. Wade was overturned based on religious principle but the death penalty is extremely popular among that same group. Obviously, there is no such consistency of sanctity for those already living. We are governed by the inconsistent religious beliefs of distorted antiquity. The principles of Apartheid where a white minority or in this case an ideology rules not exclusively on race but religion.

This practice is contrary to the stated purpose of the Constitution but has always been the case. So, the Flavian Dynasty, Constantine, and King James succeeded in devising a veiled scheme to further Rome and their personal proclivities under Christianity. It seems the further fulfillment of King James' sinister desire to elevate himself above Jesus was also realized by sleight-of-hand interpretation to create unwitting followers of King James' doctrine, not God's.

First, King James sought immortality by having his version worshiped as the guidance to practice religious law circumventing God and Jesus. As a result, rarely is a bible mentioned without the mention of King James. This incantation is a sleight of hand used in alchemy. Later, a secondary utilization was creating a pure-blooded utopia for British colonization. The iron hand method was exploiting an obedient Black slave labor force controlled by the velvet glove of religion to cultivate the land, manufacture crops, and harvest America's resources.

The psychological sorcery of an omnipresent invisible deity that demands absolute obedience and persistent suffering was superimposed over their motive for their justification and our submission. No wonder Christianity was essential to slavery at every turn to psychologically suppress Black people. It arrogantly emboldened white supremacists with their obligatory conjured-up validation. Even the Catholic Church sanctioned, acquiesced, and participated in slavery to accumulate wealth.

Finally, in 1965, they declared it a dishonor to God and took a firm and sincere posture against slavery, denouncing it. Retrospectively, the most dedicated non-white Christian populations around the world were at some point enslaved. Can this be a coincidence? Even still, how does the reverence for the Black Madonna not reject racism? Religion served European and America's expansion plan well when spreading slavery. History's monumental deceit is that taxation without representation started the American Revolution instead of what had become unfavorable business terms.

The British wanted a more significant cut of what they had bankrolled. The slave labor Britain sold at cost had no future cost other than room and board. In addition, they commonly committed wanton abuses of the worst kind acquiring this slave labor which was more or less disposable and pure profit. The American Revolution was fought over profits from slavery, not for taxation but the contract default arising from obligations regarding the funding of slavery. It was an armed musket renegotiation of sorts.

Thus, war was essential for a higher return on investments on the seed money and resources provided. Commodity trading is a fair analogy for their business transactions, as we will later learn. The war, founding fathers, and formation of America resulted from a financial dispute over profits from slave labor, not the liberty of this nation. Even many sitting presidents had no problem with slavery while staunch supporters of liberty, inalienable rights, and equality for whites.

History reveals at some point, twelve total sitting U.S. Presidents have owned slaves, which is twenty-six percent of the total presidents throughout history. Four of the first five. Sixty-six percent of the first eighteen Presidents spanning approximately 70 years until 1859 owned slaves. Also, sixty-six percent or eight of the first twelve Presidents owned slaves while in office, despairingly including no less than the two biggest offenders were beacons of Democracy, first President George Washington (317) and third President Thomas Jefferson (600+).

That accurately reflects the beginnings of the United States government and its perspective on slavery. Zachery Taylor was the last sitting President to own slaves while in the White House. Slave ownership concluded with President Grant before he held office. Yet, racial prejudices, abuses, and indifferences have undeniably continued with documented instances, utterances, and interpretations that have recently included former Presidents Nixon, Reagan, and Trump. Their guarded thoughts and motivations revealed privately in their select company can only be imagined.

Still, the detrimental public ramifications to Black people through legislative, social, and monetary policy are a nightmarish reality. Unfortunately, it has always been the American way, with discriminatory tolerances in the oval office, within every government branch, and at all levels of law enforcement. The history of the Supreme Court reflects Black representation and consideration poorly within America's history.

For example, there have been seventeen Chief Justices, none Black. One hundred and five Associate Justices since 1789, totaling one hundred and twenty-one Justices, but only two have been Black. Most notably, the beloved and renowned civil rights icon, The Honorable Thurgood Marshall, in 1967. He was the first Black Justice. So that was only two in roughly a two-hundred- and thirty-three year span. However, recently, in 2022 a third was added, Ketanji Brown Jackson, the first Black female.

Still, Supreme Court decisions have historically been against Black interests, sanctioned disparities, and upheld racist practices. George Wallace, in 1963 challenged the federal government as Governor of Alabama, protesting the desegregation of education. As a result of this segregationist sentiment, widespread student busing in the '60s and '70s became necessary. However, it was controversial with staunch resistance against an opportunity for equal education for Black students.

The Iran Contra scandal was President Reagan and Oliver North's ruse to illegally fund the overthrow of Manuel Noriega. Racially and demographically, it resulted in widespread cocaine infiltration into the Black community. The aftermath effectively ignited the crack cocaine epidemic and eradicated decades of Black people's gains while initiating the criminality of Black people's crack cocaine addiction. The war on drugs became a war on us, not necessarily on drugs.

When one form of racism or discrimination subsides or is no longer acceptable, another more clandestine and effective method replaces it along with the ensuing justification. The crack epidemic was such a replacement to disturb Black progression, social structure, and economic advancement. Some forms of racism transform while others continue simmering beneath the collective consciousness in hopes of rising again once agitated to the surface. It was most recently disguised as a political movement of conservative values. The dog whistle of racism is often blaring through the bullhorn of conservatism and religion.

It echoed Confederate ideologies and stolen electoral representation of all things. The Confederacy dogma has persisted despite their defeat and treason against the United States. Recently, once again Confederate seditionist carried their flag to overthrow the government symbolizing a foreign government takeover that was a bogus masquerade of patriotism. The civil war ended with the defeat and collapse of the Confederacy in 1865, but for it to only linger as a southern legacy.

Their appalling heritage was openly honored without much condemnation, representing a lingering racist tolerance insulting Black people directly and the United States indirectly. Where else can a loser be allowed to fly their banner and display monuments? The

Confederate flag is a direct dissent against the Union's victory and an embrace of a racist past symbolizing racism more than any other symbol in America. The Confederate flag symbolizes racism and genocide as much as the Swastika symbolizes anti-semitism and Jewish extermination.

Although unlike other wars, the Confederate flag represents only slavery, the only southern dispute of the war was economic reasons derived from slavery. Some want to conceal that the defeated rebel flag has not seen one day of treasonous prohibition or rebuke as a part of history. The Union's protest against slavery was primarily due to the unfair economic practices and advantages created by slave labor that disproportionately enriched the southern states. The bigotry is still deeply rooted and accepted, penetrating the military and government in name, action, and celebration.

Similarly lethargic, it took a full one hundred years for the 1965 Voting Rights Act to legislatively reaffirm and protect our participation in voting, politics, and government. However, the Union also eagerly participated indirectly and profited from southern slavery. Remember that Grant was probably the most renowned general against the Confederacy and had slaves during the war but before his White House tenure as President. After President Lincoln's Emancipation Proclamation, he was assassinated because he disrupted the commerce of slavery, not because of his opposition to it.

After Lincoln's death, Andrew Johnson became President carrying a racist sympathy forward. Johnson refused to honor Gen. Sherman's Field Order 15, pledging reparations in the form of forty acres and a mule for freed slaves in 1865. Former slaves fought to ensure the Union's victory. Still, the contribution was not compensated as promised and defaulted on. Again, assuring continued discrimination and generational poverty by this egregious breach.

However, the 1862 Homestead Act gave free land for settlement, but free land was given to only immigrants as had been the practice as a starter kit for slaveowners with free slaves included. Since the Homestead Act, subsidies and reparations based on race have been doled out. Native Americans received reparations, and so did the Japanese for being held in internment camps. Even countries formerly at war with the United States have received reparations and assistance to rebuild, but not Black people.

In fact, reparations were paid to former slave owners as compensation for loss of slave property. The U.S. government paid $300 per slave to slave owners to pacify abolition under the Compensated Emancipation Act of D.C. in 1862. But still, it did allow for exceptions under indentured servitude. Indentured status was slavery minus the harsher treatments. Furthermore, it is inconceivable that Britain made the last installment in 2015 from the 1835 slavery related compensation to former slave owners according to The British National Archives. The national and international recognition of reparations has been widely recognized, just not to Black slaves or their descendants.

There is no more compelling reason or justification for Black people to receive compensation. Instead, we have received continued discrimination, systematic denial of humanity, and outright carnage of our aspirations and prosperity by policy. Do we really have rights if we are prevented from freely exercising them? What about freedom, if we are restricted in the recognition of it? Those who oppose redress by default support a racial caste system designed to sustain white economic and social power or advantage.

Comparatively, descendants of slave owners have been compensated and granted favor to recoup additional losses through Jim Crow. After the Civil War, the Union most certainly equally promoted Jim Crow with the Confederate south. America was once again united by racism and discrimination. Confederate ideology marches on with racism at the helm. Today it masquerades as southern pride and conservative values when it cares to hide.

Nevertheless, the Confederate intent and persistence of racism have remained strong. Just as recently as 2021, it has been explicitly displayed to expose the enormous and robust support for its prominence with proud proclamations of its pervasive ignorance. The legacy of slavery is a shared experience with those who supported it or profited from it. Britain, France, Portugal, Dutch, Spain, and America were the more prominent countries that participated and benefited greatly from slavery. Africa itself is not without blame as well.

Africa also shamefully participated in trafficking slaves while also suffering its ravages. The others have not offered meaningful acknowledgment or compensation to Black people worldwide. The Royal Family has accumulated substantial wealth, land, and prominence from the slave trade boasting of their royal bloodline and the British empire. Maintaining the Royal family monarch façade at its core is an ode to racism and superiority claims.

Many legacy companies balance sheets have consisted of slave profits and Jim Crow exploitations. An overwhelming number of entities such as financial institutions, college universities, railroads, textile and commodity companies, prestigious families as well as many other entities or lineages that still stand today were enriched by their slave trade involvement. It is likely and safe to assume that most entities with a long history were benefactors of slavery.

The Stock Market and Wall Street were heavily involved in the slave trade. Wall Street and the NYSE were established for the express purpose of slave trading. They had been operating lawfully by decree since December 14th of 1711 as the official slave vending site in New York, sparking the building and expansion of New York City. They have slavery to thank for New York becoming a financial mecca. Most port cities were heavily dependent on slavery, even in the north.

The United States has also indemnified itself from the International Tribunal's authority and the International Criminal Court regarding its past crimes against humanity related to Black people, racism, and atrocities. Therefore, it escapes their jurisdiction and condemnation, skirting liability. The United Nation General Assembly condemned Apartheid in Africa, but the atrocities against Black people has been largely ignored, insincere, and specific changes are generally inadequate. Apartheid in Africa ended in 1994 after forty-six years, so it was fairly recent.

Suppose taxation without representation was the reason for America's revolt. Can we not consider murder, forced slave labor without compensation, and systemic racism as legitimate provocation for our protest and displeasure? The unforeseen ramifications of the proliferation of slavery, social injustice, and racial discrimination throughout America have created the seminal resistance that has prevailed as Black rage.

There is no statute of limitations on slavery, murder, or decency. But there is a hood of dismissal, deceit, and denial.So, why can't we demand accountability for the atrocities committed against us? Comparatively, whites have not endured anywhere near the degree of suffering in which they have dispensed. Yet, they are quick to bemoan and cry ouch when their privilege is diminished, or an election is not of their preference. Racism is a form of mental illness, and discrimination is a form of cheating. Psychological journals officially classify racism as a mental disorder arising from insecurity and low self-esteem. It is also an exploitation of ignorance.

Aside from the need to cheat, cheating can be defined as a deliberate fraudulent subversion of fairness and morality by altering probabilities to gain success or favor. The realization then has to become an admission that their humanity is tremendously self-devalued, when lacking an unfair advantage. These allowances bring into question the level of perseverance and achievement without fraudulent concessions. Their advantage has primarily been keeping others at an exploited disadvantage.

White America never foresaw a day when the imbalance of their influence would diminish to the point where they would have to address their abuses under the scrutinizing consciousness of history and fairness. The crimes levied against Black humanity have been obvious, and the perpetrating groups of benefactors are notorious. Still, no liability has been meaningfully accepted or imposed for the damage caused. Legally retribution is customary for damages suffered. Words are not as sufficient as actions, and empty promises have been more enduring than genuine commitment.

Conservative ideology wants to force acceptance of their deeds and beliefs upon everyone. They disregard past events and dismiss opposing views while declaring a clear conscience free from damages or redress. The past would insinuate present discontinuation, if deceitfully believed. The conservative values façade has long been used to camouflage the absolute certainty of the atrocities committed. The participating parties leave no doubt other than the needed remedy.

The forcing of their racist principles and propensities upon others starkly contrasts with even God, who grants humanity freedom of choice to believe. This acknowledgment should leave no choice but to force some redemptive actions towards an equitable resolution by ideology, government, business, and institutional structure.

ASSESSING FEAR
The fear of a level playing field looms larger than the fear of repudiation of racism or historical condemnation for the carnages of racist atrocities. The distress of reckoning with historical transgressions, which was so completely and appallingly applied, is deeply rooted in the reluctance for retribution and forfeiture of unfairness. It is challenging to visualize amends when contemplating that

maybe with equality this advantage will evaporate. The fear is, it ain't no fun when you are not holding the gun.

You fear a syndrome like the cats in the cradle and the silver spoon where you dread a non-white-dominated America may become just like you towards you. When you firmly held the stick, you beat the "hell" out of minorities, specifically us. Still, fearfully imagining yourself slowly losing your grip begging for compassion and dismissal of past grievances if the oppressed should ever hold the stick. Social anxiety is produced over the consequences, repercussions, and accountability for the nightmare of exploitation, cruelty, and oppression of others.

Consumed fully by the draining burden and deception needed to maintain by any means necessary the portrayal of a sham of supremacy. It never existed, was manufactured, and is increasingly unprotected. The fear even extends to a refusal to acknowledge the nightmarish realization that racist could have ever espoused such evil. It must nauseate the very consciousness to admit. It ignites bogusly furious denials despite a history of repulsive actions. Denial of the truth does not diminish the facts, and perhaps you are what your record says you are, or at least history says so.

Fear of looking into the mirror and reconciling the past is apparent in the current refusal to acknowledge the many advantages received and the damages it has caused. It only aggravates the problem and delays the solution. The time has come to settle the over four-hundred-year-old accrued debt. Recognizing the benefits of the advantages unjustly created for yourself must be impartially shared and made available to all others.

The change must be a diametrical shift from the systemic discrimination, deliberate persecution, and calculated economic sabotage committed against Black people. It must specifically include our recommendations for remedies for damages from prolonged racial discrimination. If you do something outstanding, you want recognition and a parade, so if your deed is not so great, why would that not be allowed to be acknowledged and exposed? Imagine if a competing team electronically stole signals, took PEDs (performance enhancement drugs), blatantly had the rules or officiation rigged to their advantage, or any other methods used to cheat.

They effectively influenced victory to glorify themselves, earning outrage at using rogue tactics. Would those gains be discredited, resented, deemed illegitimate, and in need of adjustment to ensure a level playing field and the truth documented? That is what everyone should be equally allotted, a level playing field where a standard measurement is applied equally for self-actualizing opportunities and accomplishments without exemption. In other words, equality of opportunity, treatment, and consideration.

You cannot be fearful when your actions have caused your fear. It is called cause and effect or intentional provocation. If you were not bellyaching when you committed the act, then do not bellyache when exposed, and the sanctions become due. You enjoyed the meal, now pay the bill. Reparations must be recognized as a deserved remedy for combat services rendered, the harm done, injustices practiced, and thefts committed. Black people have suffered them all without fair and equitable compensation.

It is morally reprehensible that these crimes against our humanity persist, are minimized, and dismissed. The time has come to soothe the outcry from the rampages and ravishes that sully all America claims to stand for and promote worldwide. Many virtuous claims are not practiced on American soil, claiming immunity, ignorance, or statute of limitations. Crimes against humanity have no moral statute of limitations or immunity. To categorize an action, examine the action devoid of name or race. If it is disgraceful and inexcusable, label it as such, assign the culprit to be held accountable, and prescribe a remedy to be enforced.

Finally, it is time to put a name on it, name names, and add up the invoice. Grades, credit rating, criminal record, career stats, rankings, and accomplishments are a few widely accepted measurements of you being what your history says you have been. Besides repatriation of artifacts and stolen treasures are common practices. Why not our pilfered wealth? They represent accepted systems of acknowledgment and accountability, as do reparations.

If you had not committed the action, there would not have been this reaction created. To make your fear more palatable than your atrocities, in this case, fear should not be a state of anxiety. It is an acronym and a pledge to Black people of Freedom, Equality, Atonement, and Reparations. Afterward, the offending parties' damages should be forthcoming without complaint, compromise, or delay. Being segregated and racially profiled should also isolate us for easy recognition for settling the accrued debt. What will be your manner of remittance? Cash, credit, or some other means of acceptable payment. A payment plan is also available as well upon request.

Thurston's Thoughts
Pulling the Curtain

In all fairness, the men and institutions of early America were representative of their time and the normalization of widely condoned perspectives and misdeeds of racism. A roll call and name-dropping of participants and sponsors of racism representative of that time epitomize a level of pride in some corners. Equally fitting, we would be remiss if no mention of their total significance to history went unrecognized. This country was shaped by their perspective and molded in their intended fashion.

Upon further review, their influence on the Black experience and the institutional design of every facade of political, economic, institutional, and societal structure is still apparent. Credit must be given where credit has been earned, acknowledging their dubious accolades. When we are knowledgeable of these dubious accolades, it becomes abundantly clear how what was planted has grown into what we now see and experience as Black folks.

The dye was cast from inception as a model of control, exploitation, explicit prejudice, and obvious disregard for our humanity. Naming the culprits and institutional actions starts with their motivation, endorsement, and orientation leading to slavery. Religion, fear, and inferiority were the grooming mechanisms authenticating the fiction put forth as truth and the American way concealing greed. Finally, the fraud was infused with Christian conservative values. In combination, they were used to abuse and demean the Black race.

We were considered devoid of any moral or intellectual virtue. We were deemed below humanity and treated below animals as commercial commodities. As the years passed and slavery became abolished, alternative methods of discrimination emerged to replace bondage. They were propagated by treacherous defamation of our character, and unscrupulous portrayals of us as stereotypical threats. Proclaiming Black people as dangerous by a contrived narrative and injecting menacing exaggerations.

Furthermore, the methodology was intimidation and miseducation to ostracize the Black race using fear and ignorance for society to defend and us to tolerate the atrocities committed. Later, exclusion from unimpeded opportunity and compelled complicity pacified the societal structure to insidiously suppress us. Only seeing what we have been shown projects the shadow until greater knowledge opens our minds to reject the images. Once we identify the strategies, we know how they are disguised. They only show us what they want us to see, incorporating programming hundreds or thousands of years in formation.

From Noah's curse to the Flavian influence of Josephus on Christianity to Constantine and King James' manipulation to Britain's greed and vanity. From the Founding Fathers' lack of foresight to Charles Darwin eugenics to Richard Nixon, Ronald Reagan, and Donald Trump's racist agitations. Racism has been endorsed. The agent provocateurs of racism are integrated into the religious, political, and social systems. They are masked from detection and protected by their enabler's ignorance.

They operated blatantly initially but later disguised their racial hatred and malicious intentions by denial. Critical race theory and accurate history threaten the foundation of every construct of American government and society. That is how pervasive the lies are, and America's identity is dependent on these lies. To reject the lies would be to disassemble the foundation of America exposing the truth. At stake is the collapse of identity, so the lie is preferable to avoid eliminating misrepresentations that have been accepted and maintained.

That is why racism is not roundly rejected because to do so erases the system's orientation and validation. So, the truth must be made a lie because the psychological admission of what would remain is a broken compass of identity. Religion operates on the same principle. By removing responsibility and evaluation, religion maintains a subjective faith that conforms to principles and ideologies programmed as beliefs. Everything else is a virus to the software or beyond the operating system's willingness to comprehend.

Denial of the truth does not diminish the facts as history independently explored exposes a vastly different reality than history taught. Unfortunately, the educational process is based on the thesis of training or breeding uniformity. The educational system was enforced by arrest until it became widely accepted, and resistance subsided as a submission to force. The actual purpose of education is to take an illiterate population and make them more suitable for labor. It often discourages independent or analytical thinking.

During slavery, we were excluded from reading or education because it was not essential for manual labor at that time. We were only machines of physical labor, but as labor needs changed, adjustments to education evolved. It accommodates educational levels throttled sufficiently for the labor needs. It leads to a service economy where people are the automation. That is why we were steered toward factory, menial, or service labor.

However, Black people later ensured an easily identifiable labor force reproduced for exploitation as low-wage service workers. Controlling education controls the population. Therefore, I maintain it is a marked difference between knowledge and education and the purposes and intent for each. Knowledge is the key to our ascension beyond the shackles of slavery and resulting psychological bondage. Likewise, education is culturally operating within sociological systems, standards, and practices of conformity.

As I further delve into the processes and occurrences that culminate in today's challenges, it will become clear. Our independent acquisition of knowledge from credible sources outside the conventional educational system is the only source of information remotely untainted by racist overtures. By design, the brainwashing indoctrination arms the believers as it disarms those subjected to it. Over time the policies and practices equally deceive both. It is a time-proven method to create and trigger competing fractions that are too distracted and emotionally consumed to notice the manipulation.

The instigation effectively conceals the ulterior motives, which are greed and control. Ignorance is profitable as a commodity but extremely unprofitable for the ignorant. You pay for what you don't know and can charge for what you know. So, let's take a quick spin through history, bending a few corners to check out the deceit and peek behind the curtain at some historical facts. The developmental stages of the country's birth yielded four out of the first five presidents who practiced slavery as sitting Presidents. That continued the tone and tolerance for slavery during their time.

It should be noted, some at that time saw slavery as morally appalling, but these Presidents were not among those who did. The practice and tolerance from the highest political office propelled its longevity. It was not only societally embraced but was legally sanctioned by law for nearly another ninety years. This vision is the glory and wisdom of the founding fathers that we are so bound to and afflicted by now. Their practice or tolerance of slavery was a large part of their vision of America's future. Perhaps strangely, Christianity was not a primary belief beyond control.

Founding fathers such as Washington and Jefferson owned over nine hundred slaves between them as overt verification of their vision. As for the Civil War, it was fought over resentment of the South's wealth accumulation from slave labor. Their unwillingness to depart from their financially unethical business practices of using Black people for profit-generating. The chattel or personal property of these slaveowners produced their wealth and was worthy of going to war to preserve. The treason against the government was in protest of liquidating assets, pitting the Confederate South against the Union North.

Better summed up as the free labor coercing haves against the low wage paying have-nots. The war discontinued the economic disparity, but the oppression and discrimination continued for Black people. Ironically, Grant was one of Lincoln's most noteworthy generals, which parleyed Grant to the presidency. Even he owned a few slaves, although not as a sitting president. So, it is conceivable that he was not fighting the war to specifically abolish slavery. Out of this skirmish emerged the fallacy of the vaulted Confederacy of dixie folklore and treason against the government.

The Confederate spirit of rebellion against government control persist today, except when they use the government to control others. The Industrial Revolution, known as the rise of machines, finally began to end slavery as no longer practically or financially viable. However, discrimination and exploitation remained a profitable exercise. Freedom and patriotism adopted the Dixie connotation of the Confederate spirit. Thus, racism continued as before as the prevailing standard of American society. At the sedition at the Capitol on January 6, 2021, the Confederate flag was on prominent display as an ode to their treason repeated.

The symbolic declaration that the South, having laid in wait, was rising from its shame and defeat in 1865 to now take over. That is a long time to wait, but it illustrates the insidious treachery and racist sentiment still percolating fanned by fear, falsehoods, and pseudo-patriotism. Obviously, the Confederate spirit never went away once defeated but was licking its wounds. It is displayed in plain sight in names and structures such as schools and military bases funded by public money.

In essence, this means we have helped finance the propaganda of slavery and racism. Their symbol of treason masquerading as patriotism should defy the very definition of patriotism and democracy. In this context, reparations seem unlikely from those who openly honor slavery, the Confederacy, and Jim Crow. Undoubtedly, they must disagree with reparations, if they condone the motives for it. They have not agreed yet to freedom, equality, or voting rights for Black people, let alone reparations. Do you believe they believe we should be compensated for acts they disagree were damaging or immoral?

Probably more like suck it up and shake it off, proclaiming it will be all right because no one likes a complainer, not even a complainer. The described history thus far reveals why the Confederate spirit is openly thriving today. However, that is just the historical foundation. Let's now review the fortification of the racist foundation in other facets of society. First, let's consider the primary western financial markets. It is no coincidence that London and New York are the two largest.

It is also no coincidence that port cities on the east and south coast are shipping hubs. Guess what commodity they primarily traded? If you didn't guess what, it was slaves. Their origins can be traced back to human trafficking of slaves. If slaves were considered chattel or property, they could be further classified as income-generating commodities, like stock options. The systematic and uniform trading of these less-than-human commodities' established these trading posts as global financial hubs.

Today it is called human trafficking and frowned upon, but then it was called profitable business practices and managing assets. The British Empire as the primary conductor and beneficiary was bolstered and maintained on the slave trade. As equity investors in America with shareholder's rights their dividend demand caused a disbursement dispute in the form of taxation resulting in the American Revolution. This dividend demand initiated America's independence from Britain over equity or debt repayment. The British Commonwealth alludes to some of Britain's slave trade ventures around the globe.

In just 2021, Barbados declared freedom from Britain's commonwealth rule that originated in slavery. Many countries' wealth, families of affluence and nobility, along with the most prominent institutions, including financial markets like the New York Stock Exchange and Wall Street, have a history rooted in slavery. These global and national entities that form the backbone of the largest financial and educational institutions have the shame of slavery on their income statements. We have skimmed the surface of the intentional racial impact of religion, education, the Founding Fathers, our governmental structure, the Civil War, and the Confederacy.

We have also touched on America's economic and financial building blocks along with the pervasive systems enacted to support slavery. It seemingly would be a shorter list to identify the things not associated with slavery. But wait, there is still more. More? Yes more. There are still legal and legislative elements to consider. The almighty arbitrator of fairness and neutrality, the Supreme Court has only had three Black Associate Justices with one added as recently as 2022. Otherwise, six women Associate Justices, one Black, Ketanji Brown Jackson and one Hispanic, Sonia Sotomayor. In 234 years of the Supreme Court's existence that is their minority representation.

That is only three Black people and one Hispanic or Latino out of one hundred and five Associate Justices. The Honorable Thurgood Marshall, in 1967, after 179 years, was the first Black person, so the interest of Black people and representation of minorities have been barely reflected and only in the last fifty-six years. The Supreme Court's record is less than glistening from its beginnings in 1789 by continually upholding racist policies. It has lagged behind the country's consensus and continued to fail to provide unbiased legislative leadership other than reactionary antiquated posturing.

Being duly compromised it is now on the verge of overt politicization. The interpretation of Constitutional Law is subjective to perspective and surmised intent where no original intent could have been anticipated or applied to contemporary issues. It has become a subjective political partisan exclamation of values held by the arbitrator spewed as their interpretation of intent or law. But, then again, maybe it has always been that and a farce of impartiality by its history. The ventriloquist masquerades as the companion to the dummy.

Likewise, the Supreme Court masquerades as the interpreter to the Constitution. However, we should know whose voice we hear. It is not the dummy or the Constitution that speaks. The sleight of hand is what we don't see, we ignore the hand in the back or puppet master pulling the strings. Today operating as the puppet master is a quasi-secret society, the Federalist Society of Law and Public Policy. The Federalist Society is a conservative organization for right wing ideology. They are instrumental in determining Supreme Court nomination candidates.

Their purpose is a conservative agenda controlling substantial legislative influence and interpretations including six of the nine members of the Supreme Court with affiliations. Does their affiliation disclose their predisposition and partiality regarding rulings or interpretations of the Constitution? Seemingly, this conservative slant would explain everything we can't explain. The federal court system is astonishingly worse. Legislatively, their ideology, not the Constitution, are behind the curtain dictating public policy.

The Court's composition has more influence than our votes because they control the operating manual. Legislation has always been the basis of enforcement for racism's implementation but now it has descended further into political and religious gerrymandering. Religious beliefs, social anomalies, and partisan seductions jointly solicit their favor repudiating their integrity. Economic, legislative, and criminal determinations are controlled from behind this curtain.

Therefore, conservatism is the law of the land disregarding precedence, impartiality, judicial integrity, and the Constitution. Strict interpretation of the Constitution amounts to surmised subjectivities often outdated and inapplicable to today's issues stretched beyond the Constitution's intent, limitations, and vision. It becomes a partisan tool of autocracy of opinion coercing preferences as judicial interpretation. Many applications of the Constitution are not mentioned in the document, such as abortion, so it is speculation at best presented as scholarly adjudication by the Supreme Court.

The fluctuation of conservative and liberal values makes the predictability of decisions predicated on the individual Justices and not the law. The Court has taken to liberal interpretations to invoke sub-jective conservatism as originalist intent. It amounts to pouring new wine into old wineskins. The Constitution must likewise be amend-able to new wineskins for unforeseen challenges for its preserva-tion. It jeopardizes its integrity and validity to be separate and de-tached from politics but also relevant.

This risk should not be shocking, given its blind eye to racial dis-parities and injustices of the past also being presumptions of the Constitution. By the Court entertaining restrictions on voter's rights and suppression providing favor or advantage to a political party, gives the impression that a Presidential election can be overturned or seized under the Court's protection. Furthermore, criminal law's rampant abuses of power and injustices are allowed to persist.

In some instances, they are sometimes protected by qualified im-munity overriding reform, racial fairness, and in violation of civil rights. In many ways, the mentality of slave catching and vigilan-tism is evident by disproportionate incarceration criteria and stand your ground laws. The law still routinely condones legal disparities. After racially criminalizing behavior by targeted enforcement ef-forts towards certain groups, they purport them to have fearful propensities in need of profiling. It prioritizes the doer as racially corrupted instead of the enforcement as racially biased.

A prime example is the proliferation of crack cocaine directed to-ward the Black community. It caused further economic suppression from the crack epidemic that is still felt today. It targeted us to fi-nance illegal operations to overthrow a foreign government on one hand. While also creating and stimulating the enforcement industry targeting us by the so-called war on drugs facade. Furthermore, it was government directed and sanctioned without repercussions ex-cept for mostly us.

It seems a popular racist and a complicit Congress shamefully and willfully yielded to power, popularity, and a political agenda. Yet, once again, the brunt of this atrocity has been heaved upon the

Black community. It serves to confirm racial indifference to any damages caused by government policy as recently as the eighties and nineties. But, then, tough on crime was code for tough on us imitating America's favorite pastime of three strikes. Punishment is reserved for the minions of society by racial or economic distinction, which both most often are us.

Legal substances such as opioids, sugar, and tobacco are legally pedaled. They are more damaging and dangerous than some banned substances. For example, it raises questions of marijuana criminalization. By using legality, it is an excuse to marginalize us, supply the prison industrial complex, and generate revenue for a bloated criminal justice system. More often, it is discriminately applied, destroys family structures, and economically disqualify us from significant opportunities. More than anything, drugs derailed the progress of the sixties and seventies, diverting a generation from productivity.

Finally, it impeaches these systems of collaboration of pervasive proportions involving foreign governments, American Presidents, legislative law, criminal law, and public policy. In these regards, they are infiltrated with blatant racism. It was purposefully engineered with societal land mines for the regression, slander, and condemnation of our people. These enticements are traps made attractive by desperation, hopelessness, and economic suppression. A drowning person will grasp at the tip of a sword if that is the only prospects or means of survival.

So pursuing some of these options becomes more apparent in this context as a matter of survival, not of our character. Identifying the traps and the likelihood of how and where they exist should clarify these trojan horses revealed by history. Understanding history and its structural biases should assist in understanding our condition and how or why it is what it has become. Not to make excuses but to explain it further, understanding the dynamics of its entrapments. Understanding this should also clarify where and how it requires our collaboration to help pull it off.

That is the game they want us to play, but we don't need to play their game by their rules. It always pays if we are proficiently adapt at the opponent's game and weapon of choice. It expands our capabilities, knowing that we are exceptionally skilled at ours and theirs. The opposition's weakness must be included in our strengths. It makes us hard to beat and even harder to want to attempt beating. We can't go wrong with being able to handle ourselves if pressed into action. However, it is not a battle of physical prowess but knowledge and psychological perspective.

Developing our mind as an elite machine programmed to methodically operate independently of the circumstances around us governed by the compass within us. The mind then thinks and acts in unison, accessing knowledge and utilizing capabilities instead of processing splintered logic or committing senseless acts. It is first gaining perspective and then developing our minds to follow our goals aligned with a plan to achieve them. It is fortifying our determination, prepared for the obstacles that are sure to come or cannot be deflected.

Comfort should not be prioritized over achievement. It probably will not be easy, don't expect it to be. It is a matter of excelling above the conditioned provocations calculated to elicit a particular reaction or condition producing failure. We must operate differently with applied logic. Long-standing conventional systems designed to ensnare us await lapses in diligence to complicate our path. Reparations may be a state of mind consumed by wishful thinking of what should be.

So the process must factor in the circumstances as they are and maneuver slicker than the predictability and expectations of the system. Reparation or a fair shake is not to be expected as essential to our success. Success is essential to success. Remember, stay focused and remain diligent. Peril may await, but challenges and resistance certainly does. Pulling the curtain back removes the wool covering our eyes. Clarity is the result, and vision is the reward. We must first see it to be it. Then we must become it by doing it. It is time to show it, not just say it.

Consequences arise from accountability.

Accountability arises from actions.

Shame arises from guilt and guilt from wrong.

Our shame lies in what we do not do in the future.

Not what was done to us in our past.

Let me ask you a Question

1. How many wear the disguise of respectability who were well entrenched in racist acts who are distanced by revisionist history or deceit? If their racist inclinations were evident, would it explain their actions? Is that damage incidental to issues today? How does it matter now?

2. Has the conditioning and cultivation of racism been so pervasive to normalize its impact on us? Will knowing and revealing the names urge voluntary regret or redress? How will they be held accountable? Is this why CRT upsets the equilibrium because of who and how they were involved? What are the global implications? Can we connect the global impact of Colonialism, Imperialism, and Apartheid as an ideology and not a regional occurrence?

3. How do we better recognize the instruments of racism's conditioning and implementation? Can we validate and create our own equality? If history is a ledger, does what is recorded demonstrate the need for scrutiny or skepticism? Why do they still affect us? Are we free to psychologically choose and believe differently if we still hold fast to these instruments?

4. Does it seem education is a recurring theme to assist in our suppression? Why do we insist on the same source to educate us that miseducated us? Since ideology transcends geographical boundaries, why can't our psychological awakening extend globally, not based on race but dignity and autonomy? As an ideology if Apartheid was the minority ruling among the majority, why do we still allow this desecration? How does a microcosm stop a cosmic shift, if not by mind control?

5. What knowledge have we failed to embrace? Is facts over feeling or logic over beliefs the measure of validity if we still adhere to falsehoods? Why does so much history defy facts or logic, yet rely heavily on ritual or submission? Are we counted on to remain emotional, irrational, and obedient? Is there a difference between obedient and subservient?

Overdrawn Account
Reparations and Resolutions

The solution is plain and simple in concept, although admittingly complex and comprehensive in its application. Ideally, it must also be solemn and unwavering in its commitment. The commitment requires meaningful change recognizing grievances and infringements where substantial damages and exploitation have been identified. These can be self-identifying and voluntary admissions or adjudicated and involuntarily sanctioned. The remedies should reflect the capacity and benefits of their participation in the slave trade.

War crime tribunals pursue individuals many decades past their crimes having been identified. Once their transgressions are known, their identity exposed, their location secured, and the extent of their participation verified, the pursuit is relentless. No matter how small or how much time has passed, whether they are remorseful or not, they are subject to a penalty of law for their crimes. Countries, businesses, and institutions have the same moral, legal, and societal obligations to refrain from crimes against humanity or become subject to penalty and accountability.

Under God's law and America's moral righteousness, if not by man's written law, racism must be rectified since we have always known the what, who, where, excuses, and refusal to be held accountable. Man's law and history's alterations have always sought to indemnify these abominations, manipulate reality, and contort societal structures protecting the guilty or claiming immunity. Unadulterated chronicles of history have constantly spewed forth the guilty whose deeds were so openly practiced that reparations would seem uncontested.

Unbiased enforcement of the law does not require the guilty to consent or be remorseful, only to have committed the crime. Any resolution should include guilty national and international companies and entities funding initiatives exclusively for Black people and global communities of Sub-Saharan slave descendants. Others have received redress for America's transgressions at the exclusion of us, so they have already essentially received their redress. The profiteers of slavery should be compelled to mea culpa and commit to corrective measures.

Their vile narrative as citizens of the world needs amending to reflect the sins and fruits of those sins. Also, to reflect any actions to correct or atone for committing those sins. They can openly acknowledge by their redeeming actions to offset the destructive effects of their exploitation of our people. Let history then be the future measure to judge the actions and manner in which these atrocities are corrected and a commitment to compensation demonstrated. Unfortunately, avoiding acknowledging racist elements and the resulting harmful repercussions has been ignored, allowing the accumulation of obligations to exacerbate a resolution.

Since access to wealth and equal opportunity were denied, fairness demands that it is now what must be provided. Let us not be naïve about what will or should be done. In its sincere undertaking, the objective is understood, and reparations are required in various measurable forms. The details and implementation of the means to accomplish this are complex, but the need for a determined commitment is clear. Imagine if the United States of America is a house. The citizens are the house's occupants or family.

The leaders are the parents in a cooperative and committed relationship dedicated to keeping the family dynamic strong while overcoming challenging times. Staying together for the occupant's benefit realizing the value of the individual parts, and any disruptive actions will fracture the good of the family or household. A house divided cannot stand as conditions worsen and the foundation begins to destabilize. One party cannot seek to minimize the problem because it is most slanted toward their benefit and convenience inviting a bitter divorce.

Without considering the consequences, sufferings, or contributions that have contributed significantly to the success of the household, it begins to fracture. Suppose the other party is marginalized, daring to cry out that they have a problem. In that case, WE should have a problem, and a conciliatory resolution must prevail. In America's house, regarding the context of recriminations for racial discrimination, establishing a Declaration of Resolution incorporated into the societal structure begins to rectify slavery and Jim Crow.

Only then can renovations begin to repair America's inescapable history as proud vendors of crimes against our humanity on a national and global scale. The guilty parties are interchangeable, the occurrences countless, and the despicable actions incorporated in America's history, so the impact of the resolution must be comprehensive. Otherwise, the house of Democracy will eventually crumble from the chaos attempting to sustain the unsustainable.

Any **Declaration of Resolution** must thoroughly consider the following principle-based points not being relegated to a person, occurrence, or movement but instead an unwavering commitment. It must not be accusatory but factual, implemented in a context devoid of grandiose individual acclaim but sculptured in collective obligation where everything must be on the table for examination. Finally, anoint and elevate this stipulation above all else except the cause. It creates a social crusade and not a martyr for death or a target to be corrupted.

The movement must be the leader. Otherwise, leadership becomes a target. The cause is the star, leadership may be interchangeable but not the cause. The insanity of accepting failed divisible methods must yield to practical sustainability resistant to sabotage and separation tactics corrupting, discrediting, or assassinating our leadership. The cause must be prioritized, not emotions, for logical actions and sustainability of intent promoting social justice instead of elevating personalities.

Prospects of personal gain sometimes stall objectives more than actual opposition by taking fame and money then running to the high ground, relaxed from the tireless pursuit of justice. Nevertheless, we must exalt the integrity of the objective above the method of the objection and personality objecting. The message supersedes the messenger with the change achieved sustained beyond the sacrifices to attain them. All those concerned are welcome to become agents of change.

To skim the surface of grievances that historically touch all levels of government and society, I have taken the liberty to offer these considerations with what is my humble suggestions. It can be amended or supplemented to whatever the agreed-upon or negotiated redress. Applied in the selected form of authentic actualized measures that resonate as piercingly as the indignations, exploitations, and atrocities have.

Government and legislative processes.
Government is a corporation that behaves and responds in some ways as businesses do. But, in other ways, it is insulated from certain boundaries, discharged by enacting and enforcing the boundaries against itself. Making equality, equity, and opportunity more than just words to inflate hope and deflect reality, the government must lead the charge by example. Implementing government and legislative processes compelling meaningful policy changes and enforcement is imperative. The government by applying focused statutory enactments and legislative stipulations to ensure proper implementation reconciles its claims to promote equality.

Establishing legal precedence and procedures inclusive of authentic fairness, unbiased interpretation, and accessibility in equal diligence reflects our inclusion, protection, prosperity, and participation across the governmental spectrum. A sincere government posture of equality would eliminate a sizable portion of discrimination. Many systemic injustices are encouraged by government actions or inaction to penalize violations. Tolerated violations invalidate respect for the law, equality, and claims of government opposition to racism. Codifying initiatives of Black concern or impact would establish the permanence of its impact and application. So, put it in writing as the law and enforce it.

Educational content and teaching.
Correcting educational content and teachings regarding historical inaccuracies and racist perspectives removes bigoted superiority indoctrinations. Any exaggerated white accomplishments, eugenics referenced and brainwashing propaganda, or historic misrepresentations as a matter of public education must be thoroughly rebuked. The sinister intent of material concealments distorting the Confederate heritage, supporting racist validations, and delusional impressions of condescending superiority should be expelled as educational malpractice.Portray Black history and African heritage in their authentic truth, accuracy, glory, or shame.

Education should reflect the unadulterated truth comprehensively conveyed without manipulative motives depicting an accurate illustration of knowledge and history. This knowledge should be available and disseminated at any public location where inaccuracies have been distributed. Education should be based more on preparedness for future developments and less on revisionist history. Dismissing deceptions should be a goal of education.

A curious mind craves and pursues truth with an open mind to accept, reject, correct, or improve knowledge through individual exploration and verification. An informative approach to knowledge is to know it without the need to accept or believe in it but only to understand it forming your own opinion. Understanding invites the option of participation by self-determination and clarity uninhibited by manipulation. Debatably, one of the biggest detriments to our wealth accumulation has been the knowledge or lack of involvement in various investments.

Participation in insurance, annuity, retirement fund, stock, real estate, and entrepreneurship opportunities. Also, accessibility to capital, alternative monetary instruments, and wealth-building possibilities and principles previously used to our detriment should be concertedly extended to us by the institutions specializing in them. This lack of knowledge, emphasis, and exposure which has historically prevented our compounded accumulation of wealth, is from a determined bias by fiscal design.

When finally allowed to read, participation in financial literacy for accumulating wealth was restricted along with the instruments to do so. However, expanded information has been at our fingertips for a while due to technology. So, it is incumbent upon us to independently become knowledgeable concerning topics and methods of wealth accumulation. Consequently, the educational and financial literacy gap cannot have us so far behind that we look like we are in first instead of actually being in the competitive hunt.

Law enforcement and criminal court.
The law should be impartially applied regardless of race or wealth. Adjustments and goals of policing expectations and reasonable execution of the law are required to maintain the integrity of both. Law enforcement and criminal courts are beyond repair as they are currently constituted, but that is not to say they are not needed. On the contrary, what is required is an operational modernization, and an ideological upgrade with many procedural techniques, policies, and tactics revamped.

Considering options that not so readily resort to discrimination, disproportionate discretion, or excessive force that is deadly or otherwise. Displaying discretion and empathy for the situations and struggles encountered or the individuals relegated to them, other options to arrest and punishment can be preferable. The police should also understand and familiarize themselves with the people they police through prior community exposure and interaction as part of their academy training.

Transparency and accountability must be based on admitting improprieties, abuses, and damages when they occur and are apparent.

The justifications and restrictions governing actions, intent, fairness, and respect for the public should be the parameters that law enforcement must abide by unconditionally. Standards that emphasize accountability and do not advocate blanket qualified immunity for misconduct or violations are in law enforcement's best interest to preserve appearances of an impartial disposition.

Any warranty or protection is voided after a disqualifying action or breach, so it also should be with qualified immunity. This standard should not be circumvented, subjective, or ambiguous. Abuses diminish the totality of law enforcement's credibility. Police having immunity from unlawful actions should have come and gone. Instead, appropriate conduct is demanded, and transparent recognition of misconduct is presumed, where accountability is taken as a serious responsibility of police duties concerning the public.

Our people caught up in the criminal justice system are there for many reasons. One reason definitely is some of our ill-advised decisions. But, many of these causes can often be based on limited choices and options that are frequently the result of economic desperation reflecting discrimination and lack of viable options. These causes can sometimes be a reflection of bias, poverty, or hopelessness created by willful default. Thus, making it less by choice but more by condition.

So, is it a reflection of our race committing crimes or criminal enticement by our racial condition? Nevertheless, sometimes it is the best choice out of several bad choices that seem like a clever idea at the time. When the only seemingly accessible choice is a bad choice, when chosen, it can only lead to a bad choice being taken. But, a similar bad choice when selected by someone else, the judgment cannot be different. Options unavailable to us but available to others lessen their need to consider unwise choices.

Make no mistake that two avoidable wrongs can occur by succumbing to the influence of committing a crime and the purposeful predictability engineered to encourage it. Not to justify poor decisions but to simply better understand their possible origins in thought and deed influenced by racial implications. But ultimately, breaking the law is a choice deliberately made despite the underlying influences. Although, lack of opportunity and despair often dictates the propensity for committing some crimes.

Economic ramifications and the lack of opportunities to avoid them are the basis of many crimes, regardless of race. It is sometimes part of cultural conditioning and reinforcement, considering the accessibility of alternatives for survival. Still, who is arrested and for what crimes depends disproportionately on how and in which communities law enforcement resources are directed. But, just as we expect others to be liable for their decisions, we must be responsible for ours.

Therefore, impartiality in applying the law must be uniform regardless of reason, with compassion and discretion also impartially applied. Due process of law and sentencing for crimes should statistically be no harsher or malicious with race as an apparent factor. The magnified percentages of arrest and incarceration for Black people sound very few alarms but yield plenty of baffling justifications and dubious convictions. The bail bond system, at times, suggests a caste system more reflective of economic status than the crime committed.

Arguably, the bail system is a subtle excuse for prolonged incarceration and guilty plea-provoking motivations. It often lacks consideration of actual guilt and produces a negotiated guilty plea for brevity. Lack of bail has been known to soften resolve regardless of guilt enticed by prospects of release, probation, or certainty of a shorter sentence. Cash bail needs to be abolished as the antiquated racist system it has been. As currently constituted, its application is a straight-up predisposition to penalize someone based on economics instead of the crime committed.

Bond money after the fact has no impact on the commission of the crime, guilt, return to court, propensity to commit another crime, or willingness to intimidate a witness. Bond amount does not determine these things. Still, other considerations do, such as the actual crime committed, the impact on or harm to victims, the arrestee's criminal past, and the court's ability to prevent a substantial risk of further illegal actions. The law has proven to be only as good as someone's willingness to respect and abide by it, not whether they have money for a bond. The bond is intended as a surety note meaning a financial instrument of assurance to appear, not of guilt or a guaranteed return to court because it does not assure either of these two.

Property ownership and housing conditions.

Property ownership and housing conditions, geographic housing choices, and neighborhood investment and development often leave our people in a stagnant spiral of declining or horizontal growth, reiterating generational poverty and despair. Thus, never venturing too far outside the familiar confines physically or economically of the circumstance we find ourselves. Sure, there will be those who escape this purposeful fate, but a sizable number do not stray too far away from its grip. Property ownership and valuations have long been a primary method of wealth accumulation and an effective denial by discrimination.

A job is unlikely to produce wealth because what it produces is a service to creating others' wealth. Housing is also manipulated by redlining, gentrification, and gerrymandering affecting government services, biased redevelopment, and suppressive political or electoral representation. Property tax, abatements, and other government allotments impact everything from the standard of education and schools to the services received. Lack of enforcement of housing codes, higher insurance rates, usuary interest rates, and many other fees and hidden barriers further absorb resources to impair Black wealth.

The social, financial, and political withholdings further the depletion and imbalance of resources used for our prosperity, instead secretly siphoning wealth and opportunity from us. With that said, far
too often real estate has been systematically recycled through
predatory lending practices, redlining, and foreclosures. In addition
to suppressing wealth accumulation, our communities are devalued
by lack of building code enforcement and environmental pollution.
They insidiously contribute to our health depreciation such as lead
poisoning. These are the invisible damages relative to housing that
must be addressed.

Banking and lending practices.
Banking and lending practices further discriminate by loan and
credit aversions. In addition, predatory lending practices and the
lack of fundamental capital investment create disparities and ownership barriers. Obstacles to entrepreneurship, transference of
wealth impediments, lack of wealth-generating opportunities, and
restrictive scalability in equity positions limit avenues for our participation. They have not been customarily extended to the Black
experience as available fiscal options.

Lack of capital restricts the ability of small and emerging businesses to compete and survive, with our ownership more challenging
and mandating a greater risk of failure or hardship. Seizures, foreclosures, and debt are further aversions used to discourage ventures
and present uncertainty doubting efforts to produce revenue or
ownership rewards. Given the number of banks, insurance companies, and other organizations including Wall Street, there should be
no shortage of remunerations and expertise to alleviate any prevailing harmful financial elements of the Black experience.

Being extremely familiar with balance sheets, accrued liabilities,
accounts payable, venture capital contingencies, maturity dates, and
the like, there should be no hesitancy to the existence of the obligation, even if reluctant to the terms. Refusal to calculate the benefit,
productivity, and profitability realized by properly servicing the our

community, the projected prosperity of these financial institutions is greatly restricted. Rather than empowering our productive participation and contributions, we are obstructed and rejected, but our resources are readily pilfered.

<u>Food and nutrition.</u>
The nutritional value of food is the foundation of good health, especially in young children and older adults. Therefore, the affordability and availability of healthy foods are the two primary factors in choosing what to eat or feed our family. Of course, convenience is also a significant consideration. Still, convenience can be overcome by discipline and the availability of better options. Cultural preferences shaped by generations of lack of available, affordable choices have led to a lack of healthy consumption, concern, or awareness of what we are essentially consuming.

The effect on our digestive system and organs ignites a ticking time bomb of ill health. In addition, the quality, freshness, and mislabeling, along with the chemicals and ingredients, further any damage consuming the wrong foods cause. The healthcare implications, illnesses, and associated diseases heavily prevalent in our communities can be attributed substantially to our dietary selections. In addition, our nutritional options are directly associated with our economic capacity and proximity to better food sources.

Our main nutritional health risks are fast foods, low-quality foods, and sugary drinks. Usually, the cheaper the food, the unhealthier it is to consume. Food deserts and lack of fresh vegetables and grains are nutritional considerations that affect our health as much as income inequality. It is the combination and culmination of several things. First, food co-ops and farmer markets are things our people must undertake and support, denouncing the unhealthy selections synonymous with illness.

Once supplied, we must make a concerted cultural shift to embrace a healthier diet. Nutritional education correlates to health and wellness. Consider this: Would you let your child sit and eat twelve tea-spoons of sugar or the equivalent of drinking a 12 oz bottle of a popular soda? What about another popular 12-ounce Soda that has ten teaspoons of sugar? Sugar is a drug and one of the prime addic-tive and destructive offenders hidden in drinks. So you can easily see that it is not only the food choices but our drink choices that poisons us too.

Nutritional education is essential to offset the healthcare and phar-maceutical industries' dependence on our suffering, much like the criminal justice system's reliance on arresting Black people. Black farmers are not prioritized on the same level as other farmers in the food supply chain. As a result, capital for equipment and innovation is harder to secure or more challenging to qualify for or get ap-proved. Again, this is a method to coerce them into unfavorable fi-nancial conditions and land forfeitures or debt seizures.

The discrimination against the Black farmer makes farming ex-penses unsustainable for them and their products less profitable while subsidizing the white farmer's success. Therefore, we must prioritize and designate Black farmers to offset the imbalances by utilizing their capacity to dedicated outlets. Eliminating food deserts and providing affordable quality food must be made directly available to our communities.

Healthcare and medical conditions.
Healthcare and medical conditions usually correlate with the quali-ty, the timeliness, the coverage, the cost, and the continuation of care. Unfortunately, these have all proven problematic for our peo-ple, mainly impacting other crucial areas of our quality of life. The only way to secure these objectives for those unemployed or under-employed is to take a vow of poverty and remain under the income threshold to qualify for assistance. To maintain healthcare, you then must remain unproductive. In addition, discrimination in the med-ical field has created disparities in routine preventive services, med-ications, and senior care.

Also, proper nutrition, mortality rates, childbirth, and prenatal care reveal a racially disproportionate exposure to medical indifference. Likewise, healthcare benefits are often overlooked in employment compensation packages. Mental health and substance abuse addictions are criminalized struggles, which add to our concealment and cautious skepticism of treatment. Some of our primary afflictions have gone untreated or under-treated for generations.

Furthermore, lack of affordability, medical access, and apathy to medical symptoms accounts for some escalating medical conditions plaguing our community. Lack of engagement from the medical community uncovers insensitivity and neglect that has contributed to infusing mistrust in our communities. These patterns and practices have created mistrust, discouragement, misinformation, and disregard for possibly helpful or needed medical treatments.

Quality options, proximity to medical facilities, and empathy by medical personnel would foster less cynicism. It would lessen concerns of discrimination, disbelief, and mistrust regarding medical professionals, advice, cost, and procedures. Discrimination is also an issue against Black medical personnel. In addition, these concerns contribute to undiagnosed conditions hidden in other forms of illness that further complicate our healthcare treatments. Once treatment becomes necessary, early detection or treatment becomes invaluable.

Reparations and methods of payment.

Reparations and payment methods by the profiteers should include but not be limited to money. Other options are products, services, internships, trust funds, endowments, foundations, equity, credit, ownership, grants, management, and employment opportunity. Hence these remedies should be clearly defined and verifiable. They should not be readily susceptible to corruption, misappropriation, manipulation, overvaluation, or discontinuation. Reparations in the form of services should be prioritized for at least one generation possibly two with sustained and confirmed diligence.

It should, by independent assessment, also be enforced by law and penalty of law if breached once confirmed. Whatever the business or specialty of the supplier, it is the very least they can offer. We are sure that they at least possess that service, so cash is not the only option. The government is not solely responsible for reparations. America is comprised of people and businesses that fully or partially participated in or benefited directly or indirectly from the atrocities by commission, complicity, or silence. Other countries and international purveyors of slavery are also culpable.

They should also pitch in for the solution since they were party to the problem and benefits. The cry for reparations would have ended many years ago before the issue became so convoluted if racism had been discontinued. Damn denouncing an act that has continued despite hundreds of years of broken promises, systematic abuses, and our social condemnation. Action is now required. In addition, goodwill contributions are welcome from those simply donating for a solution.

So, the most valuable reparation is the discontinuation of the oppression of our prosperity. By now, it should be apparent that the days of cotton picking and lemonade fetching are forever over. Despite the tyranny and murder rained down on us, we have proven resilient. Slavery, alleged superiority, and discrimination originally were a matter of economics but now are more of a habit of behavior. But, please, make no mistake about it. It is by conditioned learning. Technically, a display of mental illness driven by delusional groupthink colluding to maintain nonsense, revealing a primitive craving for validation using a racially disparaging comparison.

However, discrimination is required to maintain an undeserved privilege. Racism is not required but is a companion on which this discrimination is based. The terror of white privilege denied will no longer comfort this irrational masquerade. Remarkably, while claiming unfairness with simulated bravado, still afraid of a world without a rigged advantage to bolster the great fallacy, racist become even more irrational. The fallacy arrogantly seeks to excuse atrocities. Being enormously enriched by this myth, racist deny any debt or gratuity requiring compensation.

Many arguments are made against reparations, but the one that is not disputed is that whites did not commit the atrocities. That you didn't do it. That it did not happen. So next time an unarmed Black man is murdered by law enforcement, or they decide to rest for 8:46 seconds on his neck murdering him, condemn the execution. Consider it a down payment on reparations that only cost compassion, decency, and having a soul. Otherwise, material considerations as reparations are an account payable that is severely delinquent.

Acknowledgment and excuses.

The lack of acknowledgment for the contributions of our service across this country's history has patriotism used to imply whites were the only ones who defended or contributed to America's freedom and prestige. Our contributions to the advancement of America need to be appropriately accredited without the whitewash of thievery or misappropriation. Recovery, forgiveness, and grace all begin with admission and confession. There can be no prospect of redemption with persistent denial, excuses, and minimalizations.

Warring countries have been rebuilt, populations compensated, and even the treasonous rebellious Confederacy south rebuilt and welcomed back into the Union. Yet still, the leadership of the Republican party coddled an insurrection with blatant racial overtones in the Capitol Building, threatening Democracy. None of these transgressions have been a part of the Black experience, nor have Black people received this abundant generosity of consideration.

European immigrants were recruited and given land, resources, and encouraged to participate in slavery to assimilate with white America and to help maintain a disproportionate ratio of whites to Black people. They welcomed European immigrants to restock or build a surplus of assimilated immigrants pretending to be "white." That is the definition of white by the census bureau, an accumulation of everyone except Black people or Sub-Saharan. White by composition should factually be considered all others. Thus, white skin tone rather than ethnic origin took precedence over dark skin and apparently reparations.

Today to assimilate having white skin, you can call yourself Ted instead of Raphael Cruz or abandon your German heritage and grandfather's name of drumpf, claiming the confederate heritage as your own despite your relatively fresh immigrant roots. Likewise, immigrants of a white skin tone from anywhere or of white European descent can stand at a distance and be considered white and sometimes even closer if they do not speak.

But no matter how distant within eyesight, a Black person can stand and not be considered anything other than Black on sight. So you see, dark skin tone is the sole basis of discrimination. All of this is still true today for European descendants who can brag about how they came to this country and got assimilated into being white and benefited from masquerading as such to take the country back. This adopted land was brutally strong-armed and appropriated by force or deception from the occupants making it stolen property to be returned to the owners, not the thieves.

Immigration of any darker complexion people is considered undesirable. At the same time, white immigrants are favorable, maintaining and restocking the white majority since abortions, interracial marriages, same-sex unions, and white middle-class success has reduced white children's birthrate. Their birthrate and majority are waning along with a privileged white utopia. Therefore, the whites' advantages and privileges enjoyed for so long now require passing the sugar. The taste of honey has long been hoarded and requires an equitable allocation of concessions and redress to be conceded.

The implementation of equality raising the quality of life for our people will vicariously benefit all races and all elements of society, including ours this time. These gestures have been made before for immigrants, other countries, races, and the treasonous Confederacy. So, it is reasonable that the Black race that has suffered and contributed the most should now enjoy the same considerations and expectations. To no longer be subjected to malicious intent simply because of our darker hue of complexion.

For those who would cry far left-wing ideology, socialism, or socioeconomic welfare, I would submit reparations is the most far right-winged proposal imagined. Demonstrated by disbursements given to Wall Street, big banks, and big business for the health of the country's economy as being too big to fail. The act of bailing out the one percent is against the principles of capitalism and a free market. It is an unearned subsidy deemed necessary.

However, our disbursement is well-earned and should be mandatory. Never know when you will need us again, and America, you will. So it would seem wise and prudent that our people and equality are also TOO BIG TO FAIL! The same actions of correction and support are needed even if referenced by a different label or perspective, not called reparations. So you see, we are united in our prerequisite for this action, if not in our method of how. Please, regard reparations as services rendered or a down payment deposited to retain future services.

Maybe, we should pray for a magical transformation of America. It certainly won't hurt since we have had limited success praying for equality. God bless America and the wisdom for America to change for its salvation, preservation, and prosperity. Let us pray in honor of the Christian cloak of deceit we have been hidden under for so long. The nation's tolerance for inequality and the conditioning of the Black race to beg for deliverance where we are expected to forgive you for surely you deny what you have done smacks of hypocrisy.

So, let us pray.

Forgive America Father, for the Divided States of America has
sinned but has not repented nor atoned for these sins. Instead,
America has practiced and concealed these abominations cloaked in
your name to not only dishonor you but to disgrace itself. Justifying
its brutality and moral deprivation in your holy name while committing the most atrocious sins against a segment of your people.
Centuries have been spent corrupting all that should be held sacred
according to your word. America does not seek your judgment, for
surely you are not pleased, and condemnation can only follow.

Salvation has been leveraged for gold, silver, sugar, textiles, and
cotton with no regard for humanity. There is even less respect for
your holiness or the one you sent who surely cannot pay for these
sins. Without repentance, America is rebuked. Britain and America
have widely practiced racism in every corner of the globe. It has
worshipped a slavery obsession and false prophets placed above
you and the very humanity that it still refuses to also recognize as
your creation.

It has borne false witness and even murdered in your name. The
above-stated crimes against humanity for earthly riches have blinded America to your glory and its destiny. It has caused America to
pervert your word masquerading as true believers while forsaking
your honor without remorse for its deeds. America has neither been
meek, merciful, pure of heart, nor peacemakers. Conversely, it has
forsaken justice, remained devoid of integrity, imposed exploitation
on the downtrodden, and broken every covenant of yours in spirit
and action.

America cannot offer its tarnished soul for redemption or risk eternal condemnation for freely choosing to commit these atrocities. By
your word, you condemn them, but by America's actions and
words, it condemns itself! The soil is drenched with blood, horror,
and abomination from these purgatory fixations of racism, steadfast

violations, and continued denial. We can only pray America repents acknowledging its transgressions and denouncing the evil it has inflicted by the oppression of our Black ancestry.

For its horrendous crimes against humanity and religion, I fear that saying three Hail Marys and two Our Fathers is insufficient for these trespasses. Confession, repentance, and reparations for damages would suggest to humanity and God of America's remorse and redemption not only by word but by deed. And, of course, to no longer practice or tolerate these repulsive transgressions ever again towards anyone as there is no righteous justification. It might just be the difference between salvation, survival, or being judged harshly and stricken by God's wrath.

It might also be said to practice what God's word teaches, not the hypocrisy of scribes nor Pharisees worshipping the coin, politics, or a defeated President! Time to submit to a reckoning and atonement. For Christ's sake and America's, we can only pray.

P.S. This is not a denunciation of religion, just how it has been and continues to be used to accomplish and justify evil intentions by self-proclaimed conservative, patriotic, and evangelical God-fearing racist. This prayer in no way suggests a blanket accusation against all whites or evangelicals, past or present in America, regarding slave trade involvement or racism. However, it does illustrate the factual account of record. I think we can all agree if the shoe fits, it can only be your shoe Cinderella, so wear it.

Thurston's Thoughts
The Big Payback

Well, so glad you asked. Payment comes in many forms, and my brother Charlie always said to pay yourself first. Sometimes self-interest is in the best interest because it is the catalyst for motivation, but the long game is the best game. Foresight to delay immediate gratification for a more substantial compensation promotes stability indefinitely paying ourselves. So, concerning racism, what will we accept as payment, and in what quantity?

What is the agreed transactional currency of settlement? Is it correlated to self-worth, lost ambition, or time consumed? How about pain, suffering, and damages inflicted? Should the currency be bartered for consideration other than cash or only straight cash homie? Regarding reparations, it must be of transitional value to change a few things and make a difference, but probably not necessarily cash.

What do we need to do? What are we willing to do? We should not have to work twice for a payment already earned, but we will probably have to work twice as smart and just as hard to maximize any settlement received. Breaking down some intangibles into the following thirteen categories expresses a comprehensive perspective to revise our assessment and invoice magnifying implications to amplify actions.

Emotionally speaking, we need to operate less out of emotions and more strategically. We have all been owed money that has not and will not be paid. Unfortunately, reparations may also be one of those times. But just like then, this is a lesson not to be swindled again by the promise of a wooden nickel. Standing in line waiting for the government to make good on General Sherman's Field Order 15, pledging reparations in the form of forty acres and a mule since the end of the Civil War, has proven futile. Waiting since 1865 screams as long as it is owed, we will never be broke or get paid.

The emotional attachment to the damages and trauma of slavery and betrayal of the contributions made to build and defend this country is no small task to be written off. Still, like an unhealthy relationship, we must if it causes more damage than it relieves. Otherwise, we remain wounded, stagnant, and shackled to unfulfilled expectations of a past attachment. Remember, the best revenge is the ability to bounce back successfully, which always looks good worn properly. The more we do for ourselves, the less we are dependent on others to provide it. It is said that, God helps those who help themselves.

The most effective and immediate perspective and consideration to overcome these obstacles are to use addition by subtraction. We must slip the trap and avoid the challenges we suffer against our psychological liberation. No matter who administers it, poison is poison if administered by a legacy of oppression or the congregation of despair. Our primary focus should be the poison and not who is administering it. Still, it should not be us distributing it. We should resist its voluntary consumption the same as we resist coerced consumption. However, the outcome is the same, contamination. Self-harm is the hardest to prevent and the easiest to commit.

At best, the slate we have inherited is suspect, so the total reconstruction of our perspective requires redefining our beliefs and self-identification as warranted. Time to weed out the plantation mentality of limitation, scarcity, and desperation that subserviently resembles inferiority. We need to be what we think we are by our definition of us. The anger and shame, sometimes disguised as pride, need not pacify our hurt and rage nor excuse actions that are counterproductive to our well-being. We have stared these atrocities in the eyes and prevailed.

We must do the same with brutally honest assessments of where we are and how we get to where we want to be. Once determined, we must commit ourselves to that by self-accountability. Other's crimes against our race and continued discrimination are separate considerations from what we must do. No matter how we slice it, the primary emphasis is ours. Therefore let's dissect it into progressive probabilities by thoughtfully examining our circumstances.

These points for improvements have been dissected here to discuss social and cultural implications concerning us paying ourselves first despite the absence of reparations. Many of these issues linger unresolved as the root of many problems within our control. Therefore, the solutions are also within our control. The solutions are a logical protocol and code of conduct, not emotional fragility triggering combustions of rage.

Hypothetically speaking, if in our old age, after hundreds of years and a guilty conscious for the original sin, if reparations happened, it could only supplement the strides we independently achieve. Again not because it is not owed, but because we cannot wait any longer for it to be paid. The more we accomplish, the less effective the stain of slavery and discrimination hinders us. Imagine a concerted effort, integrated resources, knowledgeable application, and unified objective among our people.

For this, we only need to commit to turning aspirations and theory into practice. The proper application of the appropriate theory practiced for the maximum gain. Furthering payment of reparations must be directed where there can be only a minimal defense against it. Hypothetically, Britain is not immune from crimes against humanity and accountability for its part in the slave trade in America or around the world.

Crimes against humanity can be levied against them and their wealth, especially since the Commonwealth is the largest landowner in the world. Applying international pressure may not force a settlement but substituting legal compulsion would. With that said, why are so many of their Commonwealth lands underprivileged given Britain's wealth if not by continued exploitation and at the monarch's preference? What about an international fund for countries repatriated under repressive flags This association is not a personal attack on the Royal family or the Queen but a sober gaze at the caste system it has perpetuated for centuries.

However, the Queen did rule for over seventy years while many of these exploits continued. They are what they have been conditioned to be, just as everyone else. Meanwhile, the American government is not the main beneficiary of slavery, only the primary facilitator in America. Other non-governmental entities accumulated their wealth through slavery and can more easily be held accountable, including national and international companies. Other countries and populations may also have a legitimate legal claim for reparations.

Factually speaking, the one-drop rule is still universally claimed to dismiss skin tone or heritage as the barometer to qualify for Blackness or reparations. Determining claims and qualifications would be a circus of fraudulent assertions of racial identities and heritage. False claims of being descendants of slavery victims, since presumably no one now living was enslaved, would lack a clear definition of qualified descendants. We might be surprised who would legitimately qualify. But, by the one-drop rule or genetics, many people on earth would qualify.

The convoluted aspects of reparations must consider if an eighty year old who has lived thru the dredges of discrimination be compensated the same as an eight month or eight year old? How is a family to be compensated, individually or as a whole? What about bi-racial or persons who lineage has essentially switched races since slavery through inter-racial mating which leaves no hint of their original lineage? What about immigrants or those who lineage was not ancestors of legacy slavery descendants but are included along the way but not in the original sin?

Still further, we must settle if it is slavery based or discrimination based. Would reparations be based on isolated acts, comprehensive actions, or accrued benefits from slavery? How do we calculate discrimination to be penalized? What is the designated cutoff date Emancipation Proclamation, Juneteenth, or some other date? Likewise, the logistics make it highly improbable that reparations would be dispersed through money or by the government for some of these reasons. But that does not mean considerations cannot be secured in money or from the government.

Perhaps the source of payment and reparation expectation is better placed on the private sector and disbursed by a socio-economic metric in our communities. Government policies and programs can alleviate the governmentally allowed or caused damages. The government permitted it, but plenty of private sector entities profited from slavery. In the interest of good citizenship, they would probably be compelled to contribute once exposed. How many among them would not be clearly guilty of racism if not outright slavery participation?

Once they know that their morally corrupt profiteering is known, the disgrace and public scorn would be too unbearable not to make amends. Of course, these amends could be in services and opportunities compounded proportionately to their participation. Some financial incentives would be helpful as well. Any restitution must be based on criteria and circumstances prevalent today and not a lineage of slavery. It should address the current ramifications of slavery and maybe not the past. Disbursement can be in depressed zip codes of poverty, food deserts, and areas of unemployment.

Practically speaking, verifying who and how the profits from slavery benefited companies and institutions would be a matter of public record. There was no need to conceal the profits at the time of occurrence because it was commonly accepted and documented. Using history's revelation, government records, and the judicial process as evidence to prove the validity of class action claims. Thus, validating claims retroactively to dissolve obligations equitably against any accumulated wealth from slavery. These same entities no doubt have also participated in the systematic discrimination and suppression of Black ambition. If not by slavery, by other calculated racially biased means and methods.

Realistically speaking, the calvary is not coming over the hill, and the check isn't in the mail. The solution resides in our resolve and self-determination to move beyond debts owed. Instead, focusing on the burdens which prevent us from venturing into new horizons, not hostage to unfulfilled expectations. Reappraising our expectations toward something within our control and that is independently obtainable would produce dividends in terms of decades and not centuries. These dividends would not be by permission but by determination and beyond repeal.

It is a fictional reality to force anyone to make provisions for you if they genuinely refuse. Field Order 15 is a prime example of something in the bag but defaulted on when leadership and sentiment changed. Voting rights, untraditional marriages, and now abortion face the same repetitive challenges. All are currently under assault. The sustainability of rage is not suitable as motivation for change as it wavers, is irrational, and polarizing.

It often elicits an equal and opposite reaction. Patronizing promises and concessions of pacification often douse rage without any significant settlement of grievances. The reality is whatever concessions we receive will not be to our satisfaction. Compared to what was committed, the compromise likely to be willingly offered will not equate to the damages inflicted. But, can we realistically expect it to compare?

Medically speaking, childbirth, quality of life, and death rates can be significantly affected by rejecting everyday habits that don't involve any classic classification of illness or addictions by instead making better choices. Food consumption and exercise cannot be underestimated. As a demographic, the level and rate at which we utilize healthcare and preventive care contribute to our overall health. Lack of access and utilization diminishes our quality of life compared to other racial and similarly situated economic groups.

Medical diagnosis and treatment in the initial stages of disease and illness affect our longevity, death rates, and wealth accumulation.

Early treatment, along with nutritional choices and lifelong exercise, affects life expectancy and recovery from illness. It is better to prevent the problem than live with it or die from it. Medical bias cannot be allowed to be a death sentence or incapacitating element of our healthcare, nor can our apathy. We must take care of our body and health as a treasure and temple.

Another significant impact on our mortality rates is the rampant killing of our people by any means, especially by other Black people. It lowers our reproductive pool, endangers our communities, diminish our image, and squashes productivity by death or jail. In general, the exponential benefit is staggering if we reject genocide, embrace healthier lifestyle changes, and practice psychological maturity. Unfortunately, mental health in our communities is often dismissed as a personality quirk or categorized as a weakness of character or lack of intelligence instead of a medical condition.

The stigma attached may very well have a partial foundation in inferiority associations with racism, resulting in us denying it as a mental or emotional disorder. Mental and emotional well-being are equally as important as improving our physical medical conditions. Detrimental behavior, addictions, and self-medicating tendencies often result when mental or emotional health is not good. We cannot forget that illness does not have to be physical. Just as many physical illnesses may be beyond our control, so may mental and emotional challenges too. There is no blame or shame in getting better or help, just like any physical ailment.

Nutritionally speaking, our dietary choices and frequency of consumption are better regulated by nutritional value than by taste, tradition, or culture. Besides knowing what we place in our bodies and being more selective, the easiest way to control consumption is not to purchase it. This is one-time discrimination is actually good for us when regarding our food choices. Make it a habit to eat at home, controlling the preparation of our food, quality, and quantity.

When consuming anything, know the ramifications of consumption or overindulgence. If we can control what we buy, then most of the battle is won with what we put on our forks and in our mouths. Sugar and salt are two of the most sinister hazards to our health. If it comes in a can or a box, that is usually our first warning sign to avoid it, namely processed foods. Poor nutritional choices often lead to debilitating medical conditions that rob us of vitality and healthy longevity.

Often overlooked are the bodily imbalances improper nutrition has on behavior and learning, which are especially important for the development of our children. The gratification of consumption does not outweigh the risk or consequences of any damage caused. Whatever is consumed, there was a time when we got by just fine without it, which means we can literally live without it.

Financially speaking, money is crucial to our healthcare options and lifestyle, dictating affordability, comfortability, accessibility, and attainability. Our standard of living correlates to our quality of life, so it is crucial to be financially savvy. The difference between financial knowledge and lack of it affects utilizing our resources wisely. Our understanding of wealth-generating practices and principles regarding wealth accumulation, investments, ownership, and entrepreneurship is often the main ingredient lacking.

Knowledge is the key because we are charged for what we don't know or can't do and even swindled more easily. A fundamental understanding of business and finance minimizes exploitation, waste of resources, squandered opportunities, and theft. Investments and management of employment-related retirement funds are prime examples of wealth generation without doing anything other than just working our jobs and managing our accounts.

Participation in these programs is similar to a bonus social security or pension benefit. Secondary employment accumulating social security quarters is a good backup plan. Secondary income or a side hustle, not dependent on our main job, is another avenue to financial stability. It should be used as a bonus for purposes of accumulation. This initiative allows us to explore other more lucrative ventures while maintaining employment security.

Knowledge of the tax code can allow for legitimate tax write-offs for income-generating equipment or businesses. As capital investments, they can grow by expensing or deferring tax obligations. For example, any commonly used item can be equipment if used for business purposes such as a stove if you cater. There are many ways for various talents to dabble into ownership and entrepreneurship by cultivating a particular talent or skill. Identifying a need and filling it or participating in a staple or core necessity not susceptible to wide fluctuations of value or volume is another.

Also, point of sale and cash on delivery services and businesses can minimize the uncertainty of invoicing or nonpayment. In addition, a secondary income from self-employment creates a buffer if the unforeseeable should occur with our primary employment. This expansion can even transition to a new field or better opportunities. Unfortunately, the traditional models of college and employment are less favorable than in the past and accumulates debt. Being versed in financial concepts and practices should be our second language to accelerate our progression individually and collectively.

Priority and emphasis on financial knowledge among our small children makes it routine protocol. As they grow older they understand money and can apply analytical thinking to money as a habit. Chess and logic puzzles are excellent teachers of an analytical thought process. By starting at an early age, it becomes second nature as they mature. They become a generation acting and thinking differently, literate and efficient at generating wealth escaping cloning as a menial labor force. An entrepreneur mentality and fortitude are required for wealth accumulation.

Many of the methods used by the wealthy are available to us such as trust funds to preserve assets and shield liability. The game doesn't always have to be sold. It can also be told. The key is knowledge and how to apply it. Partnerships that pool resource and expertise are another option. In the land of the blind, the one-eyed man is king, which means having the vision to position ourselves by being different. Positioned as a source, facilitator, or exclusively essential in a process providing an exceptional or uncommon service, skill, or knowledge to create a niche.

Possessing a distinction that is in demand to separate ourselves from those without it. The clientele will always demand or prefer us if their need is there and our service is superior or scarce. The principle of supply and demand is implemented because you supply satisfaction for their demand. In this context, everything can be a service rendered by fulfilling someone's demand. So, opportunities are abundantly present for those with vision. Still, to partake in prosperity, we must speak the language of money and capital.

Astutely educating ourselves in all money matters with economics as the social persuader and equalizer. The achievement of social justice would be maximized if aligned with the concentration of our economic power and monetary intelligence. Where our skin tone is rejected, our green will be accepted, but only if our skin tone can accompany it. Our money should not go anywhere we are unwelcome, poorly treated, or disparaged. It is a package deal called discretionary spending. You don't get the green unless you accept the Black.

As a matter of consolidation, our funds, mortgages, and credit needs should be directed towards Black banks, savings and loans, and credit unions. By creating and patronizing our own financial institutions we can create a banking system conducive to our financial needs with innovative capitalization, reinvestment, and competitive market share. The cycle of financial discrimination could be broken or dealt a severe blow by an alternative option depleted of racial biases. Any concern for risk is abated by FDIC assurances as with other banks.

Educationally speaking, this is probably the most impactful consideration, only surpassed by health concerns. Knowledge nourishes the mind, and education provides navigation of the systems and structures governing society. Both equate to financial success, opportunity, and a better quality of life when properly engaged. This engagement will compound itself generation after generation if correctly done by providing the foundation or building blocks for financial success. Positive recidivism is reinforced by tangible progress, breaking negative tendencies and generational poverty cycles.

The separation in life is not often race but education. If we cannot be adequately educated by the mechanisms in place, in that case, we must continually educate ourselves outside of that influence. The new university is on our "mobile" phone via Google and YouTube information. We must ensure that our children are knowledgeable and educated beyond the constructs of traditional conformities and standard educational systems. They must expand and excel in the life skills to be most useful in their teens and early adulthood.

We can mostly agree that primary schooling often leaves our children unprepared for the reset in life when they become eighteen. Early home schooling or community based after school educational programs would further our children's progression. Supplementation and maybe even avoiding specific programming will require learning it before it is needed or worst, taught by hard-knock experiences. Knowledge is gold. Ambition is the tool to extract it. Education is the medium to transport it. We are the vessel to possess it. Execution is the method to show it.

Legally speaking, the law is mainly designed for conduct that is forbidden. We are often caught in positions of being judged, but the law cannot be used as a weaponized tool if we avoid it. Knowing the law and avoiding its judgments while on a parallel course, never intersecting with its wrath, is the best use of the law. Otherwise, applying knowledge of the law to protect and enforce our rights and interest against violations is the second best way to utilize the law.

Being subjected to it allows the law to use us. Compounding situations when resisting arrest or breaking camp by fleeing law enforcement expands the possibility that choices will be made exceeding the severity of the original offense. This mistake often results in or is used as justification for the excessive use of force. It is not an equitable exchange for them to be wrong and us to be dead. Our actions should avoid damage to ourselves. Motivated by desperation or an irrational fear to flee is a slave mentality of fear.

Fearing force, loss of freedom, and penalty avoidance consumes rationale, often over a minor offense. It is not the best way to respond, possibly risking death while compounding the consequences. However, if possible incarceration didn't serve as a deterrent to avoid the offense or not aggravate it risking arrest was not a meaningful concern. In that case, it is an occupational hazard and an unnecessarily assumed gamble.

As we should all know, if you can't do the time then don't do the crime. Complying offers a better chance for a day in court than in the cemetery. Therefore, the "talk" should not instill fear and apprehension but rational assessment and avoid impulsively acting or creating a "perception of danger." The question becomes is the crime worth it and if so, is your reaction to resist worth it? The answer is that depends on the outcome. If you are feeling lucky it may be best to play the lottery and not risk your life.

We don't need any more examples. Either you sit it out, get bonded out, or stay out the way because there is no return or escape from the cemetery. It is harder to hold law enforcement accountable and excuse our actions which created our risk by our behavior. Keep in mind the consequences of any action and their possible reaction. So control them by controlling the circumstances and our actions, letting them make a mistake or violation not based on our mistake.

Lately, it seems that one of the fastest ways to become a millionaire is police use of deadly force, so don't become the next dead millionaire. Escape is fine, but excessive force can be deadly. Furthermore for those confined, the opportunity to liberate yourself and others from the mentality that resulted in incarceration avoids the trap. Look around and see who is caught up and wonder if it is a coincidence. You cannot be ambushed knowing what you disproportionately see in a system designed to show it to you.

For those incarcerated an astute assessment of your situation would reveal a congregation, an army, or an organization if purposefully directed transforming the experience of your confinement. The regulation of time to strengthen your body, mind, spirit, and perspective could be a university of change. Thus taking lemons and making lemonade. With time as a premium, the best use of that time as a culture when incarcerated could render astounding results. It would definitely disenfranchise the system from injustices. Right now what they generally produce is job security through recidivism. You can do time or time can do you. You choose.

Politically speaking, in a democratic society, the essence of the system is by demographic interest and appeal to concerns. It directs legislature or resources to alleviate fears, promote assurances, or provide incentives. People vote for their interests and benefit. Doing so creates advantages, pledges benefits, or determines inclusion by alluring considerations or exceptions. So our disadvantage is often a result of not being included instead of being excluded. There are only so many seats at the table.

The task is having a seat at the table and understanding how politically they get assigned. One way is to be a part of the decision-making process, and another is to influence it. The goal is representation. The common interest is not represented by the vote, the candidate is, because you can only vote for who is propped up before you. The illusion is you choose the candidate, which is mostly not the case. The candidate is chosen by influences before we become aware of their candidacy or we vote.

The candidate is not bound by the common interest but instead by overriding agendas, business and political allegiances, and personal predispositions disguised as the people's will. How many people are actively aware or interested in the activities of their political representative other than the campaign fluff presented when they need our vote again? Political parties, chairpersons, and business leaders decide who we vote for more closely align to economic advantage and power consolidation. It is a power game moved by money to exert their influence, securing goodwill in exchange for a wink and a favor.

Until we know the game's rules, only then can we begin to play the game proficiently. Voting is a powerful tool with many limitations because of where it is inserted into the process. Probabilities govern the process, and we gain inclusion only by being an element in that probability. This notwithstanding, voting can be galvanized more effectively on the local levels in what is called grassroots. Building a horizontal foundation locally leads to a seat at the grownup table where the stakes are high.

Using grassroots efforts to control our area regulates the policy and assurances directly affecting our communities. This strategy works best in the inner city and urban areas. But we must maintain a constant audit of progress and access to resources to quantify our equitably allocated inclusion. With this strategy, we can influence the representative of our interest to maintain some accountability and allegiance to our unique agenda while pursuing the common agenda. Two for you, one for me is better than three for you, and none for me.

Just pass the sugar enough to satisfy a sweet tooth other than your own. Fair exchange has never been a robbery, only a disproportionate exchange is larceny. It is a game of participation and negotiation. The seat at the table requires the appropriate stakes to contribute to the gain of those already seated there. Thus, bringing something to the table which is worth the participants winning. The vote represents the ticket to the game, which is the demographic invite. Simply satisfying their greed and thirst for power makes the need transactional.

So, what can we do for them in return for what they can do for us? But, more accurately, what do they have to do for us in return for what they get from us? That is politics at work, not favors for those they deem disenfranchised or puppets of the system. Only those who matter are most considered. Usually those who vote or unless you have money. Lots of either or both. Consequently, the concentration should be on how and what moves the needle, which is votes and money. Black people politically must adopt a shift from past ideologies that have failed to produce the desired outcomes time and time again.

No longer the lover took for granted but the one who left. Our vote and resources must be courted with material considerations, no longer satisfied by token concessions. The system has always had its vulnerabilities susceptible to those who can navigate them. Only sixty years ago, the nation did not want or trust a catholic or descendant of Irish heritage as President, but now the Kennedys are American royalty. Finesse, not force. Tactical composure, not irrational emotions. Political maneuvering, not destructive protest. So alliances of shared interest, not inciting opposition, are more effective in reaching our goals.

Our goals and power are transformed by a generation of strategic voting, coalitions, positioning, and accumulation. Arguably, the time has come for alternative political party affiliation or votes not based on customary affiliations or Black skin but Black interest. Most certainly not based on political party but tangible results. As history reveals, eventually the will get what they want or in our case what we deserve and nothing less. Leverage is the motivator moving the needle.

Religiously speaking, we need to make sure religion empowers us and does not demand weakness by obedience to doctrines that defy the principles of their stated religious purpose. Religion has often been used to excuse, endure, and accept persecutions that only apply to Black folks, not the brokers of these ungodly racist actions. Those who find shelter as Christian conservatives sometimes seem so closely aligned with racial hatred that it is hard to decipher the difference.

The radicalization of Democracy, sedition, and immigration are largely self-proclaimed as patriotic and Christian conservative values forced upon others but not practiced upon themselves. The same Christian belief certainly does not allow for vastly different interpretations racially infused from the same biblical word. To grow more profound in faith, doing our research into what we accept and why we accept it may produce shocking results. It is not to question the Lord or encourage disobedience of our beliefs. However, is it mutiny of faith to reaffirm or question our beliefs, especially if they are flawed? But, how would we know it we don't?

Seemingly, it examines whether man's manipulation should have the same protections as the Lord's word. The obedience that made Joshua a warrior for the Lord can't make us doormats by the same decree. We can rest at the head or exist at the feet, having surrendered our power. Religion properly practiced should not just discourage one from doing wrong. Encouraging the willingness to do right as opposed to begrudgingly refraining from doing wrong. A self-righteous religious culture has expanded from inspiration to appease and control the masses' emotions.

The effect pacifies and disengages our minds from logical scrutiny of its doctrine and practices. Blind obedience is a prerequisite secondary to only believing, but both are mandatory. Once convinced to believe, it is forbidden to question or reevaluate. They say it is nothing but the devil stirring up doubt and leading you astray. The mesmerizing cadence and inflections of delivery or preaching are usually more entertaining than informative, often a religious performance. But, ever wonder how the imitation of preaching throughout the years has often remained theatrically the exact bombastic characterization?

The emphatic allurement tempered with a splash of condemnation is usually performed twice on Sundays at a church near you. The bombastic dramatization of the spirited roustabout messenger of the Lord inciting donations and jubilee. This jubilee only exist within the walls of the church. The congregation then ventures out armed with their faith to endure the injustices of our humanity until next Sunday's re-up. Admission is free, but the tithing plate assures you pay before you leave. By the way, was Abraham's ten percent tithe of war spoils to Melchizedek a tax, a worship, or a onetime priestly gift to God for us to observe?

After all, entertainment is not free, nor is religion financially or spiritually. It is the evolution of a cultural formula refined over time where the more dramatic it is, prompts declarations that the pastor really preached today. It warms the heart for generous tithing and an entertained membership. But let us not forget saving some souls too. The good Shepard herding the wayward flock to the pasture of salvation. The other option is the highly ritualized and structured recital as an ode to obedience. Religion can be that lighthouse in the storm and the light to lead from the shadows of peril.

However, it should not be perverted to do so by false prophets coming in the Lord's name cloaked in pseudo-righteousness. Our churches and religious leadership must direct us by a comprehensive social agenda. An agenda of strategic economic, civic, and community directives toward empowerment and ascension. That is the Lord's work as well. The national civil rights activist movements of the sixties were led by the church and their dedicated army of believers. The trumpet sounds once again to percolate a coordinated far-reaching call to action.

Ezekiel 33:3-5 "Then whosoever heareth the sound of the trumpet and taketh not warning: if the sword come, and take him away, his blood shall be upon his own head. But he that taketh warning shall deliver his soul." Our condition is upon our own head and so is the solution. The church has strengthened us before to lead the charge and can once again stir the spirit to deliver our objectives. Repetitive religious doctrine or prayers of passive endurance would not be hurt by a little organized social and economic initiative.

Domestically speaking, the family is the central nervous system of society and always has been. Like Dorothy in the Wizard of Oz, there is no place like home and family. The comforts of family return us to the shared origins and solace of our origination. So many steps along the way often began when they were with us before we knew what it was, having our back through the mud. They often are our strength when we were weak or lost. So family is not to be taken lightly, disputes too harshly, or influence unappreciated.

Embrace the assurance of unconditional acceptance, validating membership in the immediate and extended family circle because it is not guaranteed. Kinfolk is often overlooked as the extenuation of family. By kinfolk, I mean those not related by blood but by circumstances, understanding, proximity, or compassion. They are the ones you are most likely to interact with just as much or more than blood. Kinfolk have no race or gender. They usually have stood the test of time or stood strong when we were down bad putting their coat in the mud.

These close associations, when genuine, offer encouragement and correction as a matter of principle, not popularity. These influences outside of family validate our subgroup's identity and element of cohesion, be it church, friends, school, the bar, or so forth. But, we should be careful of our chosen circle of influence because the eagle does not fly with pigeons. This old analogy warns us that birds of a feather flock together, so we should have some common objectives with the company we keep. Otherwise, we shouldn't be keeping it. We can't pick our family, but we choose our friends and are often judged by our associations.

The support systems we rely on are the fabric woven within our psyche which we will resemble or assimilate over time. Family is a blessing, and kinfolk is a bonus, but neither is meant to define us. They only carry us for a reason and a season. If we are fortunate to have the support of one or the other, even to offer support to one or the other, it is for comfort and assistance, not to enable. We should not enable or seek to be enabled. It is an abuse of the family and kinfolk code which should mean so much more than to be exploited.

In tough times family and kinfolk will be all we have. In good times make haste to bond and build a legacy. A high tide raises all ships, so prosperity cannot be a singular ambition. Once accomplished, realize there are other ships in need as we once were or will be. Family and community are the extensions of self. Remember, lingering endlessly on multiple stagnations sabotages progress and hijacks our efforts while concealed in plain sight until they are addressed with determination to resolve them.

Slavery and discrimination robbed us, but we cannot be complicit in further thievery, whether or not reparations are forthcoming. We were taught to hate ourselves which has now led to us being ashamed of our features and ethnicity by virtue of our imitation of assimilations. As a further comment, with division comes defeat and assimilation comes absorption. It requires us to forfeit our identity.

Our unity, communities, families, and relationships are divided by lack of communication, purpose, and understanding for this reason. Family, we must understand that this division between the Black man and Black woman is harmful to our unity and our children's future. We can't say one thing and do another by disparaging one another.

We can't fight for one thing and surrender an essential element of its success. We fight for equality but surrender unity. All hands must be on deck and play their position. We have weathered many storms side by side to reach this point. A social agenda to disrupt our cohesion and family unit has taken over us. Mutual respect is not a provision of material objects or selfish demands. Turn the bickering and finger pointing into a tolerable settlement of interest and expectations by mutual concession to whatever amicable extent obtainable.

Blame solves nothing, nor does the nonsense of stubborn self-interest. It is a spiritual thing of cooperation and appreciation. If it must be a dispute, it should not be about something discussed. Our preferences are personal, but our disputes should be objective. Therefore, solutions are a collaboration of motive. It is situational and with a person, not a people or gender.

It you can't find who or what you want, look harder or in the mirror. Maybe change your method of attraction or your mandate conceding cooperation. Although sometimes, it will be harder to find that jewel you are looking for, but with or without them life holds many opportunities yet to be uncovered. Every foot doesn't fit every shoe but there is a fit for both.

Yet, if we can't respect each other's choices, can we expect others to respect ours? More importantly, it we don't respect ourselves, who will truly have respect for us except for someone else who don't respect themselves. This fosters disrespect among us. The goal should be to make each other better instead of the social media bickering and cultural skirmishes. There is always the option of refusal or being refused. Imagine if you sold a product in competition with similar products, could you be angry if some preferred a product other than yours?

Are you the best product or representation of yourself or the expectations set forth. What about different price levels based on quality or quantity, would that not fetch a different market? What we represent and how we present ourselves set the market for our demand, not someone else. So the current gender battle can best be summed up in the words of Don Vito Corleone, make them an offer they can't refuse. If it is refused then the offer was not sufficient to persuade them. The challenge is making a sufficient enough offer, not slamming someone for refusing it.

Life always comes with rejections, challenges, and disappointments. It's part of the game called life. Anyway, for what we agree on there is no reason we can't work together to accomplish it, especially with family matters. The collective obstacles still remain which we have a common interest in overcoming. To the victors goes the spoils, but it is about the obstacles we overcome unless we let them become the ones we didn't or won't. Let our legacy be about the ones we conquered. Our future is about the obstacles we will conquer as a sustainable net benefit.

Our task is about overcoming the past, present, and future knowing equality is not an equivalent outcome but an impartial opportunity to apply our ambitions and skills. The outcome is variable, but the process should not be. Our survival plan must include broad comprehension and application of these aforementioned suggestions. A good survival plan to guide our family's future and thriving prosperity are imperative. Ultimately, we must choose preparation over desperation and proactive over reactive. Remember, excellence is a choice. Knowledge is exercise for the mind. The mind is the gateway to success. Success is nourishment for the soul. Our destiny is our business. So, what is your escape plan from history's grasp?

The scuffle is over when we rise above it.

Losing is guaranteed when you quit or don't try.

Winning requires preparation.

Understanding entices Knowledge.

Determination, Preparation, and Knowledge repels failure.

<u>Let me ask you a Question</u>

1. What consumes our time, energy, and resources that does not invest in ourselves? What attitudes self-sabotages our efforts? Once identified, are we willing to modify them as required? Do we gain more easily by what we remove than what we acquire? Do we lack determination to do so? Should we target opposition to change to produce change itself?

2. What are the methods and perspectives of building our condition? External factors supplement not dictate our ambitions, so why do they hinder us? Patterns are evidence of predictability, so is our complacency a result of manipulation or submission? Why is our battlefield the streets and not the classroom, legislative halls, and fiscal persuasion?

3. What is the specific method to disburse reparations? Does hope of reparations hinder our progress? How will it reduce our hurt? At what point in time or ineffectiveness does anger reveal itself to be counterproductive? Why are our communities not under our control? In what ways are our viability siphoned out of our communities?

4. What detriment, hurt, or misguided perceptions do we encourage, tolerate, or harbor against our good? What about against the good of our communities? Can we blame racism for the level of violence at our functions, assemblies, or amongst our people? What is to blame? Does history impact our safety, education, prosperity, and accountability more than our current actions?

5. Is our faulty socialization too much to overcome? How do we overcome it? What poison do we feast on spiritually, intellectually, and economically? Is it our appetite or a plot in which we have fallen prey? Will our hopes be finally realized, or is it time to recalibrate? What degree of what happens to us depends on others?

Twisted Reality
Frank and Earnest

Let's get down to business, removed from the political correctness and pretenses of social graces to speak openly without regard for contrived moral consciousness, forced remorse, or reluctant accountability. Instead, let's put everything on the table out in the open to analyze present and future projections regarding racism and discrimination. Strictly speaking, it is a culmination of psychological conditioning, economic exploitation, and opposed interest which stubbornly continues to represent a delusional addiction.

The delusional obsession is an entitlement to preferential accommodations and a bloated self-image of superior character selfishly pursued at the expense of all others not historically identified as white. Racism is the American legacy that some whites clamor to maintain, directed explicitly toward Black people. We are deemed a suitable target and are easily identified by our darker skin tone used as our absolute visual exclusion. Some white subgroups, mostly racist, sustain a subculture of suppression toward us. They claim to be above all at the self-proclaimed pinnacle of the biological chain.

Thereby, they elevate their white subgroup hoisted high upon an artificial white privilege to loom above all creation. It is like the great Oz, who was not the all-powerful portrayed but a sniveling insecure little round man hiding behind a curtain of vulnerability pretending to be invincible. This facade created great fear and respect as long as the curtain remained closed. Pulling the curtain back reveals the fear and inadequacies that led to the need for and continuation of this façade.

Whites without this belief and confronted by reality, having no such advantage before God or man means the masquerade is up. This creates the stubborn need to refuse to relinquish that facade because it is the core of their being, their fabricated identity, advantage, and power. It is shocking to their core and psychologically devastating to deny the foundation of their claims despite overwhelming evidence that they are not valid.

Further, to admit the atrocities committed by cheating their way to the top is inconceivable to the psyche, so the ramifications are minimized and denied instead of confessed or conceded. That only leaves one alternative, denying its benefits and doing everything to keep it going. Otherwise, the image is shattered, and so are they. It then becomes desperation for survival of the delusion where racism and discrimination must continue for them to maintain the fallacy. To remove the fallacy would be symbolically likened to removing their oxygen, but literally, their air of superiority closely followed by its advantages.

Furthermore, diminishing their future demographic advantage brought about by fewer babies born per family while ambitiously pursuing wealth and careers further deepens their fears of being outnumbered. Due to the census bureau's classification of "white," its numbers are greatly exaggerated by the enormous number who can claim it, even some Africans. Immigrants are assigned and claim white by geographical origins, but technically Black people can too despite color.

The amalgamation of nationalities exaggerates the white demographic. Truth be told if classified as marginalized and not by race, we populate the globe as a majority. Racial oppression is international because slavery was global. Finally, considering interracial relationships of all kinds, sexual alternatives without procreation, and the death of staunch racist ideological individuals over time lends itself to a bleak racist demographic projection. The continuation of this projection is not favorable to the white male dominance of society.

On the contrary, the white male has historically had no consideration for anyone, including the white female. The one exception to Black inclusion was when and to the degree that we are needed to sustain their advantage. Their reckless actions have had unintended results that have undermined the very purpose they sought to preserve. Now it is a crisis of fear thirty to fifty years into the future when white is the minority distinction by designation, not color. Immigrants and multi-racial are already the majority be they white or otherwise. Change has long been set in motion, and more change is indeed coming.

Adaptation to change has always been the key to survival, and survival now relies upon cooperation between the human species, specifically different races and nationalities. I am not under the illusion that racism is about to end anytime soon. However, I will allow for the whimsical notion that the ideological DNA of some racists for their eventual integration may abandon it as it crumbles from ignorance and progressive change. The punishing implications attached by time as mitigating factors for change are increased racial integration, the demise of bigots, and the discouragement of racism.

Consequently, compelling the glacier shift of racists persuaded of their benefit to change their biased perspectives. There is no easy way to say it, and no need to sugarcoat it in the context of history if judged by the last hundred years or the next hundred years. A little over a hundred years ago, in 1906, it was acceptable to put a Black Pygmy named Ota Benga in a cage with monkeys in the Bronx Zoo on daily display. It was to psychologically and visually convince the public of our animalistic nature and proximity to wild cannibalistic animals to stroke public fear.

This fiasco undoubtedly contributed to his eventual suicide, but the effect it must have had on whites who witnessed it was even more lasting. The New York Times supported this barbarity as basic eugenics supposedly displaying the missing link, thereby perpetuating myths and stereotypes to be taken as fact. Such displays undoubtedly influenced many. However, there can be no misconception that there have always been decent and compassionate whites who have denounced slavery, racism, and discrimination but not the New York Times at that time.

Accordingly, over time opponents of racism numbers have increased to the present multi-race coalition. In solidarity with Black people, these co-crusaders battle the horrendous treatment we have endured by helping us to end racism, abuses, and fallacies. Fortunately, for some whites, it is an advantage and privilege they do not want or need at the immoral expense of other human beings. The key to committing these atrocities is to devalue, diminish, and dehumanize your victims to a deserving or irrelevant position unworthy of empathy or humanity.

Conversely, it exposes their racist lack of compassion. But the question then becomes, who appointed you to make such a determination of our worth? Was it whiteness alone? That determination is where religion and other reinforcement and reiterations are applied to believe, validate, defend, and promote this evil misrepresentation. No matter how sanctimonious and preposterous the justification may be, it has been socialized. The elements of this warped reality are a classic example of twisted schizophrenic behavior with a splash of paranoia.

The self-perceived contradiction to and diversion from reality morphs into a nightmarish fragmentation permitting unthinkable behavior. It lacks willful remorse, making it easy to repeat. The extreme brutality, savage demeanor, and arrogant defense of the atrocities committed under the guise of conservative Christian values go without saying. They are contrary to any actions a real Christian not suffering from an extreme devilish possession would ever commit.

So, religion may have to change for racism to change, or belief in religion is dragged into question. Compound that, by its pervasive nature, reveals a group mind control, seemingly under demonic sociological indoctrination. It results in the afflicted racist believer's faithful psychological captivity, powerless to resist its destructive programming. They are thoroughly compromised and susceptible to a programmed compulsion of moral evil and disregard for actions expecting no consequences, not even heavenly.

The portrayal of Black people as savage, dangerous, sexual preda-tors, stupid, animalistic, and so forth serves to conceal the depravity of the accuser when their actions are compared to the accused. Need I mention that the racial slur "coon" originates in hunting and killing human beings for amusement or spite. How could the indis-criminate murder, enslavement, beatings, and rape of our people not be more indicative of the savage-provoking tendencies of whites claiming to be civilized?

Now, who has demonstrated the absolute savage and animalistic predatory actions of a barbaric inclination if not racist? Rejection of the facts may be the only way to align yourself with the insanity and brutal reality we have faced at the hands of racist in this coun-try. The transference of these ghastly behaviors, identifiably one-sided against us, serves as propaganda-driven denial seeking abso-lution. The racist incubation of centuries lacks remorse, historical concealment, or convincing redress.

Understanding the extent and practices of racism helps to better un-derstand both sides' journey and current circumstances. Understand-ing should invite clarity and hopefully voluntary change. Under-standably, the dehumanizing realization of racist atrocities is fright-ening to whites wondering how we could withstand such vicious treatment. Yet, we still mostly stand for the flag, defend the country, and endure many injustices. Patriotism is the current code for alle-giance to inequality.

This brand of patriotism assigns illogical blame on others for ac-tions and disappointments resulting from the miscalculation of racist disdain. This exclusive claim to be the only guardians of pa-triotism, erodes its principles by mangling its meaning, application, and demonstration. Forced adherence to the manipulation of superi-ority into patriotism on anyone who does not look like you has cre-ated resistance to something which was never a point of contention. It has always been a demonstration against inequality.

Likewise, the current controversy surrounding voting is more suspect for voter suppression than alleged voter fraud. Surely, the day has passed when you could regulate the outcome of an election, as evidenced by the election of former President Obama and forty-five's loss to President Biden. The will of the people's vote cannot be calibrated to assure victory for them, so they attempt to suppress it against them. The Voting Rights Act of 1965 would not have been enacted in response to racism and voter suppression, if there was no need for it.

The government and many whites agreed that this was the case, and countermeasures had to be explicitly implemented to ensure that Black targets of this oppression had judicial protections for our voting rights. So, it would stand to fact and reason that neither the Civil War nor the Emancipation Proclamation abolished the slavery mentality. The ratification of the 13th Amendment in 1865 abolished slavery, which then transmuted into Jim Crow and blatant systemic prejudices.

One hundred years after the Civil War ended, the need for voter legislation recognized that racism, voter suppression, and discrimination were still the Jim Crow law of the land, on public transportation, and at lunch counters. It would then be counterintuitive that discrimination and oppression had continued beyond the Civil War, but absolutely and more sadly, it had. Affirmative action and similar actions would not exist if this ongoing oppression ended when some claim it did.

But unfortunately, many acts of oppression have continued despite these alleged remedies. It is an affront to decency for whites to have the unmitigated gall to whimper about reverse discrimination, cancel culture, and unfairness of opportunity. Allocations and access based solely on race designed to alleviate the disadvantages which were systematically imposed upon others seem very fair because it was for you when you received it or withheld it.

To deny fairness to others by declaring your plight of unfairness and inequality is to proclaim yourself stupid, irrational, or a racist. I want to think the best of you and assume that you are simply being irrational, giving you the customary benefit of the doubt. The open discrimination and exclusion practiced have been solely based upon race. Ironically, now complaining and claiming suffering by the inclusion of others while crying about opportunities you had readily denied others exceeds an elevated threshold of irrationality.

To be held liable is not discriminatory or discretionary but was inevitable eventually. Protesting cancel culture to excuse or ignore your culpability pardons you by self-granting blanket immunity dismissing your actions. It is deemed unfair by a cry of cancel culture regarding whites' accountability for racist transgression when facing societal condemnation or discontinuation of patronage. Drawing the line and adopting unpleasant consequences by withdrawing voluntary support is not an obligation to the offender but a right of the offended.

White people lack the credibility to complain. They have always been on the till with improper privilege subsidized on the public draw. Your hand has been constantly in the cookie jar, and your thumb on the scale of justice. You claim to value freedom, prosperity, and fairness but exclusively for yourselves and are quick to complain when your expectation of preferential treatment is not met. It is ridiculous to insist that such monumental injustices be swept under the rug.

At the same time, even the slightest rebuke of your privilege is exaggerated as an intolerable injustice. Just stop it, knock it off. They don't make rugs or exaggerations that huge. This strategy to alienate yourselves from blame by denying your privilege and claiming victimization again contradicts the historical facts of your actions. The mentality and allure of benefits are so great that some would masquerade as having a Confederate heritage, the ultimate legacy of racism. One such pretender was born in Canada of Cuban descent. His kindergarten name is Rafael, but now posing as Texas Ted to Americanize his image for easier assimilation into the good ole boy's club.

Could you imagine the difference in perception between Rafael and Ted? Another would claim his Confederate membership even though his lineage is German. The drumpf clan's real fortune is that his grandfather was exiled from his native land for draft dodging returning to America, where he had fled. Judging from history, Trump could be synonymous with draft dodging and not money. Neither of these persons' American lineage extends beyond their grandparents at best. Pop quiz, who is Nimrata Randhawa?

How about that great protector of American heritage whose grand-parents were born in Italy and mother in Poland in Ron "no immigrants allowed" DeSantis? Nonetheless, they make claims about their Confederate heroes and heritage despite relatively fresh immigrant roots. But white skin, anglicized name changes, and cultural adaptation allowed them to assimilate and minimize, if not avoid, racial discrimination. This pretense is the lure of white privilege while distancing themselves from their true heritage and diverting attention from themselves by ostracizing others and denouncing immigrants when their families are not too far removed from the immigration tree.

What better to illustrate a reversed crab-in-the-barrel mentality? Instead of frantically keeping them in, they hysterically keep immigrants out, designating more assurance of privilege for themselves. A sort of costume party of preferential treatment requiring adaptation of Confederacy biases. White skin alone is the prominent inclusion factor, with becoming prejudice a bonus. MAGA is an adaptation of Hitler's Germany philosophy to espouse white supremacy, which he didn't even qualify for in his lunatic pursuit. Others now don't qualify for theirs either.

Tell a big enough lie enough times very loudly over prolonged periods and people will not only believe it but accept it as the truth. It was Hitler's motto. Unfortunately, these same tactics are familiar tactics of American Republican politics and ideology today, raising the question that if the nostalgic return to a MAGA time was possible, what period would that be? To whose benefit? Would it be a time of lynching, coon hunting, forced labor, or any litany of atrocities? There was never a time in America when racism did not exist, so when? What elements of slavery or discrimination would be suitable to MAGA?

As history reveals, are these conservative Christian values returning? Lesser forms of expressing these biased values are still present, so America still resembles a lot of what it always had. Unfortunately, the Republican party has been tarnished by accepting and promoting these racist aspirations feebly disguised by association as MAGA principles. If not a return to slavery, surely the continual furtherance of white privilege by the dehumanization and discrimination of Black people specifically and minorities in general, maybe even including poor whites.

Let's call it what it is and say what is meant, predatory exploitation for greed and control regardless of color. No further proof that America is off the rails or up to its old tricks and believably beyond redemption is when more than half the elected officials refuse to denounce an insurrection to overthrow Democracy. How about maybe exclaim that it is wrong to murder a Black man by choking him out in broad daylight by placing a knee on his neck. There are plenty more examples, but what more do we need? Refusal to condemn and reject these actions actually condones them.

The reason they are acceptable is that it furthers the agenda of division. If a dog were choked out, Republicans would have been outraged because it does not further their agenda. Their compassion for the dog is probably above the dehumanization felt for our people. Do you for one second think they care about unarmed Black people being killed and sprayed with bullets as long as it is understood that, for example, whites storming the Capitol are not to be treated like the n-word?

Only one shot was fired, but a Black can be fired up multiple times in the back at a traffic stop. There was no precautionary show of force or mass arrest at the Capitol, but some would still ask what disparity? The disparity that seemingly can only be based on race. Not condoning or requesting a violent response but simply high-lighting the restraint shown when in fear for their lives from whites. What happened to the stance of when the looting starts, the shooting starts?

The Capitol was looted and violated in the worst way, there was plenty of looting but almost no shooting. On Capitol Hill yet, an overwhelmingly almost exclusive mob of whites attempted to overthrow the government as the ultimate act of looting Democracy. There was less enforcement that day than if a Nike store was being looted. Furthermore, the outcry is deafening from those being held accountable. Can you imagine their shock and indignation at being called to answer for the very attempt to overthrow the government?

When whites are being arrested for being patriots to the Confederacy, what is this country coming to? Amazingly, even Black people are somehow expecting equality and redress to boot! What is going on in this country? The discrepancies in response and expectation change when we are involved with the law as it is unequally applied, or is anyone really expecting it to be applied equally? How can one unarmed Black person be more of a fear-provoking threat and danger than a whole mob of insurrectionists?

The justification for Capitol Hill law enforcement restraint was praised, while questionable articulation for using deadly force against unarmed Black people is not condemned. Again, not advocating for less respect for white lives but equal respect for Black lives. Furthermore, there must be a comprehensive understanding, standard, and application of the law that does not give carte blanche to law enforcement misconduct and abuse of us as citizens. Qualified immunity must have clear objective parameters where protections are no longer enjoyed and resources expended for disqualifying conduct.

Law and order, crime and punishment, and wrongdoing and judgment must fall unabated on the actions committed and the person who committed them, not the exemption of their guilt by race, profession, or statutory mandate. Wrong is wrong. The guilty deed is tethered to the guilty's name if integrity is to be maintained. Otherwise, it occasionally and eventually will lead to some feeling we are left with no choice but to resist their detriment. When left with no choice, the choice is then made clear, no choice.

While police are necessary, their actions cannot be above the law simply because they are essential and less likely to impact a white person adversely. By the same consideration, police interactions are at times negatively exaggerated. Citizens are at times emotionally inflamed and apprehensively predisposed to an expectation of unfairness. The reverberations from injustices and perceptions that influence citizens' cooperation and politeness reflects our interaction with law enforcement and expectations. The point is that a recalibration must occur on both sides.

Still, the abuses of authority are not immune to the adjustments required to improve interactions. On the contrary, submitting to injustices brings about greater dissatisfaction and resistance, not to mention further injustice. This apprehension escalates into a more hazardous condition for all concerned. But on the other hand, mutual respect deescalates conflict and promotes integrity and cooperation. What encourages confrontation, divisiveness, and danger is injustice, racism, and despair.

The cause and effect are apparent, and the dismay at the resulting outrage is disingenuous and, of course, based on to whom the injustice has occurred. A plea for solidarity to heal society only becomes an objective when they are not the one making the concessions or when preserving the balance of power which has shifted away from them. Once the political tables are turned, a plea for bipartisanship is uttered. Again, the priority of moving forward together in healing a fractured country at a fragile time is encouraged by others' submission.

Bipartisanship is only if they stand to lose or have lost something like the 2020 election. This plea is unconvincingly done and not done when Republicans have political leadership. Renovations are always best when you are already working on reformations requiring only one overhaul. Suggesting that grievances are delayed for the good of the whole would somehow benefit us is contradictory when your concern historically has been to benefit only yourself. So many times in the past, this conciliatory posture has only resulted in a delay. This ploy is not for improvement but is repeatedly revealed as a sadistic prank.

So, let's suppose this is truly a time of healing and bipartisan coopcration. In that case, the Republican leadership should try to cast at least one bipartisan vote to signify their sincerity. A gesture of willing barter or exchange of sorts. Maybe extending the olive branch for once instead of demanding concessions to conform against conventional wisdom and our best interest. Having exhausted all your deceitful persuasions, your advantage by inequality has run its course leaving you fearful of the void. There is plenty of work to be done, and time is squandered not resolving the issues that cannot and will no longer be silently suffered.

The accumulated depletion of will and resources will not accomplish your objective since your preference is no longer the only consideration to be considered. Compromise and cooperation cannot be adverse abstract principles only for us. Compromise and cooperation are the way forward for you too. You cannot persist in taking pride in obstruction and destruction to exert a waning exercise of power tied to the dying ignorance of racism and absolute control. History is undefeated and has proven that resistance to change and stubborn ill-fated indecision has led to obsolete power and a doomed extinction.

Many world powers and nations have met their demise due to civil disorder and refusals to make changes. The societal collapse is often preceded by extreme economic instability and fluctuations, infrastructure and labor deterioration, hunger and chaos, and finally, governmental collapse. But unfortunately, the arrogance of America will not let it recognize warnings or change its actions. Balance and equilibrium are universal laws, and imbalance, by its nature, is unstable and prone to collapse. Due to the inequalities of racism and oppression, societies worldwide are currently wobbling.

The question is, will the change or the collapse come first? I do not believe it will change because of its opposition and the universal foundation of deceit that has lasted this long. It is collapsing under its own weight of deception and denial. Think about a celestial gravitational collapse that occurs due to the contraction of its weight pulled inward, succumbing to chaos and disorder. Why is America exempt from collapsing from contraction caused by resisting the harmony and order of the universe, God's will, or decency?

There is no need to look to the sky since history and anthropology can confirm the earthly demise of civilizations that once had great power. The turmoil of 2020 was a premonition that cannot be survived repeatedly, especially with the tailwinds still being felt. Progress and transformation to form a more perfect union not defined or restricted by the past is the only hope. Those who long for the past are afraid of the future. Uncertain of their prospects and secure with the status quo without regard for advancement but clinging to stagnation to prolong their significance. Thus, inadvertently hastening their demise.

By nature, the young become old, and the old gives way to the new. A new path is now required. Building this country on racism and the ill-gotten surplus from our labor is its structural flaw. Without question, vast wealth and resources have been accumulated and shielded from Black people. Can there be any further denial of that? Should there be a recognition other than words but in redress? Damages cannot be undone or life restored, but mending can be pursued. Since I have stated my pessimism or realism about meaningful change not being forthcoming, let me express what could or should happen.

The first restorative action that will have the most significant impact is to cease and desist the nonsense and somehow just knock it off. Despite all the lives lost and mangled, the economic imposition has far more implications than the murders. No more apologies, ineffective methods, or promises are needed. The deaths caused and atrocities committed cannot be rescinded. Still, the wealth benefits denied can be recuperated, like when stolen artifacts are returned. The government, businesses, and institutions should pursue more than conversational remedies since they actually receive real monetary benefits.

Money and resources would be a suitable substitute for words or holidays. These words and holidays are like a new vehicle with no keys, nice but useless. Still, do not be deceived, slavery was about the Benjamins, so the Benjamins must be deployed. The government should not be the only payer. Services are the most likely form of payment that only require tendering the services, terms, or business you already provide, such as free higher educational opportunities as discretionary scholarships.

Generations of descendants of slave owners have significantly benefited from their racist endowment to pay it forward for their ancestors. We are still suffering from the plight of our ancestors. So it seems only reasonable that they would have a connection to their obligation by the continued benefit still enjoyed. The primary distribution could be opportunity, development, and investments but first, recognize the imbalances for us to receive a fair shake. Since presumably no white person today has owned a single slave, it seems only logical not to carry the racist ideology forward.

But, indeed, being recipients of racist privilege and ideology enjoying the benefits of bias constraints have its advantages. The inherited courtesy enriched American society by entrenched bigoted practices resulting from racial abuses. So it is not unfair that we would get a fair shot after your road has been paved by discrimination. Forty acres and a mule was the unfulfilled promise, while the elimination of discrimination is still a dilemma. The future impartial allotment of economic viability, equitable opportunities, and equivalent resources now requires a social accounting.

Abolishing the act of slavery set the parameters for economic profit-sharing. As a result, the North received a more equitable distribution of the profits. A more sensible voluntary method of extracting the surplus of exploitative profits from our labor based on our people's lack of options and suppressed conditions. The South received the ability to continue operating ideologically as usual. The adaptation of the new extraction method without bondage, using supposedly voluntary labor with adjusted profit margins aided by the Industrial Revolution.

Both North and South adjusted well to their prevailing economic and social arrangement but still at the peril of Black people. They also both received plausible deniability. The dehumanizing treatment remained pretty much the same. Many freed Black people still worked on the plantation scratching out a living at the master's behest. Only now, the new and improved way of debauchery was called Jim Crow.

The Industrial Revolution began in 1860 and greatly influenced the end of legal slavery. It was the most probable cause of its abolition because it transitioned from sole dependence on human labor to machine labor. It created new models of efficiency and manufacturing, making the old slave model obsolete. Still, it did not eliminate the need for a permanent underclass to manage the machines and incidentals. The massive migration of our people to the north more equally spread the abuses and the resulting benefits instead of lessening it by relocation.

Instead, it lessened the method of physical labor required and increased the productivity for greater profits to be more evenly distributed between the North and South. Thus, the master-slave relationship became the boss-to-worker relationship model still practiced today as the basis of the economy with many of the same philosophical principles regarding labor, including the term boss. The master-to-slave mentality and dichotomy persist despite the rise of unions. Unfortunately, this mentality has a residual effect that still exists but has dissipated over time only slightly.

Some whites become indignant at the very suggestion that discrimination exists or the audacity for us to expect relief from it. We share a polar opposite of a dual personality disorder. Racist whites' psychopathic character traits are devoid of compassion or remorse contrasted with our people's submissive need for permission, validation, and conciliation. The refusal of whites and the begging of some of our people regarding reparation and equality display both mentalities. If they are delusional, are we imaginary, or is that the other way around? It is hard to tell.

Centuries of bigoted behavior still leave us in the position to beg for what an overwhelming number of whites refuse to give or recognize but enjoy. However, the context of slavery and the psychological realities created a subculture of survival for our people, which manifested itself in our saving grace and sustained resilience. The missing piece has been cohesion that secures an identifiable targeted objective with a solitary concentration. But, we lack unity of purpose.

We need targeted penetration into isolated and sustainable components of society using relentless incremental campaigns focused on
building scope, scalability, and momentum. So, if reparations are
forthcoming, then beautiful, but until then, we must forge ahead
from a position of fortitude, focus, and resolve. A shift in the paradigm of our perspective is the most efficient and assured way of
securing equality. Previously suffering from an extreme deficiency,
we now have sufficient agency to pay ourselves first.

Meaning no permission is needed from others for our assurances of
equality and economic viability. But, as always, we must renew our
efforts from where we are now with what we have to build alliances
and coalitions for prosperity and equality starting with us. We have
enough, plenty, but the division of our resources and purpose cannot continue to be counterproductive or diverted. Discipline is
needed, certainly not separatism, since we have paid too much for
inclusion and deserve to wet our beaks equally.

Repeated requests always transform into pleading, which is always
distasteful under any circumstances and rarely effective. It grants
someone else the power to refuse or grant the request. Far from
downtrodden or self-pitying, we should be encouraged by how far
we have come, what we have overcome, and how near we are to
conquering the final frontiers of racism. We were strangers in a
strange land, prevented from finding our way. They never had the
right to dominion over us, so now we do not need to seek their
permission for our self-determination.

Reparations are for their salvation, not ours. Again, the most valuable gesture would be to knock it off. Still, either way, we have
made tremendous gains to close the immense social gap, notwithstanding the gap that remains. Rest assured that their children
will not face the retribution of our actions but will have to adjust to
the extinction of their white privilege. Their survival as a race is not
endangered as ours was, and their claim of fear mainly realizes the
elimination of their advantage, not their race.

The privilege or displeasure of white America will no longer be the paramount concern on which society operates. Whites' substantial resistance should be more productively directed toward rectifying the problem, not denial and concealment to continue their comfort. The hypocrisy of denouncing bullying as being too strong for bullying does not extend beyond being too weak for racism, perhaps the most extraordinary form of bullying. The fragile racist psyche and mind are dependent on the intimidation of racism.

Racism is the poisoning of a feeble mind believing that white skin somehow makes you divine. Deprived of privilege, your means of survival will not be like our constant struggle for existence flung to the lowest socio-economic ranks in society. Your future will not be sabotaged by the systemic injustices you have consistently heaped upon us. The injustices of slavery and Jim Crow is the crux of many issues experienced in the Black community. Jim Crow will not be anything you will have to contend with as contributing influences of dysfunction in your communities, only as a haunting nightmare of your past actions.

Black is not only a reference to a race but has been a condition that has amassed an extreme toll. Debt for atrocities and crimes against our humanity developed over centuries. An overdue tariff is owed in this realm but may be collected in another, punishing your racist soul. Deflection or denial of these conditions cannot be independent of issues confronting the Black community. Close examination will likely reveal a correlation to slavery, discrimination, or the psychological trauma they caused in our communities. Not to mention the generational poverty created and perpetuated.

Therefore, the repeated insistence on deflecting onto other problems in the Black community does not absolve them of their infractions. It does not justify our exclusion from equal treatment under the law or equivalent opportunities. A three-dimensional understanding of a four-dimensional problem leaves one dimension short of a resolution. The Confederate heritage and the American legacy have been synonymous with each other since this country's inception. The founding father's vision was indistinguishable from the discrimination and exploitation of Black people. At the very least, they didn't have a significant problem with it.

Suppose the founding fathers were as wise and incredible as they are portrayed. Why was slavery allowed to be woven into the fabric of America's DNA? Little consideration was given to the detrimental effects of slavery projected over time. It was intentional and may be why some whites think they need to take the country back for white exclusivity following its initial purpose and concept. This notion fully ignores that it was occupied long before them and strong armed away by them. So, it has never been a white utopia. The founding father's guidance and influence are still the overriding authority today suggesting their vision has transcended hundreds of years of governance.

The constant square peg in a round hole predicament of stretching the interpretation of their intent on matters they could not have envisioned essentially expresses the intent of the current interpreter or agenda. As antiquated as it is how much further can it be reasonably stretched. The emphasis is then on the current interpreter subjectively conveying their particular understanding and surmising the original intent or interpretation. Stretching it to their will. Is clarity of interpretation the paramount objective or enforcing the selective choice of a subjective interpretation?

Either way, it is still conjecture. The confusion and misconceptions of understandings and allowances of iniquities have traversed, deviated, and wandered over time regarding the subjective translations of constitutional intent and purpose. Still, the one constant has been civil and economic exploitation by racism, and that interpretation has remained relatively consistent including the High Court. The founding fathers should have calculated the compounded effects and centrifugal implications of racism in their infinite wisdom.

So therefore, they never envisioned one day having to address the restitutions accrued and the adjudication required to resolve reparations or racial injustices. Accordingly, it was later recognized that restitution was owed but reneging upon the forty acres and a mule promise still didn't dissolve the obligation. They should have had the foresight to envision that it would become one of the perils of the country surviving just as the Civil War divide had. Refusing remedies to offenses unjustly enforced creates a domestic threat to stability from dissatisfaction. Only this time from white's dissatisfaction.

Isn't it ironic that white supremacy will destroy America while attempting to maintain its advantage? Meanwhile, opposing and suppressing anyone or anything that supports change, even the government. The last time it was called the Civil War, and this time it is called Trumpism, MAGA, Patriotism, and the Republican agenda by deed or declaration. Trump's leadership is reminiscent of someone much more ancient than McCarthyism of the 1950s or Hitler's antics but back to ancient Rome and Commodus.

Commodus initiated the fall of Rome setting the wheels of civil war in motion. Rome never recovered. Likewise, the ramifications of slavery, racism, white supremacy, and injustice reverberates beyond the past and present into the future if not reconciled. The expansion of time amplifies the ramifications and compound the difficulty of resolution. If my words, tone, and honesty are harsh, then the reality has been more brutal and bitter for us to experience over centuries. Feeble attempts to misrepresent, reduce, or quantify our damages expose the unwillingness to understand our injuries, thereby preventing a resolution.

There must be a recognition before there can be an understanding leading to a settlement. Then by accepting the problem and through the spectrum of the casualties, they can endeavor to rectify them. Racist ideology and whites' resistance to being held accountable leave me unconvinced that meaningful change or national reparations are on the horizon, but collapse is impending. With an inclination of self-righteous arrogance, the combustion of racism and economics fuels the pending downfall as symptoms of the illness. The arrogance of racism is symptomatic of the transitional changes needed.

If repeated reminders of discrimination and disregard for resolution are any indication, the racist compulsion leaves bigots powerless to resist and hopelessly cursed. So they are destined to be like the scorpion's sting, being in their nature to sting even if it destroys them in the process. No genuine remorse can exist without redress and consequences to address and satisfy the wounded. The truth is that there can be no healing without remedy. While some hope and wish, I am well beyond the age of believing Santa Claus is real or us soon achieving real reparations or recovery.

P.S. Be sure to wear your seat belt. We are expecting some severe turbulence ahead in reshaping the nation. Assuming the fetal position might help, but it is not advisable fearing the outcome if caught tooted in such an exposed position. Be careful, anything could happen.

Thurston's Thoughts
Madness to the Method

Slavery had its economic advantages and motivation bolstered by greed, fear, and the European influence of classism. But its roots were in dark skin tone and labor valuations by racial distinctions. Driven by the European conquest of Africa, resource depletion, and oppression, the slavery practitioner brutally made the slave fearful in proportion to their own   fear, depravity, and quest for dominion. The geographical upheaval alone posed an insurmountable obstacle but nothing near what the stubbornness of racism has been.

The foundation on which slavery and superiority rest are not actual determinations of superiority or morality, just pure ignorance and racism propagandized. Excluded from most advantages, our people were subjectively designated inferior when we only lacked opportunity, education, familiarity, and cultural integration. Hatred and exploitation led to subjective confirmations and judgements based on race. In this context, racial equality dispels this biased subjectivity, lessening the misconceptions and motivation, thus eliminating the justification.

So, in essence, racism comes down to preserving and excluding benefits by fear and deception for greed and separation. Race fundamentally not as motivation but instead as justification. The deception lingers and has yet to be roundly rejected, maintaining an unfair advantage by preventing equality. There was never a time when the imbalance of advantage has not suggested an elevated white self-image. Inequality has become an element of white character, often oblivious to or willfully ignored not as a practice of discrimination but of ignorance or comfort.

The dread of removing a system that assures this advantage creates uncertainty or, more specifically, the certainty that no such benefit will any longer exist based on race. However, any lack of expectation being met produces sour grapes that will then be blamed on our racial infringement upon their privilege and prosperity. The level playing field tilts their reality, magnifying their fear of sharing or replacement. Fear and deception have a dual impact causing different effects on whites and our people, on the one hand, apprehension of change, and hopelessness of change on the other.

Submerged below the racial classifications are the ideologies that sustain them. Within the establishment of this structure, there are multi-level dynamics to examine and understand, considering them, us, and the systems in play. To clarify my references, by them, I mean the ideology of inequality and advantage held by racist. By us, I mean the ideology of equality and marginalized experiences. And by the system, I mean the prevailing constructs and socialization that support and reinforce biases.

So, for example, the prism of race is subjective to color differences and extremely limited in understanding the basis for the beliefs, processes, and behaviors associated with racism. So this is not in the context of race but conditioned behaviors, experiences, and assumptions. It is beyond the physical onto the philosophical. Consider infants are born in innocence into a world having no reference point. They are challenged by the unknown, needing guidance and cultivation to adapt to their environment.

Born only with the fear of falling and noises, all other fears are learned and vary significantly among the human species depending on cultural behavior, experiences, or geography. Consequently, it is chosen fears that grips humans. Where no such learned behavior or experiences exist, assumptions are substituted to support or reject anxiety of the unknown. Racism comes about from learned behavior, transposed experiences, and projected assumptions. Infants know no racism. It is taught or learned, so we find a starting point there.

From infancy, the process of imitation and assimilation has long been set in motion to navigate the world as we grow older. A primal fear of socialization is not belonging to a group that affirms our identity and being defined by that group's norms, practices, and standards, which creates a sub-group. Sub-group membership is categorized together with any other group of associations comprising the totality of our identity and connectivity. Loss of identity or change in prestige or status within the subgroup removes a portion of our self-worth altering the benefits of its inclusion.

It results in a fearful void, anxiety of unaccustomed or rejected connection, and an insecure definition of self. That is the power and lure of a caste system and its membership to reject those deemed unworthy. Those deemed unworthy aspire to be validated as worthy by seeking inclusion. Removal or discontinuation of association conjures infantile emotions of abandonment, stirring the primal need to belong and be accepted. It is a powerful dynamic upon which family is built as the first order of membership.

To be removed is to return to the womb, being born again metaphysically and searching for attachment but fragmented without one. Who, then, are you when you have no reference point? You are made dependent without identity or definition. Stripping away identity was a crucial principle in our people's psychological impairment facilitating slavery. Symbolically, those longing for what was lost returning to the past, preferring the comfortable familiarity of the sociological womb. Racism is not genetic. It is narcissistic.

It is an inverted fear to desperately protect and promote an identity which by rejecting is too self-deprecating to face the truth. It is similar to when your job becomes who you are, and you are incapable of separating from it. It is no longer what you do but who you have become consuming and defining your existence. But, without it, you are nothing because any expectation of separation or rejection is a request for self-destruction. You become severed from your identity.

From this perspective, the persistence of racism and possibly the method to rebuke it can be better understood. But as stated, when racism is the primary symptom or consequential impairment, it becomes the dominant identifier of the sub-group. Any opinion or ideology proven is measured by the sub-group consensus and bias metric, systematically comparing and establishing it, justifying exclusion or subjugation. The resulting comparison by this measurement generates the subsequent ideology, deficiency, and misrepresentation.

Reaffirming but not being representative of or recognizing other lesser differences or variations as long as the main one is met. The standard is developed and verified in one sub-group and then applied outside that sub-group or culture, assigning discriminations as less favorable by comparison. When viewed in a larger context, the biases and exclusions practiced are not solely based on race. Still, many other distinctions are not considered unless you belong to the relegated group demoted from equality of consideration.

The same dynamic exists outside of race, and these distinctions produce alternative perspectives desensitized by those whose advantage it benefits that do belong. The distinction of gender, adult or child, an employer over employee, religious belief and choice, income or education, and sexual preference or moral judgment are shallow divisions. Furthermore, tall or short, heavy or thin, city or rural, and other trivial methods of comparison are used to claim priority or authority because race might not be used, but other differences are used. It can get confusing and convoluted but rarely relevant.

However, we are all different and don't fit into many of others' subgroups, just as they might not fit ours. Still, you may belong to the subgroup based on race alone but not by other differences. As the desirability becomes more specific regarding sub-groups, some don't include you. For example, being white gets you membership. But are you a straight white male, Christian, Catholic, tall, educated, affluent, right-handed, fit, rugged, healthy, same race marriage, without southern traits? Are you a legacy American without immigrant roots, racist, and so forth?

So at what point do the distinctions stop when you don't control or fit the qualifications? At what point does social cloning start realizing the insignificance of the criteria? Penalizing all differences leaves you isolated and singular, a unique subgroup of one. Self-awareness would inform you that we are all different from each other, and there are no duplications of uniqueness within humanity or even snowflakes. Consider the diverse population and entities of heaven before Eden under God's harmonic gaze. It was not homogenized.

The faulty earthly assumption becomes evident by the logical application of skin tone not having any significance outside the social orientation of sociological deceptions to exploit differences for advantage. The origin of skin tone is evolutionary ancestral exposure to sunlight. The variation of color perception is the degree of reflection or absorption of light. Both are environmental influences absent any implied superiority or inferiority, only adaptation. Any other method of evaluation is fabricated to further an objective.

Racism is the persuasion of such fabrication. In the distinctions mentioned in the above paragraph, much the same has been fabricated or stigmatized. Biases manifesting discrimination and insecurities in many forms are based on exclusion from a group you aren't reflective of by comparison. When not validated or preferred, its preoccupation can be devastating to your fundamentally projected image and beliefs or to receiving fair treatment. This fixation can be readily observed by style and fashion imitations, duplication of mannerisms and personality traits, and body transformations to conform to images, expressions, and attitudes.

The anticipation of receiving a similar validation by vicarious association and impersonation is consuming. This replication would seem unrelated to racism but is the same core motivation to assimilate with a group identity consumed by belonging based upon a romanticized advantage for inclusion. The seed sprouts the tree, so it is the orientation that sprouts the identity that robes or confirms the self-image. This conditioning is inclined to emerge based upon association or familiarity with other races when the predisposition of determination is racially biased.

So the tussle is not with the outside world. It is from within your-self, uniting your self-image to fit society's expectations. It reflects a continuity of psychology by cloning comparable components. It even produces similar variations from and among similar deviations of the same identifications. These internal expectations are the reg-ulator authority incorporating a specific confirming perspective. This conformity is the Karen syndrome to coerce compliance to their approval or curiosity.

The urge to exercise unreasonable expectations of control is sup-ported and reinforced by behavior removed from reality or having actual authority. It is associated with racism because that is the closest resemblance of this anticipation and desire to control some-one without recourse, especially of a different race and usually Black. But racism, human trafficking, and involuntary servitude have been practiced by every race and continent around the globe spanning time immortal. Africans were also guilty of slave trade participation and tribal atrocities.

Slavery was an ideology initiated into practice to support greed, conquest, or subjective subgroup characteristics. However, men and whites feel everyone outside their subgroup is inferior promoting sexism and racism. Racist beliefs are not the domain of only whites. Still, in a historical context in America, it does apply excessively but not exclusively. Others are racist, including Black people, but whites have had the most significant outlet to express and practice it while stubbornly refusing to relinquish it. Therefore, to attack the person is to attack the result, not the cause.

Based on orientation, the result is convinced that their perspective is justified based upon some subjective criteria steadfastly believe. They are sometimes determined and accepted without the benefit of experience but by assumption devoid of personal knowledge or ex-perience. Once this weed spreads, it is incorporated as organic, con-suming any rational perspective. The expectations, stereotypes, and generalizations suggest the slave master's steadfast commitment, supporting their arrogance and impunity.

They are convinced they are correct, even morally right. Any material validation or accomplishment as a measure of value and virtue is propagated as being solely possessed and exhibited in their cultural differences or desired social qualities. Hopefully, revealing the underlying ideology leads to a better understanding of the core forces and processes undermining equality. It must be addressed at the factory, in its infancy, before it festers into deep-rooted biases refined over time by socialization and mass production.

Again, racism is not always caused by racist thoughts. Often, emotional engagement overrides logical reasoning resulting in tunnel analysis reverting to habitual indoctrination or outburst. This predisposition triggers social conditioning exhibited as racism. Likewise, a child who is repeatedly initiated and deceptively conditioned into an intellectual and emotional acceptance of inferiority interprets any images that exclude their self-worth and self-identity as a perceived reality based upon the consistency of their exclusion.

Inferiority and exclusion becomes their reality. That is what makes role models important. Exclusion instills insecurity, while inclusion instills confidence as an impression of self-validation and hope. Of the many years of primary schooling Crispus Attucks, Eli Whitney, Booker T. Washington, Harriet Tubman, Frederick Douglas, skip to Dr. Martin Luther King Jr, and Rosa Parks were the only Black people who deserve a mainstream passing mention.

There was disdain for Malcolm X. if mentioned but onward to The Honorable Thurgood Marshall, followed by the recent addition of President Barack Obama. A few others are scattered across the landscape of history, but just like their image and presence make an enormous difference, so would the many more absent. Yet, we are inundated with European history, figures, and events but no mention of any African history. So history presented as education resembles an anemic reference outside white existence and accomplishments.

Many more noteworthy Black people and Black communities contributed to our history in America. But slavery and suppression are
the primary narratives purposefully campaigned. It is simply not
true, but it is incumbent upon us to promote our prosperity and contributions and not expect it to be taught in school. It will not be
taught in schools, especially with CRT opposition, because it considerably changes their narrative.

Considering the history of slavery in a global context, the duration
of America's version is limited. If it is forbidden to teach Black history of America, Africa, or around the globe, what is the purpose
and importance of European history to us? Although slavery has
been practiced since ancient times and was not exclusively based on
race, America's is the most recent and atrociously blatant since medieval. Surprisingly and historically, most often, race in the context
of color was not the determining factor for slavery. In contrast,
America's slavery is exclusively color based.

The continued outrage in America is America's claim to Freedom
and Democracy for all, but with vastly demonstrated exceptions
contrary to its declaration and continued denial of equality. The
stain on America's character and dignity lingers for these reasons,
mainly its false claims, weak denials, and divisive refusals. Meanwhile, America is exalted as above reproach with exemplary dignity
and unilateral freedom. Whose national character is worthy of
praise but foreign to any resemblance of fairness to many outside
the white sub-group it promotes by privilege, representation, and
fictitious reiteration.

Images of Jesus accomplish the same task as many portrayals on
television, but particularly religious depictions. Estimating the extent and effectiveness of its propaganda on unsuspecting minds just
ask a small child the color of Jesus. This inculcation of propaganda
is implemented and set at an early age, with entertainment and visual portrayals as the prime miseducation. Eventually, either identifying with the symbols of hierarchy and white pride subliminally

installed as education, entertainment, and religion or degraded by submission to the same images.

The pledge of allegiance is a chant of devotion echoed so many times as to implant it in your subconscious, circumventing any conscious analysis by appealing to emotions and automatic submission without hesitation. The American Flag is an item of life-sacrificing worship despite any atrocities and inequalities inflicted. It is a method to ingrain obedience and loyalty. Patriotism and Nationalism are invoked under selective and beneficial conditions depending on how advantageous its recognition and necessity is to include us.

Otherwise, there is a distinction such as African American or minority, not of lesser numbers, but as disadvantaged. Never just American. The Olympics is the only time we are simply American. No other race or nationality are referenced by a land many of them never visited and ties dating back over four hundred years. They at least have a country instead of just a continent of origin. However, many have populated this country to have the interim title removed from their designation, simply being called Americans.

Undoubtedly, the ability to Americanize one's image for easier assimilation diverts attention from themselves, especially by ostracizing others, particularly Black people. Those who arrived by immigration now bemoan immigrants while concealing apparent hints of their immigrant origins. White and light complexion immigrants easily assimilate into the white culture or middle class and are excluded from adverse comparisons and discrimination. Once incorporated, they quickly develop no allowances for a diversity of perspectives or cultures not rejected by their new identity and cultural spectacles.

Their culture is surrendered in exchange for a new identity welcoming them to the Americanized white subgroup. Not having their identity stolen but surrendered, they fail to see the damage and trauma caused by never feeling or escaping the prolonged ostracization our people have faced. Regarding the "African American" plight, they don't know the half of it. The sting of the whip or the noose around the neck of it. They instead become members of the system by white association. The system and the integration become indistinguishable.

People are molded to be inflexible and dismissive, while systems are designed rigidly but fickle. Taking the country back for conservative values is maintaining the violation of church and state for religious values to mandate legislative foundations supplementing sociological biases. These customary biases and identities are preferred as normal behavior well entrenched, while any deviation is abnormal or fearfully anticipated. The imbalance that produces their comfort disregards the aggrieved party's demand for consideration, essentially minimizing and dismissing claims with indignant outrage.

The way it has been is prone to narcissistic impositions by rejecting the evolution of intolerance and discontent to instead embracing inclusion. The majority inclination has shifted from the majority ideology of controlling minority populations. Yet, the now racist minority ideology resists the changing times seeking to rule the majority. The ignorance of the past attempts to paralyze the present and remains opposed and fearful of future possibilities and expectations. Redefining the constructs of society, self-identity, and equality is deemed a threat.

Marginalized society is no longer happy with whatever scraps procured, instead wanting whatever possibilities and considerations advantaged white's receives. Wanting equilibrium of opportunity and social treatment impartially available and applied. The contempt and discontent are prevalent and pervasive on many levels regarding a biased irrelevant and suppressive application or standard.

However, a stark difference exists, whether it is gender inequality, pay inequality, religious discrimination, educational gaps, healthcare deficiencies, lifestyle orientation, and many others, not just racial profiling and social injustices. Moreover, many deep traumas have been directed towards all subgroups not representative of the dominant controlling group despite being members of other dominant subgroups such as educated, male, or the double whammy, Black and female. Every subgroup has a learned behavior with defining expectations and benefits and is subjected to judgment from other subgroups' prejudices.

However, the problem arises when it minimizes or infringes on another subgroup to be defined by the standards beneficial to the dominant subgroup. Thus preferences are common to all humans or specific taxon, but the exercise of dominance and privilege where none exist based upon a manipulated interpretation or advantage violates humanity. Continued practice of this violation is not a deterrent for change, it invites it by unfairness. On the contrary, it dictates perseverance because to concede is to assure the imbalance of identity, perspective, and privilege continues.

Discouragement must be persistent punitive condemnation and removal of incentives that perpetuate prejudice. The system is very efficient in producing the desired outcomes by instituting behavior patterns and instigating reactions. Perhaps the focus should be at the earliest development on the most impressionable, similar to the current sociological practice. CRT threatens to disrupt this approach by replacing the pipeline by making changes in the supply chain. The focus probably should not be on the people who exhibit these traits of entitlement and discrimination, but instead on the pipeline.

By focusing on the supply chain, understanding the process of how it occurred to reduce its influences would produce more beneficial progress. The creation and impact of these influences predict the intended reality, so restricting or changing the production affects the flow. Interrupting supplies or preventing reinforcements is an effective military tactic. This combat premise is socially applied in a civilian situation to govern and regulate by implied manipulation garnering voluntary compliance and submission to the threat, penalty, or outcome.

To understand the dynamics at play, look no further than the puppet performing in a presentation controlled by the puppet master from behind the curtain, illustrating a fabricated reality. Mesmerized by the conditioning, symbols, and images, we dance on a string manipulated from behind the curtain of power and greed, suggesting involuntary ritualized behaviors and compulsions. It is never resolving the source of the problem to remove the problem but only treating the symptom, allowing the infectious dilemma to return repeatedly.

This cycle is often done under the misconception of freedom to dictate control but actually promotes less freedom for those not in power. This myth is the ultimate social pyramid scheme operated like a Ponzi scam robbing Peter to pay Paul, exaggerating the benefits, and destined to collapse from instability when due. A level of ignorance, foolishness, and trust is required. Ignorance of being unaware, foolishness disregarding the improbabilities, and trust absent verifiable proof creating the deception. Racism is a mass delusion based on skin tone, rationalizing our visual difference as being of substance, validating the delusion.

Black is demonized, biracial is ostracized, and White is worshipped but criticized according to a system that benefits those sufficiently positioned by the chaos and division. The social Ponzi scam is an inverted pyramid expanding deceptions dating back thousands of years carried forward designed to dilute or contort beliefs, history, and motives over time. The origins of our social systems must be known through world history to examine the mechanisms and reasons for its structure and ideologies. Conquest and submission are dominant factors in both. The defeated submits under the conquest of domination capitulating to the conqueror's narrative.

As conquerors rotate so does narratives, beliefs, and justifications. The meek shall inherit the world once run by the mighty as a matter of repositioning when the cycle repeats itself. All that was once mighty have either fallen from the heights or risen from the depths. It is usually where delusional and imaginary visions cross paths with reality. Imagine a superpower such as China spearheading a competing organization. Let's label it BRICS+ and a growing coalition of disenfranchised countries joining together.

Let's further assume that Mexico joined and under a union with say China struck an agreement to not only house weapons and military bases but to build a wall isolating America under house arrest. Imagine America protesting to a government whose people America has shun and government America has son(ed). Imagine say Canada chooses to remain neutral for self-preservation further isolating America. What recourse would America have other than a daunting war having been weakened from a geo-political musical chair of politics and economic seduction?

Can this new coalition of marginalized insurgents be relied upon for guidance by the Marquess of Queensbury rules of civil engagement and rest breaks? They certainly would not dare attack the default currency status of the U.S. dollar which has precedence established long before even Roe v. Wade. Surely, while America is consumed with racism and politics they would not dare seek advantage striking us when we are down during such a perilous time for America. Then again, I guess it is a succession plan, only not the one Republicans now pine for so badly. Furthermore, consider Mexicans ARE simply returning to a home they occupied first!

Seems self-destruction or mutual destruction is often more palatable than the uncertainty or unknown consequences of losing or sharing power. When you have known no other way but power you cease to exist by identity, ideology, and relevance. Either way America wakes up to a cold and empty bed slugging through its stubbornness to evolve as they no longer have a need to smile in America's face all the while trying to take our place. A house divided bickers as it burns with no hands on deck to extinguish the blaze when it was just a flame. The intoxication of power and prestige can cause an addiction greater than the organism's will to survive.

But, back from the brink of imagination to the reality of now. When it is simply a matter of who retains control or authority to designate policy, by default, others are methodically rejected and suppressed to further sustain this reign. Understanding this decline from dominance trembles the sociological and psychological paradigm triggered by the process of change. When the privilege to grant permission or demand conciliation is removed, the associated identity crashes along with the declining perception of its power. Yielding to declining power incentivizes its desperation.

No matter how fearless or justified, repeated requests empower the petitioned party to be recognized with the authority to refuse others' self-determination. It is a form of begging to repeatedly request anything once your intentions have been made known once. Begging is always done from a position below. The meek begs waiting to inherit the world in the sweet by-and-by where the strong don't roam, but the submissive abide. Timid requests are usually met with firm denials tempered with a hint of anger or force. The arrogance of refusal or the act of pleading invites authority over the displayed weakness of the requesting party.

Reparations fall into this category in many ways, waiting by the mailbox for the check to arrive. It was never mailed despite the many assurances that the payment was in transit. There are other means to secure the American Dream despite reparations or obstructions. As currently constituted, a glimmer of hope shines on the horizon brighter than in previous years but the battle wages on to enhance the progress already made. The fight against racism is against the concept and practice, not focusing on people only to the extent of hindering their ability to spread it. It will go away by social suffocation with no source or escalation to incubate its ideology.

Its death will be the same as its birth by sociology and psychology. Being accusatory or confrontational invites resistance as a defense mechanism instead of the desired persuasion. Digging into a position evokes the fight or flight reflex. It is not to accept or excuse historical atrocities and injustices but to move beyond them as a psychological and sociological impediment. It must be realized that some people, especially those profoundly biased, will not be convinced or converted, maybe even you among them. Finessing the cause is a more effective use of energy than force-feeding transformation.

Change is often painful and slow, but even more so when the most efficient and effective methods are not used. Once comprehensively embraced and reinforced, primary, secondary, and contingent objectives promote the progression of equality and identify its violation to initiate change. Otherwise, it's a merry-go-round arrangement spinning the scenery sequenced repetitively without modification or variation. The carrot, out of reach, is being chased by the mule as motivation to participate.

But, never being rewarded with the carrot for its efforts is a resignation to failure regardless of the effort. The objective is to be the vision that projects the image seen, not the mirror reflecting what is placed before it. It takes courage to be different, to say what is required, to say what you feel, to stand on principle, and to declare your autonomy. If you are not ten toes in, you might as well be totally out. It is not always possible to be unscathed or without resistance when extracting revelations of knowledge producing change. The evolution of change is discovery followed by acceptance and practice but preceded by ignorant opposition.

Aristotle stated it is an educated mind that entertain an idea without accepting it. It is also an educated mind that accepts an idea's veracity despite its unpopularity. Epicurus stated we must know our flaws. So our minds and self-identity cannot be too fragile for correction or debate. To coverup knowledge, ideas, flaws, or debate relegates us to continuity of our existing state. The systems and motivations are interconnected and a foundational understanding of its connectivity and operation require a solemn examination. Therefore, we must be blatantly frank and earnest when untwisting the reality.

The mask only conceals the façade, actions reveal the composition.

Choices are often subdued by voluntary compulsion.

Habit is only repetition self-duplicated.

Psychology, socialization, and systems set the boundaries of replication.

Courage changes them.

<u>Let me ask you a Question</u>

1. Can we detect the exact opposite of the same dynamic but different behaviors? If we can clearly see and understand theirs, why can't we see ours? Does the system create the racial simulation dependent on ignorance, obedience, and faith?

2. Do we control the systems or do they control us? Is it dependent on our disposition and participation? If chaos has a pattern, so must human interaction, but based on what fallacies do we tolerate or promote it? What do we judge by but refuse to be judged?

3. Is the lion King of the jungle because he thinks he is king or don't care who doesn't? Can equality be the same? Why is the lion

never a victim? Why may the lion lose but is never defeated? Can we be only delayed, not stopped when having the heart of a lion and courage of two? Does conquering the enemy within defeat the enemy without?

4. Are reactions sometimes automatic expectations of things not present but presumed? Is an easy dishonorable submission preferable to a difficult principled stand? Is fitting in or belonging a higher honor than standing out?

5. If we are citizens of the universe and thus equally privilege indivisible from infinity past and future, why are we concerned or obstructed by disturbing matters without making adjustments? Are racism and discrimination the same mindset as inferiority and inequality? Are we responsible for our programming or is the system? Are we detached from a logical response disguised as free will hopelessly shackled to ideologies, indoctrinations, systems, and beliefs aligned in oblivion or by choice?

Happy Emancipation
When the truth is a Lie

Rejoice! Hallelujah! Free at Last! Happy Jubilee! Juneteenth is now a holiday. Finally, a day our ancestors never thought would come. Perhaps a day they only dreamed about, but could it be only a pseudo-Freedom of which they had repeatedly fantasized? How about a mirage or day full of promises that would go unfulfilled? Could it be a day yet to be seen other than symbolically? Civil Rights, the Voting Act, Black History Month, and Dr. Martin Luther King Jr. Day brought some of the exact lofty expectations and excitement.

Please make no mistake about it. It is progress, and we will take it as part of an ensemble. However, it is oddly questionable as acknowledgment or satisfaction of meaningful change. Let history in the future look back and judge if June 19th, being declared a national holiday is signaling meaningful change or just another layover along the way. From this vantage point, history reveals some very curious methods of demonstrating the Freedom and emancipation of Black people in America since that initial day of liberation in 1863.

First and foremost, many have diligently worked to bring about awareness and recognition for this holiday as a heartfelt endeavor. Second, many more rejoice in the celebration of the symbolism of this day. Third, the relief and swell of pride is barely contained within the satisfaction of its recognition, declaration, and celebration. Juneteenth, at the very most, is a celebration of symbolism. By no means do I want to diminish or criticize the insinuation of its importance, impact, or impression for those feeling the triumph or validation of its meaning and achievement.

However, I wonder if the wave of pride felt is really a symbolic fountain of hope or otherwise an abstract pacification. I really wonder, reasonably considering the eventual unsustainability of its concealment and the summary of its actual historical limitations beyond notification. Seemingly, we were only told when it could no longer be kept an open secret but remained an open practice. Certainly, the notification was better late than never. The notification at this point was reluctantly received by racist if not reluctantly delivered.

One can argue that it was the end of concealment, not the completion of notification. Skipping past the inadequacies of its subsequent impact, it has to be contemplated where is the meat on the bone? At its core, did it deliver as promised? Governed by the reality of its intent, purpose, and application by legislation, what was really "given," promised, or protected by this notification of Freedom. This notification was two and a half years later. Lincoln's Emancipation Proclamation regarding legislative decree changed the method, not the mentality or tradition of slavery, only the procedure by legal context.

Some states still have not received notification because it is still on the state law books. I imagine the rationale is probably just in case, you never know. Still, although the law and announcement had occurred, not the complete notification or earnest undertaking of relief. It appears there was no urgency to enforce it, ensure its observance, or guarantee its notification. One hundred and sixty years later, there is still significant resistance to justice, equality, and liberated acceptance for Black people in America.

So, is Juneteenth a memorial to the atrocity of slavery or a celebration of relief from it? If this is a celebration of relief, why are we still subjected to the injustices of discrimination rooted in slavery? How about a symbolic day of reverence honoring our ancestors and furthering our unified objective similar to a day of Memorial? Mourning the indignities suffered and the struggle endured does little to shake the remnants of its ideology. But, is it a day to suspend our diligence instead of pursuing the intent of notification, the freedom from racism, or equal protection and application of the law?

Should it instead be a day of strategizing an agenda to achieve the stated liberty? That achievement would be truly festive and a reason to celebrate. Both seen and unseen, slavery's implications are effectively, overtly, and covertly still practiced in principle and purpose as racism. As a result, legitimate questions surface when quantifying and contextualizing the reprieve against the sinister practices still limiting our claim of Freedom. When, how, and where freedom did take effect spanning Jim Crow to racial profiling and marginalization were we free from the inequality of slavery's principles?

Was it only in words or more prominent by deed, wishful thinking, or imagination? A quasi-end to slavery and its overt methods gave way to the beginning of pseudo Freedom and Black people's everlasting crusade for equality. The two-edge sword cuts efficiently on both edges, but the handle is safe from its wounding damage. The blade is slavery, and one edge is longingly reminiscent of their dominion. While the other edge is gratefully relieved from its mutilation and wholesale atrocities.

Same sword, two different realities, so which edge is celebrated depends on the edge you reside, dominion or mutilation. We are only familiar with the side raining down mutilation. The handle controls the power wielded and damage delivered directed by the system. The system or power directs the blade and the blow, deciding which edge delivers its fate and to whom. Whoever controls the handle guides the cut, thus the reality. So, what was really given or received on this day of notification, other than the notification?

Was pseudo Freedom not granted in 1863 over two and a half years prior, subsequently making the notification amount to permission to know? It doesn't seem like there was any rush. This lack of urgency is the tale of Juneteenth and its extended perspective of racism, slavery, or freedom from it. Its authentic observance still lacks urgency today. It is not the celebration but how and why it is celebrated, achieving what purpose of significance. Furthermore, General Granger's Field Order 3 language in Galveston Texas on

Happy Emancipation
When the Truth is a Lie

June 19, 1965, may reveal the true sentiment regarding freedom of slaves and the disregard for its liberating message of freedom.

Then it would follow why would you celebrate the delay of the information or change above the original day it was enacted into law, January 1st, 1863? Not much had essentially changed, except now everyone knew about it. What about those who had already known or where it had already taken effect? What day do they celebrate? Celebrating the notification seems like a consolation prize for participation. It is like a job title without the pay or promotion but increased duties. The delay of Freedom's notification to finally reach the outer regions granting Freedom seems like the beginning of social placation and the official beginning of Jim Crow.

They appear to be two different things, but upon closer inspection in practice and law, which one does it seem like we received the most? Slavery was followed by Jim Crow and its many variations of systemic racism and injustices. Remember, over one hundred years later, "Colored Only" water fountains and lunch counters existed in plain sight well after the Juneteenth notification. Ask Claudette Colvin or Rosa Parks about Freedom to ride the bus without being required to give up your seat to a white person.

How easily are we now deceived or pacified by our need for acceptance and validation by no less than offerings of a holiday? Fortunately, we can look forward to another holiday when we exit this holding pattern upon notification of what we are still waiting. We now dare to celebrate a day that did not deliver on our expectations or the sincere interpretation of its intentions. But have we forgotten what was promised or the hollowness of that promise? It did technically mostly deliver on abolishing physical slavery. Still, it did not deliver on Freedom from not being treated as a slave or inhumane.

Emmitt Till, Rodney King, George Floyd, and Ahmaud Aubrey are examples that we have a ways to go yet. But then again, what it never promised was the assumption of justice or equality along with

Freedom. In essence, it never promised equality or freedom from injustice, just freedom from bondage. In many cases, forced labor became coerced labor, and no education became limited or scripted miseducation. Accordingly, this granted freedom is tilted heavily towards our discouragement and disqualification from equality and prosperity.

In many ways, there is no definitive way to deal with the horrors of slavery other than to liberate ourselves by instituting a meaningful change of substance and perspective, not by accumulating holidays. The only question is whose change or perspective, ours or theirs? Unfortunately, many of the necessary solutions haven't changed, nor has the unwillingness to pursue them. We must implement the solutions without reservation using the necessary actions dictated by the circumstances.

For example, removing economic barriers, securing quality healthcare, education not designed for lowly social orchestration, loan and banking modifications, criminal justice system reform, and restricting qualified immunity for law enforcement. Many other reforms or proclamations would have far more reaching substantive benefits than a holiday celebrating something that in principle has yet to happen. So, it is not only enough to give Freedom, but you must also enforce it.

Generally, it would be better for the Black condition if certain things were discontinued instead of celebrating shallow holidays. As a free nation, do we not, as everyday citizens have the right to celebrate any day without that day being a national holiday, for example celebrating your birthday? Then why do we need the government's permission to celebrate any day of collective importance to us? You know they sell ribs, beer, and fireworks for celebrations other than government-sanctioned holidays. Our culture, observances, and celebrations should be determined by us and our method of expression.

Maybe we can celebrate a week of non-violence to build towards a demonstration of our unity and humanity towards each other. Why do we hold other's celebrations above our own? For that matter, we have Kwanza, which is largely ignored. At the same time, Christmas is widely celebrated as a government-sanctioned holiday, and credit is given to a white myth. Pardon me, I mean Santa Claus. Thus, it could be misconstrued that we need government approval and validation to determine our cultural celebrations. Of course, the lack of a holiday has not damaged the Black condition as much as our challenges.

Still, many societal and institutional injustices have, so why not address them? Our grievances won't disappear with a holiday, but they might with stipulations that address inequities. There are no holidays from dignity or social justice. We need reciprocity to share in what we have contributed to others receiving. What they received in equal value, context, and quantity has to also extend to the principles of our Freedom. Freedom redefined should be Freedom from discrimination and systemic obstructions to our unhindered participation in the American dream, where any racial biases are functionally irrelevant.

The extent of our skill and ambition are the only factors, no more or no less than anyone else's, as Dr. King put it, the content of our character. That should be the interpretation and understanding of any Juneteenth intent with a forward gaze, not pacifying anyone's guilt or outrage by celebrating either. However, we have yet to receive that kind of Freedom where race is irrelevant. Juneteenth is a participation trophy where nothing was won or given of value. A holiday can't be given to instill pride and validation in a race of people.

Because, at its essence, it shares the same psychological bondage as slavery, permitting us something within our power and dignity to grant ourselves. It is frivolous to celebrate because they finally decided to endorse celebrating it. What is the intrinsic metaphorical value of freedom if not courage? Even worst to celebrate something within you because someone allowed you the courage to express it. It is a reflection of how far we need to progress psychologically to claim our pride, identity, and self-acceptance, fortifying our strength by self-determination. Our validation is a singular journey of mass undertaking to reject social confinement.

It gives rise to our collective ascension by removing ourselves from being individually part of the problem and collectively demonstrating a calculated representation of the solution. To be counted in our progress and removed from our stagnation. Like in the Wizard of Oz, Dorothy was told she always had the power. She just needed to recognize it. It was a matter of awareness. Juneteenth, in many ways, was a matter of awareness, not a promise fulfilled. It has yet to be realized because slavery was transformed into discrimination. That discrimination has operated since the notification of Freedom reached the far regions of the country.

But somehow, it has yet to fully reach the distant regions of modern society. Time has carried the water of this ideology while we are bailing ignorance only to have some who are refilling the vessel with hate. Therefore, celebrating this holiday has a minimal effect beyond another reason to fire up the grill. When the celebration ends, and the congratulations are done, there will still be more pressing issues that await us. So we will have to get back to the work of substantial practical progress and remain diligent. We cannot let the celebration douse the commitment and resolve needed later to focus on the task at hand.

Fortunately, any solution endorsing Juneteenth's purpose and intent lies between the ears of those who champion or oppose its principles, not on paper. But unfortunately, that is where the problem started and continues to hide secured in the mind. The mind conceals or reveals the perspective whereby the problem and solution rest. But for now, let us celebrate this day as creating temporary possibilities. A day to pacify a truce of perspectives and notification of slavery ending while not addressing its remaining evils. We recognize slavery's termination in 1865 but ignore its ideological revival in a different form.

If this seems cynical or ungrateful, I ask, should I be celebrating gratitude that it is now only discrimination? Freedom from bondage implied the accessories of Freedom from discrimination and suppression. Freedom, in its essence, obviously could not have been given if, after a century and almost a three-score-long fight, it has still not been received. Seeing but not touching, smelling but not tasting, spoken but not heard and although slavery ends Freedom does not begin. So there goes that delay again, and all its trappings held in abeyance. Once again, cut by the blade of racism and the delay of equality.

As the handler of the sword, the handler is impervious to the damage from the blade. While those who are cut continue to cry out, where is the relief, the Freedom from damages? We continue to cry out. Should not the one injured be the judge of the injury's severity? Of all our requests, is a holiday the one to be honored? The truth is a lie when proven false and can't survive scrutiny. Or when it is brutally honest but so truthful that it is repulsive and rejected as a falsehood to preserve ignorance or dignity. So, which is this truth, a lie or too repulsive? The biggest lie ever told is the truth when you do not want to accept it. The lie begins where the fact ends, and Freedom from racism and discrimination never began.

Warning! Straight no chaser.

Truth is similar to quicksand. The more you struggle, the faster it engulfs you. So, there can be no opposition where there is no resistance. Likewise, there can be no resistance where there is no opposition. It's a silly notion that the last day of notifying us of our Freedom made all the previous transgressions evaporate once we knew. The transgressions only lessened or evolved. Only the coercion of free labor, not fair labor, and physical restraint diminished while other ramifications increased.

Therefore, are we free from the consequences of being free? Seemingly, by all accounts we are still burdened by the refusal of our equality and denial of our humanity. We were not promised or given Freedom. They essentially stopped robbing us of it. It was not theirs to take, so how could they give it? Now no longer a slave, are there still those who do not know this? Despite slavery or Freedom from it, why are we still not fully afforded our rights and social justice? The facade of Freedom without conviction is the problem.

Consequently, being free but unaware until notified gives us a mental perspective devoid of physical suppression but a psychologically dependent one reminded by discrimination. Better techniques are now used to accomplish the same effect. The question is, what is that perspective and technique? Does it require permission and validation to be obedient to conformity and restrictions? Do others' actions suggest we are still not free, or do ours imply that we still don't know we are free? Capitulation is surrender. Submission is a willful defeat.

But both primarily come from a weakened spirit, so beware and protect yourself from both at all times. We no doubt have the spirit to persevere, it is tested and proven. However, the ghost of slavery still haunts us. Our perspective and psychology lingers behind our progress stagnating our growth and prosperity. Our options are either resistance to the stagnation or willful submission to it. The system will submit you regardless of race by defining the rules and narrowing the prospects demanding complicity and conformity, especially if you are Black.

Although there is no mystery often regarding the rules, to smell success, we must overcome the obstacles anyway because we ARE Black. The motivation is for the smell of it because we have proven that is what we do, overcome. Boasting of the obstacles that have

been overcome smells better than crying over obstacles that over-
came us. Mental toughness and an analytical resolve supply our
minds with the tools needed to overcome any barriers. The stench
of slavery should motivate our resolve to smell the roses of true
freedom and self-actualization.

Any breach allowed to penetrate our mental perimeter weakens our
spirit. Be careful what ideas are served that we devour. We must
consider the menu and motive before consuming it. Don't believe
the hype. Look for the substance. Therefore, this celebration is diluted because the holiday benefits everyone whether they want it or
not, whether their ancestors suffered or not. Our experiences paid
for this day, so where are specific concessions for us with practical
solutions to our condition? We are hustling backward for what we
have already labored.

Everyone else is now along for the feast when before they have
feasted without us. Amends for transgressions against our people, it
seems reasonable to assume any concessions would be specifically
directed toward our redress without exceptions. Many issues linger
despite the late notification or recent holiday. We are still patronized
by ignoring vital changes and unresolved grievances. A social benefit analysis reveals the sum impact of the holiday is probably not a
substantial gain. Its practical benefit is not much more than if it had
not been declared a holiday. It is devoid of any meat on the bone.

Granted, the holiday is an absolutely appreciated acknowledgment
if you accept payment in holidays, not practicalities. So is this a
trick or a treat? Are we dressed up to masquerade as free for one
day? Freedom is a concept manifested more in what is not taken
than what is given. It is the availability of presented choices unhindered. Freedom gives you more options and a better selection, but
not what is available from which to choose. Instead, only what you
can choose from, not the selection but what is selected.

How available and accessible are these choices for us as our options? Freedom restricts what you cannot do while defining what you are allowed to do and your options to do it. Freedom taken is not returned, it is stolen by the passage of time. America's dignity is violated during that tarnished time and its sin is compounded by continued injustices. Still, receiving permission for a holiday by their notification indicates the veneer of Freedom yet to be realized. Unable to take or grant either Freedom or dignity leaves only the lingering psychologically afflicting bondage of spirit and mind to be shaken.

We freely control that unless we relinquish it. We need to stand on it, stand in it, but don't loiter around it. Time mandates the wise use of our provisions and opportunities to avoid another century of tribulations seeking justice and equality. Loitering is a sign of lurking hesitation, hesitation invites delay, despair, and stagnation. We need to claim it, not wait to be told it. Therefore, we are always free, but our options are constantly regulated. The mind evaluates our Freedom's reality, our actions are the exercise of it.

Whether we are notified, already knew, or since come to believe it, it does not affect its existence. So it was not the Emancipation Proclamation of January 1st, 1863, or the last notification made on June 19th, 1865, that freed the slave. It was being told, but we will only truly be freed when we tell ourselves. This exhibits the four minute mile barrier mentality. We must know our self-worth within our minds without being told or having to ask. A strong will and a knowledgeable mind are formidable opponents when the mind becomes an elite intellectual weapon. A weapon always at the ready, rendering us unable to be disarmed.

Our mind is the final frontier of contention to be conquered by us to guarantee our Freedom by our permission. Like Dorothy in the fairy tale land of Oz, we always had the power. Knowledge is the currency of prosperity, which is why it is always forbidden. Knowledge is Freedom. Know that, practice that, and become that, knowledgeable and free. We must master our minds. We must be made to remain ignorant to remain a slave, obedient, or perpetuate a slave mentality. Ignorant of knowledge but mainly of their schemes, our autonomy, and our possibilities.

A piece of paper signed or late word spread is no longer sufficient control to restrain our minds or liberties. Only our lack of discipline, determination, and vision can restrain us, otherwise infinity is our captivity. Information is knowledge expanding our radius of understanding, prosperity, and possibilities. Remember, my people are destroyed for lack of knowledge according to the bible. They are also punished for rejecting it, referring to knowledge.

As Ten Bears said, no four corners of a paper can hold the iron. The iron is in the tongue when you speak, and it is in the actions you take. And if I might add, the iron is in the mind's thoughts and heart's determination to defeat any obstacle placed before us. We must know that by now! It is time they know it too! There can be no holiday that denies or relaxes our dignity. The holiday of discrimination has lasted and been celebrated for far too long. Time for us to issue a long overdue notification of our own. No more. Never again.

Anyway, Happy Juneteenth to all, and enjoy your Freedom and holiday or Freedom from this holiday. Courage has no holiday and nor should our exercise of our Freedom.

Thurston's Thoughts
Regifting Freedom Again

We must define and understand the terms, conditions, and definitions set forth thoroughly, comparing apples to apples regarding the
concept of Freedom. Once defined, we discover there are levels to
the concept of freedom. The levels outline the parameters beyond
our freedom that are restricted. The granting of Freedom was the
lessening of brutality regarding captivity, which was in their power.
In principle, it was the absence of bondage, not granting the essence
of freedom, but granting movement while still confined by the ideology.

In the attempt to satisfy expectations, the deception is that the absence of bondage produces the presence of Freedom. On the contrary, the fundamentals of slavery have continued because they did
not grant freedom to inclusion or freedom to become equal first-
class citizens. In essence, they granted Freedom of the body but not
mind or spirit and definitely not opportunity. Removing the physical shackles, but other restraints were substituted with Jim Crow,
injustices, and beyond. Various forms of brutality persisted but now
since less acceptable means remain vaguely concealed from public
view.

Furthermore, the systems accomplished what the individual racist
use to dispense. Freedom of mind is the one freedom that cannot be
granted, taken, or withdrawn. It is freedom in its purest form. It
must be surrendered as an act of complicity or compliance. All other varieties are shadows as stoic philosophers believed freedom res-
onates from the mind outwardly. It emanates from within, affecting
physical movement, environmental conditioning, to abstract application. It is well known that freedom cannot be attained if not by an
embraced concept within the mind.

So the question of why Black people were not free when legislated
on January 1, 1863, is not because we were not told but because it
was not psychologically accepted. Some may argue it still isn't psychologically and socially accepted by them or us. On June 19, 1865,

the last regions of slavery divulged the two and a half year old secret. Still, the slavery sympathizers could not embrace the concept of abolishing slavery in their minds, only in their words. So, essentially having not embraced emancipation, racism has been allowed to fester like an open sore.

By enabling the degradation of our humanity to persist, the racist Confederate heritage to simmer, and the systemic biases to flourish transformed slavery, but not abolish its mentality. It supposedly was banned when the south was allowed to rejoin the Union. But you cannot legislate or abolish thoughts or inclinations in someone's mind if they choose to harbor them. So, the pledge was an action dependent on a thought, not the mentality to produce the action of Freedom.

Therefore, what freedom, pledge, promise, and liberation all have in common is they are not physical realities. They are mental concepts manifested by physical actions that require trust or belief, willingness, and behavior. These physical actions are neutralized when the actual manifestation does not measure up to the perception. The perceptions are then always pursued, seeking to meet the elusive expectations. Both are subjected to effort, integrity, and opportunity to sincerely be realized.

Opportunity defines the concept of equality of availability. Equality is access to equal possibility, not of results, and the application of impartiality to both. So, equality is relative to the expectations of equal opportunity but not to actual equal accomplishment because of it. Opportunity and outcomes are subjective but should not be prejudiced or undermined. The presence of opportunity does not dictate the presence or absence of achievement when, in truth, they are unspecified possibilities.

The twisted comparison and perception lies in the absence of physical oppression being different than the presence of psychological, societal, and structural suppression or obstruction. These non-physical oppressions formulate the supposition making it plausibly deniable that the remnants of discriminatory conditions do still exist. The quest for Freedom from the reality of the psychological effects, social conditioning, and the systemic structure's harmful effects on our people and whites' mentality has never been definitively addressed.

The seismic shift to the foundation of America's self-righteous identity plagues solutions to maintain the deception. The same is true globally in many societies to maintain an exploitive advantage. The struggle of the disadvantaged portion of these nations is preferable to disrupting the identity masquerade of the advantaged portion, fully convinced of their purity by sheer nationalism, ignorance, and privilege. The mind rejects what is inconceivable to process, categorizing it as false, irrelevant, or non-existent.

Psychologically breaking down the self-image and core identity, which is opposed to history and the truth, requires a degree of self-destruction. That degree of self-destruction is what they will avoid at all costs but is also what our people have suffered to overcome since 1863. So, where does the burden lay? They have theirs, and we have ours. But we both have a shared one. There is no argument it occurred, no consensus on a resolution to find a remedy, and dubious debate about the lingering effect, even with our proud denial.

But, there is plenty of avoidance of its disorder. Our burden is alleviating our condition, which is different from erasing their burden. History consists of memories, and memories are reminders of what is sometimes preferred not to be dragged into the present. The triggers of history bring forth different memories based on experiences. With that said, is Juneteenth a reminder to us of inferiority or a celebration of racism of the good old times? Juneteenth is a memorial to the Confederacy in a racist mind that has never abandoned its principles. It is questionable what it is in the minds of non-racists or our people. All can agree it is not a celebration of liberation from prejudice.

With the relief being marginal by what hollow standard, stated or implied, is an expectation met for a reason to celebrate while the battle still wages? It is as premature as it is overdue. Celebrations are best reserved for victories but let's calculate and evaluate the reprieve against the veiled and disturbing observations that have limited its impact. Is a day of sorrow more appropriately transposed as a ploy instead of atonement minus the compensation or rebuke? The acknowledgment is sarcastically ceremonial, problematically symbolic, and sluggishly aspirational.

Holding the carrot out of reach but within range of belief maintains its principles while denying its practice. So are we celebrating the promise of freedom, the delivery of freedom, or the hope of freedom? Like the carrot, all three have proven to be just out of reach. Would there be a need for debate if the illusion of Freedom had become a reality? A full and tearful confession is unrealistic, and wholesale rejection of deep-rooted conditioning is improbable. The ledger of progress from 1865 until now has had some milestones.

Still, it lacks sparkling recrimination of racism that was not diligently challenged for its cruel effects and intent for nearly one hundred years until the Civil Rights act of 1964. Since then, the transfer has been from oppression to suppression, exclusion, and now just oblivious denial and bodacious posturing. Why do we celebrate a holiday while our voting rights are mangled? We must understand a primary reason for the denial of racism is that it is so fundamentally established it is invisible to many making it synonymous with the structure of American society.

It is also resistant to evolution from a society built upon a pyramid based on race with our people as the exploited foundation. However, the actual order is based on economics and ignorance, and that is where we should focus since only the distraction is based on race. The have-nots are primarily preoccupied with race incited by the puppet masters. The haves are preoccupied with control and accumulation. Conditioning or social engineering and economics is the direct force to be conquered on the path to social justice and equality.

So we are conditioned to play their game. But, it is hard to get mad when playing with someone else's ball when they take their ball and go home. That removes the essential element to play the game. We need to get our own ball. Even a snowball beats no-ball. That is why we are still subjected principally to injustices and discrimination by our lack of ownership. Yet, somehow, many of us can sustain despite the limitations, but sustaining is not obtaining or advancing. Stagnation and molasses moves at nearly the same pace.

Coincidentally, so does our conversion to ideologies, actions, and behaviors that liberate us from the past. Subliminal reinforcements are the subconscious perpetrators of racism, whether intentional or accidental, with most being culturally inherited and socially accepted. The identification and rejection of them lessen the stereotypes and ideology supporting racism. Symbols of white racial superiority are interwoven in the DNA of every facet of society, education, and present within the government infrastructure. Participation is the most effective way of teaching, followed by a demonstration and repetition.

Racism penetrates the mind on a level avoiding the scrutiny of its origins, intent, or validity. This avoidance of scrutiny is where the crux of freedom is compromised. We must attack racism structurally at its roots, the socialization of the mind, not by emotionally vilifying the individual. The racist spirit mutates among individuals, so the spread is the villainous idea and the individual is simply the host.

Case in point, the Judiciary act of 1789 established the Supreme Court. Has America not been "free" to nominate more than three Black Supreme Court justices by accident, coincidence, or oversight since 1790 in over two-hundred and thirty-three years? Justice Marshall was a civil rights icon, but the second is viewed by some as a spectacle of self-subjugation and corrupted principles of self-identity and heritage.

This second justice opposes the extended expectations that Juneteenth claimed to have provided as a level playing field. How to provide it and if it is required would depend on the effects of its imbalance and who it disadvantaged. Staggering starting positions and adjustments for racism are essential to fairness, thus redeeming allocations to mitigated proportions to achieve balance. Affirmative action is restoring the balance that, for many years, the Supreme Court struck down with separate but equal.

Affirmative action is a settlement of racial transgressions independent of others' circumstances but specific to the wrong done. To settle some other grievances should not eliminate our settlement especially since affirmative action is a recognition and admission of systemic discrimination toward us. If the damage continues, why would the remedy not also continue? To stop taking your medicine before cure or to maintain health attracts deterioration. Is the Supreme Court willing to continue undoing its damage, not to mention America's deterioration?

If opposed to affirmative action and so-called set-asides, would military service credit be essentially the same? By adhering to fundamental or originalist interpretations of the Constitution, the Justices effectively promoted racism then or reject remedies now. Their interpretation of that document was never very favorable to our people or the three-fifths of a human being it did recognize. Are there not remedies required? Affirmative action's time frame is a fraction of racism and discrimination and even lesser compared to slavery's.

Considering the benefits of affirmative action, it is miniscule compared to America's benefit from slavery. It is short sighted and revisionist. The Supreme Court interprets and dictates the law of the land and traditionally without the benefit of a diverse perspective. The slant is toward narrow determinations often averse to social justice and equality or demographic consideration. By concealing bias patterns, injustices are structurally cloaked as normalcy from law to educational content, economics, and history.

So we must dispel the centuries-old notions of judicial and Christian salvation that have permitted social and moral abnormalities from America's origins. Also, refrain from expectations of a sudden conscious awakening from racism or the voluntary grace of reparations. These pacifying expectations I am sure have merit but have proven to be the long way around, in fact, centuries. Time to focus on something more realistic, like what are the probabilities of waiting any longer or further pleading?

Not to harp on the past but to clarify the future, a future operating from a position of strength and vision more fully aware of the persistent underpinnings of this equity divide. We must do our part to secure what was not promised, equality. Excelling by another metric of assimilation, association, or identification that is not reliant upon consent or concession. The dynamics of today mandate a deviation from what has been relied upon in the past. Perhaps, we are going about it the wrong way, using methods and strategies that are not the most effective. We cannot step and fetch our way to equality begging for what our courage will deliver.

Dignity demands equality while begging erodes it. Our protest must stay off the ground and out the gutter, literally and figuratively, and remain focused on an efficient and effective strategy. As with any journey of peril, we will not all make it, but we must save who we can. The key to survival is evolution. Evolution is the ability to change and adapt to circumstances and stimuli. The advocacy of the sixties is the foundation and motivation of today's protest model but reevaluation and improvisation for this much different time are necessary. It starts with the concept of freedom.

Freedom is first a state of mind before it is a state of being. Freed from the physical plantation but controlled and maligned on the psychological plantation. Both are real places. One we lived on, and the other lives in us. Any mentality of hopelessness must be cultivated over time and repeatedly reinforced by punishment for resistance and rewards for producing compliance. The mind then normalizes the hopelessness to be internalized. It self-replicates even when the circumstances have changed. Over time, this consolidation of mind, body, and perspective results in actions that magnify despair instead of encouraging hope, ambition, or action.

To an extent, we have fallen prey to this trap of self-fulfilling prophecy or expectation of inequality. To expect it subjects you to it. Emancipation was a physical concession to relieve our physical pain, but never alleviated the mental anguish. The psychological plantation and slave master mentality continues today and, in many cases, by social default, if not purposeful intentions. The purposeful intention is the design of the system, not necessarily the cognitive principle knowingly being practiced.

The hidden implication of racist actions and mentality is they can be unrecognized and defensible by ignorance of that fact, honestly claiming not to be what they are as racist acts. Kill the head, and the body will fall, so to control a person's body, you must control their mind rendering their actions predictable and subject to manipulation or ignorance. When this identity distortion is created, it blurs the line of logical detachment from the habitual responses and vacuums constantly seeking validation or acceptance by that standard promoted as superior.

It expresses a basic human need to belong and believe, even when fitting in is counterproductive or unreasonable. Bowing to conceptual inferiority breeds mental contempt of spirit, denigrated behavior, and relegation of body producing acquiescence to a subservient existence. Freedom is a choice, but as an acquired taste, it is first realized in the mind projected outwardly, proclaiming it, not begging for it or apologizing for exercising it. Times have changed, and the obstacles are not insurmountable monuments, just challenging and inconvenient hurdles.

Now the major hurdles are internal and by us ascending psychologically displays the emotional resolve needed to lessen the impact of biased external influences. The gatekeeper's control is no longer the only means to enter the gate to accomplish a goal. Being tethered psychologically to a past reality is the next frontier to be dismantled to realize the freedom promised and sought. Both sides must not be convinced because, on both sides, there will be those who defy logic and change and are unable to adapt to an evolving reality.

Therefore, it is useless to expend time and focus where progress is improbable. Instead, leave the improbable for last to expire or comply under the weight of evolving times around them. Diehards die hard, but they do die eventually. Consequently, the perspective installed in its place must be amended regarding the concept and exercise of freedom. We must have the fearless audacity to live and exercise our freedom without concession or permitting incursions the same as those who have always been accustomed to it.

We must also realize ours may come with a price but you get what you pay for and we have paid dearly. Consequently, we must now define our freedom, realizing freedom and courage has never been free of consequences with both subjected to resistance. Still, they are free within our minds as concepts exploding into reality. However, if we are to be free from discrimination, we must have the courage to relentlessly declare our non-negotiable humanity. That is the nature of survival, in concept and reality, unyielding in principle and truth.

Therefore, never being free of risk or the mandate to not fold under pressure until veracity of its merit is either proven or negated. Remember, there is a partition of facts between us being proven wrong and them telling us why they are right. The divide is objective verification as opposed to subjective confirmation. It is a matter of conviction and persuasion, not doubt or justification. They have always held up a flimsy justification cloaked as facts or biblical history.

So, prove to us why we are wrong instead of telling us why you are right. An ideological reckoning is imminent sustained by truth not faith or patience. Patience and faith will no longer suffice. It is hazardous business to wait for something to be given that can be otherwise pursued and acquired by fearlessly handling our business. In essence, expecting someone to give up their advantage for our benefit is very risky at best and unlikely at worst. Where grace does not always prevail, diligently applied leverage might.

Grace has had a limited historical impact on improving our condition, so sustained inducement tactically directed might work by attrition. The wise use of intellectual, economic, and integrated resources produces the best probability to whittle racism sculpting our tangible social gains. What is a readily available resource constantly at our disposal to establish and maximize our objectives and achievement? Knowledge is the artillery and shield of prosperity easily accessed through technology, the new gatekeeper. Knowledge is Freedom.

The most significant material gift a parent can give a child is knowledge and education, aside from a flush trust fund. A strong back benefits a strong mind, but a weak mind must have a strong back. The mind is a tool of labor, not only the back. I stated that there is no opposition where there is no resistance and no resistance where there is no opposition. One must exist when the other exists, but you fight fire with water, not fire. When opposed, exploit their weaknesses, neutralize their strengths, and minimize their options. But resistance involves fortifying our weaknesses, expanding our strengths, and maximizing our opportunities.

Furthermore, harnessing and utilizing the force of the opposition's arrogance and mistakes to ensure our objectives prevail by hook or crook. But WE cannot continue to succumb to the same tactic. The best game possessed has an antidote to the best game presented. Know yourself and your opponent equally well. To state an uncomfortable truth, I submit that flesh, ego, and vanity are instruments used to distract our aspiration with superficial appeasements, much like this Juneteenth holiday. Snared by the tarnished expiration and glitter of fool's gold substituted for considerations of substance and generational prosperity.

It allows us to enrich others for their symbols of social validation and the conceitful confirmation of our value by imitating theirs. Pleasures of the flesh, ego exaggeration, and vanity are easy enticements that influence our mentality, actions, and finances far too often. Considering the holiday, would codified voting rights, categorical affirmative action, and poverty directed investments be more beneficial, impactful, and compelling to foster progress? The goal clearly stated must align with the actions clearly taken.

The walk has to match the talk, even in outrage, protest, or times of self-correction. Our motivations and pacifications must be corrected where token gestures will not suffice. When we correct ourselves, it lessens the need to be corrected. Correction, by definition, is an improvement. When veering off the path adjustments must be made, steering to remain on the road or crash. Therefore, corrections should be acceptable if we do not have any objections regarding our progression.

If not, then progress is not our destination. The substantiation and justification for nonsense restricts our movement keeping us in the same box since 1865, seeking wholeness as a people. Pointing to others does not lessen our responsibility or accountability to ourselves. Similarly, pointing to ours does not lessen theirs. If racism damages our progress, let it be without our collaboration but let progress by our actions be our ringing affirmation. We cannot occupy ourselves with distractive matters and ignore priorities during times of progress or crisis. Thinking creatively is not breaking the rules. It is not being restricted by them.

On the contrary, it resists mental restraint and is the foundation for all discovery and greater knowledge. Instead, independent thinking will expand willing minds cultivated by us to operate at levels above us. A curious mind and analytical reasoning are encouraged and stimulated when each one teaches one, passing the game down to be improved upon by our offspring. Essentially a student must have a teacher as stages of development progress to expand the student's knowledge and awareness. However, the teacher appears when the student is ready, meaning knowledge is always present if only we recognize it and its dissemination is accepted.

The student exceeding the teacher is the pride of the teacher. Each subsequent generation excels on the foundation of the previous one handing off the baton for the next leg of the challenge. In a relay each leg performs its optimal function to present the best opportunity for the team at the finish line. As the social, political, and economic paradigm shifts and the portal of opportunities eclipses the regulations of exclusion, the prospects have never been better. However, we have not yet ran our best relay or performed to our potential.

Think of it as the modern-day gold rush, where riches are excavated and wealth generated. But, the gold we dig for is knowledge and information leading to prosperity. Emerging technologies and transitioning economics reflecting tomorrow's reality should be our focus now. Catching up is not the goal. By the time we arrive where others have been, they are gone leaving their unwanted scraps of opportunities. The key is leaping into the future avenues of tomorrow's possibilities and projections of prosperity.

Now is such a time combined with the expanded capabilities to explore intellectual resources and learn independently. The initiative and emphasis must be on us to be counted in our progress and exponential growth. Unity of our economic and political resources curves time and multiply our power to be major brokers in any equation of influence. Accordingly, our focus must be acquiring knowledge and information not frivolous mindless consumptions of voyeuristic curiosities labeled as entertainment.

Culturally speaking, others enjoy many advantages simply because they have the unity, knowledge, and exposure. They are not always advanced by the privileges of active racism but by their preparation. Race may play a part, but it may be more of their preparation. Other dynamics other than race can be the difference. What are we missing or lacking? Creative curiosity? Commitment, what is it? Often it is a question of having the qualifications to compete. If we are denied based on our qualifications, we must enhance our qualifications by stepping our game up.

Therefore, we need racism to be why we are denied and not our capabilities. When our capabilities are sufficient, we remove that excuse from the scenario narrowing the confirmation to possible racism. The one equality we absolutely have is equality of time. Everyone have twenty-four hours in each day. The separation of equity begins with what is done with those hours. Our minds are free to roam the possibilities only limited by our imagination further defined by the wise utilization of our time. We cannot afford to squander our time.

Knowing that, we must recognize the possibilities as an attainable reality by being adequately prepared. We must conceive of achieving our vision by drawing from our freely exercised aspirations, ambition, and time spent determined to conquer the goal. Considering the number of affluent Black people and available mentorship, excursions into other professions and markets are more possible than ever before. The lack of specified education and opportunity has hindered our entrance into specific fields, but this is not the obstacle it has been in the past.

The past is filled with atrocities but doesn't tell the whole truth and definitely doesn't dictate the future. There has always been successful Black businesses going back to Freemans. The market for support or incidental services and organizations is a gold mine untapped from a unified Black business perspective, especially within our community. So, creating a business can be an alternative to finding a job. We can create ourselves a job more easily than at any other time. There are many skills and transferable experiences when cultivated can be monetized.

Our concentration should extend beyond CRT to GRT and the knowledge to transcend our history in America. Like the celebration of Juneteenth, there are doubtful benefits of forced CRT education for history's sake. Still, CRT has some benefits in eliminating ignorance or misconceptions from the past and many times it is ours. We should be knowledgeable of our true history and the instruments of discrimination used against us. With that said, we have always been much more than what slavery has portrayed.

The portrayal of slavery has caused lingering damage to our self-worth because of the degradation we have survived and the opportunities denied. We have also colluded to sometimes accept and perpetuate these stereotypes. The positive aspect of our existence and achievements have been either erased, appropriated, or minimized. Likewise, the study of ancient sociology could replace CRT to acquire the knowledge revealed by manipulations in history and the evolution of beliefs and behaviors. Racism and GRT are the results of global sociology and its many extensions.

Sociological norms set the terms of inclusion and exclusion based on religion, social agendas, ignorance, greed, and wealth accumulation. The more significant ramifications of Juneteenth and GRT are they reveal an assault on the truth transparent throughout history. Skin tone was the identifiable justification, sociology was the vehicle for normalization, and denial is now an attack on the facts. The global trade routes and transatlantic slave trade adds context and clarity to our plight in America as a smaller part of a larger scheme.

Thus, they had to cover themselves with all manner of justifications. The separating and identifying factors for racism were the darkness of our skin, making it easy for anyone, even foreigners, as immigrants to seamlessly assimilate over time if they had a light complexion. Therefore, our dark skin did not allow us to do that, so the distinction was based on the only thing it could be, the eyeball test. The eyeball test still dictates people's psyche of racial fear and biases, giving more favor to the lighter complexion of all races, probably rooted in revisionist religion and slavery ideologies.

Immigrants whose appearance is visually associated with whiteness only need to lose the accent and pick up the mannerisms and attitudes to assimilate after having passed the visual test. We will never pass that test based on skin tone alone that elicits negative denotations, even sometimes among ourselves with colorism. So, the dogma surrounding Juneteenth's freedom certification must off something that transcends metaphoric notions with tangible skin tone blind actions. What is seen when looking at us must be redefined first by us as we see ourselves, which will erode any socialization of negative connotations or stereotypes.

Then we will always be free by our own standards and declaration. Freedom and fairness are utopian aspirations regulated on a spectrum of subjectivity within the perspective of a sub-group. Whether it is nation, race, gender, wealth, education, sexuality, religion, or every variety of preference and measurement within life except simply humanity. Freedom and fairness have persistently eluded humanity, although the human species is separated by the thinnest of veils, which is the depth of the skin tone.

Freedom is a concept, while liberty is a right requiring an action. The Industrial Revolution diminished the forced labor of slavery, the freedom. The socialization went unaltered, the liberty. The quest for social dominance was never relinquished, the action. The constructs of today have their adaptation prescribed by the industrialist from the late 1800s and early 1900s. They are based on an economic business model, specifically money, power, and greed. Race was the most lucrative exploitation for wealth and power accumulation. The ideology never changed as time advanced so the replica for exploitation, socialization, and domination lingered.

The wealthy formed a system to facilitate their control and prosperity, thus wielding social power through economic wealth. Since then, the only Freedom to exist within the system has been monetary. What do they know that we refuse to recognize? Could it be the true power of the dollar bill beyond purchasing power but its influence? The process of maintaining the system is currency transformed into power. That is the motivation of voter suppression now, to sequester the system's capacity by greed to generate money dictating policy.

Or it could be amassing power to generate money. But the winds of change have blown, arousing the ire and frustration of the public awakened from slumber by time but still on the brink of ignorance. The pendulum, having swung, gives way to knowledge and technology, now dispersing wealth and power to the sleeping giant, the public, awakening it to the vampire's drain. Meanwhile, we still wallow in the social distractions of the underclass, determined not by race but by economics as a new dawn of transformative opportunities approaches.

This social distraction will prevent our participation in the emerging economic transformation remaining as members of the underclass. The underclass is preoccupied with race while government movement towards a ruling class meritocracy based on money goes unnoticed. The cycle and model repeats itself since the earliest days of civilization leading to an autocracy of the underclass. What is understood need not be spoken, so past grievances are inconsequential to prosperity in the future. Likewise, a holiday to celebrate a day delivering a concept largely disregarded and yet to meet our expectations is tiny to a giant.

Meanwhile, we are once again expected to capitulate our interest to supplement everyone else's. If there be a penalty, so be it, but we must unapologetically claim by any means necessary that society will not be balanced on our backs this time. We have been controlled by our division, needs, and vulnerabilities attempting to avoid penalty at all costs. The conviction to directly confront the penalties must be traveled as evidenced by history as the path to shed its sequence while always avoiding the bully eventually becomes too consuming. Our current cycle is at the point of breaking its sequence if we don't reenlist for another round of subjugation.

Our progress requires changing our focus, behavior, and expectations accepting accountability for our navigation while anticipating the requirements and possibilities of prosperity along with adversity. Courage devours adversity on its path to victory. So, we must courageously set our sails with the winds of change. To make our next move our best move, we must empower our future by preparing for and participating in the transition. As the social echelon shifts, it is our opportunity to taste the nectar of social relevancy and undeniable dignity.

We control that by exercising our freedom and expectations of parity by having them respected. If your freedom and rights are respected, so must ours be equally respected. Insults to our dignity cannot be tolerated and humiliation to succumb to circumvention of our autonomy will not be accommodated. Our voices cannot be bullied, penalized, or shuttered because of yes sir bossing its expression. We cannot continue to have our voices compromised for the sake of outraging those who despise our courage to speak as freely as they do. How can we expect them to respect our humanity without our conviction?

Next, impartial inclusion in economic dynamics or take our ball (money) and go home as economic leverage to not play that game. Then, not be pacified and patronized by a holiday devoid of substance or any other gesture lacking a practical impact worthy of our contribution. Also, dismiss the notion that reparations are realistically forthcoming, or we can wait on the voluntary honoring of the equivalent of forty acres and a mule. We are still waiting after one-hundred and fifty-seven years without compensation. Trillions upon trillions have been spent on wars and given in foreign aid, so the debts or assistance the government wanted to pay they have paid but still not to us. We must shift our demand for a compensation package to agreeable terms that can be recovered.

Therefore, considering a different source and manner of reparations, but our actions should not be contingent upon it. Likewise, reparations are not more attainable than the exchange of fairness,

liberties, and freedom from exclusion. Namely, the equal consideration and application of our liberties, rights, and opportunities. Lastly, it is outrageous to believe words, documents, or declarations devoid of verifying efforts and actions have any significance beyond
symbolism. Action moves the needle, not words, so our actions dictate our progression and their action their intentions.

Consequently, we must switch gears from the emotional grasp of
needing racial validation to the principle of self-confirmation, projecting the images we want to be and others to see. Of all our concerns, a holiday is not the answer because "Freedom" is no longer
disputed if secured in our minds. Still, transacting dignity, equity,
and opportunities are the next frontiers to breach. With the physical
restraints no longer present for oppression, our fight for Freedom is
over our minds and perspectives. Society's next task is unconditional consideration and application not obstructed by systemic biases re-calibrating away from historic social deceptions.

It is impractical that we would still be fighting for, in principle,
what has been so-called given many times before, freedom and
equality. Equality was never promised, and Freedom is the gift that
has been regifted since 1863, while reciprocity that addresses unfairness has proven to be a different pursuit. Dr. King spoke of the
promised land. It is not a destination but a journey of self-determination by declaration, not permission. Being led to the promised
land is a utopia of the mind. In the fertile promised land of our
mind, at least we are free to declare ourselves free by our actions on
days other than holidays designating such.

Grant ourself the Freedom to celebrate ourselves, declaring ourselves the holiday to be celebrated. Picture the sun as the nucleus of
society with the planets rotating around it in a fixed orbit. This is
the ecliptic and universal majesty of the number nine. The planets
or concepts and ideologies orbit on a linear plane rotating within a
defined range. Around each planet and sub-delineation such as stars
is a composition unique to that planet creating different conditions

such as heat, ice, or light with variations in between. This is the circumstellar disc. But, the planets do not emit light they reflect it.

So the system is a sphere or cycle depending on the axis of a regulatory radius controlling its orbit according to the nucleus. The rotations and orbits do not veer to far from the confined regulation of its origination or nucleus. They are a reflection of a larger system controlled by forces unseen but orchestrating the symphony of chaos. This is the operation of the solar system but in the context of society it explains the limitations, orbits, and radius of chaotic ideologies very well. It is the cocoon around its ideology.

To maintain its ideology the atmosphere must remain relatively static adhering to the earliest stages of its development. This is good for planets but not civilizations. Many social foundations are symbolic of the solar system with abundant hidden revelations repurposed. That is possibly why there is evolution to keep the river of life flowing avoiding stagnant waters from becoming contaminated. Society is at risk of contamination from stagnation. Antique and vintage should not apply to an advancing ideology of evolution depending on what has evolved instead of what is evolving.

Incarcerated by hypotheses of past misconceptions impedes the mind's natural inclination for discovery and development. Can this be a global coincidence or the global purpose with each country or distinction of separation only concerned with their ideology not allowing for other orbits to exist. The cosmos exist in synchronicity with competing orbits far vaster than our socialization. The yoke of the past harnesses our minds to be herded by mentalities conforming to the slumber of ignorance. Humanity obsession with inhumanity might be psychological conditioning from hunter gathers days but time has evolved to a new paradigm not governed by the rearview mirror of hoarded knowledge.

Knowledge and exposure of wayward beliefs and perspectives discredits the axis and nucleus of our sphere of socialization. We cannot replace the sun but we must replace the faulty machinations thousands of years old. That reality is not this one. Slavery, free-dom, racism, equality, and celebration as abstract concepts applied to our sphere of reality operates as reflections of their nucleus. The radius of their practice and deviations are ecliptic with each on a circumstellar disc according to the central concept of their origina-tion. Their orbit is defined by the plane of its ideology.

They rotate around a foundational concept whose perspectives are aligned within a range of interpretations and latitude. So these con-cepts rotate around a central supposition or nucleus while their per-spectives rotate around them. The observable characteristics and extensions remain restricted by their origination or ideology. It is a cycle dependent on a larger cycle. As such, needing a big bang the-ory of socialization comprehensively discarding the old configura-tion producing a new social system whose orbit is not prescribed by the limitations of primitive concessions, observances, fallacies, or obedience.

The current social dynamic cannot stretch beyond its ideology without that ideology being overhauled or replaced. The systems lag behind the people pursuing expansion beyond the orbit of its structured biases. So, the population of the globe must have a col-lective perspective scrutinizing the systems that limit their radius. There is no shortage of funds or commitment for control and war but humanitarian abuses and neglect could benefit greatly from the same dispensation of resources.

The machine feeds the machine around the globe. Racism is just a raw material fed to the machine. Strong armed regimes use a differ-ent raw material to feed their machine. Consequently, they all feed some form of marginalization, exploitation, and desperation to the machine while disbursing glimmers of hope, faith, or endurance but definitely compliance. So can a mind or government imprisoned by their ideological captivity grant emancipation to anyone beyond the limits of their own confinement or ideology?

Any celebration is within the limited scope or relevance of those rejoicing within an ecliptic. The nucleus dictates the orbit of this ecliptic's rotation and celebration. However, liberation beyond the gravity or internment of history, indoctrinations, and beliefs cannot occur acquiescing and capitulating to quarantines of thoughts or autonomy. The reality of mass dissatisfaction suppressed by mass psychological captivity vents by emitting hostility towards anything receptive or socially relegated as a soft target.

It is far easier to persecute than to confront your persecutor, to blame than self-evaluate. So, a real commemoration is declaring the courage to reject the mind numbing conditionings that lead to subjugation or submission of anyone's humanity forfeited to the system's appetite. That would be a substantiative reason to celebrate, a universe that also include rotations around us. Rotating around it creates a pseudo-freedom devoid of the orbit of emancipation.

Thoughts in the privacy of our mind afford unlimited Freedom.

Freedom is a state of mind.

Freedom is a byproduct of Knowledge.

Knowledge produces equality.

Equality is a reflection of belief.

Belief is a conviction of the mind.

Let me ask you a Question

1. If hesitation waits on encouragement, who or what are we waiting on to encourage us, if not history or a brighter future? What will it take for emancipation from indoctrinations of psychological captivity, fallacies of history, and distortions of religion? When confined by mind controlling boundaries is mental rejection possible while adhering to its confining principles?

2. Does defining freedom limit freedom dictating and dominating the exercise of it? If under the liberation of freedom why do we need approval or agreement to exercise it? Is our expression a cause for apology for having the audacity to express it? Equity, equality, impartiality, and parity are defined as the same but why not for us? Why not the same freedom, opportunities, or expression expected or extended?

3. Is our mind our commodity or our body our currency? Is our constant conciliatory inclinations to get along a hindrance to the mobility of our freedom? Is the greatest threat to our freedom our reluctance to stand on it and not other's racism? How can we abandon our own to placate perceived violations of their freedom or injustices by silencing ours? Isn't that also against us and our freedom, to silence our narrative to promote theirs?

4. Is it too much to expect standards to be consistently applied? Do we know by now that because it is said doesn't make it true? Because it is taught doesn't make it fact? If our narration is an algorithm of experiences and indoctrinations what does that reveal about the probabilities of its benefits? Can we allow others to denigrate our freedom without defending it but remain respectful of theirs?

5. For what Black History month didn't do, what does a single day of Juneteenth accomplish? Are party favorites at the back door of society as second class citizen for so long pacified our expectations, behaviors, and tolerances? Despite the price of great hardships,

oversights, losses, and indignations what pieces of the puzzle are missing to propel us to self-realization? Do we realize it is not further suffering, capitulation, or forfeiture of our humanity?

Disturbing Display
Inner City Blues

Black folks, it is time to face reality and have the courage to speak the truth. We have indeed faced hundreds of years of racism and oppression in America, and any atrocity that the mind can imagine has been committed against us. That is a given, and the damage of those actions and consequences are still evident today, but we have proven to be resilient. There can be no denying that there are many reasons for the Black condition, but there can no longer be any excuses. We have a right to tell the truth about others, but we also have an obligation, to tell the truth to ourselves about ourselves to improve our condition.

We may not want to hear it, but truthfully, we should listen to it from ourselves. Believe in what you see more than what you are told. You can be shown better than you can be told. Actions always speak louder than words, so what is understood need not be said but observed. If we do not like the truth, we should make it a lie by changing the reality, not the conversation. Then, they can't dispute the obvious, and we won't have to defend it. Our current liability is not imposed on us, we impose it on ourselves. Who is going to pay for that if not us. There has been no redress for the slavery debt. Nor is it likely to be paid to our satisfaction or the extent of the damages done.

Yet, it is no secret in our inner circles what we agonize over the most in our communities, and it is not the police, racism, reparations, or the white race. We may be marginalized directly or indirectly by many, but we don't agonize, cringe in disbelief, or are afraid for our safety regularly because of that. We barely see the police or interact with them in some of our neighborhoods. Our crimes are mostly us against us. If there are whites in our community, they are a scarce minority, if at all. Besides, those who are menacing or violent towards us are even less.

Racism has always tipped the scales, so it is nothing new and nothing we can't or haven't overcome. We are not fooling those outside our circle because it is plain to see and increasingly harder to conceal. We cannot use racism to conceal our actions any more than they can use our actions to conceal racism. Some of our actions are as desperately urgent to eliminate as racism. That is why detractors can keep reminding us and deflecting from their actions that hurt us because sometimes we damage ourselves more.

So we give them something to talk about and discredit us. Could we be wrong more so than they are by our actions in our communities? Just as two wrongs don't make a right, it doesn't make us even either. In this case, it makes us odd. Odd to harm ourselves in a struggle against mistreatment by others. Odd to ignore our detrimental behavior and dysfunctional perspectives. Odd even by contributing to racially stereotypical projections in competing proportions. We slander our image and portrayal by proudly and willingly exhibiting behavior that can only be viewed as damaging.

Oddly enough, how can we be, and why are we equally as wrong as the forces we complain and protest about, asking them for our equality and safety from them? What about our equality and safety among us? What do we demand of ourselves in our predominately Black neighborhoods where we practice a different form of cultural racism and genocide? Why is it easier to point the finger at others as the source of our problems in OUR communities where they have a minor physical presence?

We cannot pretend to have submitted our consciousness and condition to their influence when they are not present. It doesn't make sense unless we admit to the frailty of our minds to be so thoroughly conditioned to perform atrocities against ourselves without their presence. We have to keep it one thousand family. Sometimes, we do it to ourselves. Do they invade our neighborhoods and litter? Do they conduct themselves in a disrespectful manner inconsiderate of our children? Do they force us to not be unified in the improvement of our communities?

Do they pedal poison in substance and thought to our people? If so, why do we allow ourselves to be the instrument by which they do? Do we allow them to saturate and infect our families and communities with dysfunction and detrimental profiteering? Do we create our hardships as much as they do? How many of our actions play directly into a narrative which are used to justify their reaction? Whenever the police kill an unarmed Black person, it is always a crime and tragedy. But how many more would be at the dinner table if we were not killing our own at an alarming rate in these streets? What of this can we blame on racism or white folks? I am sure we know who's to blame, and it is us.

How many innocent children would continue to play? What about reckless gunplay killing innocent children without sustained outrage instead of our capitulation? We have even resorted to murdering our women and our women committing murders at unprecedented rates. It has become dangerous to attend any function for fear of gunplay erupting. Friday to Monday morning is the most dangerous time to be a Black person in our urban communities because of the homicide rate among us. How can we blame this on racism, slavery, or the police? This is on us.

Black folks we have a problem that we need to address. It is our funeral homes bustling with business and families devastated by senseless death. How many tears have been cried, and how many more will be? How many families have had generations damaged by violence and the drug game? This sh-t isn't normal or gangster! Why is it so unsafe in our communities from those who prey on those who look like them, us? Never leaving the neighborhood to commit a crime but would claim Black lives matter to them. So much of this is in our control or our lack of it.

Who do we blame? Who else can we blame but us? The Black man is emasculated for lack of the two primary things he must provide. That is protection and courage, to defend the family orbit and stand on principle as an example of both. Why are our Black women disrespected by us and treated in ways anything but respectfully? You choose how to treat people you deal with, not their behavior. If their behavior don't allow you to treat or be treated properly, leave them like you found them.

Still, the Black woman is the straw that stirs the drink mixing the ingredients to bring forth birth and stabilize the family structure. They make the family cohesive despite many challenges and under-appreciated recognition for that attribute. We make it happen and they figure it out. Okay, I hear you, playboy, and that may be true, but what about checking the man in the mirror first or having regard for your mother, sister, or daughter? What about not violating your integrity despite provocation or emotions? Big boys do big boy things, including unconditional protection of and provision for our women and children.

That said, our Black women also must maintain the dignity befit-ting universal respect. Is it proper for our women to project images appropriating others' cultural beauty standards to their impression-able daughters? It diminishes the empowerment and dignity of their child's self-image or self-love by obsessively demonstrating other-wise. It also influences your son that is the standard of beauty and not you. What about restricting the freedom of your actions to pro-vide an example of avoiding any devaluing of your dignity? Role models influence the replication of what they represent.

Frantically pursuing images that discredit your respect encourages others to do the same. Black women deserve an oasis for your uniqueness and value but must avoid distorting or erasing admira-tion for your intrinsic worth. Instead, Black folks, we must ask our-selves, do our self-esteem and character reflect our integrity and principles by our conduct? Is our image more critical than fronting for others, imitating others, or tolerating nonsense? Is our example the example we want to reproduce?

Whatever interactions we voluntarily participate in should not require us to get out of our hookup, head jump time, or wear a jacket that doesn't fit our character or preference. Are we that fragile in our thirst for validation? How do our conduct, perspectives, discipline, and ambition positively impact our children? What about for other races to be more respectful of our humanity by our presentation? We have proven ourselves to be a resilient people but not as collectively progressive as we should have been.

We cannot normalize or excuse the behavior that holds us stagnant as others surpass our condition while holding us in contempt. We have worked hard, but now we must work smarter to produce a reality that aligns with our expectations and demands. Instead of focusing on the negative not within our control, we must focus on the negative within our control. We cannot overlook our behavior and reasonably blame others. Our bed will be hard if we contribute to making it that way. Decisions can have unwanted consequences, so our choices have lingering effects.

We are often hindered by emotional displays as an outlet with outburst of feelings erasing our meaningful gains. The domino effect of our individual actions extend beyond ourselves whether positive or negative. Positive brings pride while negative brings shame. It is time to truthfully reassess the normality of our dysfunction. We can't only see what others have done. It is cognitive dissonance of our reality. It is group deception to accept and overlook the self-imposed hazards haunting our communities.

So, it is time to be candid and transform if change is to happen. The grind will take extra effort, but the rewards will be abundant. By using the principle of addition by subtraction we move closer to our goals. The innovative substitution of traditional education and rejecting self-defeating socializations rids us of many of our problems. That along will greatly improve the quality of our life and communities. We will have less need for relief if we handle our business. We can have what we deserve by providing it to ourselves.

It reminds me of the Godfather of Soul commentary on social equality in the sixties. We don't want nobody to give us nothing, we will get it ourselves if the door of opportunity is opened. Enough doors are now open, and we can open more doors for our prosperity and progress, but we must position ourselves advantageously. A change in our mentality and specific education outside the structured socially engineered diagram must occur. We must shepherd our resources wisely and stack our educational, economic, and cultural advancements and achievements.

Nevertheless, we make that more difficult by a self-sabotaging mindset and dysfunctional behavior. Many of us know the rules of the streets and how to survive, if not thrive, but it is time to switch the game up from the nonsense. All money isn't good money and we shouldn't sh-t where we eat. Some of us tell ourselves this is our only available way. There are better and more beneficial ways, but it will require something more of us. We can't convince ourselves that it is economic-related because there are many ways of making coin that doesn't hurt the community in which we live.

It is not always the economics but the mentality and lack of applied ingenuity toward obstacles that prevent our economic stability. True hustlers for real are not limited by whatever they hustle. Instead, they possess the ability to produce. It is not what you are hustling but how thorough you hustle. So switch the hustle to prosperity that builds instead of destroys. Otherwise by your actions how can you be distinguished from the enemy? We must carefully consider the methods by which we move or we are the enemy.

Life will present challenges, but we should avoid the damage we do to ourselves, our image, and our communities. Unfortunately, some aspects of Black culture have taken on a detrimental mentality that significantly contributes to our dysfunction. We should not adopt negative labels or harmful behaviors and embrace them as a positive cultural appropriation endeared as somehow characteristic of our conduct. It encourages and conditions others to associate the tainted conduct as an invited reflection and acceptable prejudice.

Must we assimilate to these negative images and expectations perpetuating disrespect and distorting our culture and humanity? Has the delusion become the reality or reality the nightmare? Can we continue to deflect our self-depravation onto anything other than ourselves? What we immerse ourselves in becomes our reality and desensitizes us from the cause and effect of its impact. Unfortunately, the nature of some of our television and music choices from the earliest ages conditions us with destructive subliminal suggestions and indoctrinations.

That forms our perspectives and behaviors dictating what we accept, conform to, and aspire to become. For example, look at the historical depiction of our people on television which continues today. Every negative aspect of grimy behavior and clown activity is used to culturally slander our image. It usually insinuate that we are scandalous by nature, prone to buffoonery, or inherently vicious and treacherous. Is that what we call entertainment? There is some positive images but far too many negative. Still, does that influence our behavior or do our behavior influence the depiction?

We need not imagine the obvious psychological impression to migrate other's expectations to accept such defamation as an accurate representation of our character. They are essentially convinced if there is little presentation to suggest otherwise. It is fortified when actual encounters trigger impressions confirmed by our indications and mannerism to forecast that conclusion. The double edge cut is our behavior and allowing harmful depictions which verify their assumption. So, instead of changing their mind, we contribute to making up their mind perpetuating the negative association.

The metamorphosis of racism's power lays in its subtleties to be practiced and presented in a concealed manner. The mutation of our perspective is focused on it not being what it was instead of what it has become. Furthermore, we have succumb to the masquerade cloaked by our participation as appeasement for allowing our representation although it is sullied or subservient. Sullied by the stereotypical slander or subservient by willingly submitting absorbing the sludge of our characterization. But, what about our preference or dislike concerning our image?

Why don't we protect our image as others do theirs? Anyone can sponge us in line or take our lunch money with a conciliatory gesture for us to either suck it up or maybe next time. What does the summation of our images project that is honorable? We can't blame their menu. We must blame our appetite. We enthusiastically condemn certain entertainers as corrupting our children but powder the bottoms of those glorifying murder, mayhem, and materialism. Which is actually more detrimental to our communities? Is our clear conscious and exemplary pursuits to be forsaken for a dirty diaper of capitulation to and coddling of dysfunction or destruction?

Someone's alternative lifestyle has not racked up nearly as many bodies as the degenerative mumblings of trap. We honor and are amused by "trap" and the categorization of our women as scandalous thots. Consider the sexualization and thot image of Black women championed by society where there is little or no discernment for the diversity of their presentation. The monolithic expectation is of Black women are impulsively twerking, fighting, bickering, and materialistic as a majority.

Why are Black women obliged to twerk when twerking is not a part of the scenario or context at hand? The mirror supplies the short answer but the socialization or culture provides the question. How many depictions of Black women result in twerking or some defamation of their character? We must respect ourselves to the level that we expect others to respect us. Why is the highest level of credibility or esteem that a Black man can achieve is being thugged out, street, or a real one? This mentality has been detonated in the Black community to wreck generations of destruction concealed as culture.

Analogies to war torn areas of the globe are embraced but ask yourself a few questions to see if they are comparable. Is theirs by choice? Is theirs committed against those who they claim to be allies with in a common fight say against racism? What is our division, our objective to commit genocide? Why are we frightened by us and them and why should it be both or either? We have some social issues which need deprogramming to remove the haze of deception from our self-inflicted dehumanization and destruction.

The military tactics of MK-Ultra or psychological warfare presents a textbook application to the our community and its effective weaponization against ourselves. A principle of firefighting is to contain a blaze for it to extinguish itself until there is nothing left to burn. The inferno of genocide in our communities rages out of control. However, have you noticed that it is contained to our communities to rage until it extinguish itself by its destructive combustive behavior. The music is a primary accelerant for the social arson of our hopes to shed the exposés of inferiority.

This genocide is so comprehensive that it even violates the communal affinity in the animal kingdom. The deployment of our music endorses every manner of vicarious and salacious violence displayed by natural predators and adversaries as a manner of evolutionary survival or predisposition of their species. What is ours as a behavioral assessment? We have none except for the one that is implanted. Implanted by who and for what reason can be senselessly argued but the effect cannot be ignored.

The pride of the Black man cannot be the destruction of another Black man especially over the repetitive nonsense that we are grieving. The shame of the Black man is to not stand erect and tussle with incursions foreign or domestic upon our dignity, families, and communities. It should not matter who it is even if it is us. It has to be rules and protocol as a code of conduct. Imagine if any race was being killed, maimed, or family units destroyed at the rate we are by our own but by another race.

Wasn't that a primary element of what slavery was using as enforcement? Do we now practice a similar atrocity against ourselves for whatever purpose? This is not for the condemnation of the individual but as with the entirety of these articles to illustrate the systems, their operation, and impact. We can see how it impacts us but now imagine the impact on our children as their inhibitions are stretched and distorted beyond our dismay. The curse of Noah does not now follow us but the curse of ignorance does. It will also follow our children too as demonstrated by our actions.

The genesis of the system is its renewal to be more deeply rooted every generation it recycles itself. Are we really stealing cookies from the cookie jar if someone else is replenishing the supply for us to take? Aren't they actually regulating the cookies in the jar? When they stop the supply of cookies, what is left to take. They can stop us from damaging them, but do they condemn us to damage us? Can we regulate our cookies, our damage? Can we stop ourselves from ravaging our children's future? We must determine and regulate our consumption and presentation to guard our imagery as gold.

Imagine a sporting event televised around the world and the image of Black people as gang banging was televised. What would viewers think about our people and gang culture? What if this was propped up as our hero? Well, sadly we don't have to imagine it. It happened as half-time entertainment to be the best half-time show ever. But was it the best portrayal of us? Did he walk it like we talk it or display what he values more than social justice, gang affiliation? What credibility or sincerity can he have to reject gang activity when he promoted it on international T.V.?

These innocent moments are where our image is questionably magnified while the white guy paid homage to social justice at the same halftime show. Pardon me as we digress. We must be diligent about what we expose our children to, primarily if it promotes negative images concealed as entertainment. It is not entertainment. It is mind controlled manipulation by conditioning. We must then ask ourselves, what do we benefit from mimicking these actions and behaviors? How does our communities benefit from celebrity affirmations of gang affiliations which have decimated our neighborhoods?

Can we expect to be anything other than dysfunctional when the stimulus we bombard ourselves with is tainted by violence and indifference as our regular primary programming? Instead, we have tricked ourselves into devouring it and blaming others for our appetite and their perception. Just weigh the benefit against the detriment and compare it to what is observed in our communities. Black man, we must reacquaint ourselves with what it means to be a protector, provider, and example or role model for our families and communities by providing veteran leadership and knowledge-creating stability.

Kinfolk, it is time to lead the charge unflinchingly as a pillar of courage. Let's end any misconception of our character by changing our negative projections so that our children don't pay a higher price later for emulating them. Look at the composition of the juvenile centers population to see who comprises the pipeline. Our ego or being a tough guy or a "real one" cannot displace our obligation to our family or contribution to our community. The bravado is an allegiance to a broken spirit of weakness disguised as swagger while riding for despair and destruction, but not respect or progress. This is what is labeled as toxic masculinity because it is a hollow measure of substance.

It takes effort to build and larceny to destroy, but whose future are we robbing if not ourselves and our community? It might not be your shoes, but too many of us fit them well. I have asked many questions, but maybe they were not questions but solutions or concepts that may lead to solutions. I cannot be ashamed to say that the generation of the eighties and nineties became distracted after significant gains made in the sixties and seventies against stern social opposition. I say that to say the fruit today was from seeds planted then, just as tomorrow's fruit will be the seeds planted today. What are we planting today that will grow tomorrow.

We must regain our compass and set a course of self-determination and self-realization that requires no one's consent, just our grind. We can't wait on reparations or equality. We must create them. You cannot be made to feel a way you refuse to feel. To seek personal equality indicates you personally feel inferior. Collective systematic equality in the form of institutional fairness will take far too long waiting for decency to be granted. We grant ourselves equality by the strength of our perspective, actions, and integrity. We cannot overcome injustice or operate from a position of weakness where power is required, not granted.

It is never good to ask or beg from a position of frailty and it is always from a position below. With that said, let us pay ourselves reparations first through our conduct and progression, creating an atmosphere where nothing less than our respect and equality will be expected from others or accepted by us. We need to respect our lives, stop killing each other, and stop hindering each other. That is some soft shoe sucker activity to throw a rock and hide your shaky hand while dispensing destruction as an act of social cannibalism. But cannibalism of the worst kind, only devouring your own.

If it is that important to blast, put your pride on the line and throw down or better yet, let it ride if it causes more problems than it solves. The cycle is broken by being avoided. Don't let these angry or foolish moments destroy you, your future, or another's. More of our people need to make it home, not just from the hands of the po-

lice but each other. Time to break the chains and systems that enslave our minds to move beyond internal conflict. To move beyond
stagnation and protest to action and advancement. Then we won't
have to whisper but can say it loud and clear that indeed we are
Black and Proud.

Progression requires a transition of perception that becomes an obsession manifesting a realization. We must find ways to get it done
instead of yielding to why we cannot. Reasons are why you do
something, and excuses are why you do not. It is all learned behavior needing to be unlearned. No excuses allowed is the battle cry.
Our call to arms is loyalty to the determination not to harm our advancement and to excel beyond obstacles and conflict. Determined
to reframe from genocide in any of its forms whether its flesh, image, or ideology as a matter of honor.

The movie depiction of the honor and commitment of a real-life
navy diver displays the fortitude that may be needed when you really want it and won't be denied even despite outrageous discrimination. Let the healing begin within us while the solution resides outside the pitfalls of social engineering but well within our control
and determination.

We have made it this far, dragging psychological and sociological
chains that must be carried no further, especially by us. Much love
to my brother Charles Edward Thomas (Jheri Curl) from East St.
Louis who stood on principle and pride. He always spoke of Black
pride being resilient and resourceful. My hope is we don't live it
any differently but with dignity and abundance, by avoiding these
disturbing displays of self-mutilation.

Booker T Washington coined the phrase "crabs in a barrel" to reference the mentality of people to not want to see others advance
above them. This is especially true among people of the same race,
condition, or class. It intensified with the hostility generally felt between "master's" house personnel and the field personnel. It is

probably still the lingering animosity behind colorism. To hold another back assures that misery will always have company. Sprinkle in a degree of desperation and you have a volatile cocktail of a selfish jealous vindictive regulator of others' success.

It plays out as the drama of life. Real life drama disguised as art is presented in the Squid Games as entertainment. How about the frenzy of Black Friday sales? How far are you willing to go or be made to go? Desperation is a hell of a motivator. It suspends morality, logic, consequences, and emotions. We all know the Squid Games is a game orchestrated to exploit hopelessness by giving them a way out. The probability is low but the risk is high. It is a study in sociology, ethology (animal behavior), and induced aggression. The crab in a barrel mentality is fine tuned to not only prevent other's progress but to desperately pursue yours by any means deplorable.

However, in life why would someone else's success prevent yours or not create a chain whereby many more can escape the barrel of despair? In life there can be more than one winner, so a cooperative effort seem logical. Analyze the Squid Game we play and the motivation for it to continue. There is none except for programming aligned with circumstances that no longer exist outside of our creation. The ploy invokes a structure and context to elicit a piranha or predator reaction to devour anything in our pursuit without reservation or restriction.

Our condition is no less of a sociological game than this show for the twisted entertainment and experimentation of an entity to control us. But, in a larger context so is everyone else playing the same game funneled down from an elite perch. We are all made to be desperate or separated by it as a piece of the puzzle. Race is the great separator and we are inconsequential pawns when we volunteer to sacrifice or eliminate ourselves before the game gets underway. Slavery started us from behind but we keep ourselves behind until we reshape our reality and psychology.

Courage to claim our rights, freedom, beliefs, and psychology is the price of admission to equality. When we display the weakness and acceptance of inferiority by our actions and mentality others will too towards us. Those who do not resemble an accusation feel as if you can't be referring to me. So, to become upset concedes a measure of resemblance or some other inferior classification. If it were flattering the reaction would not be contempt but honor.

Whether Black, LBGTQ+, woman, left handed, or many other arbitrary distinctions that yield anger is an acknowledgement of difference. Those things considered "normal" or "superior" does not bring forth the same connotations. Each of these "disparaging" classifications will be normal when they no longer arouse anger or justification. Beside, we all belong to at least one of them. Left-handed people were roundly thought to be of less intelligence. Primitive and ignorant assumptions are usually based on unfamiliarity or fear without any factual basis.

The Taxonomy of Black people are similarly situated with an echelon and perception among our classification to further distinguish within it a hierarchy of Blackness. Within the Black community the terms African Americans, n-words, Black people, Bi-racial, and person of color all have a different meaning. Likewise, all those of African heritage from the transatlantic slave trade dispersed around the globe have different identities although we all originate from the same continent, Sub-Saharan region, and lineage. Our only difference is the socialization of our geographical slave experience.

Taxon is an identification of species or classifications like humans from other mammals or fish. You cannot have a higher classification without the original classification from which it derived. In this context racism is illogical with an empty kettle blowing steam and noise running near empty. The presumption and distinctions separating humans are irrational and ignorant when based on generalities not vetted on the individual's composition. We are not a monolithic block but far too many subscribe to the identity assigned us unable to reject the social addictions that binds us.

Groups, sub-groups, nationalism, patriotism, social classifications, and social distinctions are the same as currency. They are only as valuable as the belief in them which is the thing that gives them power, value, or barter. Many of these misconceptions are like the puffer fish or blow fish who swell to ward off intrusion but their posture must eventually deflate. So must the fallacies and socializations of deception. Our inner city blues are a result of our disharmony displaying a disturbing pattern of behavior and ideology entrenched in our minds blocking our vision. If only we had eyes so that we may see. To see the real game being played might be us playing a sinister caricature of ourselves.

Consider the ruses being played and the mask that are worn to distort or malign our self-identification recklessly displayed and incorporated by us as racially representative of us. Any such mask is a form of self-rejection and sabotage by default or commission. What we seek to become or replicate cannot further the insinuations and stereotypical slander as our mentality. Society forges assumptions and images by which populations assume. The resulting ideologies and behaviors extenuate to further incorporate fractional conclusions creating polarities based on interest, position, or conditioning.

It results in stereotypes and defined mentalities generally accepted. For example, slavery was the slander. Stereotypes were the assumption. The fractional conclusion were reenforced propaganda or observation. The mentality is the degree in which we resemble the accusation. We pull down our self-esteem and reputation by littering our image with the debris of violence, crime, and bodies. That leaves our image shook, our credibility took, and our humanity overlooked. It is our mentality that is toxic to our ascension.

We need every variety of individual in our communities to become a messenger regardless of pass transgression or status. There are corners that only some can reach where others cannot. Honestly, we definitely need those corners to be reach the most. For those who have operated in those environments their service is desperately needed to provide their clout to spread the new message. Respect the messenger if they respect the message by reaching those who language they speak and image they reflect. The ministry is the message spread to improve our mentality.

Therefore, we cannot afford to disparage the messenger because who else is capable of doing it. The many ways we contribute to exploiting ourselves offers plenty of messengers an opportunity to spread a constructive message. Every manner of socialization, economic, educational, health, healthcare, political, criminal justice system, and many more need voices raised and boots on the ground to rationalize and extend a new liberating perspective.

For those already holding things together but could use some more helping hands and voices be encouraged that the calvary is coming over the hill. Remember, if nothing is done, they will continue to have it their way at our expense. But, can we continue to let them. More importantly, can we continue to let ourselves.

Thurston's Thoughts
Hustling Backwards, Gains and Losses

The number one rule at the casino after winning is never give it all back. Play too long and the house always wins. In the end, you stayed too long and lost it all, much like the dope game. Life is, in many ways, a reflection of a casino where many games are played with varying percentages and probabilities. Much is potentially possible but actually unlikely. These algorithms all disproportionally favor the house. It is the industry's structure to lure you by the optimistic temptation of gain but more likely inevitable loss.

It is a gamble, a fantasy activating euphoria. The euphoria sweeps away logic and caution only seeing the prospects of paradise. However, the only realistic hope of winning outside of pure luck is to understand the operational principles of the game. Thus, gauging its vulnerabilities that yield the highest percentage of advantages in your favor, the odds. So, knowing when to hold em and when to fold them helps minimize your losses. Sociology is understanding The social rules that comprise the operational principles influencing the laws and behaviors of society and humanity. It is life's casino, the uncertainty of life and possibility.

Any sociology is usually manipulated and sculpted by design to favor the house or dominant group. However, a fool without the rules usually plays at a disadvantage, only adding to the house's accumulation of gains. The spectrum of sociology reflects the prevailing psychology, social norms, and beliefs replicating behavior, traditions, and cultures conforming to that standard. The sociological standard is sometimes obsolete and without merit or application to current relevance except for being resistant to a more suitable replacement. It becomes mostly a ritual demonstration of a conditioned inclination disguised as culture.

This conditioned proclivity is the method to control populations and the minds of the masses through traditional and cultural influences. It fosters the exploitation of your interest by deception, despair, or promise of participation for a more significant benefit. By definition, your participation defines someone else's exclusion. Because for it to be exclusive and desirable, it cannot be available to the unworthy and those who fail to qualify for its rewards. So, for its intent and purposes, sociology is shaped not by accident, chance, or choice but for the desired outcome that is socially preferred.

The desired outcome can be engineered for the worst outcome more easily than for the best. It is always much easier to destroy than build and sometimes to deny than to accommodate. The present concern is the future, not the past of how we arrived at this current juncture. The past has less significance than the journey ahead. Nevertheless, we must retroactively examine it to establish its sociological and psychological influences. It helps us navigate a path forward to avoid and reject our complicity compounding our struggles. We know the appalling historical occurrences to nausea.

Therefore, a perspective of brutal honesty where all discussions are on the table can't yield any fewer results than dwelling on an undeniable history. As well as we know the historical atrocities, we should also understand the sociological and psychological mechanisms used to perform and perpetuate them, thereby avoiding past patterns in the future. More specifically, the origins of the indoctrination have been thousands of years in the making, evolving throughout history. Its survival and concealment have promoted caste systems, racial distinctions, and societal segregations.

The patterns are incorporated into the human experience by nurture and environment, so it is naïve to believe we are not subject to them in ways inconspicuously practiced. Racism is the byproduct of the practice, the symptom of the disease that afflicts rational thinking. Once planted and reinforced, it replicates itself just as inferiority does. To examine the practice, we must explore how the seed from which it has grown and replicated is cultivated. Racism survives by replication as an ideological organism in form and function.

It compulsively reproduces its corresponding engrained characteristics, attitudes, and methodical patterns of beliefs. Still, racism can be substituted for many other socially held beliefs or compulsions of social design. Often oblivious to its acquisition, these compulsions are automatically fixated upon in mind and culture beyond the physical and historical implications. The social component insidiously infiltrates normal channels of resistance by youthful imitation and assimilation. It penetrates the very psyche as culture, conduct, and assumption becoming an overwhelmingly defining perspective.

To illustrate this, let us use a seemingly harmless example and expand beyond its innocent ramifications, Santa Claus. Remember, all indoctrination is not racial but societal. First, I am sure it is nothing, but for consideration or coincidence Santa has something in common with someone other than Jesus of biblical note. Perhaps the literal presentation and interpretation obscures the symbolic connotation and denotation. Then again, perhaps not. In a game of scrabble Santa can be re-arranged to spell Satan.

Notwithstanding Santa's signature and symbolic red suit which he and Satan both share an infinity for the color "fire" red and deception. However, they also present the duality of obedience. With Santa obey or you receive no gift but with Satan by disobeying you are awarded his prize. Either way your prize depends on disobedience. When viewed in that context, it is easy to trace how it became racially charged to achieve a secondary purpose besides obedience. Anyway, on to the Santa story and more.

The charade of Santa Claus is widespread, but not so much the origins of Santa Claus. Let's follow his journey to prominence today to become fully aware of the extent and longevity of his celebrity. Santa Claus is allegedly from Saint Nicholas of warm weather Mediterranean origins near Turkey and adopted by the Christian faith. Over time, he was relocated to the north pole and transformed his identity and appearance as if in the witness protection program. He changed his whip from on foot to riding a goat, a flying horse, a flying wagon, a flying dragon, and from one reindeer to multiple reindeers.

His merry making gift delivery was initially in early December but was moved to December 25th, and oddly associated with Jesus. Co-incidently, Mithras known as the giver of gifts, the Persian sun god, allegedly was born on December 25th of a virgin and had a resurrection from death. Santa has been celebrated in some form from about 270 AD until now. Santa was making his round before Jesus' birthday was celebrated on December the 25th. However, Jesus, the savior's birthday, is now celebrated on December 25th after being celebrated from early December to January 7th by old calendar standards.

His birth is also believed to be in early spring or early fall, even on September 11th. The conception opposition to abortion is probably loosely correlated to the belief of Jesus' conception and crucifixion being on the same day. His conception on March 25th is used as evidentiary for a December 25th birth. Yet still, Emperor Constantine declared December 25th as the day in 336 AD by Roman rule. By dispatch, Pope Gregory also promoted it to be December 25th following the new calendar. Gregory also believed Anglo-Saxons, who coincidently are of Germanic descent to be fair skin blonde hair angels. Not so coincidently, December the 25th is also the birthday of the unconquered 'sun.'

So fa-la-la-la-la, there you have it. Seems like they just picked a day, but how? Why? Did the many significant roman events, calculations, miscalculations, pagan rituals, Saturnalia, winter solstice, Scandinavian yule, and many more merged to make this the day of celebration? The day of our Lord and Savior Jesus Christ is a more or less random symbolic consolidation of fractional beliefs. It appeases and unifies various fractions for maximum acceptance and worship. If it is any one or more of these reasons and Jesus name is plastered onto it, what manner of deception is afoot? How did Santa Claus enter the picture, is it his birthday too? Who is Odin? What about the Sol Invictus or Helios, both translated as sun?

But wait, why don't all religions that believe in Jesus celebrate Christmas? Nevertheless, come all ye faithful joyful and Invictus, I mean triumphant. However, if you are a true believer why honor the Savior's birthday by committing the acts of a heathen as outlined in the Bible? Aside from the religious ramifications, there were the economic implications resulting from the productivity of the sun returning to futility. Let us not forget that Christmas is the number one commercialized holiday generating economic stimulus over the winter months, months generally of less productivity.

However, in case the implication was missed, it is the Winter Solstice associated with sun-worshipping and the days becoming longer. Even the name Christmas derives from Christ's mass, the mass after sunset which started at midnight before sunrise or the sun's return after three days of stillness or rebirth. Furthermore, Yule was a pagan celebration long before Christmas and mistletoe symbolizes fertility. It could be an extreme coincidence or maybe just social engineering at its finest.

These are some of the histories which are probably unknown by many who steadfastly observe and practice Christmas through ritual indoctrination. Much of which has been determined and manipulated by means commonly unknown. The Roman Catholic Church has influenced those who don't actively follow its doctrines by socializing its concepts and decrees to those unknowingly ritualized. Beyond even those considerations, Santa Claus is to be feared and obeyed while portrayed as a white man with magical powers and the power to punish us if we are naughty. Santa Claus, like God, sees it all and knows our deeds, especially disobedience.

Jesus has greater command of the same powers granting salvation as a reward for obedience. Still, Jesus covered our sins by his death. When knowing better but not doing better, we become submissive to a savior or validator mentality, giving reverence to white images of worship and obedience for a reward. It is all-encompassing because we all fall short of perfection and thus are all included in the guilt and judgment-seeking grace. When not falling short of God's grace, thanks are rendered for the protection to rise above it.

So, all bases are covered despite our conduct. This cover is where the submissive, obedient, and racial twist is injected if we want the prize. Oh, I almost forgot to mention there is a penalty associated with it called the fires of hell and the devil. This disobedience gets us the scrabble Santa, Satan's prize. Still, violations abound even by those who claim obedience. Not to question or arouse deities but to see if race has any effect on extenuating perspectives, obedience, or who is the punisher. Why is it important for Jesus to have a color or race? Why is it necessary that it is white with blond hair and blue eyes? Why is a sun disk usually present with his depiction?

Any image of Jesus is blasphemous in its observation, not to mention its worship. Any image is technically an idolatrous violation and was created at least three hundred years after his death. With no composite description, how is his image accurate but ever evolving after three hundred years until its last alteration in 1941? Can you create a precise depiction of your ancestors from three hundred years ago without a reference point when the technology was not available as it is today? How about two thousand?

Even today's technology cannot do it because it has no lineage in which to begin. Why is Jesus' white complexion in conflict with the darker complexion of inhabitants of that region at that time? If his color does not matter, why was it made white? The sociology of selective images establishes the white race as dominant on subliminal levels undetected by the conscious mind, especially when they demand obedience without examination but defy logic. A single problem like racism explored can lead to a multitude of questions and unintended knowledge and consequences. So, what is the foundation of our beliefs? Do we worship someone's imagination or deception? The truth or the sinister directive?

How about Saturday being the Sabbath and the day of worship God gave? Many go to church on Sunday which is the first day of the week and not the seventh day which God rested after creating the world. Sunday is the day of the sun or sun day. Monday is the day of the moon or moon day. For that matter Saturday is name after Saturn which has a whole back story which may surprise some.

Furthermore, Isa or Lucifer the Prince of Darkness is known as the Morningstar or Venus light before sunrise. Lucifer translates into shining one or light bearer. Not to discredit anyone's beliefs but to illustrate the vastness of knowledge beyond faith. A little knowledge is a dangerous thing but a lot is enlightening because it extorts the truth.

Ancestors of Native Americans lived on the Bering Strait or land bridge more than 15,000 years ago around the last ice age. Asians from the same region 25,000 years ago. Archaeological records of humans from the region date back 30,000 years. God created the heavens and earth in six days and rested on the seventh holy day. The earthly Adam and Eve are only 6,000 years old but their origins doesn't start there. It starts in heaven, but what was their identity in heaven?

Furthermore, did their age start there or on earth? Is time also a chronological constant in heaven and why? Did you know the stone age, wheel, spear, bowl, and club are older than the 6,000 year old Adam? Older than the biblical population of earth. For that matter if God made Adam from the soil in God's image and breathed life into his nostrils why is Adam white when dirt is not? Not that it matters until it matters. But more importantly, was Adam an angel demoted to a man or a mortal among angels. Either way, was his angelic form or human form the image of God? Does God has wings as depicted by images of angels?

Can we be the image of Adam and not by extension the image of God since Adam was decommissioned to a mortal form? In whose likeness were the other entities in heaven fashioned given the variety of their purported appearance? Even more importantly, how is all this pre-earth or heavenly knowledge possible and what is the source? Limited knowledge, faithful assertions, and irreconcilable disparities assumes the highly questionable to be absolutely unquestionable. Still, it is conveniently explained without the source of its faithful assertions, unless by faithful leaps and bounds over many discrepancies.

Notwithstanding religious beliefs, the spirit of celebration arguments, or rejection of anything not aligned with your coding but strictly consider the sociological adherence to traditions of which you may have little or no understanding. That is how racism is also permeated. First by blind ritual adherence, then by refusal to reevaluate, and finally by irrational protection of the practice without logical confirmation. So complete is the effect that if and when knowing the truth, you still refuse to reject it, instead seeking the comfort of conformity by being assimilated into the deception. So racism persist as well as Christmas as two of the largest deceptions of humanity.

In addition, God's image was rebranded once again by the insinuation of likeness to white Jesus, further religiously marginalizing those excluded from social consideration as inferior by our distance from the likeness. This socialization still plagues the 21st century by establishing institutional and foundational psychological predispositions of negative impact on the Black race. For another example, the law is often a dichotomy of preference and protection for whites but control or punishment for our people. Race and economics are the metrics by which it is decided, unbalancing justice by social appraisal.

It is an exercise in societal status on how the law is applied, while race is usually implied. The lowliest of whites can feel superior to the highest of Black people by skin color alone. It is inbred as a psychological entitlement. Conversely, inferiority is also inbred as psychology enhanced by sociology. Feelings are subjective, and we must agree to feel a certain way for that to fester. There are fractional effects of racism to varying degrees, either in support or in dispute of any manufactured suggestion.

The racial suggestion may be mutually inclusive of other similarities or differences other than race as evidence to bolster the suggestion and association. In other words, it is a mixed bag of considerations of possibilities. They are not simply based on race but can be racially inconsistent with or inclusive of suggested stereotypes. For example, some whites hold a favorable perception of Black people, just as some Black people have an unfavorable perception of whites and vice versa. The contrarian view of whites having disdain for other whites and Black people having contempt for other Black people also exist.

It is based on conditioning, experiences, and an environment that impacts the prism of perspectives. This self-affirming prism of perspective is then carried forth and replicated either negatively or positively. It then becomes the limited scope of evidence that validates realities outside the radius of greater considerations. In essence, a small sample size determines the vastness beyond our knowledge. Being pragmatic would be to evaluate the sample size and why we acquired that belief as universal beyond its limits. Even if situationally justified, it can't be universally true in all situations.

Therefore, it must be independently assessed. It is common to entirely embrace and conform to symbols and concepts that regulate and formulate our overall perspective without evaluation. But it is also foolish. However, it also reveals the sociological pathology of not considering the possibilities, nuances, or empirical facts that deviate from our assumption. Without consideration, it thereby eliminate an objectively informed perspective. So, the perspective of one subgroup's self-interest is simply a function of preference over another's self-interest, jostling for the survival of competing views.

It is fire being met with fire intensifying the flame to avoid it being extinguished. The same conviction can be seen if converted to the opposing subgroup's viewpoint, so it's situational to one's perspective or lack thereof. Therein lays the problem and the solution. Both are three-fold. Further inquiry reveals the three options are either cooperation with consent, control by coercion, or convincing persuasion. So, there is a rhyme and reason to every element of social orientation. The origins and purpose may surprise us but rest assured that detection is obscured or denied while promoting the intended agenda.

If we are not falling for the old buzzer in the hand routine, why do we continue to participate or succumb to control mechanisms that our ancestors underwent? Everything European is taught as standard curriculum. Our culture or history are taught as vaguely existent or a special study. It is not their legacy, tradition, or displacement of which we are ignorant. It is our lack of knowledge of ours. Furthermore, we accept, observe, and commit transgressions with comparable results as the intended measures used to sustain oppression. In fact, if they discount us, do we respond by discounting ourselves as a counter-offensive to shake oppression?

Does the outcome make indistinguishable the prey from the predator? What results do we not see as counterproductive by our conduct? Consider this, a group of people conspire to exploit another group. Avoiding the repercussions they devise methods where they can accomplish their debauchery without it leaking back to them. The group to be exploited unwittingly falls into the trap. The "trap" automatically resets triggered by the activity, not the groups exploited designation. Only by exhibiting the targeted characteristics will the trap spring and reset. Over time some have figured out that they can escape the trap's fate. Others continue to be baited into the trap and reset it for others.

The question is are they being trapped or are they entrapping themselves and others? Is the trap set to ensnare exploitation and not the designated group if those who escape avoid what triggers the trap? So is exploitation the prey or the predator? Regardless of position prey or predator, which one are you if your actions are to or would be similar in activating the trap? To take it further, if the damage is the same does it matter which one you are, prey or predator? The trap or control is a cyclical paradox of exploitation functioning directly or indirectly based on ritual ignorance.

Remember the prey is always concerned with the predator while the predator is unbothered by the prey except to devour them. The ideology is the predator and those who succumb are the prey while the trap is the means to lure and psychologically confine. From an empirical perspective of achieving the objective by means other than force or direct confrontation blame is avoided. Can the predator be determined or have any liability fiduciary or otherwise for our actions? Furthermore, the whole Christmas spill was a cursory excursion into the beliefs, methods, and social indoctrination widely accepted and practiced that have a basis other than the perceived one, a trap.

Likewise, the application of the law is from a similar establishment of practice, protocol, and enforcement which cannot be objectively administered if the basis is tainted or favored. The law's resistance to change dupes one into accepting a perceived faith despite the realities of its injustices. Both represent systemic beliefs that to question are desecrations of public faith. Not because of their veracity but instead by our ritualized conditioning forbidding them to be questioned. There are few absolutes in life due to evolution, erosion, or discovery, but our societal structures and rituals resist the very laws of nature which is change.

Nothing is immune from change. But, many social quirks and practices are inoculated by obedience, faith, or ignorance. We as a species arrogantly consider things as primitive not acknowledging we are still practicing the same primitive notions. To refuse change is to refuse progress by improvement or trial and error. The error of some of our ways leaves nothing but improvement by changing them. The obstacles of self-infliction by their design or our commission nets the same results. So, we must escape the traps which impairs our progress. Despite the technological advancements, we continue a primitive mindset as an overall species in general and our people in particular.

Humanity is resistant to change bound by history mesmerizing our logical discernment. Black people as a sub-taxon must accelerate our perspectives while eliminating conditioned ritual obsessions. By eliminating obstructions within our control, we precede change in others when we make the necessary adjustments to expand our perspective and etymology of behavior. This process produces the most effective method by logical default affecting the transformation by our conversion, which transitions their opposition. By extension, for maximum expression, the change must be incorporated internally, then demonstrated externally, not the opposite.

Speculating on what remains when coercing external conversions, would that not still leave the internal obstructions regardless of how they came into being? Always preaching it but never practicing it. Persuasion by self-realization converted into cooperation has the most profound impact without the accompanying resentment. Willful change is always preferable to forcible compliance. That is how we change others by them changing themselves. The existing sociology may have resulted from slavery, racism, and discrimination, but at what point are these ulterior motives no longer the justification but the programming?

Debunked justifications are Plato's cave of illusion denying a larger reality. The shadows were created by those outside the realm of the cave thus shaping the projection into the cave. We must exit our cave of illusion holding us stagnated. We then have the ability from outside to project the image shaping the cave's reality. We are also free to script a new path outside the illusion. The rays of knowledge illuminates that path. Sociology must be factored into the solution to neutralize its effects, illusions, and practices.

Primitive deviations and ideologies restricting the current reality can only reconcile to the application of past realities. Their relevance to a future reality blocks the fluidity of progress according to current circumstances. Adaptation and improvisation are decimated by the regulation of change. Change by evolution, erosion, or discovery will eventually expand beyond its primitive confines where it becomes unacceptable or ineffective. Reprogramming is necessary to repel habitual socializations where we perpetuate the trap, resetting it to lure others.

So conversely, if our internal obstructions such as sociological and psychological tendencies were rejected or eliminated, that would be of substantial benefit to affect external perceptions. However, regardless of external perceptions, to minimize their impact and efficiency our core foundation must be fortified against it by reprograming it. Either way, our internal adjustments move us closer to our goals, with or without others change. What we debunk combined with enlightened progress accumulates to contemporary gains and perspectives replacing primitive boundaries. Otherwise, we are hustling backwards throwing the good after the bad.

These patterns of accepted beliefs and behaviors within ourselves and others reflect and project sociological images as associations and identifications characterizing our perceptions. British, Roman, and European composites of rituals, beliefs, and practices that formed America are still woven into the societal structure established and concealed as normalcy. This normalcy propagates a class of aristocrats and racial hierarchy above certain economic classes and races, most notably above our people. The implied acceptance promotes a tradition of approval routinely practiced without reservation or sometimes even awareness. Including our celebration of hidden indoctrinations.

The inverse effect is for us to expect and receive the opposite of what they experience creating the opposite normalcy for us, expecting discrimination. But, yet we imitate their normalcy instead of our reality. White privilege can be described under this dynamic where some who genuinely benefit are unaware of its benefits because it is standard for them. The resources unavailable to us are unperceivable to them because they are not self-aware beyond their limited scope of not being impacted. Self-interest and benefits experienced as undue consideration blur sensitivity to the unfairness of the actuality or practice as customary, which results in anticipations and entitlement.

So whether it is willfully or unwittingly indulged, the outcome or observation of racism is so close it is hard to make distinctions. Furthermore, individuals, sub-groups, groups, and institutional or systemic networks are sometimes matters of personal affiliations where race is incidental to the determination. This practice affirms motivations for nepotism as a reality also dispensed by familiarity or similarity, not always race. Close but slightly different. Again, the distinction is often slight, although not racially discriminatory, resembling racism by the criteria's omission of us.

Also, being kept from positions of power limits our ability to practice nepotism or cronyism as a matter of preference regarding our affiliations too. Although it is not always racism at play, it is sometimes what it appears to be, racism. Often feelings of anguish and anger are influenced by disappointment and rejection where no alternative explanation is feasible but racism. Either way, the opportunity is denied if by metrics outside of qualifications. The totality of context and criteria should apply to reserve harsh judgment when not justified before playing the race card.

It cannot be liberally alleged or smeared when expectations are not met or presented with adverse outcomes. The race card is only to be played like the Big Joker, appropriately and shrewdly. It may be some other method coincidental to race, gender, or whatever have you that the decision is actually based. Fairness is the overriding reciprocity where race or any other discriminatory metric is not the determining consideration for exclusion or injustice. When reciprocity is violated racism can be a likely candidate but not always.

Transcending the racial barrier requires reexamination of current circumstances instead of historical implications to factor the evolution of its sneaky insinuations. Above all, we must amend the narrative by which we contribute to our negative socialization. Rejecting self-limiting socializations, questionable self-identifications, and indoctrinated miseducation designed for our psychological confusion and trauma will lessen the cause and effect of their perpetuation. Any negative impact on us independent of others' prejudices must be identified, addressed, and improved. This socialization is usually disguised as entertainment, culture, and sometimes religion to project and reflect the stereotypical images that diminish our character and intelligence.

As for entertainment, we are often depicted as violent and untrustworthy cutthroats with a propensity toward criminal activity. These depictions make for an easy association and sometimes even among us to believe that our people are of low moral character and always on the prowl to commit a crime. Reality contorted to this fiction justifies and enforces tolerance of its harmful effects to shape our psychological development and economic probabilities. Our opportunities are affected by impressions convincingly propagating prejudice accepting the narratives presented. If it quacks like a duck or only ducks quack is used as validation. In other words, if we resemble or imply the insinuation then we validate the entirety of it.

The method and resulting damage is concealed in plain sight under disguised rituals, traditions, generational teachings, and our entertainment choices. Without the benefit of diligent examination the context of origins or intent remain as silent assassins slandering our image. Look no further than the sitcom depictions of our people in the '70s and '80s on television and the movies. For that matter historically. Also, these traps of characterizations have evolved into the drug addicted, drug dealing, woman abusing, murderous, unscrupulous, immoral, violent, and promiscuous characters far too often depicted today.

Desensitized to the ramifications, it has become a commonly accepted accurate portrayal by some, especially if removed from firsthand experiences or interactions with Black people. The overwhelming perception becomes the reality. Mystifyingly, the music is more of a violation by glorifying genocide and misogyny than the visual depictions. This assaults our sensory perceptions since hearing penetrates the mind more than sight. Hearing can be passive while seeing is active.

It seems more than a coincidence or innocent entertainment compared to white's portrayals and cultural appetite depicting them. These are not forced consumptions but preferred indoctrinations sought by our conditioning of the Black archetype and our selection of available choices. Even how we receive our news may display Black faces but not Black perspectives. Role models and representation sculpted as intellectual crusaders promoting our positive perception to mainstream need more of our support.

They provide a much-needed service to shape perceptions and our portrayal. For example, BNC (Black News Channel) would have produced more benefits than reality TV by entertaining our minds instead of our fetishes. Independence of thought and the radius of honest depictions and perspectives are essential for our people to observe and not to envision. But, we must support it for it to continue or grow.

Otherwise, we are passively oblivious consenting to relegation by repeated and continuous bombardment of degrading and psychologically damaging inculcations by our choice. Rejecting these definitions and portrayals would reduce the pleading needed to solicit actionable redress since 1863. On the contrary, deception abounds in many forms as a trojan horse. The appearance belies the theme. There is a revenue generating phenomenon sweeping the globe and swelling our psyche with pride. The results of the experimentation has been wildly successful.

But, we may be deceived by the message seduced by the messenger. So, beware of what is said and not who is saying it. We cannot be enamored by the pageantry of the messenger to accept the message. Thus, the two edge sword is swung again offering participation in exchange for propagation. We receive a fictional homeland, a cross breast or "X" salute, an assigned identity, and wonderful toys we refuse to use. They receive the propagation of a race who shutter to actively defend itself, are stricken by Stockholm Syndrome, docile and conciliatory, and content with hiding and self-relegation forever.

Once again two equally marginalized groups combating each other unable to unite for a common interest as allies. In the end the group representing us has fallen for the old banana in the tailpipe again and are very forgiving. Why must we always end up eating cornbread off someone's anatomy and bent over forward ankle grasped and hoping to get it over before someone sees us like that? Sound like something we have experienced many times before now more creatively presented.

The new twisted sociological shift projects that ideology and image to the world at a fee while we eagerly grin resembling its overtures. Peace at all cost even our dignity despite having superior resources. Wa-kind-a nonsense is this. We can only Marvel at the subtleties of its subservient psychosis even in victory. Did the movie benevolent theme betray the party and comic regarding self-defense forsaken for conciliation? Was it Black versus Black or color versus color both instigated by who else? The title Forever would even insinuate an inescapable condition disguised as a testament to eternal longevity. The trap of validation has been sweetened to reveal the entrapment of identity diaspora searching for a home and identity.

Perhaps it is retail therapy since we pay to receive the cajolery. It used our sociological cravings to urge perceptions and metamorphous by association to supernatural knowledge and power but still reluctant to leverage our resources. But maybe I saw a different movie similar to the first one but my conclusion is not a cinematic review but a psychological commentary. They don't force-feed us the behavioral engineering. We voluntarily consume it. The shameful and annoying disappointment of caricature integration into our self-image makes mockery of our serious consideration. The results should be enough to change the method and approach to achieve our objectives or at least not allow them to achieve theirs.

Either we step our game up or force them to step their game up, but the old buzzer-in-the-hand routine has played out. A calculated and tactical approach to identifying and rejecting detrimental sociological and psychological influences that impair our perspective, self-image, and autonomy is needed to wake the slumbering giant, the Black nation. These normalized and ritual perceptions are engineered lullabies to neutralize our autonomy. So, if these things must be, they must be without our consent, subsidy, or participation.

A methodical approach is the most immediate and comprehensive way to strengthen our communities healing our trauma by changing our sociology and psychology. Changing its core to expand beyond the regulated programmed scope into other spectrums of prospects, interactions, and perceptions. Time to break the psychological chains that bind our minds and the minds of others about us. Our symbols of prosperity must be directed towards practical gains rather than egotistical validation or damaging imitations. As a result, resources should be sent into social battle to establish generational wealth through knowledge and education. The validation, equity, and equality will follow. The purpose is reinvestment in ourselves for sustainable gains.

The returns on investments will be evaluated by collecting businesses and ownership that generate cash flow, equity, and a better quality of life. The savior we await is within us by removing the poison of slavery and its institutional deceptions from our minds. We no longer remain under the misconception that anyone can give us anything that already belongs to us and must undoubtedly reside within us. The American Revolution, Industrial Revolution, Social Revolution of FDR, and Technological Revolution all gave way to each other after a generation had passed. The next one will be the Sociological Revolution.

It will be initiated by the dissatisfaction and knowledgeable awakening to the social engineering and abuses of human rights, religion, economic suppression, disparity, and systemic exploitation. Racial discrimination as a thread in the social fabric, along with regimes of absolute control and abuses of humanity, is becoming unwoven by repulsion of global proportions. The curtain has been pulled back by globalization, technology, and information. As a result, the mutual problem is no longer known by many names but by a unified rejection. The humanity of humanity will prevail when courage and knowledge combine to explore a future freed from the past.

Consequently, we must consider the unprecedented times and resources available to affect the changes needed conducive to our expectations for our future. The train is leaving the station, and we must be on board with our intentions and expectations packed for travel. The destination is the reconstitution of our minds, ambitions, and perspective. Making our life matter makes others' lives matter. Removing yourself from the problem adds to the solution. Change is always about courage, vision, and determination.

Life, opportunity, and potential are too often squandered or gambled away, pursuing misconceptions that are doomed by desperation. There is a proven process to follow, so there is no need to gamble. It is only gambling when the return on investment is not inevitable and left to chance. So bet on yourself as the house, you will inevitably always win. It is not gambling for the house, its random collection. It is just randomly unknown how or from who. The standard set is the standard to be met, sort of like the wager. Still, the wager or standard must be faded to participate.

We have to play for a chance to win and we also risk losing but we have to try. However, there is no need to gamble at meeting others' fluctuating definitions when we meet ours. We must take our gains off the table, careful to retain them. It is a game of percentages and probabilities that produces winners, not luck or prayers. The underdog wins when they play the odds or overcome them. Don't play the house. Play the odds or become the house.

Otherwise, we will lose eventually. You know we are winning big when they have to call the houseman, so when it comes to our

Freedom, equality, and social justice, call em. Time to settle up or change the rules. Improving our psychological and emotional intelligence should reduce loss prevention, especially of freedoms repetitively given. It's the same old dog with tired old tricks and repetitive results. So, let's not be swindled or trick bagged out of our fortunes by loaded dice. Sometimes a dog can't just bark, it must also bite.

Good and bad are not only in the eye of the beholder but also the doer.

To see evil but not condemn it is worse than doing evil and not see it?

Self-harm ensures that someone is always on duty, us.

Therefore self-destruction is the most avoidable destruction.

Self-actualization produces the most affluent prosperity.

<u>Let me ask you a Question</u>

1. How much progress is surrendered when throwing the good after the bad undoing social gains by what we do or fail to do? If we are free to behave a certain way, why are we not equally free to refrain from it? Do we hesitate or depend on others for our provisions in our communities that we should control? How are our communities reproduced as a holographic entanglement where racist agendas occur with non-racist even when racist are not present?

2. Does our actions exploit our condition or does our condition exploit our actions in a pick-a-boo of prey and predator? The psychology of self-image is the foundation of existence, what is our foundational identity? Did we choose it? Is it better to focus on what is lost or what is to be gained? How does our behavior resemble a child seeking attention and validation? How far can a regressed mentality flourish in a strategy of advancement?

3. Why aren't we responsible for our detrimental and dysfunctional behavior? How do we better obtain the knowledge and perspective to better assure our progress? If the building blocks add up to the structure, why do we feel we lack the necessities to build with what we have? Where has the questions not been asked or the change not sought? Can we learn more easily from what not to do than what to do regarding our conduct? Can we not see how economics is more of a problem now than race?

4. What can we learn from the courage of David to slay Goliath casting a stone to his third eye slaying the giant oppressor? Where is our courage to cast our autonomy slaying the psychological oppression of our self-identity? Can we stand on our dignity as Muhammad Ali did secure in our self-validation? If our mind controls our body, what and who controls our mind? Do we lack the critical analysis to filter the inconsistencies of social explanations, religion, and pacifications?

5. Can we not see the detonation of self-harm in our communities with the fallout contained among us? What about the explosion of our unity and dismantling of our family structure to isolate our resistance and progress? When and how will we recover from slavery and racism without the resolve and perseverance of our ancestors? They have passed us the baton, what are we going to do with it if not finish the race

No N-word Allowed
But Can We Stop?

The time has come to discontinue the deception associated with using the N-word. We cannot deceive ourselves about the historical usage of this word. Deception is most effective when employed with the complicity of the deceived when they are oblivious and totally clueless to the truth, but we are not oblivious or clueless. Deception is mainly used to promote an acceptance of falsehood to gain an advantage or incentive by voluntary compliance. Yet, we voluntarily insist on being compliant regarding the N-word.

Any deception is a form of delusion that requires acceptance and thus influences reality, causing a manipulated behavior or reaction disguised as free will. A fantasy or illusion is created, establishing fiction as a fact that is then acted upon as factual. Again, self-deception is the most effective form of deception, creating delusions of convenience and justification but rarely of any sense.

Delusion is a mental disorder, and the more extreme it is practiced or embraced, the more significant the psychological dysfunction and detachment from reality. Delusion allows one to staunchly and adamantly accept and defend a belief or position that has been exposed and discredited as contrary to the truth. The greater the dysfunction, the more danger it poses to the deceived one's lack of awareness of reality, the deception, or its delusional affliction. The clinical term is schizophrenia or being detached from reality. In this case, the reality of this word.

The concept of an enemy disguised as a friend is a common deception creating a delusional reaction to lull one into passivity and ease. It is the wolf in sheep's clothing syndrome. We are at a fork in the road in history to definitively restore reality to the poisoned legacy and use of the N-word. At the same time, we still grapple for specific treatments of equality. The N-word is a constant reminder that complicates equality as a continual reminder of its negative connotations.

The perpetuated effects on our people, in particular, and the structures of society in general have and will restrain our mental health and progress if this N-word defines us. The courage to recognize and confront the truth is the first step to correcting this deception and the first action to shed its grip. In nearly all dictionaries, the N-word is defined as the vilest and most insulting word in the English language. However, some have argued that we have appropriated the term to change the connotation, embrace self-love, and honor our Blackness. If this is true, why is it insulting when other races "honor" us by calling us that?

Reflecting on the historical use of the N-word, the meaning has not changed in our minds to an empowering and appreciative word when used by others. On the contrary, it is an insult worthy of inciting outrage or violence. Meanwhile, we still use it in a derogatory manner against each other when angry or describing foul behavior. Yet still, it is often used as an insult describing ourselves in terms we claim to despise and most certainly are not meant to be flattering. But, also used as a gender distinction only for Black males, a traditional target of degradation.

Stockholm syndrome develops through affection or sympathy for your oppressors or captors by assimilating with their ideology. It is a sort of mental surrender and survival mechanism. Stockholm does not promote a mutual partnership but a subordinate designation of dependency as a hostage or slave to a captor or master. It is an integration of your humanity as an eager hostage to the ideological bondage of your captor. Furthermore, it is essentially your justification for their actions for having held you hostage to their rogue authority.

The N-word can be interpreted as such by embracing and using it. We welcome and protect it with an entitlement reserved only for our use. Plato's theory of reality further explains a correlation between thoughts and corresponding actions regarding social organisms. Society, from the beginning, has required the labor and servitude of a depreciated class by choice and design. Either the power structure deems you unworthy, or you deem yourself unworthy. That is the concept behind aristocrats, monarchs, and royal families.

You accept your place beneath them as of little significance other than to serve as second-class citizens. In Britain, they are called commoners. In America, they are called N-words. Yet despite this, we insist and persist in its use to self-identify. It continues even as our use of the N-word contradicts our claim to be freed from its other horrendous distinctions. Meanwhile, we are begging for equality but projecting anything but equality by using this word that has a much different historical definition to others.

Lima syndrome is where the captor becomes sympathetic to their hostages and feels remorse for dehumanizing and imprisoning them. Much like owners of pets. Imagine a captor who is white, insisting on inflicting dehumanizing treatment on a hostage, who is Black. Now imagine the hostage, Black people, adopting or insisting on the vile treatment used to dehumanize them by using it on themselves. The N-word can again be interpreted as this by us adopting its usage.

When they discontinued using it, we did not. We embraced it instead of being free from its burden. No doubt, it is psychological slavery so complete that they can't even prevent us from abusing ourselves when they have stopped. So, whose culture is it, urban or slave? If we appropriated it, was it worth appropriating, or is it our implied psychological surrender? Is this how we define and refer to ourselves with such a vile historical reference?

Emotional bonds and coping mechanisms beyond what was needed for survival have now, oddly enough, become self-imposed conditioning. How can we disassociate the method of trauma oppressively enforced using the N-word while raining down atrocities upon us? In other words, what the N-word stood for is synonymous with slavery and Jim Crow, now used by us as we denounce the lingering biases and discriminations associated with this word. How serious can we be to love this word more than we hate what it has and still represent?

Seemingly, we haven't gotten enough of it unless someone else is using it. But then we are mad, demonstrating that it still has the same sting it has always carried. So, the claim is they better not, or they don't have the right. But, what is our exclusive right or why do we want it? Aside from as a reminder to them by depreciating ourselves, why do we use it? Yet, we refuse support from anyone else to help us insult ourselves. We got this, nobody can do it better, and they better not try if they know what's good for them. How dare anyone try to use the N-word to disparage us! We can demean ourselves just fine without assistance, thank you very much.

But how do its meaning and origin change subliminally for us or others based on who uses it? Does our use damage our self-image as much as it damages our image to others? This extends beyond the border of mental illness and identity crisis. It is accepting and maintaining an outdated coping mechanism of acquiescence at worst that must be considered mind control at best. Begging for identity and approval is the manifestation of the conversion of a hostage accompanied by acts of sniveling appeasement.

It encourages yes sir bossing it to prevent penalty and show obedience. Seeking validation for what was damaged inside us and asking for permission from the one who hurt us reveals a simmering inferiority pathology. It is foolish to claim power from what was used against us except to demonstrate what we have overcome. However, have we really overcome it when using the N-word? Plato described this well in his Allegory of the Cave of a limited reality defined by the wall shadows.

It describes a reality based upon limited knowledge and the refusal to adapt to expanded understandings by clinging to the illusions of the initial conditioning. It resembles self-confinement by the mind when free to reject previous restrictions. This confinement renders you unable to grasp or function outside that illusion, convinced that it is your decision or no choice but to conform to the limitations of your experiences. It is psychological captivity by submission and conditioning. Therefore choosing the freedom and comfort of ignorance over the undefined possibilities of liberty and knowledge.

Essentially not wanting to know or knowing but rejecting the reality free from illusion. Basically, the cell door is left open but refusing to escape or leave, maybe even shutting the door as a thankful courtesy to the captor. The expression of our need for validation from the source of abuse instilled this inferiority complex in us we still do not feel worthy of vehemently denouncing. The N-word's use is not a way of seeking relief from the brutal historical systemic racial subordination we have long endured. The back and mind bares the mark, the whip does not. The whip has forgotten more than we can remember.

Still yet, what does the noose remember that we have forgotten? Are we so willing to continue using this word that we would deceive ourselves about the atrocious history of this word and what it has really done to us? By our use, we do not vigorously reject the assumptions of the inferiorities and inadequacies associated with the N-word. We cannot denounce all it has represented but sanction this word with such a horrible history. The historical meaning and application of the N-word can never be erased or sugarcoated.

When we demand change from others, we must also self-evaluate and require a modification in ourselves to truly be about that business. It should never be culturally acceptable to demean ourselves by voluntary association with this word. By contrast, no other race or culture self-defines itself with derogatory terms used by others to demean themselves. Others may use those terms but not refer to themselves or allow others to refer to them insultingly. Sadly, this is not true of us. Using the N-word to self-identify as a group is where we get it wrong. It guarantees the word will continue its derogatory implications for another four hundred-plus years.

The negative connotations continue to be falsely assumed as accurate, especially by those with no point of reference. It becomes assumed as factual. We correctly understand that we must forbid others from using it against us or about us. However, we must realize that we must also stop using it to refer to or define ourselves. At its core, the N-word is not a term of endearment because it feeds an inhumane dichotomy of ourselves in opposition to our interests and humanity.

We must first convince ourselves that we are something else before others are convinced that we are something other than what we have allowed ourselves to be called. Then, by definition, we cannot be n-gg-s if we want to be respected and treated equally. If we cannot or will not stop calling ourselves this word, why should others not perceive us as that, even if they don't call us that? Maybe we should not say it for them to hear, just as we don't want them to say it for us to hear. Don't they also have a right not to hear it? Perhaps no one should hear it, which means no one should be saying it, most of all us.

Our social justice expectations no longer request a change but demand change. We are in a position to expect and achieve these changes but could accelerate it by our actions, by what we do or refrain from doing. What behavioral changes are we willing to make to bring about these equalities sought against social injustice? The question then becomes, is it realistic to expect change without us changing or making concessions that facilitate the desired changes?

Systematic atrocities have been conceived and committed using this word. This word has accompanied slavery, lynching, buck breaking, rape, coon hunting, Jim Crow, and many other lesser atrocities to this very day throughout history, with the N-word as its constant and loyal companion. Those who have subjectively dehumanized, oppressed, terrorized, and murdered our people have used this word to justify their actions. It has been used to justify their barbarity against a supposedly genetically inferior sub-human species broadly identifiable by our dark skin.

Being just an N-word is below consideration as a human being and to be treated accordingly. Claiming we are animals was their rationale for denying our fundamental human rights. Is this the nickname we concede our identity to by using the N-word? This N-word has been stamped upon us along with the extreme sufferings that have always accompanied its use. We must define ourselves and not fall victim to others' historical definitions of us.

Just because we have been egregiously and systematically wronged, we cannot pretend that there are not things we subject ourselves to that we must address to improve our people and condition. Build our culture, not perpetuate theirs. Heal our wounds, not continue the damage. Some argue this results from intentional conditioning or social engineering, which may be accurate, but that does not dissolve our responsibility to resist it. For far too long, we have had to endure. Now we must begin to flourish and reject self-inflicted socializations from slavery.

Physical wounds have visible damage and healing, but psychological wounds fester under an invisible scab, only detected and revealed by behavior. More than anything, behavior indicates our character and self-worth by our actions and not by our words. Therefore, we must identify what actions and behaviors are counterproductive to our collective interests and obstacles to our advancement. How does the N-word benefit or advance us? What is its net value beyond a constant subliminal reminder to others of our alleged inferiority?

It is not always the boogie man. Sometimes, our very own perspective is just as frightening. The betrayal of our humanity and interests can be considered high treason and enslavement of the spirit. Certain self-portrayals do nothing to dispel some of these stereotypes. Instead, it is supported by practicing this N-word lunacy associated with over four hundred years of atrocities. This word has survived many societal, legal, industrial, and technological evolutions. Still, it remains robust and resilient, now overwhelmingly by our support. It is a disservice to ourselves. More importantly it is an absolute abomination to our ancestors.

The deeds that so methodically degraded us were done using this word. Denouncing these atrocious actions as evil, the N-word must also be identified as evil and a symbol of the rebuked evil actions. The immorality of this word is undeniable, reprehensible, and unredeemable. The word cannot be repurposed or rehabilitated. Human sacrifices have been made, brutalities endured, and unfair repercussions overcome for the price long ago to be paid in full. Paid to no longer be considered or treated as N-words. Should others honor above us what we should honor more?

Unity of our objective must prevail where division and, yes, ignorance stagnates our interest. A unified commitment to our equality establishes an axis, standard, and discipline that must be the basis of all our actions as a foundational change. The next frontier is promoting our next generation beyond the limits of past restrictions to explore future possibilities. Possibilities beyond the limited images on a wall of deception or hopelessness. To finally envision ourselves as anything possible except for an N-word. Exponential advancement to incremental progress depends more on us than on anyone or anything else.

Playing our position or managing our post to hold ourselves accountable, being part of the solution and not the problem, is our needed individual contribution. We must recalibrate our perspective, discarding what does not serve us by rejecting its deceptions and illusions. We must declare an elevated reality that does not sabotage our efforts. We can only deny ourselves, and we do not need others' approval to proudly be the best representation of ourselves. Be the best representation of, not an abomination to, our culture by cultivating, promoting, and nourishing excellence that demonstrates a worthy portrayal of our character. Let this be our culture. The results will motivate self-acceptance, generate impartiality from others, and display our renowned honor. A singular journey and purpose becomes our collective reality when aligned with a common pursuit, social justice, and equality.

The philosophical theories of Plato and Socrates are interpreted to mean that words reflect thoughts, and thoughts govern actions. They shape perceptions that restrict our realities which define our limitations within that reality. What thoughts does the N-word perpetuate within us and others to compel specific actions or attitudes? Does it create contrary perceptions and manifest realities that produce the images, constraints, and obstacles contributing to our condition by our consent?

Black folks, kinfolks, and all folks, it is time to bury the N-word in an unmarked grave, never again for us to offend or be offended by it. If others are not permitted to say it or can stop saying it, we can too. Remember history's use of this word and that it was the last word that many Black people heard before death, and not in a loving way. Reportedly this was the last word heard by Ahmaud Arbery. Respect the young brother by replacing that word with one we can appreciate and be proud of no matter who uses it. As a protest, honor ourselves and those who have been taken from us by not using the N-word. From now on, no N-word should be allowed.

I remember Big Momma used to say it is not what they call you but what you answer to being called. It is a matter of self-respect. Mom used to say be known for what you do and make sure not to bring humiliation upon our last name or ourself. It is a standard of self-awareness. Those who need reprogramming to fill the N-word void should initiate a challenge to creatively replace it with something conclusively empowering and complimentary. It is a symbol of self-love not to allow our humiliation. There is a vast vocabulary out there or create a word, just not that word. Maybe even consider the horrors attached to it and our current claim to want to escape the ruins of our psyche.

Let me ask you a question. Would you be willing to abandon the use of the N-word if it meant greater justice for our people? What makes you think it won't? It seems like a small sacrifice for us to pay for the potential psychological reward it would provide. Yet, it is the right thing to do for our children's legacy to grow up, not embracing a vile reference to themselves no matter how we twist it to be all love. Remember, the restrictions of our mind constrain our movement and ascension by encouraging harmful perceptions.

Therefore, no N-words can be allowed in our declaration of equality or first class citizenry. Otherwise, why get mad if others use it? After all, it is all love. But, love of what or who? Certainly not ourselves. Next time you decide to use the N-word, envision your young, innocent child stretched rigidly on the floor like a rug at the feet of a rocking chair with a white master's feet warmed on their belly. Your child used as a cushion to warm your master's feet, and then imagine the psychological damage done to your child. This is the history of the N-word.

Nevertheless, we must recognize the disservices we commit against our children with unbridled sensibilities or this word because damage is damage. We should never be rugs or N-words again! Treated and convinced as an N-word at a tender age the memory lingers a lifetime, and the programming is well underway regenerating the psychological virus. The nature of a virus is to infect a host to sustain continuity of its vibrancy and spread regardless of the damage to the host.

Degenerative ideologies, pathologies, and psychologies are no different except they are mental. The N-word is a conduit for the blasphemy of our dignity and identity. As such ask yourself if this word has any redemption for anyone and what damage we cause by conditioning our children to identify with the normalcy of its historical insult. I guess when appropriating nonsense, we should be thankful that we didn't adopt having our children used as mud mats to remove the sting of that experience too.

Imitation is the sincerest form of flattery or, in the case of this word, ignorance. In bygone days, it was fighting words to call another Black person the N-word. Now, where is our honor or indignation? We somehow see no evil in speaking this evil. But rest assured that no good can come from it. Being a real N-word is to find you on the floor with someone's feet on your belly, whip on your back, noose around your neck, or worse. Have we forgotten? Do we care?

Obviously not. Otherwise, we would not desecrate our ancestors by using this word as a proud moniker. I wonder what is our actual definition of this word. Is it our highest level of prestige? We have lost our way regarding this word, but I can assure you we definitely don't want to be real N-words again. After all, I thought that is what we are fighting against. If this is true, don't ever say it again. If not, don't protest it being said by others because you are obviously not offended by its use.

Thurston's Thoughts
Speak no Evil, Do no Harm

Attempting to isolate parcels of cognitive dissonance regarding race, let's think outside the box to detect and examine the contents within the box. Often emotions misrepresent the origins and purposes of specific adaptations of developing racial coping mechanisms. Cognitive dissonance requires the distortion of reality, usually rooted in misrepresentation and appropriation for physical, psychological, or emotional protections.

These protections will often justify perspectives and behaviors or establish and maintain an alternative reality that supports that perspective or behavior. Either way, they are subjective reactions to a stimulus, either supported or rejected, that is not objectively or factually upheld but is primarily an avoidance technique. These subjective reactions as cognitive dissonance contradict reality separated as perception while closely synthesized to resemble each other, with the perception becoming a reality.

Together they are exercised as independently formed assumptions interdependent on fabricated and artificial responses to reasons that complete and confirm the contradiction by comparison. This cycle of contradiction relies on a misconception to exploit the mind and emotions, provoking behavior and expectations by scripting self-fulfilling realities. This sculpture of illusion is then self-imposed and disassociated from how and why it began, lost for a reason but enforced by behavior.

Far removed from its origins, subjective reactions, or cognitive dissonance justifies or rationalizes destructive behavior. It is cloaked as deliberate decisions unaffected by the underlining sociological originations. The futility generates a constant plea to petition validation by submitting to and vying for approval from a racial system designed to suppress our reality and self-identity. Worshipping images and adhering to ideologies supplanted to diminish our humanity and control our minds delivers a reduction of our self-worth by comparison.

That reduction results in self-hatred of our likeness by fostering insecurities. So, by extenuation pro-Black is anti-something or another including our assigned self-image. The flaw in our psychology is the seminal displacement of our identity invalidated by indoctrination and grooming priming us for inferiority, exploitation, and submission. Many of our standards and beliefs were given to us either modeled after our oppressor or some denigration of our dignity. The vilification is not exclusive to whites. We have the preponderous of the slander upon us by perpetuation of dysfunctional behavior, induced captor adoration, and obedience to implanted beliefs.

The standard set to ascend above the historical pitfalls is the blueprint of rejecting impediments and enhancing our transformation. The standard set is the standard to be met. Still, the standard is prejudiced to maintain a historical advantage based on color, which we can never overcome in a color-based paradigm. So the dilemma is not to be judged by color in a society built on color since our color will not change to meet that criterion. Other changes must obviously occur to impact the change needed. But, we control the most efficient and impactful change and that is us.

Other factors outside of race must become directly proportional to the degree and substance that adversely and inversely affect equality, independent of historical distortions. This difference reveals the great divide and the substantial disconnect of societal chasm to minimize color as a characteristic of judging equality. A closed mind is necessary to perpetuate these differences, refusing to consider modifications and alternatives. It creates a crisis of separation from conditioned conformity and a reluctance to dismiss it by recognizing the prevailing realizations or evolving socialization.

Not supporting and by rejecting the contradictions or misrepresentations are essential for change. The primary preference is to maintain the familiar confines of reassuring conformity rather than invite discomfort by change or equality by fairness. By definition, the conflicting perception opposes the change, preferring to preserve justifications for beliefs and behaviors entrenched by obedience to deceptions and fears projected as truth. The sub-groups or races subjected to these definitions of deviance are stained as morally defective and criminally dangerous to support a false justification.

This contortion of perception creates fear by identifying differences to be fearful of and protected from based on those specific characteristics, often race or immigrant. The perception mainly depends on the constant systemic reinforcement of racial portrayals and supporting events and images. Any unfortunate instances are highlighted or exaggerated substantiations of behaviors that cause fear. The negative portrayal of our images is counter-propagandized, contrasting whites' supposed moral and intellectual superiority.

The cycle constantly repeats itself as a self-confirming construct embraced by those who have no point of reference by interaction or have had a negative experience. The other way to confirm the construct is for us to demonstrate the behavior that supports the contortions as fact. Thus, the perception must effectively change to change the belief, altering the behavior. Adjusting the perception by shifting the perspective is a cause and effect that changes actions by changing thought patterns.

The social structure can then be altered by either initiation of or re-action within that change when it becomes a normalized pattern. It is a two-way proposition whereby we manage our end of the equation, thereby affecting the other end, creating equilibrium. In other words, recognizing our contribution to negative social components and positively recalibrating the process favorably achieving a measure of balance or positive normalcy. Under this concept, all actions of change rest with us to change the common denominator for transforming the outcome, once again us.

The equilibrium is linear to expectations and predictability establishing the social balance of our introspection and projections. Water seeks its own level as synchronicity of perspective aligns with progression in a symmetry of actions, presentation, and demonstration. It is an almost electromagnetic correlation between actions and probable results which are identifiable as scrutiny or re-evaluation worthy based on results. The self-evaluation and knowledgeable verification of solutions must be an empirical reflection with the courage to change the outcome.

The first principle of clarity is to harness volatile emotions understanding that these emotions are protections and reactions to hurt, not a solution for them. Our expectations are not benefited or restored by emotional reactions or outbursts. Our feelings are soothed, but the situation is not resolved. So if the goal is to comfort our feelings, that is fine, but it is not for conducting the business of resolution. The second principle is to logically rationalize a response that will resolve the dilemma by assessing our options, vulnerabilities, and strengths which will enable us to obtain the best resolution.

Third, to have maximum impact with minimal repercussions and utmost assurances of obtaining objectives while lessening friction. Countering racism and its effects involves eliminating or minimizing the impact of instruments and images facilitating its sociological implementation. With the root being sociological, then the solution must be sociological. Minimizing the benefit discourages the action. Racially insidious actions are adverse and harmful in direct proportions to the relative racial distortions disturbing the social paradigm. The conditioning is equally binding to the perpetrator and recipient by innocuous repetition and habit.

Perhaps to some degree, all races are partially blind to the consequences disguising the foundations of racism. Ethnic groups substitute instruments of oppression and judgement as assumptions of realities instead of conditioned intolerances, unfamiliarity, or fearful projections. It is often anticipated as notions of overt and subliminal insinuations, creating a presumption reflecting the prescribed assumptions of good or evil. The source, pervasiveness, and method of conveyance authenticate it as believable, thus making it true.

This belief is especially true if that is what you want to believe or have the predisposition to believe. Cultural differences are usually a matter of geography rather than ethnicity, more or less according to relatable or similar circumstances. The commonality of circumstances or purpose makes for understanding and unity among similar experiences and of unlikely fractions when in the same boat. By logical reasoning, if being the same circumstance, it would have to encourage both or discourage both, but not divide inviting clashes unless influenced by scarcity.

Also true is that coexisting beliefs and images contradicting these distinctions and assumptions can routinely be held by applying different interpretations and responses. For example, the same belief or behavior that justifies violence against a particular sub-group or race while also requiring obedience and endurance from those endangered by it would not if applied against themselves. It produces a different standard and thereby either a fluctuating injustice or a bias exemption.

Imagine a group of juveniles gathered where the only difference is their race and not their activity, getting different treatment from law enforcement. Under scrutiny, the reasoning would prove faulty or immoral when inversely applied, giving a different interpretation and result. The inducement should be a uniform discernment, not a different sensitivity. Still, it is all in the interpretation and resulting perspective, proving that power and perspective is the overriding determinant of application, not actions. We cannot underestimate the systems within systems and their hidden impact.

Allow me to demonstrate the subtleties of identity and interpretation. Jesus is in the likeness of his father God. Whites are in the likeness of the portrayal of Jesus. By deductive reasoning God must be white and male. As such since God is to be obeyed unconditionally as the epitome of authority, it is only reasonable that whites should be too. God is perfection, so whites can do no wrong especially while ordained under God's rule and Jesus doctrine to be righteous in their actions. This is a stated and implied superiority by vicarious connotation of their purportedly endowed godly attributes.

Conversely, the N-word overwhelming association conjures images of slavery and degradation. Slavery denotes captivity to the impulses of a master and inferiority to whiteness. By deductive reasoning, the use of the N-word is a claim towards us as being inferior. As such any dehumanizing treatment is conditionally justified according to the diminished status of N-words and dissimilarity to Jesus. Being not equal and treated as such. So for Black people to call themselves the N-word reaffirms and acknowledges the denotation to inferiority. Then, the result and implication is a defamation of our humanity by our accusation when we use the N-word to identify us.

To examine it to a further extent of innocuous capitulation, Santa's real assistant is not reindeer but his twin brother Krampus. Krampus is the opposite of Santa and handles the dirty work of dealing with the naughty. He is evil and is half goat and half demon but not white and jolly like Santa. You probably already guessed it, so I won't say he is very dark skin, except to add that he has horns and a tail. Anthropomorphic is when animals take on human characteristics and behaviors. It is also when humans prescribe supernatural powers to human like deities worshipping them as Gods or divine spirits.

Supernaturalism promotes misconceptions and distortions of biological processes and attributes that transcend probability and earthly restrictions. Magical powers, flying, underwater breathing, exceedingly strong, controlling the elements, and many other infatuations of the imagination qualify. The tendency to explain these phenomenon provides a connectivity to an envious admiration or faith beyond reason elevating them above human as deities or supernatural. The persuasion of powers beyond the human capabilities to establish immortal divinities or superheroes appeals to the intrinsic psychological disposition to submit to anything portrayed as greater than us.

Racism and religion can be viewed from an anthropological perspective in many aspects. Not to commit heresy, but to explore the intellectual concept aside from religion or faith to consider the similarities. Also notwithstanding the infinite powers of God, but by human standards and knowledge reconciling the many miracles, extraordinary lifespans up to 969 years, command of the elements, and many more supernatural occurrences. Faith and belief is the partition between religion and earthly realities. What is the difference between miracles and magic? Between seeing visions and schizophrenia?

What about being directed by mysterious voices? Between believing in things that don't exist except for in your mind even if it is a collective belief? The difference is interpretation and acceptance. If it is religion based it is acceptable but if not it could lead to medication or confinement. Seeing images, hearing voices, and otherworldly beings is demonic or mental illness except for in a religious context so race cannot be the motive but instead sanctioned control. The results of sanctioned control is rejection of knowledge as a precursor to what exactly? The bible is used in the opposite fashion by promulgating the book but not the essence of its teachings.

The power is the book and not necessarily the observance of its idealized contents. So, by the book or belief it controls the masses and corrals rationalization producing worship of otherwise rebuked concessions to magic, alchemy, pagan persuasions, or insanity. Same thing but different subject, interpretation, or source and acceptance.

Ghost, spirits, divine possessions, glossolalia, and supernatural phenomenon are trance and spell states religiously recognized and blessed. So, anthropomorphism is identical to fantasy but somehow different from religion except for the inspiration or source but not the conviction. A consensus or conditioning relegates the validity of beliefs which deeply imbedded defies rejection, scrutiny, sanity, or proof.

Racism, religion, self-image, and racial assumptions anthropomorphizes attributes and illogical impressions widely believed without analysis. When we are afraid to die, we are afraid to live. Afraid to claim our humanity unfiltered by the implementations and mechanisms of control we refuse to confront or dissect. We cannot examine race without examining religion and the correlation between our struggle for equity and our continued belief in some tenets of religion. The psychological and spiritual folklore, traditions, and mythologies captivate us by fear and obedience to an irrational cajolery holding us hypnotized.

When analyzing things we must keep an open mind to evaluate it thoroughly. We should refrain from forming absolute conclusions because it is within the context of the limitations of our knowledge that we presume. Being open to expanding our knowledge and accepting the findings by exploring curiosities without forbidden beliefs or concepts restricting our understanding and operating conclusions. If we believe something we should personally know what it is we believe and why. Should religion get a pass?

According to systems thinking every component of a system must be evaluated for efficiency, effectiveness, necessity, and alterations or elimination. There is no question that religion has played a significant role in our systematic captivity both physically and psychologically. Likewise, we may find our anthropomorphized imagery as N-words based in religion which we subconsciously perpetuate by clamoring for white validation while using the N-word substituted as our unworthy declaration. Modern day Pharisees tower of control crumbles when their spell of deception is broken no longer scattering our mentality and confusing our interpretation or communication.

We worship fear and limitations which define our obedient psychology to assimilate to the likeness of God by psychological submission to whiteness associated to God. We desperately want to please God, our father, and cannot reject a psychological likeness to him, whiteness. Thus, we seek misplaced validation and approval from whiteness equated to our father figure, God. Likewise, the N-word is a designation of disapproval from which if we can't beat them, join them in misappropriating the word for our use to pretend it doesn't mean what it does. But, can we erase the sting? Inequality is connected to Blackness and non-likeness to God or whiteness.

The use of the N-word is more than a word but the submission of our accepted dissimilarity to God. Our identity, culture, and spirituality has been erased with the resulting amnesia replaced with longing to please God or whiteness. By extenuation white is a power greater than ours with our inequality a given. So we are reluctant to dispose of the most deeply rooted remnant of slavery, their religion. They used it to enslave us and we now use it to keep us enslaved. We are fearfully convinced to reject it would be to reject a mystical salvation. It is the standard by which we judge ourselves in a society that exploits and judges us by it.

This judgement illustrates the separation and imbalance of cognitive dissonance needed to sustain compliance by perspective or, more precisely, psychological conditioning pertaining to self-image, depending on which side of the judgement you reside. From the influence of England or Great Britain to the Founding Fathers, throughout slavery, Reconstruction, and Jim Crow, onward to the Social Darwinism of inferiority and superiority among the human species, embodied by separate but unequal racial distortions, racism has been upheld as an acceptable institutional structure. This construct is how it was implemented, but how is it now furthered?

At the foundation is religion but the coding registers across the realm of society's racist inspirations that continued from some of the founding fathers imitating British imperialism. These beliefs are sustained with a diverse twist of insanity invigorated by Charles Darwin's justification and prophecy of Eugenics. It furthered the racist sociology supposedly backed by science, further assigning racial inferiority to Black people amidst a white utopia. Perhaps, it is no coincidence Darwin was British or religion was implicated.

Eugenics, along with the Albertus Magnus, Albert Pike, and Hiram Abiff masonic-inspired fraternal order of secret societies inclinations and supremacy of exclusion by special order influenced the structure and sociology of American society then and now. Now The Federalist Society of Law and Public Policy shapes the exclusion landscape disguised as conservatism. Once again religion is implicated. Not only systems within systems but agendas of not so secret societies sculpt the invisible radius of our circumspective journey for equality.

Educational suppression and indoctrination is controlled by curriculum. Subdual of opportunities and ambitions is controlled by constriction. Many more, including voting restrictions and the deterioration of our family unit shape shifts the social paradigm for camouflage of its application. These agendas amount to a society of structural biases based on race. The system still does, even if one foolishly suggests it no longer has any relevance or impact. On the contrary, its very structure and existence cannot help but have adverse residual implications based on the longevity and pervasiveness of its racist practices. The systems replenish based on ideology until the refinement is punitive and not suggestive.

The longevity of its impact is evaluated in the context of Stockholm Syndrome, which resembles gorilla pimping for submissive behavior. Lima syndrome begs for relief and sympathy from a helpless and hopeless subordinate position seeking compassion. Both prompt repetitive behavioral responses mimicking Pavlov's Theory using reward and punishment methods to convert or sweet-talk reactions. These psychologies can best be demonstrated as a compulsion defined by the restrictions maintained to sustain the deception or compliance.

Combined with Epictetus's Theory that reality is created in the mind governed by what is in our control or beyond only leaves the task of placing it in the mind as reality. Integrated limitations shaping the radius of options, ambitions, and hope within this reality are well defined and resistant only to the individual's choice for what they choose to be controlled by or accommodate. These beliefs, images, and psychologies create the thoughts or reality of perception that regulate perspectives and the resulting actions, which at some point are chosen, even if conditioned.

Once again, perspectives form perceptions while the resulting perceptions reinforce the assertion sustaining a self-contained cycle of manipulated choices. It is psychological surrender to the confines of an engineered reality, often without awareness of the surrender built into the system. Furthermore, yielding to the balance of power establishes dominant forces extorting submission to avoid suffering or punishment, solidifying assigned roles of dominance and dependence.

The resulting power disparity dictates the rules, the rule-makers, and the penalty limiting options. Participation in submissive actions to lessen the impact of hostile power prolongs its reach, giving it breath. It is transactional for safety in exchange for compliance while suppressing resistance. Thus promoting submission by fear and anxiety, avoiding an anticipated outcome while suffering a current abuse. The current abuse is preferable to the imagined consequence. Understanding this can only result in damn the torpedoes if the victims are to overcome the oppression willing to face the consequences.

A fundamental concept and weakness of power is it must be recognized and accepted for it to be most effective because you always have a choice to refuse or disregard it. Outside of its realm, it is non-existent, lacking jurisdictional authority. Therein lay the key to operating outside its realm conceding no control to its influences over us. We must declare our sovereignty over ourselves, our thoughts, and our actions despite the penalty. Power get its authority from not the penalty but the avoidance of it.

The method is to control what is within our control without consent or exemption from another, just our willingness to exercise it. Following the fearful stampede rarely leads to safety, meaning the beaten path has never produced a trailblazer or major rewards. Our fearful disengagement compounds the burden of those who brave the challenge. So, don't get struck out with the bat on our shoulder. Go down swinging, accountable for our time in the batter's box. We are ultimately responsible for making our determinations and the accountability of its yields.

The accountability for any liability caused by participating in self-harming activities for surrendering power damaging our self-image or complicating our achievements should concede blame to ourselves. Coerced compliance is one thing, but voluntary surrender is another. Of course, our harm must never be voluntary. Still, the process of how it becomes voluntary or reflexive indicates the origins of its intent and consequences as an instinctive pattern of reaction.

Self-deception disguised as free will is the most effective deception, dictating actions by conveniently repeating impulsive associations. Subsequently, unwittingly projecting an identity that deflects the damage done to our self-image while simultaneously damaging our image to others. Thus the deception replicates itself, and the extenuating damages promoted by the activities and perspectives are enticed as a psychological dysfunction. The cognitive dissonance of self-abuse is created by being historically abused and discriminated against unfamiliar with what its absence look like. Seemingly, the expectation of bias and some of our behavior strangely invites it.

From our infancy in America, the psychological dysfunction began from the deviant brutality of being subjected to violent psychological capitulations. As a result, we developed a psychological defense mechanism for survival from this brutality. From that time onward, oppressive situations and biased authoritative prejudices have altered and largely penetrated our psychology. Superiority and inferiority are two sides of the same coin of conditioned entitlement or absence of privilege, power, or obligation. Entitlement is the "you owe me" or "I have that coming" attitude where no such obligation exists or is acknowledged.

Entitlement is a narcissistic personality trait for individuals equally applied to groups, nationalities, and countries. White entitlement is reflected in elements of Black entitlement. Is it not Black entitlement to insist that we can use the N-word even in mixed company and at our leisure but expect no one else to use it because it belongs to us? What other words belong to a group of people unauthorized for use by others? It appears to be a conflict of interest and a mite dissonant, or we should reconsider our fondness for the word.

Any state of mind believing that entitlements or privileges are rights and that they are to be expected as a matter of assumption is irrational. No one has an obligation to concede to another's entitlement, including the N-word prohibition. Reparations, whether a right, privilege, debt, or obligation historically and morally owed, are undoubtedly an unsettled receivable, but if, when, and how will it be paid is the mystery. This long-due claim hinders our progression by waiting or expecting a past-due liability and expectation to be compensated. So, it is not an entitlement but it has become a delay tactic distracting from more attainable compensations.

It is not to be forfeited, but it should not be a psychological ploy to camouflage a stagnant expectation distracting from our progression. The accumulating penalty and implications of slavery's psychological and sociological impact have exceeded their limit. That is the actual debt to be addressed, which we are still paying unwittingly. This stagnation is the debt we can no longer afford to pay and is no longer necessary as it was a mechanism for survival. Instead, the chains binding us are ripe to be broken for an account we should no longer psychologically fund.

As an alternative, we must begin to see the evil before us, which we persist in prolonging by our perspective, activities, and self-definition. A few of the most troubling conversions of perspectives remaining have been our use of the N-word, the weaponization of religion, our carnivorous genocide, and our conformity to engineered socialization. All were instituted to break the mind by first incapacitating the spirit and then creating obedience through hopelessness and submission. The flip side is chaos and mayhem over frivolous and misguided provocations.

We tend to highlight the positive aspects of a chosen option and negative elements of rejected alternatives but rarely scrutinize the totality of considerations. But what about the negative of chosen options removing the rose-colored glasses? Likewise, even the positives of rejected alternatives need evaluation. The N-word leaves no doubt of being without merit, no matter how it is sliced. The N-word and religion are not separate as being mutually exclusive from perspectives that prescribe a variety of discriminations, including racism. They are not exclusive but are inclusive of social ills by practice and design.

Also, we must make the distinction between believing in a religion and that religion's history of being weaponized against us. Please remember that this religion was forced upon us as a condition of slavery. Undoubtedly, the indoctrinations were used as coerced methods of passivity and obedience, not as an interest in our religious salvation or refined social graces cultivating morality or equality. Some aspects of religion have now become ultra-conservative and racist, central to an interpretation of Christianity far removed from the inclusion and love of Christ. Religion has been used as the ultimate shield of inequality, atrocities, and genocide.

Truthfully, this has been the case historically from the Knights of Templar and also against races other than Black people. A concentrated effort to force Christianity upon populations or death has been practiced since medieval times. Many wars have had their disputes in religious differences since the beginning of time. The Romans influence is still cleverly concealed and observed today, oblivious to many worshippers. If religion enormously establishes morality, what role did religion uphold in supporting immorality? What about slavery? What about deception?

A caste system defined social prejudices based on classism, even among the same races. The haves and the have-nots are a theme as old as time. The exaltation and envy of those adorned, anointed, or possessing the accessories of wealth or prestige has always been the distinction of separation, even if it was only cows or chickens. Asking for the nature of humanity to change is a tall order. However, we can position ourselves in the caste system's coveted categories by wealth and education if not by race.

History repeats this process of redistribution over time, whereby privilege is taken and given depending on a revolving echelon. With that being the case, gatekeepers have constantly disrupted the continuity of social evolution to preserve their pecking order. Usually, causing chaos and disruption among the masses keeps the masses distracted with infighting over inconsequential matters while being obediently robbed of a greater prize.

Historically, the Ku Klux Klan, among others, has disrupted the social evolution after Reconstruction giving rise to Jim Crow. Their objective was to maintain the ideology of slavery despite the change in law. Ironically, they were formed to oppose the Republican Party of Lincoln, who supposedly opposed slavery proving history's revolving echelon. Now, white supremacists support the Republican Party and find comfort among their leadership and rank thinly disguised as conservative values.

The Republican Party now obstructs social evolution by spewing poisonous ideology and revisionist accounts surmounting to outright lies. Their desperation lacks the physical violence of the Klan but is more damaging by its cover of conservative values and lies. As obstructions and reversals of social progressions, the Republican Party has absorbed the disdain and dread of the Klan. The Klan was a feared group not because their numbers were overwhelming but due to their sanctioned brutality and clandestine sympathizers within the power structure.

They were bolstered by the uncertainty of who was involved and when or how they would rear their dreadful and violent hoods. Their ideology insidiously spread within the power structures of

America. Though concentrated, the fear of their actions permeated beyond their measure by corrupting the law with vigilante justice. Their ideology and memory lives long past their actions having a psychological persuasion to infiltrate government and law enforcement. For that matter, confirmed Klansmen have occupied the "White House" and Supreme Court!

Little doubt that in the Black community, the hatred of snitching to and fleeing from law enforcement has its justification in the Klan's legacy and slavery. These ideologies and memories have destabilized our identity for hundreds of years, attempting to dilute our value by fear while still molding our psychology. Devaluing the object, population, or goal is necessary to discard us as inconsequential, especially by inflaming passions of danger, fear, or retribution through long-established misrepresentations substituted as truth.

Even worst, this disdain effectively rejects aspects of commonality as exoneration. The N-word is a reminder of the devaluation of Black lives, our liberty, and a shoutout to the fervent slave and Klan ideology. A statement not only to those outside our race but also, sadly enough, within. The context of the N-word's origins and the aftermath of its appropriation, referencing the "culture," is what culture? Is it the Klan or slavery?

When applied to social norms, the N-word's appropriation by us refers to fundamentally hijacking or strong-arming its disgrace and shame by our unmitigated audacity and entitlement to use it. Some would say we own the word now as ours, but I would reply, how and why? Has it become an indispensable primary designation of our identity? The use of the term has also been extended beyond race to gender. Equally used as a reference by our women referring to the Black male. I find it disrespectful. Many find it acceptable. So not only do we disrespect ourselves, but our women do too.

In addition, imagine if white folks ran around referring to each other as Klansman or worst, I doubt if that would sit well with us or them. We would also be forbidden from using the word or face what they face now for using the N-word. If one plus one equals two, then it would make sense that two minus one equals one. The truth can often be determined by if the reverse is true. The word does not empower our image or interest. Quite the opposite, it undermines our integrity to demand the dignity of social justice and for Black lives to matter by not being treated as a N-word.

So, on the one hand, why is it affectionate and self-affirming when used by us but offensive when used by others if it means what we claim it now means? On the other hand, is its meaning and use conditional and fluctuates by subjective standards and selective exemptions? Are we the only ones allowed to promote dysfunction as a representation of our cultural affinity, forbidding others from reminding us of the devaluing and derogatory nature of the word?

It would seem that we would have a different preference for ourselves, evidenced by becoming outraged when used by others. However, our use does not vigorously reject the assumptions of the inadequacies associated with the N-word. We cannot embrace this word with such a horrible history but denounce all it still represents. It has been used as a weapon against us much longer than our appropriation of it. Yet, to many, the meaning and connotations still haven't changed, adding to the confusion about its use. Our entitlement to the word has been well compensated by our pain for its discontinued use.

It really has been well paid in trauma for its banishment from use by anyone. We have earned that right. To a substantial extent, white folks readily recognize that right by compliance with not using it, but we will not stop, can't stop. What else will we not recognize affecting our actions and our advancement? If words matter, the N-word is an invitation and incantation conjuring generational curses and self-deprecating impairment of our identity, perspective, and value. An alchemy of disgrace and submissive relegation that we insist upon.

The alchemy of cultural transformation is prevented by its use, fulfilling the self-realization of its damaging psychological impact. Plainly put, we assist in keeping the foul impressions alive by the word's use. Time cannot reconcile the discrepancies of those whose experiences have not been shaped by prejudices represented by the N-word or negative stereotypes when we promote them. So, there can be no opposition where there is no resistance and no resistance where there is no opposition. We don't resist using the word but oppose others using it.

We don't oppose it but they resist it. This is the twisted reality of our demands for its use by us. We must oppose these characterizations and resist their portrayals as our identity. What would be our response if the N-word were on an application or government document? Have we not fought and suffered enough for it not to be, but it might as well be if we still insist upon its use to identify ourselves?

Chanting the N-word affirms its curse and derogatory orientation, subconsciously diminishing our self-worth and confirming our association and likeness to it. How could our self-esteem not suffer? How could others' projections of us not suffer? We are encouraging association with strictly negative connotations. There are no positive ones, none. We even disproportionately use it as a derogatory reference rather than an endearment.

My avoidance of the N-word is not to be socially or politically correct but to not add energy or acknowledge any power to the word. I will not concede it any significance, even by my speech. To use it is to promote it and, to an extent, self-identify with it by association. In a vast vocabulary, another word of expression must convey an image not steeped in trauma and slavery. If not, it is time to create one. The assumption that the N-word can be rehabilitated is an insult to our history of slavery. Certainly, our ancestors and all the atrocities that Black people endured for us not to be called or viewed as a n-gg-r or n---a, flat out. Yet, we continue to suffer immensely under this word, unable to rise above its use if not its implications.

Game recognizes game, and game recognizes lame. Nowhere are they one and the same. It is a preposterous proposition and weak persuasion that the word has been repurposed and appropriated by the culture, our culture or any part of it. But let's examine the culture where this nonsense lacks constructive justification whether used within or outside our culture. The easy part is that everyone should be able to use the word if we so freely use it. Considering others' presence, disgust, or discomfort when hearing a word they can't use or is offensive does not license us.

Why would they want to listen to it if they can't say it? Why can't they also use it to honor our culture? The only logical reason is to punish them for all the times it was said when our ancestors didn't want to hear it. Maybe, we don't want to hear it if we get so offended or our head jump time becoming inconsolably angry. Otherwise, it makes no sense to be emotionally triggered. Who can argue that the N-word has enhanced or propelled our social ascension or agenda by appropriating a vile term vaguely disguised as honoring our Blackness?

If this dishonor is not true, why is it insulting? Can we still protest others treating us like that? But how and why? Reflecting the historical use of the N-word, the meaning has obviously not been changed in our minds to an empowering and appreciative word when used by others and sometimes not by us. It has a dual meaning even to us as derogatory when angry or describing someone foul. It dilutes the message of not being viewed as or called the N-word when we insist that we have exclusive use of the word, indicating our fondness for it.

We remain under slavery's grip, marginalized by and subservient to the sociology and psychology of an inferior and derogatory distinction, but we most definitely cannot contribute to it. Not as entertainment, culture, or deed as leftover fragments of survival and coping processes, but more accurately ignorance that stagnates our progression. Conversions and adaptations appropriated or evolved from systems and practices designed for submission, disparaging our self-identification, and previously accepted beyond reproach must be challenged.

Undertaking the next step in our cultural evolution we must utilize the knowledge and analysis of the systems and behaviors that restrict us by our submission. As time and circumstances have evolved, we must engage new perspectives and methods to achieve old goals and new horizons. The N-word has no place in that strategy or our future, no matter how we twist it to be insanely embraced. For the tongue it is a brief moment of indiscretion but for the mind's memories it is tormented agony with centuries of deliberate appalling and atrocious inflictions.

Our ancestors suffered the highest magnitude of its abuses. However, if we too had suffered the most egregious atrocities we would know the deepest meaning of the N-word and the trauma built as a fence around it. We surely would not use it if it were our personal experience, but it is ours as well. No embellishment is needed for the ferocity or barbaric actions that accompanied the N-word.

For those who resist forgetting about slavery as if it never happened or champion reparations, by us using the N-word we have already forsaken both. By remembering its history we must forget the N-word. Severe adversity was our ancestor's teacher by experience but they are our teacher by perseverance and we should never forget it when it comes to the N-word.

Remember, Bosses lead with their deeds, having no stomach to concede.

They call their shot, making their way, witnessed and proclaimed by what they do and say.

When put to the test, the foregone conclusion is being the best.

Bosses never claim to be, instead when you look, you can describe what you see.

The title Boss is often thrown around, but we know everybody can't fit the crown.

When it is time to do Boss things, who among us will claim the ring?

Boss up. Playtime is over. If you can't handle it, run for cover.

Queens and Kings don't do N-word sort of things.

Let me ask you a Question

1. Do we realize the power and influence of white imagery? Can we surmise the negative impact of our people's imagery and the N-word that promotes projections of inferiority or discrimination? What if the N-word in rap lyrics were replaced with a derogatory term for other ethnicities or sexualities, how long would that last? Could therein reside our answer regarding the N-word or other derogatory terms being used in-group but having a different meaning to those outside the referred to group? Is that a sign of acknowledged degradation? Why does our psychology deny the intent of their indoctrinations and ours? Is religious adherence obstructing our resolution and clarity? Can we honestly assess our knowledge of what and why we believe what they do or what they told us to not only believe but trust?

2. Do you worship and obey the Tetragrammaton, Elohim, Tammuz, Hemes Trismegistus, or celestial beings? Do you know the difference or is there one? What knowledge of Rosicrucian, hexagons, pentagons, circles, "X," and triangles are we missing relative to religion, sacred geometry, and each other? What are their hidden meanings? Do they promote fear, obedience, and weakness as religious symbols, hierarchies, and ideologies? How was slavery insidiously influenced by any of this? What about GRT (global race theory) sociology and imperialism? Are we so accustomed to the mind and identity mill herding us that we cannot detect it?

3. If our bodies are physical what is our souls comprised of that is flammable to burn in hell by fire which is a physical element applied to a spiritual state? What is our soul's composition if not breath, spirit, or energy? Why is every inconceivable religious anomaly attributed to a bat utility belt of blind faith? If religion is a quantum entanglement of spiritual existence (belief) and nonexistence (proof), what if it were a human relationship would we feel deceived or cheated on to find out the truth is not what we were observably led to believe? What if the premise is true but the narration

is false? If this is true of religion, what is true of our social indoctrination?

4. Does the whitewashing of us out of the Bible and history not raise questions about why? If God, Jesus, the angels, Adam and Eve, and every significant figure mentioned in the Bible is white and in the image of God for his people or children how does that include us to believe except by inferiority? Is that the crux of a slavery and inequality mentality, religion and ignorance but not racism? Does the one who oppress the poor insult their Maker, God, as stated in the Bible? Didn't Moses marry a Black African woman and Abraham descendants marry Canaanites dispelling the lineage of Blacks as cursed?

5. How do we worship the name Jesus when the letter "J" was not used until some 1400 to 1600 years after his death and the last "s" added to make it masculine? Did you know Jesus' name was Romanized before becoming what we call him today as a derivative? How much of our psychological vortex of racism, slavery, and inequality is hidden by our refusal to examine contrived certainties which we accept absent the knowledge of history, religion, and self-identity? Can we continue to faithfully take their word for it forbidden by the rebuke of God? If religion is any indication of our psychological confinement, what other social swindles do we accept? From these contradictions can we not see the connectivity of socialization to entrench N-word programming undetected?

Tactical Protest
Objective Campaign

The intent and purpose of protest are to demonstrate the objection, frustration, and dissatisfaction of circumstances denied redress, which can no longer persist without correction or change. Civilizations have been toppled over disregard for the people's protest of conditions that will no longer be tolerated. Protest can be stifled, but eventually, it resurfaces and overcomes suppression being the people's will from an indomitable spirit. History always repeats itself in this regard, and change prevails or extinction occurs.

The more widespread the objection, the higher the expectations for change. Thus, the more likely a revolutionary demand emerges that requires radical adjustments to the system according to the people's will and acceptability. Effective methods of protest vary with the extent of outrage and the ramification of its leverage to force change. Additionally, the passage of time influences the efficiency of protest methods used to settle such grievances. Still, violence and force have usually been the method, given their effectiveness and primitive ease of first resort.

The method of protest for the specific modification's ultimate purpose and other expressions of frustration should not be confused or diluted by the actions used to achieve that desired modification. The circumstances under which the demonstration is conducted must be focused and flexible to maximize its effectiveness. Also, mindful to minimize the harm to the protesters and their exposure to being suppressed by force. Radical responses have erupted during protests where force has been met with force.

Peaceful protest has also been met with force. Harmful exposure of protestors should be minimized to preserve determination and is equally important as the cause. However, it may be time to adjust the tactics more aligned with the changing societal climate, economic persuasion, and distress from the political shenanigans still lurking. Using more strategic, socially effective, economically targeted, and conciliatory tactics conducive to the desired change would make the outcome more attainable.

This is not to suggest not keeping the pressure on or lessening the expectations to appease opposition. But to achieve objectives differently galvanizing resources more efficiently across a broader spectrum of solutions and support. Any protest should consolidate active and passive support. It should refrain from alienating resources or allies that can be an asset by supporting change or, at the very least, not opposing it. The total Black population is roughly 48 million, or 14.5 percent of the total U. S. population of 330 million, leaving approximately 282 million people other than Black. With 67 percent estimated at some point to support racial equality, it is clear that any additional percentages would be helpful.

Taking it to the streets with bullhorns had its place in the past and may still contain a level of effectiveness, if not efficiency. However, today a precise concentration of tactics combined with efficient use of human resources applying technology, leverage, and citizen coalitions can disseminate messaging and informational exchanges beyond physical confrontation to gain more of a universal advantage.

More modern tactics can resolve some significant concerns and limit the negative impact on protesters, the alienation of allies, and the alternative actions or narratives levied against the protestors. However, protest tactics, methods, and ideologies must be updated and operated with surgical precision, not blunt force. It is not the skill of the sword but the skill of the swordsman that directs the blow. Destruction is an emotional reaction to frustration and disappointment which is not equivalent to passion or progress.

Reactions are usually an emotional reply that lacks intent and is more of a passive reflex to provocation. On the other hand, a response has an intent that should be logically formulated to affect an assertion or reprisal to an effect. Reactions are instinctive, undermine legitimate efforts for success, and squander opportunities for logical action, resolution, and advancement. To avoid random destruction or ill-fated confrontation, the objective should be to respond with or facilitate focused disruption and transformation.

A tactical advantage has the purpose of engagement with a minimal footprint for retaliation but maximum effect. The goal is to inflict disruption and affect changes without being subject to retribution and to resist dispensing collateral damage to innocent parties not involved in the engagement. Specific tactics can define most responses by manipulative design, thereby aligning the reaction with the purpose of the tactics while working to position the objective for success. Success can often be attainable without conflict when the opposition's energy is converted or depleted to benefit the protest's objective.

You cannot lose unless by surrender when causing methodical attrition to the opposition. Conflict is always an option but becomes exhausting and depleting when recklessly deployed as a default reaction. It should be the last resort even when conflict is the first chosen action. This is not a doctrine of non-violence but a perspective of principle to not become or commit the very violence and oppression against which we are protesting. It only justifies the response, fear, and treatment of us, forming a perspective contrary to change while enforcing resistance.

Resistance needs to be weakened by our actions and not fortified by our emotions. It serves no meaningful purpose to destroy or loot except to indiscriminately inflict pain upon someone who has not harmed us directly. Those harmed may be sympathetic to the protest's objective or the plight of racism. Protest awry presents the opportunity to express anger, emotions, or repressed personal vendettas by offering an emotional outlet under the disguise and protection of collective outrage for the cause. The business of protest is not personal. If concerted, the collective objective will be primary while providing some resolution for many personal vendettas and emotions.

Destruction for the therapeutic purpose of soothing angry feelings or emotional outbursts is not practical or efficiently convincing without focused goals to achieve. Being under the influence of a mob mentality or raging emotions undermines the collective purpose of tactically maneuvering to accomplish our stated objective of social change. Avoiding compromise by self-imposed distractions and not succumbing to emotions is essential to executing a strategy for change.

Our anger turned inward against our communities is illogical and counterproductive. Destruction of our resources can only be justified as a last resort when preventing them from being used against us. It is foolish when it sets us back, or when those resources were used for our benefit. We can never resort to destroying businesses that serve us in our communities. If there is a gripe, it existed long before the current conflict if it is not the reason for the conflict. As an economic or ownership issue we condone exploitation by our patronage. The primary way to fight injustice is to not commit it against ourselves, our communities, our interest, or by our financial patronage.

Emotional intoxication impairs clear thinking and promotes regrettable actions alienating allies from supporting our cause. It further clouds our claims of underinvestment and lack of economic development in our communities. Retreat into our deferred pain or submission to displays of emotional rage prolongs our condition and lessens our community's viability. As the past has consistently proven, anger subsides with time and is an unsustainable expression. Anger is fleeting and an unreliable motivation to propel protest or change.

Pent-up emotional frustrations must be controlled, transformed, and refocused for any protest's sustainable strength and integrity. The mind must be engaged, not the emotions, for logical actions and sustainability of intent. The insanity of our same approach without results is evidence that we have traveled this road many times to find ourselves on the same old road again. It is beyond time to change approaches for a result other than being angry, stubborn to self-examination, or resorting to destructive behavior.

Confrontation is the lowest level of persuasive negotiation or communication, with the greater force usually dictating the terms and conditions over the lesser force. Overcoming a more significant force or power requires not a direct altercation but a strategic and analytical negation of their advantage. Primitive expressions of anger from past pain are counter-productive to future gains. Anger disregards intellectual pursuit and persuasion, surrendering to and conceding an inability to reason or debate our objective convincingly.

Commitment finds a way to achieve by not succumbing to surrender or outbursts when faced with obstacles but instead engaging by adaptation. Our strategy's methodical and foundational principles must remain firm in their conviction but flexible in their concentrated execution. It must promote the expansion of our influence and support the acceptance of our objective. Cultivating our base requires that they be informed of the purpose and the method of achieving it.

When efficiently deployed, their determination, resources, talents, and skills will optimize their contribution to the collective objective. The methods used should be surgical and fluid in dissecting the obstacles to the objective's realization. The impact can undoubtedly be predictable and quantified when the methods and techniques are organized and unified. However, when we do serious business, we must keep it strictly business. Doing business with tangible results verifying measurable outcomes must be structured by expressed policies and concessions aligned with our agenda.

Appealing to one political party or ideology has historically failed, bouncing from one extreme to another, never achieving the wholesale changes sought. More realistically, it has led to being conquered by exploiting our differences and personal ambitions instead of being unified by our commonality of interest and circumstance. Due to this division, we have no applied focus, momentum, or process to make demands, much less change of a monumental impact. Maybe a holiday is declared, but nothing of a quantitative difference.

Clearly, change has occurred since the bullhorn and rhyming slogans formed the focal point of social justice protest. But, the insanity of the same old protest tactics has lately yielded glacier changes and progress. Unfortunately, as a result, perceptions remain tainted (theirs and ours), assurances are hollow, and equality is still elusive. That is not to discredit the efforts and accomplishments of those who have gotten us to this frontier. Instead, it suggests that embracing tactics conducive to current sentiment and public consciousness would seem wise to fully benefit and further the threshold of progress.

We must avoid repeating the same disheartening cycle where destruction overshadows progress and expectations. Instead, a multi-dimensional approach must be utilized, confronting the systems and perpetrators of injustice and those who align themselves with justifying or concealing their institutional and societal violations. Political and legislative recourse is the most pervasive and effective way to universally isolate and identify systemic injustices to punitively and economically persuade or penalize transgressions and transgressors alike.

It is imperative to use all those who would align themselves with our objective of equality and fairness to address both major political parties. Implore them to propose, pledge, and produce programs, legislation, and penalties to resolve injustices. Not specifically for our benefit but to establish an equitable reality. The precise agreed-upon procedural implementation and application should be transparent, obvious, and most importantly, enforced. Changes to existing structures in violation must be urgently undertaken and remedied. Visibly effective actions would be the only acceptable verification to honor any assurances of change.

Our political and economic courtship must be accompanied by this bouquet and by any other suitors who would seek favor with us. However, since beggars have never been choosers, for us to have a choice, we must develop further options to empower our interests without others' permission. Therefore, we must make it necessary and in their best interest to create a coalition with us essential to their own success. It can only be demonstrated by their actions seeking and validating our trust and support.

Political and economic prowess is fundamental to being respected as a force to be reckoned with and afforded the same first-class citizenship considerations as any other group. A major cohesive political initiative is needed to consolidate a coalition of grievances to remedy historical and systematic discrimination. Any redress must include our grievances, interest, and those marginalized within the diversity of our ranks instead of random pacifications. While political influence and legislative reform are essential, economic protest is the most immediate and convincing consideration to facilitate change.

The bottom line can alter mutual goals, shared results, cultural awareness, and systematic bias. Fortunately, the almighty dollar has been known to change things quickly. Maximum effectiveness can be derived from imposing strategies that impact and weaken the financial interests of those in opposition. Let our spending do the heavy lifting against immovable obstacles and prejudicial resistance. Money penetrates many stubborn resolves and keeps our coat out the mud.

The most impactful initiative is preparing, educating, and directing our base in our preferred way of resistance or financial persuasion, similar to the bus boycotts of the 1960s. Financial withdrawal puts us at no physical risk, allows us to remain lawfully blameless, and is an exercise in our spending discretion. It can be heard without ever being seen but definitely will be felt. It is called discretionary spending, and it is our prerogative. The tactical concentration of resources and the creative application of proven techniques reverse-engineered and effectively used against us can also be effectively used for us.

Hostage negotiators seek to humanize hostages to captors, making them compassionate and reluctant to harm the hostages. The most prevalent is self-identifying with the hostages and reflecting on their similarities to elicit empathy from the captors. They must be made to see themselves in you or see your similarities in themselves. Lima syndrome techniques can be used effectively towards those not hopelessly entrenched in their ideology or stance. It encourages empathy for those they have wronged, inflicted harm upon, or suppressed.

Their injustice is their shame which they feel compelled to resolve by civilized impulses of compassion. The same technique can reverse bigoted social engineering to reject racism and instill a more socially compassionate affinity for equality. Conversion of the ideologies and perspectives of people must hold a more significant enticement to change old thoughts rather than adhere to them. The logic of change instead of the irrational stubbornness of bigotry. First by converting and disproving their antiquated bias beliefs through their realization.

Next by instilling a genuine voluntary acceptance of the change where their hurtful actions become vile, distasteful, and regrettable to themselves. It must be voluntary because changes not aligned with people's core beliefs result in resistance as a survival mechanism as if they were personally attacked. This personal attack is then internally mutated by defensively confirming those thoughts and actions to reconcile their beliefs as justified. Therefore, any required change must be a self-revelation where an acceptance or realization transforms those actions and attitudes into a separate set of core beliefs aligned with a new perspective.

The concept of addition by subtraction seems counter-intuitive. Still, much can be gained by what is taken away or eliminated. It is far more challenging to remove and replace a thought than to place it there initially. In this regard, social engineering must be addressed as it relates to the perpetuated racial inferiority or superiority complexes. Spreading these complexes must be prevented, reducing the ratio of people who learn, are taught, display, or are made to feel either.

Repetition and reinforcement of these concepts led to their prevalence. When reversed, it can also lead to these concepts being rejected. Time and patience utilizing reverse socialization of the propagation of these concepts presents an opportunity for an overwhelming insertion of a preferred concept. It also provides the absence of the unwanted concept leading to the extinction of the unwanted behavior. Like potty training, it instills a level of widely acceptable, socially compelling, and enduring conditioning at an early age to be practiced throughout life.

Aside from the many psychological and behavioral modification techniques available, procedural adjustments can be similarly effective on institutional and structural entities. These organizations are entirely comprised of people operating within those systems. They are either governed, restricted, or compelled by some parameter of conduct or procedural mandate despite their personal preferences. Adjustments can be implemented when and where an understanding of their protocols, mandates, and operations are utilized to ensure adherence to those guidelines.

Intimate knowledge and understanding of these parameters can nullify, neutralize, restrain, or mobilize their resources for our purposes. Conflict is short-sighted when others can do the heavy lifting for our purpose by the design of their systems. For example, resources can be either used for our protection or against us. It depends on how we influence or maneuver their interpretation of our actions and intent. Let their muscle support our objective against any known antagonist intent, as the national guard did for school desegregation in the fifties and sixties. Changing our methods requires a responding change in their tactics or approach.

Case in point, to lessen the possibility of conflict and be equally effective, refrain from a massive crowd assembled in one place. A mass assembly shuts them down, but a disbursed assembly prevents them from shutting us down. Without a specific practical agenda for our collective assembly it is not tactical or practical. To spread their resources, we must spread our enticement. Our mass assembly results in their assembly as a stronger, more fortified consolidated force. However, to dissipate their strength, we disperse their response and organization by separating our assembly.

Peaceful assembly locations should be carefully chosen, and agendas precisely directed and fully understood, with contingency plans against conduct clearly undermining our purpose. There must be no tolerance for egos, flexing, insults, emotions, or agent provocateurs. Only our confirmed objectives and goals calculated for conveyance to negotiate precise solutions. Our concerns should only be addressed by those with the authority to remedy them.

Any conduct while assembled under our flag reveals whether you are with us or for yourself, in which case unwanted activity damages our purpose. Our protest must occupy the high ground morally, intellectually, and geographically to move separately but in coordination while converging collectively into a specific purpose and method to achieve that purpose. Disbursement into smaller crowds that spread opposing resources and divide their command demonstrates our clear, peaceful intentions. It minimizes herd mentality on both sides and communicating our message can become more sustainable and direct.

If a breakdown occurs, it is isolated to that location and not descend into collective chaos like a massive assembly. Law enforcement has to respond to any protest as a contingency and paid captive audience. So instead of yelling, insulting, or confronting them, why not try to convert them or at least salvage the ones who may find themselves marginalized within their own ranks. Those sympathetic to our protest and objective will not oppose us if tactical diplomacy is used. It is a marketing opportunity since they cannot leave, and exposure to our ideology cannot be avoided.

This time and opportunity can be used for them to hear or see our message and promote it in places we cannot. By the same measure, the key is not conflict, but if not conversion, then their expense and attrition. The more they stand there, the larger the expenditure becomes until it becomes too much on the city budget. City officials will want to negotiate a resolution because law enforcement will also complain and protest their conditions and attrition. It will then become a matter of wasted resources and weakened morale. Law enforcement, city officials, and the city council can be required to meet with the public in any number of safe environments.

We can then put a name and face with a promise or proposed action at that time. The police department must always accept complaints, investigate them, and give a disposition to the submitting complainants, which can become overwhelming. Churches, schools, community centers, and government facilities can all be utilized for community events and meetings with officials. If they can't come to us, we can always peacefully assemble and go to them or meet them in the ballot booth. Fortunately, systems and resources are always susceptible to being inundated and incapacitated.

Eliminating the overseer, occupying force, and adversarial culture of law enforcement's mentality to be above the people they serve is crucial to better policing. Changing the officer's expectations within the department to be less statistically driven as the basis for the court system, jails, and general fund revenue generation. Additionally, training needs to be directed at mental and psychological options for compliance, self-control under fearful or stressful situations, and de-escalation techniques that simulate reality. Indeed, a different type of training and increased training is in order.

Also, reevaluating the cause and criteria for enforcement. By engaging the political and legal process at the municipal, county, and state levels we can change their composition and processes. Targeting the city charters, county operations, and state laws to mandate more accountability and transparency discourages many instances of abuse. The other component to remove abuses is to actively remove those who obstruct or violate the intent or equal application of the law.

City Charters can make the Police Chief accountable to the public, not to the mayor. However, the mayor is always accountable to the public. So, in essence that makes the Police Chief vicariously subjected to public discretion. The law contains many remedies that are not currently utilized or aligned with the people's will. The political structure of this country is established upon majority rule, even if that majority is slight.

If and when we have the majority we must leverage our advantage. Therefore, the path forward seems clear, we must keep what has served us well in the past. Embrace that which reveals itself to be effective moving forward. Discard that which has yet to produce the desired results. The use of technology, emails, and social media are powerful tools to disseminate protocols, actions, protest, and objectives.

Information is the new currency, and collective education is the manner of transport to expose the iniquities of history and the needed corrections now and in the future for advancement. Voting is the leverage and overt demonstration to generate consideration, if not change. The objective must be sustained beyond the sacrifices made for change. It must remain elevated above the method of the objection with the message superseding the messenger. When distortions are made possible, it is no longer the message of the messenger but propaganda to dilute its conveyance.

Therefore, all concerned are welcome to be agents of change under this directive that reduces harm to the integrity of our concerns. We must practice policy-driven protest, not random emotional exhibitions of rage or extortion. Unfortunately, some more effectively utilized methods, such as voting, are contingent on legislative and social circumstances subject to partisan subversion. However, we must amend our methods to adjust to the opposition's techniques.

The development and implementation of effective alternative methods impervious to being easily undermined must be employed. In addition, seditious forces endeavor to legislate and criminalize specific actions to abolish or lessen their use and effectiveness by making it more difficult to protest, vote, or by alleging violations. Laws proposed as countermeasures to suppress voting and protest have been indicated or announced. Usually, by gerrymandering, labeling it unlawful, or treating it as riot-inducing activity to prohibit the lawful exercise of our rights.

Suppose the attempted overthrowing of elections and the government were not too farfetched. In that case, we must not be lulled into believing we are immune from direct efforts to neutralize social justice efforts. These attacks will probably be linked to First Amendment Rights and biased interpretation of its use if voter suppression fails. Among the many disparities is one of Black people being unarmed and ill-prepared to survive under less-than-optimal conditions. The extremes to which we can anticipate opposition should not be minimized, including blatant vigilante force reminiscent of the past.

Resorting to the Second Amendment will lurk as a threat of recourse if we persist beyond the prescribed conciliatory submission to the status quo evoking terror. Make no mistake that a radical fraction exists, not restrained by reason or compassion. There are those radically intent on revolution by civil war to preserve racism under the cloak of patriotism, religion, and conservative protections. On January 6, 2021, an attack was made on the Capitol by anarchists hell-bent on imposing their Confederate allegiance, suppressing social objectives as woke, and obstructing the incoming administration.

McCarthyism of the 1950s has been reincarnated as Trumpism by subversion and treason, causing a racially enchanted stupor of fear and ignorance. We are not equipped for revolution by force and should not be so inclined or baited. If the choice is not ours, then self-defense has been chosen for us. However, the chaos of it moves us farther away from our goals. On the contrary, the times are ideal for evolution, with the circumstances ripe for the proper strategic approach that illustrates the absurdity of racist ideology.

The surgical attainment of our prime objectives should aspire to minimal exposure and maximum benefit. With that in mind, adaptation and progression do not have to be glacier, but it will take some time and sustained effort. To survey the factual landscape and assess the most effective course of action, we first must control our emotions and remain reasonable about the sequence and scope of our goals. We cannot succumb to the emotional compulsion to express our frustrations through destructive methods that yield only a release of anger but limited results.

Instead, a military mind and approach are needed. They must not rely on violence or force but on a tactical strategy. Our use of violence or force in the form of civil unrest and civil disobedience, as it is termed, has minimal long-term effect. It is usually localized at best and a squander of human resources at worst. The butcher's tools generate casualties and opposition by employing force and confrontation. Their reaction is to reply with strong-armed suppression. Evolution is the tool of the maestro akin to a chess mastermind anticipating their move and checkmating them by outmaneuvering the opposition and manipulating their action by intellectual persuasion and strategy.

Direct confrontation and engagement must be critically weighed as a course of action. Many of our methods have historically been the same, and support for them has waned along with the results. Consequently, examining their obvious weaknesses exposes new paths to success in need of pursuing. We must logically analyze our available moves and the playbook against us for vulnerabilities and deficiencies that require improvement. Their ideological numbers have weakened. Ours have been strengthened but should not exclude contributions of those willing but unable or situationally restricted.

For example, some have aged out of active protest in the streets. However, they can still significantly contribute if an avenue for participation remains within their capabilities. The same holds for adolescents who can contribute in their own particular way or persons who would need to remain anonymous for their own preservation. Anyone who would love to contribute if provided a way. All hands on deck, contributing what and how they can.

The racist or conservative values' ideology has to be exposed for what it is and the lack of inclusion of some who support it. Some do not realize they are not included in that ideology except for helping achieve a goal that will discard them. Some are even the Clayton Bigsby's among them. Some conservatism is rooted in the puritan past and influenced by racism. It does not include alternative lifestyle choices, gender roles that are not male-dominated, interracial relationships, immigrants who do not look white, and more. These are the fractional ideological divisions and vulnerabilities which needs exposing.

The 2020 election and the strategy utilized are symbolic of the horizontal attack on a vertical establishment. It proved the legs can be removed to make the head fall. The divide-and-conquer tactics that have been so effective against us, redirected against the social intimidation used to sustain the stain of racism, can also topple this system of discrimination. Change is inevitable by isolating racism's systemic methods and motivations, compelling revision for society's benefit. Bigots wither and are ostracized isolated from the broader acceptance of change.

The implosion of maintaining their discriminating ideology will collapse when starved for an outlet. The pen must be mightier than the sword, and the briefcase more effective than brute force to have their incentive redirected for our purposes. The prototype is to build a horizontal coalition targeting as many local gatekeepers as possible, from the school boards to the city council. The infrastructure that governs them by vote, city charters, or other legislation can either change their policy, personnel, or function. It also promotes the compromise needed for our redress.

The shifting demographics of those by their designation whose specific interest would more closely align with our objectives for fairness or their benefit has grown. The number of those who would oppose or actively resist has diminished when put into the context of supporting racial and economic oppression. Focusing on the horizontal social foundation is where the legal changes will be more attainable and extensively affected at the grassroots level.

However, new socio-economic norms not constricted by race, gender, or other forms of discrimination will require more vertical institutional infiltration and persuasion. It would be regrettable not to fully benefit from this diametrical shift of ideologies spreading across the board. Confronting this plague of racism that has persisted for centuries has spilled out into the open. Therefore, we cannot refuse to update our strategy conducive to achieving meaningful change.

There was extreme civil unrest in 2020 as clashes of ideology and incendiary incidents and practices occurred. However, that certainly seems less of the case in 2021 regarding social justice, although incidents continue to erupt. We cannot use the same method of protest for friend and foe, for allegiance and disdain. If this Biden administration is so inclined, the chance to benefit us from the highest levels of government should be unencumbered by behavior that undermines their efforts or strengthens the opposition. It effectively frees us to focus on others or areas of more specific complimentary gains.

By demonstrating their actions and those appointed by them in 2021 and 2022, they have demonstrated more willingness toward fairness than we have been recently accustomed. So let us do our business while they do their business unencumbered by each other and in support and coordination towards a mutual objective. We can use all the help we can get and cannot afford to squander our allies or resources by our emotional behavior or lack of logical strategy. The struggle for social justice, equality, and equity is fought on many fronts by many methods.

The most inflammatory reason for recent unrest is law enforcement's excessive force and misconduct. Many protests are in response to the loss of life of our brothers and sisters by law enforcement. The aggrieved family gets constantly bombarded with reminders of their loss and at times it is exploited for reasons other than their loss. They deserve closure and resolution reflective of the pain they have endured. We need to provide the progress to help minimize their loss and provide some measure of comfort.

So, let us not get too wrapped up in our anger to exacerbate their pain without achieving the progression needed to result in honoring

THEIR loss. We must embrace their well-being and ensure they are provided for while we claim our actions are on their behalf. Our actions cannot disregard their wishes or not empathize with their circumstances and grief. Their loss is not a commercialized or self-aggrandizing opportunity for others but for their support.

Remember, it is about their families, their loss, and the protest collectively, not us individually releasing anger or gaining fame. We must remain diligently respectful of their loss. Any self-aggrandizing, profiteering, or sullying behavior has to be blasted. United, we must stand erect, consolidated in purpose, and with integrity to demonstrate our convictions, the family's justice, and demand accountability.

Prevailing by using a strategy of war tactics applied to peaceful thought processes guiding social movements that reflect a methodical approach. The logical application of our perspectives and resources is not to create conflict but to create evolution and progression. They are designed to minimize conflict and self-inflicted collateral damage while rationally ensuring success in overcoming obstacles. Our method dictates our success. Again, the perspective of tactical protest is wisest when there is an objective to everything that is done, not demonstrations of emotional outbursts.

So, the question is, will we end some of this nonsense or wait for others with less incentive? Their bidding must not be done by us to support any justifications that are detrimental or jeopardize our mission. The mission or objective is the flag which matters more than the flag bearer, to be carried forward without compromise regardless of the flag bearer or opposition. Not all who protest join for change, some exercise hysteria, not protest. Remember, protest is not defined by confrontation but by resolving legitimate grievances.

Still, focusing on the problem can't be allowed to obscure how we obtain unconditional solutions. We must not continue to consider ourselves as other but included as the same. We must not present or consider ourselves as a physical entity but as a kinetic force. If we believe in the transformation of religion, why not our unconditional DNA to the source of religion, the immortality of energy, and the evolution of ideology. The reconstruction of our protest is to radiate the achievement of a symmetrical experience purified of biased distinctions for impartiality. Our method must remain tactically strategic and unified. Likewise, our ideology must be with tactical objectives fully engaged.

We Are The Force, A Social Storm of Change!

Accompanied by the thunder of knowledge.

Propelled by the winds of determination.

Striking with the lightning of revelation.

Washed by the rains of purification.

Ushering in the dawn of a new horizon.

Thurston's Thoughts
Power to the Purpose

When dealing with a problem, it must be identified and examined from a brutally honest perspective considering internal and external influences, the causes, and prevention processes. That which can be controlled and that which cannot. That which is the trigger and that which is the result. The ability to deal with these contingencies builds power and control over yourself and, eventually, the circumstances.

Social justice challenges are fairness, the uniform application of penalty or reward, and access to equal opportunity and prosperity. Four pillars of power converge, significantly impacting social justice objectives. The skillful deployment of each will harvest substantial and deliberate results. They are a focused plan and clear objective, practical protest and effective demonstration, accumulating political power and economic influence, plus stimulating change and sustainable progress.

The method is to first use the path of least resistance when possible, only escalating when that proves to be the most effective alternative and application. Escalating measures can always be deployed, but why use an elephant gun to subdue a fly. The right tool for the right job is needed. Escalation is the last resort of practically exhausted options. Unless escalated against, the preferred method should be to outwit and outmaneuver.

The second consideration is to suffer minimal damage in the process, whatever method is utilized to hit without being hit. Defeat can only come by surrender. However, surrender only comes if our will is broken. The third is to remain determined and resilient once the decision is made but flexible in achieving it. For example, it was said that an invading fleet would burn their vessels once onshore to ensure their commitment to the task and maximum effort. This provides no path for retreating, with victory or demise the only options. So, detecting the vulnerabilities of the challenges positions it for submission by logic or pressure, eliminating its benefit.

No resources are to be squandered or capitulated to recklessness. No engagement should be provoked to cause a forceful reaction. We should only provide responses to engagements deliberately initiated by us or responded to for a specific purpose by picking our battles. Not to be drawn into unfavorable skirmishes. The sequential order of these four pillars is for prioritizing efficiency and effectiveness from a position of strength. More importantly, the foundational plan is designed to ultimately bring about the resulting change for the needed progress.

Focused Plan/ Clear Objective
The first order of business is to stop the begging. It reeks of weakness, lacks initiative sending the wrong intent, and is vague without a specific directive. To be strong, we must be perceived as strong, and then we will be taken seriously. Power is measured by its acknowledgment or dismissal. Power is the equalizer and the motivator as leverage in many situations seeking relief or improvement. So, no doubt gains have been made, but many of the same gains are repeatedly in dispute for lacking power.

Take the Voting Rights Act of 1965. We are still fighting for something supposedly granted and protected back then because its protections should have been permanently mandated. No such dispute can be applied to the women's suffrage movement that rightfully mandated women as voting citizens without future review. It is not repeatedly up for reconsideration or dispute. To secure more gains, we must first secure those repeatedly in dispute but allegedly already rendered.

The placation of our expectations can no longer be compromised by surrogate gestures lacking meaning, intent, or permanence. Once the objective is procured, it must be sealed from future contention. This linear observation certified by irrevocable legislative confirmation must be acknowledged as settled, unquestionable, sustained, and enforced. As time and social awareness have evolved, so should our expectations and tactics, improvising an offensive targeting racism's insidious causes. The previous successful methods and strategies may not be sufficient now.

For too long, we have targeted the symptom and not the cause. Progress has been slow, emphasizing the symptom rather than attacking or eliminating the cause. Without the cause, there is no symptom. The methodical attrition and deliberate actions impacting the cause can either add to elimination or subtract from propagation. The resulting squeeze from both ends will likely produce the most productive results.

The cause is the socialization and psychological predisposition nurturing misconceptions and distinctions based on subjective comparisons. This invites moral evaluations as better or superior instead of different. Differences are then forbidden outside expected conformities or comforting projections of similarities. That is the problem because if there is a preferred difference, the interpretation follows it is better or right by that applied subjective prejudice.

America's racial and social ailments have persisted because of this perspective supported by societal biases and structural foundations maintained by those indoctrinated by its ills protecting its social purpose. However, ideology within the system often conceals and suppresses the biases' existence and effects on those not subjected to its biased harm. This is where the primary emphasis on changing the systems should be placed, on the people who operate and support them. By doing so, the foundation and indoctrination are neutralized before it is entrenched to replenish, corrupt, or preserve the system.

Thereby both ends can be stricken, the source and the consequence. The socialization and psychological justification produced by the ideology utilized racism, religion, and morality to solidify exploitation. Ever since, it has been incorporated into every facet of the truths believed to be self-evident, namely the delusion of white racial superiority and privileged entitlement. How could the resulting structure deviate from the founding father's blueprint approving racial inequality? As time has progressed, it has become indistinguishable from ordinary discourse.

That normalcy must be rejected, but to do so rocks society to its core perception and operation. Clinging to the fallacies of historical racial calibrations is the direct consequence of refusing to denounce or change them. Accordingly, they persist, and so do the many misconceptions of white self-characterizations. An unprecedented avalanche of societal critique has led to the current social unrest and political upheaval. It has crossed a major national threshold that has breached this characterization, compelling change and fair consideration outside of whiteness.

The leverage is reasoning and knowledge used to influence perspectives overpowering misconceptions driving change to reject primitive social conditionings that defy logic or morality. The resources and energy concentrated and applied effectively leave the least damaging footprint since damage is not our objective when amassing influence and power to effect change. The bull in an antique shop or butcher rather than a surgical approach may be effective eventually but is rarely the preferred method of efficiency or practicality.

Using economic patronage, technological message dissemination, and moral indignation to denounce, expose, or oppose injustices have moved beyond physical confrontation to efficiently exploiting ideological defects. An accelerated expulsion of racial fallacies initiates a transformation of perspective by logical examination. Contemplatively and empirically the conversion to fairness and equality would essentially reject white's attachment to its value of superiority by the misguided association of color.

Some will be incapable of accepting this transformation of the only truth they have ever known, conditioned and socially convinced psychologically of its validity. This psychologically devastating devaluing of their racial advantage must be considered a factor in opposition to any transition. A new reality requires adjustments to previous realities where a cycle of fallacies supported each prior and subsequent fallacy. To break the cycle, the fallacy must be disrupted.

Social unrest is the combustive reaction to frustration and resistance to that disruption. They must hear the roar if they do not hear the whisper. So, in many ways, social unrest has been necessary to get the necessary attention, but it is inefficient. Cajolery invites voluntary resignation but coercion festers resentment until the time is once again ripened to rebel. This has been the case with lingering discrimination and the simmering confederacy as history lessons of obstructions to achieving permanent progression.

Lessons learned using the current public recognition of systemic ramifications to alter the racial imbalance would seem wise. By revealing discrepancies, distaste for practices and policies are morally galvanized against the country's prejudiced past. Consequently, re-socialization is the answer. In addition to the opposition's re-socialization, we would have to undergo our own re-calibration forsaking our instinctive compliances and dysfunctional behavior.

A concerted and relentless initiative directed properly undoubtedly exacts change. Still, it is enhanced by our refusal to participate or further any pursuit counterproductive to our advantage. All parts of the strategy and objective must move independently but in coordination, merging collectively to achieve the purpose. While we cannot rely on others' provisions, moral or otherwise, we also can not invite opposition where none exists.

Some will not enter the fray and should not be invited, decreasing resistance by default or neutrality by choice. Empowering an adversary only weakens us, contrary to the necessity to remain steadfast in our convictions. The methods to achieve that conviction should not hinder its success. Consolidating active and passive support and assembling resources and allies as supporting assets best positions our objective for success. Operating indiscriminately from frustration or anger defeats the likelihood of attracting concerned collaborators by offending their sensibilities, unintended consequences, or collateral damage.

Anger obscures reason, inhibits negotiations, and is unsustainable over time as cohesive and concentrated intent to achieve lasting and definitive results with quantifiable identifiers. So adaptive tactics and techniques should be developed to minimize collateral damage, enlist demographics outside our own, and accumulate resources for sustainable progress and unrelenting change. Varied methods of persuasion should be deployed first to attain voluntary and conciliatory consensus accumulating a diverse coalition of supporters.

Suppose the goal is fairness and non-oppression of liberties. In that case, the uniting persuasion should consolidate like causes and like minds. The causes have the same basis, combating socializations demonstrated as biased tendencies spanning the gamut of intolerances and victims. Historically, friends can often be made when they share a common enemy, in this case, an ideology of prejudice and exclusion. The apparent strategic vulnerability rest with the ideology's socialization before the system can be toppled. Otherwise, same game, a different name, and unresolved blame.

Practical Protest/ Effective Demonstration
When a protest is fueled by anger, it is likely to result in conflict. When the reaction is fashioned by intolerance, conflict is expected. When both anger and intolerance are present, then conflict is usually inevitable. Protest subjected to a conflict should produce a clear ambition and a victorious objective. Protest, by definition, doesn't have to be confrontational. It only has to be effective, a statement, or disruptive as an observable or conveyed objection.

Peaceful protest is inconsistent with a demand for redress by its passive nature. Only Blacks and hippies subscribe to peaceful protest for change as a submissive form of obedient discord. However, violent protest invites retaliation, so our people were relegated to turning the other cheek so it could get swollen too. Not advocating violent or destructive protest but determined resistance un-flinching in the face of adversity or self-preservation.

Understand that adversity is woven into the process accordingly to the degree of change sought and the opposition to it. Protest is termed demonstration as a contradiction because the demonstration is showing our cards of dissatisfaction instead of making our move a tactical objection for creating change. Protest should be for the corrective action, not the complaint's display of emotional begging. Destruction is an emotional reaction to frustration lacking remedial substance.

However, as a statement of emotions it parades a forceful or fearful exclamation. Emotional release is the most inefficient implication of protest and least satisfactory long-term if it results in the exact repetition of that frustration. The problem is still unsolved despite the emotional charade or patronizing acknowledgment. Unregulated emotions create exhaustion and further frustration instead of invit-ing reevaluation of the protest method. The methods must be im-provised using the right technique for the right circumstances.

The protest ideology to achieve an objective cannot be a show of might when the might rests with the opposition. It must be an act of subterfuge with selective demonstrations for calculated impact. The infiltration of resistance to impede their functionality is preferable to a combative assault when at a disadvantage. That is why espi-onage is so effective where war is not. The psychology of guerrilla warfare applied to political initiatives and social protest enacting concealed methods with obvious intent lessens an effective re-sponse.

Using various effective methods of protest with elements of sur-prise or unorthodox tactics, remaining preemptive, and forcing a predictable response by reflex manipulates the course of events into a trap. Logical maneuvering does not necessarily involve direct al-tercation but avoids unnecessary harm by strategic and analytical application of engagement. Each action or engagement is calculated for future positioning, implementation, and gains. The flexibility of efficiently deployed methods will increase their impact and resiliency to withstand collapse.

Methods must be used to separate and isolate opposition challenging their specific motivation and cohesion. Summarily removing the incentive with viable options encouraging inevitable change instead of conflict. But, it requires a military mentality while playing psychological chess. The issues must be highlighted and articulated by the actions taken, not so much defined by the individuals taking them. The individual can only be the objective when transcending the cause as the catalyst.

The individuals are moving targets and forever changing, only replacing a different perpetrator performing the same action. Attack the action, whereas the individual is the distraction. Just as our leadership must remain secondary to our goals, although they are valuable, they can also be forever changing. When the goal is primary, it remains unchanged by the changing of leadership. Subsequently, the goal remains until achieved without interruption. The primary focus and objective remain, dismantling the seminal instrument that plagues us.

Moving beyond protest to redefining our leadership to aggressively confront racism not as an act of nonviolence but as an act of declaration and assured expectation is long overdue. Begging discredits our intent and resolve when fairness is not optional nor negotiable but required. Racism's shame and disgust cannot be discounted or minimized when the actions, processes, and structures continue to prolong injustices. At the same time, we are strung along with hopeful possibilities, prayerful expectations, and eternal promises.

Possibilities, expectations, and promises must materialize as results. Ultimately the confrontation of racism's reality is the protest's results. Exposing the sheer disgust and making the rejection of racism more palatable to the soul are incremental to results. Although the ultimate change remains in the socialization of the population, the systems must be audited for discriminatory practices and corrected. Tangible practicalities, not fanciful pledges, are the unilateral transactional appeasements quantifiably accumulated.

Temporary or limited results will no longer be sufficient or pacified by holidays or promises. Change is uncomfortable, so it must be made more painful not to change. Therefore, evolution must be preferable to revolution, choosing improvement over injustice as a matter of humanity, morality, economics, politics, and national survival. Likewise, the caterpillar stretches beyond its cocoon into awareness and comfort beyond the restrictions of its previous reality, and so must society. Through evolution, the caterpillar is destined to become a butterfly.

Otherwise, it will never reach its fruition for survival and perishes within the confines of its tomb. So has the encasement of America by racism that has prevented it from fulfilling the promise and possibility of its greatness and humanity in concept and deed. Abandoning unjustifiable oppression would seem as necessary as the oppression is indefensible simply as a matter of humanity. So, America remains at the crossroad regressing and repeating the transgressions to salvage denial, thereby prolonging racism's application.

The recollection of the brutal nature of prejudice and its defense horrifies the sensibilities attempting to deny, disassociate, or suppress its damage. But, this realization must be confronted as a therapeutic rejection of its furtherance by admitting, identifying, and discontinuing its impact. Suppressing facts of atrocities associated with history or actions committed provokes shame only when refusing liability. It diminishes their self-image not by being too humiliating to admit or accept responsibility but by refusing to take corrective actions.

By avoiding acknowledgment, no one can pretend this is not a reality needing correction, it will continue to fester. The systemic privileges favoring whites often prevent them from feeling how it disfavors others. This is narcissistic human nature at best and racism at its worse, which, by its fragility, resists needed change and deflects the elephant in the room as invisible. Effective protest and complete examination expose these privileges, brutalities, and fallacies put on full display.

Denial is no longer a refuge from either atonement, willful resemblance, or privileged association. On the other hand, perhaps the revolting nature of reality has led to unconscious repression to protect their self-image and preserve their indoctrination. The mind can often easily reject what it knows to be true, even if it is painfully obvious. Either way, they are defense mechanisms that would explain the unreasonableness of ignoring racism, pretending it no longer exists. Yet, at the same time, it is openly hidden in plain view and conspicuously practiced.

The internalized fear caused by the guilt and shame evoked by association rejects reality and history. So maybe racism should be addressed as a group dynamic exhibiting psychological dysfunction. Racism, superiority, and for that matter, phobias are classified as psychological disorders to varying degrees. The schism of mind, society, and perspective played out as a distortion refusing to participate in reality. This distortion preserves the social status and self-image by fabricating alternative justifications, perceptions, and perspectives.

The fight or flight mechanism is triggered when stirred by reality, resulting in resistance and denial. The strategic approach to racism engaging the fundamental cause might be better protested and demonstrated by a mental health and awareness approach exposing its absolutely ridiculous basis. Revelations of the ideological and emotional instigators prelude the physical and visual display. The conditioned mentality initiates the racist demonstration provoking oppression, suppression, or aggression. The threat of either are the traditional tools of intimidation.

Physical conflict and destruction is an impulsive primitive reaction where either violence is impetuous or self-restraint is abandoned.

Anything out of control risks damage to whomever or whatever it contacts, intentional or not. It is also a conditioned behavior we refined from its use against us. The precision of an ideological and psychological approach is overwhelmingly needed for transformational change of those resistant to social progress.

Expanding the amendable demographic is not a novel idea. It has been used against our people for centuries by concentrated manipulation. That is how we arrived at this point, so reversing it as concerted persuasion produces the opposite effect. The demographic afflicted by racism has descended to a level where they feel threatened under the guise of their liberties being attacked not by population, but by the tumbling numbers of racist. It is an indication when they cry out that they feel the intense winds of change storming their resistance to bend or be broken.

The dwindling of racism given oxygen incites a blaze that will grasp any opportunity for survival by responding with anger and outrage with desperate times calling for desperate measures. So desperate to even mangle democracy and the law once again. Now spinning out of control, attacking what once protected them is a desperate act of last resort. The civil unrest and protest for social justice, peaceful or otherwise, trembled their racist nucleus. It agitated an insurrection on the Capitol and seat of America's government when disillusioned fearing the lack of their racist protection.

So let their heads jump time while further illustrating an irrational, dysfunctional break from the inevitable reality of fairness and equality dawning. Extraordinary lengths consumed by desperation reflect a seismic shift well underway toward what they fear the most, the removal of their advantage by fair play. Monumental change is by revolution, but the evolution of revolution is to implement new non-destructive ways to obtain this change. Progress will render racist obsolete.

The battle waging for social justice is for awareness, inclusion, and unbiased liberties versus the dysfunctional and biased exclusionary element promoting the status quo. Same story interpreted by a different generation producing an enlightened conclusion for an unbiasedly tolerant outcome. However, society will no longer silently tolerate or accommodate bigotry under forced conservative values and lies, whether it is racism, sexism, and any other phobia or ism.

Conservative values, when forced, violate the right to freely choose values as they were allowed to choose theirs. This violation is contrary to assertions of supporting freedom. Force and hate are often companions. Hate consumes the hater first and attempts to infect others next. Under these circumstances, hatred and control become the prevailing recourse, outraged by the courage of those who are different or choose differently outside the conventional standard of conformity or conservatism.

The coward's mentality must be understood, feigning bravery to conceal fear and weakness. The majority's cowardice manipulation forces others to be fearful of deviating from the path of conformity. Deviation risks loss of acceptance and resentful punishment. Courage to resist is either a display of insanity, invite of condemnation, or defamatory abnormality. Since they lack the courage of self-determination and independent thinking, shackled by a crowdsourcing mentality, how dare you differ. By condemning differences and individuality outside their conditioned similarities of cowardice, obedience conceals their weakness.

It is a behavioral disorder expressing buried insecurities attempting to elevate and validate their self-worth. It is a dissociative disorder disguising envy as outrage. Being governed by consensus, they are envious of any refusal to submit. They despise those with the courage to be different despite peer disapproval and being socially shunned. Despising those daring enough not to be controlled by others' conditioned judgments and expectations. Their cowardice is on full display. Being understood for what it is, jealousy of any courageous disregard for conformity, daring to be different, to be you, to be free.

Condescending judgement can confine the mind to a rigid reality that cannot break free from its narrow projection. However, the unapologetic demonstration of self-expression is the ultimate protest. When you are busy being yourself, you have no desire to control someone who is being themselves, extending the same courtesy afforded you. Instead, being controlled by constraints and expectations compels them to control someone else by those exact limitations, becoming judgmental of you for not conforming as they did.

They secretly despise your courage as inversely offensive similar to the morality of racism, although the difference poses no harm to them. Likewise, how could someone's skin tone alone pose any threat, black, white, or otherwise? Microcosmically what they resent is their discomfort of differences. Differences allowed and similarities realized prevents distinctions used for bias exclusion and tainted judgment. Protesting this nonsense with illustrations of its irrationality, isolating and disrupting its shared patterns and perceptions, or galvanizing opposition discourages the benefits of its assimilation.

Participation in preventing injustices sometimes requires contribution from people and places inaccessible or more convincing by proximity to reach the crevices of resistance we cannot. Shrinking the equality disparity and expanding the perspective of tolerance and consideration requires new shoes for a new journey and taking new steps toward furthering progress. Judge not superficially least ye be judged superficially and perhaps harshly. Display and develop the understanding to promote the change. As such, we are the polarity of our protest and declaration.

Political Power/ Economic Influence
Throughout history, there have always been three considerations that governed human events and influenced or sanction religion. They have been political power, economics, or control. They are socially intertwined and self-promoting but also complimentary. The three kinds of political power supposedly have a distinct sepa-

ration by law in America. They are executive, legislative, and judicial.

The redistribution of power and wealth often does not stray too far from their statutory influence. If we want to get in the game, be a player in the game, or win in the game, we must learn how to play the political game well. It is like multi-level chess, where a move on one level must be accounted for on another, always having implications beyond its own level. The four levels are municipal, county, state, and federal.

Every level has an influential person, a big fish in a small pond on its own level. However, when that small pond influential person moves to the next level, they become a small fish swimming with bigger fish in a bigger pond who are more influential. Essentially existing on an echelon or lower level only in service of a higher level. As the pond moves to a river, then a lake to an ocean, there is a succession of boss of bosses or the big cheese. But even the cheese is subject to influences.

The political system is similar, constantly feeding a larger body with more powerful players having further-reaching authority and influence. This is the key to our political empowerment controlling the small pond, which is our communities and expanding to affect city and county leadership. That base expands to state and federal representation, not necessarily based on race but political interest. In this scenario, promoting our interest takes precedence over race. Consequently, it seems they are often the same, where our race promotes our interest more frequently but it is not necessarily true.

Still, we can change behavior through political empowerment. That is why voter suppression and gerrymandering are critical to controlling voting preferences and representation to minimize our influence. By dissipating our voting power, it diminishes our progress and prosperity. This is where the focus must shift from the individual's indoctrination to the systemic and structural inclinations. The building materials and management tendencies must be addressed before we can address the system manager operating as prescribed by the structure.

Changes in the political systems most effectively and efficiently targeted should be directed towards the systems that directly impact our objective and relief. In many instances, this is a bottom-up approach at the local, county, and state levels. Not neglecting efforts on the federal or executive levels to affect change but producing an impact from the bottom and the top. The foundational level of politics is the municipal level, following home rule and loosely adhering to the regulations of higher levels of government, most notably the legislative and judicial.

The legislative branch makes the laws governing the land. It sets the standard to be adhered to in a hierarchy of continuity. Therefore, anything can be legislated in or out of practice. The judicial branch interprets the law, its application, and its constitutionality. The criminal and civil courts comprise the judicial system for punishment and redress. The judicial system has two objectives which are protecting citizens' rights and interpreting the law. All parties work on behalf of the government except the defense attorney.

So the deck is automatically stacked in favor of the system against change. The judicial branch at the highest levels is appointed, not elected. The manipulation is injected by the ideology of the appointer and the interpretations held by the appointees. That is why conservatives must stack the Supreme Court's ideology with perspectives and interpretations that last decades. The short-term ability to change the law is hindered by this process. Obligated to the predisposition of the placeholders and the ideology that placed them there.

Even with elected officials due to set terms, they are discouraged from actions and decisions outside their political party or support base. The undue influence of party politics, money, lobbying, and campaign opposition magnify selfish motives to hang onto power and prestige, making any change equally tricky. The ability to affect the appointments or elections bypasses change. It reinforces the status quo unless the influencer is for change.

That is the strength and vulnerability of the system, the Achilles heel. Grassroots-induced change starts with the municipal and City Council level providing a refuge on the most immediate level that affects us. Then, by resolutions, ordinances, and city charters, control can be exerted over specific actions, policies, and processes as a matter of policy, procedure, and statute. Municipal or City Code sets the practices and legality of procedures by adopted resolutions or passed ordinances.

The mayor is in an elected position that should reflect the sentiments of those they represent, not just political or business interests. The Police Chief is usually appointed by the mayor, so the mayor should be held accountable for displeasure with the Police Chief or police department's performance. The Police Chief serves at the mayor's discretion and can be changed at any time for any reason. The County Sheriff is also usually elected along with the County Administrators. We hold them accountable by vote, transparency, and public pressure.

Supposedly, all elected positions are accountable to the public. So, why are they allowed to persist if not for lack of voter turnout, an abundance of voter indifference, or a majority of consent? The referendum of the voting public either sanctions or rejects according to our degree of indulgence. Protesting in the streets with rhyming slogans is less effective than exercising these referendums and doesn't require begging, being assaulted, or being granted concessions.

The majority vote in the next city council or municipal vote settles any dispute by the ballot. A valid petition is another way to address concerns and preferences by legislative and judicial decree. Protest and demonstrate by your vote and influence to persuade others to vote for a more equitable system by statutory resolution. This addresses the system while deterring conduct and persons who oppose it, but it too, must be vigorously enforced.

County court acts in the name of the State, usually under the Court of Common Pleas or some similar designation. It deals with all felony violations of the law and civil grievances. Its judges, for the most part, are elected. Understanding the function and composition of these legal and governing bodies exposes how they can work for us or against us. It is insufficient to bemoan the process and function when they result from deliberate guidance as a symptom of the procedures, laws, and determinations that direct them.

These systems work according to the structures and influences comprising them, the interpretation of those who operate them, and our tolerance or indifference. The vast degree of discretion or interpretation allows a subjective application. It is often in line with biases for or against a particular disposition when the selected criteria yields that result. Law enforcement is the arm to enforce social norms. However, social norms disguised as the law or community policing at times unjustly regulate and inflate problems where biased solutions can be employed.

But, rather than adjust to changing needs, methods, and circumstances, they prefer to equate change with defunding the police and restricting their authority. Law enforcement is not immune from change or the law, just as no one else. The need for them is great, but so is the need for them to change. Consequently, many will leave law enforcement ranks when brought to accountability, complaining that their hands of injustice are tied. Bemoaning their inability to do the job, outraged by the audacity to restrict their misdeeds and rogue conduct.

Law enforcement should police themselves to avoid broad indiscriminate condemnation. Bad apples should not receive the same consideration as good apples. They only taint the whole barrel or profession. The refusal to police themselves has gradually eroded their prestige and credibility. So, the blame lies within their ranks and power. The governmental and legal systems configure public policy, perceptions, and ethics, creating performance patterns and the application of their interpretation, discretion, and resources.

For example, when law enforcement resources are directed primarily at Black or low-income minority communities, the statistics are twisted and used to justify the enforcement practice. Likewise, you can't find crime where you do not look, but it is justified by stating that the resources are directed where they are needed. But, curiously, the economic development is not also directed where it is most needed.

It should be noted that often in these impoverished communities, the crimes are likely created by poverty. Therefore, addressing poverty, opportunity, and viable skills would certainly decrease crime. But keep in mind crime is a big business essential to government revenue and employment. Seldom are the historical and deliberate causes addressed, such as discrimination, lack of opportunity, or poverty.

So statistically, traffic tickets, arrests, searches, force, and violations of rights occur in areas perpetuating the intended systemic conditions. It justifies fear and the enforcement measures taken while compounding the burdens of the underprivileged. It is a system of catch and release or, better, taint and discard by criminality. Just as a plea bargain is presented as a tool for your benefit, it actually benefits the system by freeing it for increased capacity and functionality.

For our people, the disparity in prosecutions, bail amounts, and sentencing is discretionary for assorted rationales that disguise them as standard. This configuration of ambiguous discretion applied to statutory options discreetly supports discrimination, inequality, and also, strangely enough, crime. It is not a function of law enforcement to address these issues but a function of society that defines law enforcement's duties and responsibilities. Many social issues are treated as a criminal matter blurring the lines and overloading the criminal system.

Jail is not the answer for many things in which arrests are made. The legal system avoids overload by presenting plea bargains and bail as relief valves for the operational health of the system. The demands for jury trials, speedy trial, discovery, and rejection of bail would force personnel, housing, medical, and transportation nightmares beyond the system's capacity. It would also stop frivolous charges, biased procedures, and selective applications resulting in a fairer discretionary judgment or alternative considerations to preserve resources.

Briefs and requests for documents alone would bog down the system forcing change to eliminate overcapacity. The politics of policing, tough-on-crime rhetoric, prosecutor's personal ambition, and career-enhancing imbalances without the merit of justice would no longer be an amenity of the system. The abuse of the criminal justice system for enhancing the ego, appeal, popularity, or power of individuals, parties, and politicians could no longer be supported by the weight of its improprieties.

Convincing the public of chaos, stroking fear, stirring emotions of outrage, garnering maniacal support, and being wary of dreadful consequences frightens the public into indifference or submission to extreme measures cloaked as necessary. This is one of the ways excessive force is justified, as danger always lurking, even if not in that particular situation. It stirs the pot, mixing possibility and uncertainty with reality while discarding facts, probability, and reasonable articulation.

It is a control mechanism triggered by fear, unaccountability, and ignorance, promoting conservative values suggesting that crime results from liberal beliefs. State legislatures make most of the criminal laws that affect our communities. City ordinances govern most misdemeanor crimes. Most criminal justice agencies follow some guidelines set by their own internal policies. Each has a protocol or memorandum of operation that they follow as internal regulations.

The public knowing these internal policies and procedures assures if they are adhered to or if they are in violation. The juvenile justice system, housing segregation and financing, board of education and public school systems, and addiction programs are cleverly disguised shelters for bias application and discriminatory practices as social norms. Among them, the violations are rampant as matters of policy and procedure.

At the same time, the racial disparity shows a numerical discrepancy by cursory observation. Accordingly, discrimination as a policy violation is determined by conduct or procedures sometimes reflected in a numerical inconsistency or irregular application. Building horizontal coalitions of shared interest provides eyes, ears, and seats in the room placing our issues on the table present to help make the rules, not just be subjected to them.

Also, assuring that violations are exposed and any lawful duty to maintain integrity is unbroken, thus rejecting unlawful activities and policy violations. Enough is on the books already, but there is a lack of courage and an unwillingness to enforce them with the same vigor as the fundamental social war on crime. Independent review boards, transparency, and auditing activity may be necessary as a balancing and compliance measure.

Society is becoming more racially, politically, and economically polarized under deteriorating caste conditions. It includes unprecedented groups that blame other groups for their decline in prosperity. Fearful discrimination fills the void to deny others by deflecting the source of their loss to another group instead of the greed of a failing system based on control, racism, and exploitation.

The underlying concern for most Americans is the economy and financial uncertainty, which makes people susceptible to agitation and panic. The distraction is socially concocted and promoted to circulate and inflate fears exaggerating primal triggers of scarcity prompting a retreat from civility and order. Meanwhile, resources and wealth are siphoned and hoarded in a hierarchy based on status, feeding off the middle and lower classes. The upper crust continues to party and feast like its 1793 in France while as Marie-Antoinette suggested, for the peoples provisions, let them eat cake.

Stimulating Change/ Sustainable Progress

Change and progress are voluntary even when forced since we can always choose otherwise despite the penalty. Our choice is eliminated only when we seek to avoid the penalty. Some forms of protest fall into this category depending on how the protest achieves the change. The manner achieved impacts its longevity and acceptance.

Lasting change is a self-revelation requiring a concerted effort whereby an acceptance or realization alters attitudes and actions. Thereby, adopting modifications voluntarily for transactional expectations or in exchange for an improvement. Change doesn't always equate with progress and is sometimes a vastly different reality. Change has occurred where progress has not. Conclusively, appraisal of progress is the primary objective to quantify any meaningful change.

The cynic would state that the election of Barack Obama was a precursor or preemptive provocation to unleash and justify the bigotry subsequently displayed while questioning his effectiveness against tremendous opposition. Otherwise captioned, the election of Barack Obama as president was advertised as progress. It was in a specific context, but primarily it was change. The change was the catalyst that signaled progress, causing concern and opposition to the conditions that allowed it to happen. As evidence Mitch McConnell openly boasted of how he personally obstructed the presidency of the Obama administration as his badge of honor.

Analyze the changes and progress made since his election. It will reveal a societal regression or a sum loss to some who feared the racial hurdle and promise of progress signified by his election. President Barack Obama's success in getting elected was a combination of the popularity of his personality and the hope of his message forging a hopeful future. Another main contributor to his electoral success was circumventing the power structure and targeting its vulnerabilities.

The grassroots embraced him, but the establishment resented and obstructed him, vowing to not be outmaneuvered in the future. The previous method of winning a skillful fight would no longer suffice, so a brawl was the only chance against this new reality. So, in totality, regardless of the circumstances of President Obama's election, the aftermath is undeniable regarding the escalation of racial tensions inflamed by his successor. It had its radical appeal and shameless divisiveness flaming racial hostilities not recently openly exhibited.

The rise of racism is poorly disguised as conservative values by Republican politics of latent fears of eliminating discriminatory privileges. It exposes the feeble psychology which has culminated in frantic and fanatical dread of the new reality. No longer comforted by psychologically remaining in the womb under the founding father's protection. The protection has been shattered, and there is fear of a new emerging birth of progression.

So, the birth of progress was delayed, and the efforts to further sabotage it are underway. The blatant demonstrations of racial nostalgia and longing for inequality are last-ditch survival efforts for an existence whose light has dimmed. The resulting dimming has created the fear of uncertainty and loss of identity. It is all a matter of semantics. Equality, fairness, and social justice are micro labeled under humanity or human decency. The implementation and acceptance of compassion towards humanity to deliver atonement is still unable to change the past but affects the future.

But only for those who want to look forward and see the future, not look ahead at the past. The past, whether a memory, a dream, or a nightmare, is gone, consumed by time. The destination of the past has vanished and expired, partitioned off from any longer being a possible reality. History and time has outran the racist narrative, justifications, and ideologies. Yet some brazenly persist in the futility of stuffing the toothpaste back in the tube, freezing time, and social regression to retrofit history's deceptions. The past and current injustices don't have to be future ones.

Venturing into the future unleashed is the promise of what America could be if not under the influence of the caste gatekeepers, greed mongers, and chaos hustlers. A racist narrative had to be resurrected to stir racial tensions to levels not seen since the sixties to attack the nation's gravitation to diversity and a unified racial perspective. The movement to denounce racism was a youth movement and the movement to double down is a conservative old-head attempt to block change and prevent progress.

Feeling threatened by uncertainty equated to an ominous foretelling of change created the atmosphere for the boogeyman. This identifiable enemy to be afraid of is defined as the dark-skinned insistence on change that forebodes equality by stirring awareness of traditional retorts of racism. With two sides to every coin, we know what equality means to us and how much it would change. However, consider the inverse effect on those who have been snuggled by the privileges of inequality. Now we can measure their resistance in context as being just as meaningful to them.

Fear and certainty of doom are illusionary concoctions of the old guard to hold onto power and privilege. It promotes and sponsors the divisiveness needed to stimulate and sustain a prejudicial structure. The refusal to concede equality avoids any equity in sharing the prosperity or suffering while claiming the bulk of prosperity but dispensing the preponderance of suffering. It is like when an older sibling has their way without regard for the younger sibling, who is expected not to challenge the older sibling's authority or suffer the smackdown.

It puts an end to that bullying nonsense when the youngster sprouts, making it no longer a free lunch. So, voluntary recognition of change or a struggle is inevitable. Now the danger is your candy may be taken, or at the very least, your candy taking days are over. So it is with us that the time has come when past actions will no longer be tolerated under the shifting dynamics and outgrown past. The smackdown has become a throwdown. It is time to reimagine and restructure society admitting that the grand experiment called racism has failed despite its social intent and integration.

Its failure was not only due to its principles but to its practices in a so called democratic society of freedom. The decay was baked into the system and should have been removed after the civil war during reconstruction. It was a farce now evident by the number of symbols, policies, practices, depravations, suppressions, and injustices allowed and supported by society and government. This has been hidden in plain sight and worshipped instead of condemned. The rot must be amputated, not treated, because it has been left to fester far too long, endangering the entire democratic body.

The shift in society's diversity of opinions and tolerances has become a threat and motivating factor in supporting change for progress and America's survival. A legitimate reconstruction is required. Social justice and reform require a willingness to consider implications other than yours regarding race and marginalization. Unfortunately, well-intentioned people are sometimes misled and galvanized by the deception orchestrated to propel hidden agendas furthering a divisive purpose.

It should be noted that this ideology and tactic is used across the spectrum of society and politics to increase support by deception. Otherwise not supported or attracted by logic. Often the incentive is to avoid a penalty or accept a concession to maintain the peace, thereby sustaining the effect by acquiescing. Denying diversity and equality ensures an ideological clash, perhaps another civil war, or the republic's collapse.

Resisting adjustments where just practices match just principles will seal America's fate, duplicating the demise of history's greatest civilizations toppled by discord. It is a bleak outcome and a colossal risk. Still, we must be willing to risk that penalty just as they are willing to instigate the cause and consequence to maintain injustice. No measure of destruction is preferred, but our unflinching blink amidst a stare-down is compelled since avoiding the penalty or making a concession has proven averse to our progress.

Once built, if not modernized or evolved, a society decays and dis-order occurs, denigrating into unrest, instability, and self-destruc-tion. Time and circumstance have mandated that the adjustment be made for us rather than once again by us. No more come along to move along. Time for us to make a stand, not for more concessions. So let the patriotic fervor reveal a love of democracy above a love of injustice. If not, it will be at the expense and destruction of what they claim to love so much, America and patriotism. It won't work both ways.

A choice must be made since there can be no return to the level of bigotry historically practiced. The genie is out of the bottle refusing to reenter. Black people have witnessed other group's rights and redress acknowledged for a list of grievances, internments, and wars. Such as the Confederacy, WWI, WWII, and many foreign countries and governments, only for us to be moved backwards in the line. As a kid, they called that sponging, which was not tolerated when you were next in line. We are next in line but should have been first.

It would be wise and prudent to ensure a true Democracy rather than an injustice where there is nowhere to exercise it. Not a threat but an observation that Democracy and America as we know it is doing the stanky leg, wobbling badly from more than just racism. It has ideologically expanded beyond its structure, bursting at the seams. That is not our choice, but we have declared that the racial imbalances will no longer be balanced on our backs.

We are at the bust-out where we cannot submit to these manipulations under penalty, concession, threat, or force. They were the sole purveyors of power and determinants of change in the past, but that is no longer true or acceptable. The cocoon of social consciousness has expanded to see the only remedy is to evolve society. Most of the younger generation gets it, but the old way is stubborn, seeking to corrupt the impressionable.

The young must lead us out of this predicament of discrimination and ignorance for the future they wish to live in as we have lived in ours. Time eventually takes its place and replaces all things through change or expiration. Can most current leaders who were teenagers in the 1950s or 60s expand beyond their social conditioning or possible racial biases to envision future possibilities? It is like the ridiculous assumption that the founding fathers could have predicted the present reality or made provisions for it. Instead, time has passed them by where less restrictive vision should apply. It is time for fresh vision to relieve weary eyes.

Adaptation is the key to survival, and it will be ours too, according to the universal law of evolution. Therefore, we cannot get caught up on color by neglecting the larger context of discrimination and the crushing blow to tumble this resilient giant's history. Progress depends on the plan of attack galvanizing all sufferers of relegation below first-class citizenship and dignity. The same ignorance that wounds them is just a different facet of the same prejudice that harms us. These things that diminish us also diminishes them in a different context but still an injustice.

The battle is essentially outdated clashing with the newly renovated, sometimes it is not a classic, it is just old. It is often systems born of ignorance and intolerance with connectivity to the same ideology or expression, whether it is race, identity, gender, sexual orientation, economics, opportunity, or whatever. These battles waged cannot be individual insulated struggles instead of a united war against the indoctrinations and ideologies that reproduce themselves across multiple oppressions.

This is the two-horn approach flanking and encircling the shared objective. Us and others must realize that their struggle is ours with a different pronoun describing the affected group. The pronoun is interchangeable. Black, Latino, Jewish, LBGTQ, women, poor, disabled, you name it. Accordingly, enlisting the solidarity of their plight to join ours builds a coalition against a common affliction, nullifying any minor distinctions for the common good. How can you champion your right but stand against ours when it is the same marginalization?

Not to dilute our cause or any collaborator's but to consolidate collaboration where our interests converge or overlap. So our progress involves us being sensitive to and avoiding inflicting upon others the poison we are contesting. Likewise, they must also refrain from such actions. Remaining consolidated while traveling the path together until the road to our destination differs from theirs. Being of assistance while being assisted is a win-win alliance if the target is a shared fundamental, not an ancillary whim. If this thought process can be applied, consider the universal effects and conditions it will impact or eliminate.

The common good to remove abuses and violations improves the common condition simply by changing primitive stupidities that have a collective implication. The psychological trauma due to the relegation of humanity by discrimination has restrained our mental health and societal progress. Re-socialization must originate with the only ones we control, our individual selves. Just as adaptation is the key to survival, knowledge is the key to progress, and discipline is the key to exercising it.

Knowledge, education, and healing are needed as our foundational trifecta for progress. Knowledge distributed as a mandatory rite of passage. Infused for our purpose on our terms for our benefit to our people. Education affords guidance and mentorship for operating within the system, while healing nurtures thought, perspective, and aspirations. At sundown, our cause is our problem, although help would be nice but not necessary. Regardless of others' actions, it does not relieve us of our duty to pursue the knowledge, education, and psychological healing that promotes our future and well-being.

Mandating progress by law with discretionary enforcement is often ineffective since it only succeeds as much as someone's willingness to comply. While attempting to regulate forced progress, it is easy to instigate an adversarial mentality induced and distracted by resistance inviting conflict. When unforced, although progress may be different in appearance and incentive, it does facilitate change that can morph into a replica of its purpose and intent, encouraging compliance. But still, it remains no coincidence or surprise that the cycle of contention continues generations later.

Seemingly, a meaningful change comes only every sixty to eighty years, producing moderate change and glacial progress. Obviously, racism continues to be practiced and promoted despite any previous interventions or progress having the desired impact, except one. It is our ascension. Our elevation and self-determination to become a force to be reckoned with by our intelligence, skill, character, and economic impact proactively applied to breach the door of inclusion. Once breached, it can be leveraged and opened the way sports, entertainment, and business have been. But, we have been betrayed by our tacit complicity to become distracted and pretend shock about what's primarily unspoken but often seen, felt, and understood.

Progress, like respect, must be earned or taken because, if granted, it can be regulated or rescinded. Considering this, our path has been the rough side of the mountain. Still, we continue to ascend over time. However, the summit is within sight, but we must finish the climb with intelligence, not force, and change how we do business with ourselves and others. The goal is the summit, and the path is diligent ascension by our actions, behaviors, and acquisition of the qualifying knowledge. Namely, the breadth of knowledge exhaled into our psychological captivity generating a genesis of revelation aligning our true identity and purpose.

Marcus Aurelius said, "The impediment to action advances action. What stands in the way becomes the way." Let our obstruction become our instructions to proactively advance our actions. Let it become the way, forsaking past hindrances and self-indulgences obstructing our progress. The flexibility of our methods without compromise of purpose elevates our ability to maximize progress and the improvisation of contingencies to achieve it. There is sufficient strength in our unified numbers and solidarity of purpose, even if achieved unaided by others.

We can't wait any longer for the social calvary to arrive. Analysis of the obstructions points the way to the solutions needed. It continues to point to what has always been needed, solidarity. Be mindful that the shortest distance between two points is a straight line or the least obstructed path of resistance. We must be prepared to go over the mountain, around it, through it, move it, or bring it to us. Remember, what obstructs the way guides us along the way.

So, that is a critical distinction that requires extreme emphasis to consider and utilize for securing progress. What has held us back? What is within our control that does not require begging, and what can we further do to facilitate our progress? The integration of change must be proactively accumulated to counter the obstructions. That is the path to progress and prosperity. Similar to setting up chess moves in anticipation of the ambushes set in place. Without revealing their detection, we more easily manipulate, prevent, and overcome them by using astute counter measures.

Outmaneuvering by using a superior strategy, shrewdly employing the element of surprise where the plan requires us to be deceived or disenfranchised. The predictability of future outcomes has always been forecasted by past events when demanding historical change. The old becomes the new. It is the mystery and certainty of change that repeats itself. It is the universal social cycle of life where primitive ideology is exposed and discarded to better understand and wonder how could it have ever been so foolish.

Our goals must be complementary. Advancement by accelerating the replacement of racist sociological ideology by emphasizing knowledge, compassion, and equality. Furthermore, exposing the irrationality of racial superiority's stupidity as self-deprivation, exploitation, and a display of psychological distress. Condemned as an attempt to suppress others' opportunities by hoarding prosperity based on concocted justifications. The final alignment is to consistently dispel its notions by our actions.

Misconceptions, dysfunctional socialization, and dangerous hallucination keep the racist believers and practitioners ignorant and fearful of associative equality where the opportunity computes the same as being equal. The sorcery of racism and discrimination necessitates a ridiculous devotion to an identity crisis projected as condescending judgment disguising a personal or group anomaly. Affirmed without merit by pompous comparisons lacking a rational basis but bolstered by a cycle of insecurity posturing as superiority describes this syndrome.

Extracting this debilitating mental supposition impeding social justice will likely only be accomplished by the piece mill exhaustion of its rationale to break the cycle. In essence, for the cycle to be broken, misconceived justifications must be supplanted by association of a more preferable self-identification and socialization. The power for progress comes from the people driven by its purpose. More importantly, the youth as the cycle renews must be unencumbered by fallacies, fears, and conformities of history.

They can be hoisted above our limitations to the psychological higher ground of social impartiality instilled with fortitude to change, power of an inclusive purpose, and priority to progress. The children are the future, while the adults represent and impose the past, preventing future progress by clinging to past comforts and pains. Legislation on the books will not suffice alone, while under-enforced or grossly misinterpreted for the rejection of bias, a youthful infusion is mandated. Fear is not an option, failure is a submission, but change is perpetual.

We have come too far and paid too dearly. Remember, reasons motivate while excuses discourages. Still, we cannot afford or accept excuses any longer neither can the next generation. The next generation takes the baton, better positioned to achieve in their lifetime what we have only seen the possibility of in ours. Just as my grandmother believed we would never see a Black President, my mother lived to see it. What will we live to see with a greater focus and ambition applied for the next generation to see even more?

Fashion, music, liberal expression, and the hip-hop culture have done what legislation has not. They promote inclusiveness, commonality, and tolerance among the youth in the world they will inherit not defined by color or race. But, the emerging social consciousness is more generational due to social media interactions, school integration, shared cultural interest, and music. The rejection of bias has been hampered by the controlling older generation's power and reluctance to evolve, offering an inheritance of ignorance. However, time is constant, and so is change.

Title VI, enacted against racial discrimination in 1964, the Voting Rights act of 1965, and even the Civil Rights Act of 1866 regarding equal protection under the law, have not produced the progress mandated. Nevertheless, the effectiveness of unconventional measures and perspectives arouses the possibilities of progress by social dynamics unrestricted by the conformity of traditional boundaries and biases. Consequently, the rejection of binary definitions and solitary perspectives are creating seismic reverberations across the globe by challenging conditioning, control, and inhumanity.

So, maybe in hindsight, progress will come through a revolution generated by the youth's evolution to reject the ignorance of their forefathers and mothers, namely us. Confucius said everything has beauty, but not everyone who sees it sees its beauty. Youth rebellion may just be a beautiful thing. It was for us to liquidate dusty assumptions and behaviors. Just because it has been this way doesn't mean it has to stay that way or that it was the best way.

According to physics, everything is in a state of constant change. Nothing ever remain the same, none of us, but each generation chooses for themselves. This next generation seems to be choosing more wisely that any before them. They have to live with the world THEY create. Our time has passed, and hopefully, racial division and other mechanisms of prejudice along with it. The global colosseum of conflict structured for exploitation and control is crumbling under the revelation of its deceit and coercion.

The vitriol of division disrupting the harmony of humanity in a chaotic revolution of events by cyclical evolution has curved time's trajectory. The time has come. The day is upon us. The hour is near. The minute has yet to arrive. The seconds of urgency no longer awaits. But father time is steady ticking toward change and so must we poised against the bigotry of tyranny, racial or otherwise, refusing to participate or hopelessly and silently wait.

Every hand on the back is not to propel us forward, some are holding us back.

Fear and unfiltered obedience are the same psychologically and emotionally.

A narrow perspective is the dimensional cocoon preventing the blossoming of new realities.

Dare to probe the infinity of our imagination and possibilities.

Time and change evolves either around us or us along with them but neither waits.

<u>Let me ask you a Question</u>

1. Is passivity and revolution the same only varying in degree of overt resistance? Is overt resistance preferable to covert resistance? Is force used to gain a purpose different from force used to maintain an advantage? Can we decide the instances, manner, and degree of engagement more tactically? But how? Can we rely on the social construct and economic blueprint designed for our subjugation to lead us out of it?

2. Must a racial struggle exclude those who are not targets of racism? Can we protest in the evening what we comply with in the morning? How can we achieve change without a transmutation of perspective, psychology, and complicity? Is our ideology of equality stagnant? Does the reconciliation of our humanity and identity reside within us outside our experiences in America?

3. Should our protest be internal to reject detrimental and stagnated concepts and inculcations? How far are we willing to go, burn the boats or keep the car running? What lessons can we take from history to establish power or policy? What diminishes our power? Has racism morphed into a different mountain to ascend needing a different method to ascend it?

4. Is our protest more a result of our emotional trauma or for the advancement of our progress? Can we more effectively galvanize our political and economic power or the use of it? Why don't we? Why are we selective in the indoctrinations that we protest but not religion, education, or economics? Are some forms of racism remnants of our past or consequences of our present compliance and actions?

5. What are the implications of destructive protest when we never leave our communities to commit it? Is that self-expression or self-harm? Can we hold an unidentified face more accountable than the face in the mirror? If we fortify our resources will that make others less regulatory of our fate or fortune? If our purpose is sufficient for

the task, why not our resolve? When has it ever been better or easier to institute change?

Don't Say It if We Don't Mean It
If we Talk it, we Walk it

There are causes and consequences to everything. Both interact as a development from some trigger, tipping point, or condition. Some are foreseen, and some are not. Some are intended, while others are unintended. However, causes and consequences have a domino effect until no more dominos are left to fall, seemingly reaching a conclusion. This is according to a universal symmetry calibrating probabilities rendering specific outcomes of observable cause and effect.

However, some causes, effects, and outcomes are not readily observable but in reality creates an infinite loop of progressions. Thus, there is an invisible replication assuming a random determinate instead of a definitive origination causing a reverberated process. Accountability balances out the aftermath of consequences assigning credit or blame correlating to a judgment or standard confronted by the truth of the results. Integrity and character are the human measurements to concede conclusions in accordance with the observable truth.

Society is the superficial judge, but the mirror is the actual arbitrator and appraiser. Although not of our appearance but the truth that we hide from everyone else and sometimes even ourselves. The little lies that swell into large deceptions. But, we know, just as an astute eye or ear can detect the masquerade, certainly deep down, we know, the mirror knows. Our intrinsic nature defaults to denial, attempting to conceal weaknesses or insecurities and protecting their existence while projecting the opposite.

The fears, anxieties, and insecurities accumulated over a lifetime and supported by life tribulations are magnified by our thirst for societal validation. This validation is conditioned justification for our actions and perspectives. No matter how much we deny it, we know by human nature, our nature. Our ultimate humanity is measured by how we adjust to the discrepancy of what we are to determine who we are or what we want to become. So often, we surrender to the masquerade of what we want others to believe we are, requiring the continuation of that image by fronting and stunting.

So when we fall short or backslide, personal accountability is painful, so if we are not careful, we deflect by using rationale easily escaping blame. It is easier to cast blame or comparisons around when our anti-self-destruct mechanism does not allow us to accept accountability. It is a self-persuasion that sugarcoats the reality of our disappointment with ourselves, unable to accept ourselves in our infinite beauty as unique human beings with limitations, mistakes, and imperfections. These limitations are individual and not racial but evolves with knowledge, understanding, and expansion.

Limitations come in many forms, but mostly we play the hand that is dealt us. Consequently, in many regards, if it is of a nature that we cannot change, we accept the ramifications. Many circumstances are subject to change or improvement. As such, we can often take action to form a better hand overcoming the limitations of our circumstances. But, sometimes, unbeknown to us, there are consequences associated with a better hand that proportionately expand our obligations.

Simultaneously, improving our position also comes with a distinct set of challenges and responsibilities. To whom much is given much is expected and to whoever expects a little, it is also given. The higher up the position, the longer the fall. The steeper the incline, the more precarious the decline. The more you accumulate, the more you have to protect or lose. The crux of societal advantages complicates its pursuit or voluntary rejection of its benefits by the draw of self-interest and personal aspirations to pursue it. So if we take it, we take the bitter with the sweet and the progress with the ensuing obligation.

Consequently, there is an operational protocol within the systems of society that evolve slowly, stubbornly, or differently. On the other hand, dynamics outside the system evolve quickly because we have the control to not only trigger the dominos but to our benefit or detriment. The best speaks for itself because everyone loves a winner superseding almost all other considerations, the objective is to supersede the standard. To accomplish this distinction also require criteria specific to their acquisition to get in the game, possess the needed qualifications, or maximize the opportunity.

In some endeavors, it is natural talent or gifted genius, but that applies to a small percentage of people. For the majority, it is obtained through determination, resilience, and dedication. These are available to everyone costing only the willingness. It is the multiplier and game changer for return on investment for time well spent. But, like the lottery, we must play it to win it. Therefore, nothing invested guarantees no return and no comparison to those who have heavily invested their ambition, regardless of race. Not to seem naïve on the rah-rah pom-pom parade because many obstacles lie in wait, including racism.

But there are many more such as sexism, disabilities, religious intolerance, geographic nuances, abject poverty, and you name it. So we name our poison, and there is someone who would gladly exchange theirs with us, feeling that they could make it with ours. Our specific obstacles are interchangeable and compounded challenges like everyone else's. But they are ours, thus of subjective importance. On the other hand, there are times when we look at someone and wonder how they could have made it, given the obstacles they face.

Likewise, how could another not succeed, given the advantages at their disposal? The answer is always in the mirror. So we must learn to see in the mirror a reflection of why we can, despite any complications of why we can't. The more we do this, the more it becomes our default mechanism of not being denied. Building willpower to dedicate ourselves to not the task but the fortitude to accomplish it. The task is specific, but the fortitude transcends all tasks, ever present to be summoned at will to put in work.

Consequently, we look at the atrocity of slavery and the stain of racism from a historical and collective perspective to protest the consequences and implications impacting us as a group. This approach is acceptable from an observatory perspective but not as a call to action for nullifying and rectifying future ramifications. Nevertheless, there are some aspects to be undertaken as a racial subgroup recognizing that there are subgroups inside our racial group whose interests are diverse and not necessarily subjectively compatible.

Their experiences may not be ours and our experiences not theirs' or to a lesser degree. For example, the dichotomy between racism, sexual preference, gender roles, colorism, economic status, and religion may have us all under the same racial umbrella but not the others. In other words, one size will not fit all, so the solution has to be multi-faceted. Accordingly, each participating subgroup's interest must be represented in the solution or benefit. It cannot be independent outside the scope of the commonly shared solution for it to roundly apply.

The diversity of the issues complicates solidarity beyond the common good if there is not a common problem or cooperation. What autonomy would we concede to another in exchange for exercising our transactional autonomy? Not so much for theirs but so that we can secure our benefit. But more importantly. how can others be denied when their problem is the same as ours but by a different adjective? This is where the coalition of similarities must supersede the differences of division to secure the common goal of elevating each participating subgroup.

Cooperating to at least remove the common concern as a point of contention, suppression, or discrimination. That notwithstanding, the parts are not greater than the whole, but the whole is an assembly of the parts. So, we must assemble the proper parts for the whole to operate fully functional to its purpose. This is where we have fallen short and been turned back repeatedly. Either individuality expressed detrimental to the whole, acting in our own self-interest, or not encompassing others that complement the goal.

It is often undone by direct harm, lack of commitment, or refusal to support the goal. If it takes a team effort, how cohesive is the team? What about the willingness and dedication to be assembled despite pursuit of individual accolades and coveted treasures? It satisfies a personal agenda showing limited commitment but not attaining the ultimate objective. The task must be based on the reflection in the mirror as to what we constructively contribute. Assembling that in the collective vessel until the vessel overflows, igniting progress and shattering the narrative changing the reality shaped by our actions.

I have sought to frame the narrative, obstacles, and viable solutions historically, emotionally, and pragmatically. The part A articles, which are historical assessments and facts, are used as the foundations for the part B interpretations, which I apply a logical perspective and examination. Part A, B, and the resulting questions contextually examined the established misconceptions of history, truth, and belief. Keep in mind faith is not to be question but is different from belief. Faith is believing in something. It is above reproach and a personal right. Belief is a conclusion of why we have faith, the reasons. Without belief we cannot have faith.

However, we can have belief that don't require faith but for that belief we should just simply ask, why? Remember, integrity and character are the human measurements to concede conclusions. The courage to conduct a thorough examination of the factual and impartial information. Also, the courage to apply the facts to our interpretation and not our interpretation of the facts. Let the facts tell the truth and we accept the unbiased findings. If the answer is not what our faith is, we must reevaluate our faith altering our beliefs in response to our findings.

We must eliminate our faith proportionate to the accuracy of the findings. If the findings ever exceed a disqualifying level of faith, our faith is not justified due to impartial examination, dismissal of deception, or truthful deduction. Otherwise, it corrupts the perspective to salvage the belief, contorting it to justify the belief. If the deception and excuses expand to hold on to a lie we know to be true, it's a lie. The mention of faith can be substituted for racism, inferiority, superiority or whatever adjective. The process remains the same, asking ourself, why?

Then, if we cannot justify it, change it to something we can. If our actions do not create our reality, ask why not? So, changing our actions changes our reality. By extenuation, our actions are a result of our perspective. Reversing the process retreats back to substantiating our belief and faith. If it is not knowledge, it has to be ignorance, socialization, or indoctrination. All are by design as a construct which requires cooperation and participation. Now we are into the what. What is our contribution to it and how?

Can we continue to be so careless with our beliefs, faith, and actions which lacks veracity. Are we fishers or bait, the cause or the effect? Still, we cannot dispute the outcome or the reality. We change others by changing ourselves. We starve the system by not participating in its nourishment, by feeding an alternative. The what and why of it hopefully stir the evaluation of our actions, responses, and socialization in the context of social self-analysis. Contemplation that lead to change by rational assessment makes improvement the goal.

Thus, performing a little psychological mind cleaning including a complementary perspective modification from enhancing our knowledge. There is a method to the madness. Only seeing ourself as a solitary tree instead of in a universal forest produces the psychological inferiority of separateness. A perspective of differences without regard for similarities. Consider that similarity creates one forest where differences symmetrically blend into the forest concealed as part of the whole. That is the essence of equality. It is a concept of totality and distinct to an inclusively broad category.

According to our actions, what perspective controls incentives important or essential to inclusion? Is it undeniable knowledge and economic persuasion? Why not? The power is there, but the emphasis is not, nor the accountability to create it. Accountability to and for oneself is the catalyst for individual progress leading to our collective gains. Social justice is attainable, whereas individual equality probably is not as currently defined or imagined. Equal application of the law, government resources, schooling, access to benefits, banking, and employment opportunities are attainable if our consideration is within the equality definition.

There should be no distinction within qualifying classifications other than the level of competency and production but none among comparable levels of opportunity and performance. The principle of equality will always have some level of imbalance. However, it should not be systematically or arbitrarily based on discriminatory characteristics. In any endeavor, some will excel within the grouping beyond others in that group. So equality is only an abstract theory when applied as a material contrast or comparison.

Recognition of a quantifiable quality within the group is a reason for inequality based on ability. Very few should dispute each according to their contribution, skill, or qualifying metric. I point that out to illustrate the vulnerabilities in the system and the methods outside the system to influence it. The logic of complementing our expectations of parity with impartiality to attain progress by equity. Parity is uniformity, while impartiality is fairness. Both have specific applications. But, by nature, fairness should be consistent and objective, while parity conditional among like contributions and contributors. Equity is vested according to worth or value.

So, for example, you cannot treat the best and worst workers equally. Then there is no incentive for your best worker to excel or the slacker to improve, especially if the best worker is you. Now that is discrimination and irrational, but under the theory of equality, the treatment would be the same. Even though they are not equal in value or production. Their equality and impartiality are maintained but their equity or value are much different. That creates an inequality on another level and devalues the process.

Historically, our challenge has been the denial of the opportunity or being judged fairly by our qualifications or like contribution. So we must play the game until it no longer serves us as part of our plan. As a result, it is not always possible to build our own. Still, the thought is not ridiculous. While the reality is that we often must operate within the systems we find ourselves until we can improve upon it, improve ourselves, or have better options. Within these systems, we are regulated and relegated to the whims of the system or those operating them. But, only we can regulate our reality and have the courage to produce it.

Therefore this should always be temporary, biding time until favorable influences can be introduced to either remove the circumstance or remove ourselves from it. It helps to be good at what we do so that our value can be welcomed and appreciated elsewhere. This effectively removes the thumb off the scale of suppression. It also assures high turnover and the lowest production and quality of services aggregated over time. Lacking quality personnel retention or loss of production ends the practice or the entity. They need us or someone like us. However, we only need what they provide.

When we are valuable, others will need what we provide while providing us with what we need. So don't become defeated or complacent, remaining beyond our necessity to be there. We must hunt opportunity. It will not stalk us. In any endeavor, remember that we are there to fulfill our need. Their need is a byproduct of them fulfilling ours. We serve at the discretion of our needs, not to remain trapped in an exploitive situation.

If we find ourself in this situation, the appropriate response is to gain whatever knowledge or skills necessary to elevate or laterally improvise provisions to fulfill our needs. This is where operating legally outside the system independently of suppressions with an entrepreneurial spirit to provide the same service or different service elsewhere according to our talents. Exercising available options and choices, maneuvering ourself into our best position.

We are not always to blame for our circumstances, but the most efficient way to overcome them is by our own device. Therefore, expect the system to fail us so we will not be thrown off by its inclinations, knowing that more will be required from us now to rest better later. Systemic changes have a wide-ranging effect, but individual changes primarily affect us, with others receiving a residual benefit. Enough individual changes cause collective changes leading to systemic changes.

It is the domino effect of consequence, both intended and unintended. Consider that sports and entertainment were the primary areas of emphasis in our community because it was probably the most accessible and affordable. Consequently, concentration in these areas has produced remarkable changes, representation, and power. Now imagine if our communities' overwhelming influence on youth was academic and business centered.

Consider how much our representation in these areas would multiply. Such a dynamic would quantitatively place us in more positions to make decisions absent the historical biases we have faced. Consequently, more diversity would be available for those who could benefit or have been excluded. So the equality we seek is an apple-to-apple comparison. An apple-to-oranges comparison becomes selective according to preference and not quality or similarity.

Even within apple-to-apple comparisons, the apple quality matters most for its taste, not its ancestral pedigree. So assuming the same, there could still be an assumption and application of inequality based upon the differences within equal consideration. A differentiating factor affecting the qualitative or quantitative contributions meeting or surpassing expectations rendering a subjective selection. That is why you have starters and bench players. So skill and production comes down to the basis for the inequality.

Often the inequality is race-based because of the exclusion from the criteria to get the opportunity. Even when qualified, the familiarity factor among subgroups and socializations appears as racist. It can be more a result of the effect, if not the intent. It is an understanding removed from emotions that we must implement to position ourselves differently. It is like musical chairs. When the music stops, you don't have a chair which seems fair until you consider when the music routinely stops to intentionally disadvantage you from getting a chair.

There are many possible explanations, and race is just one of them. Still, without any other viable reason, race would seem to be the main reason. So to respond in a non-emotional way, we must resist default explanations as race being the reason. Of course, there may be other reasons we reject out of convenience or projection. But, whatever the reason, we are left without a seat in the game, and that is what we must deal with first, the position we find ourselves in, followed by why.

This identifies starting and ending points where our opportunities and resources can be cultivated for specific outcomes. Unfortunately, our starting point often differs due to historical systemic biases, making our needs entirely different to compete with additional barriers to success. This enables historical racism to prevail by system proxy where active racism may not apply. Nevertheless, the lingering effects and insinuations do exist and are innocently disguised biases as preferences.

Many depictions and portrayals perpetuate stereotypes, reinforcing what many people, including some Black people, identify as a racial distinction and characteristic. Any behavioral distinctions or characteristics are learned as a consequence of socialization and probably geography. In the right environment, you can turn the most civilized person into a barbarian if their will to survive overtakes their civility. Behavior is conditional and situational, just as you can tame or domesticate most species despite their nature.

With that said, the current portrayal of us has been unfavorable for many many years. Ranging from intelligence to temperament to promiscuity and beyond. Likewise, other races' perspectives representative of us are impressionably supported and promoted instilling a derogatory image. Subliminally, sociologically, and psychologically engineered exaggerations and misconceptions damage our image. The terror becomes the screen, not the picture, meaning the race, not the individual. They are made to be indistinguishable and inseparable, casting wide racial aspersions.

Just the same, many a negative truths are included too. Arguably, the most dangerous and deadly profession in America may be a rapper, basically a musician. Why is that? Unfortunately, we too often contribute to trauma and negative images through our actions and projections. Violence with little or no provocation is normalized as the preferred method to resolve asinine conflicts, real or imagined. Done often without regard for collateral damage.

Black men are generally portrayed as thugged-out predators. Black women are objectified and sexualized as being of low morality. Black children as unruly, sassy, or of slow intelligence. Any depiction or action to slander our image or advance a damming narrative is morphed into a collective trait. Acts by most other races are individualized or isolated and disassociated from the collective, deemed an anomaly. This is a bias of perspective routinely applied to the same act. Still, we must bear responsibility for our damaging contributions.

From reality television to mainstream T.V., movies, and music, it is labeled news or entertainment. Seeing Black folks represented in the worst ways whether dooming or amusing is deliberate. Sadly, we patronize these images and assimilate our behavior to imitate portrayals that would never be allowed to influence other communities, especially their children. Ever wonder why rap music and the culture were so frightening to white America when their children started emulating it?

Nonetheless, it was more frightening to them when it was a method and symbol to enlighten and elevate our awareness and spirit. Instead, it has largely been hijacked and weaponized as a tool of dysfunctional depictions and numbing resemblance. Since the early days of rap is crap, now we find ourselves with rap as a tool for them instead of a tool against them. Its origins were not a tool against us, but the greatest modern-day heist has flipped the script even worse than our use of the N-word. Our greatest enemy will come from our own bosom, by our own words, likeness, and representation.

Promoting violence, drugs, misogyny, and mayhem constantly bombarding dysfunctional messages lures impressionable minds into programmed imitation as predisposed instructions. Its sorcery is mainstream, similar to the N-word. It most certainly promote the images and music. Still, we make it as weapons formed against ourselves in pursuit of shiny things. Foolish games are being played, but they're not the only ones playing them.

Music is currently being used to promote our disfunction, genocide, and female sexualization poisoned by the complicity of our mouthpiece, behavior, and cultural identity. Ask yourself, whose culture is it really if it discredits our dignity and purpose? I point these discrepancies and dissonances out as self- destruction and more akin to psychological slavery than cultural affirmation. This illustrates the subtlety of the game within the game, the hidden prevalence of demeaning archetypes. The flip side is behind door number two, sub-dual of images and role models as positive prototypes.

It is widely recognized that a Black woman as a Supreme Court Justice is encouraging for the Black image and aspirations of our youths, especially young girls. Yet, we pretend that these contrary rampant thotting social betrayals are not harmful. Why is equally dysfunctional and derogatory messaging not directed toward other communities or races if there is no harm? When we speak of diversity and equality, portrayals and representations of us should not be betrayals of our image or moral decency.

So do we provide reasons? Equality, diversity, and inclusion all have positive and negative implications depending on what they are applied to and how effective their application may be. However, all are numerical quantifications prone to interpretation and, thus, manipulation. Often these interpretations and manipulation are weaponized against our image forming foul perceptions of us. Our inclusion or exclusion usually has other determining factors outside the superficiality of race and is sometimes determined by behavior.

Inclusion can only be available to those who have met the requirements to be included but only in context. It is not carte blanche for all outside the context. Outside this context, it would also include those undeserving, which resembles discrimination in an abstract sense by promoting those not more qualified. Do not construe this as a condemnation of affirmative action to remedy discrimination. Instead, just against those who don't qualify or have not been discriminated against seeking its benefit. Qualifying elements must be met for consideration and inclusion unless there are none.

However, redress should follow where harm has been done to obtain a level of equilibrium. That is the principle behind rules to apply the same. So in a social structure, it also makes sense when applied to the reasons where the opportunity is not uniform, mandating adjustments accordingly. Nepotism, favoritism, and cronyism are elements of human nature that cannot be legislated out of existence. In most cases, in and of itself is hard to prove, not illegal, and to some degree socially acceptable although generally despised.

The intent may not be race-based, but the impact can most definitely be misconstrued as racism. The resulting reality is often so close you can't tell the difference. This is one of the challenges of diversity. Diversity should reflect the demographic served, those with interest in participation, or that comprise the organizational structure. Especially if a public institution receives or is funded by public resources. If private, then our discretionary support by spending and patronage would speak to our level of displeasure.

Patronage is voluntary, as the bus boycotts of the 1960s proved, but also quite an effective protest. Disruption and loss of revenue are even more effective. Leveling the playing field by impartiality, qualifications, or leverage objectively opens access to opportunity. Inclusion and diversity often leave us short by not having the requirements, thus justifying the exclusion when others do. By that standard, it ultimately produces a loss of productivity and human resources by restricting opportunities by our lack of development and cultivation.

Suppose certain irrelevant criteria or information is deleted from consideration. In that case, relying solely on qualifications will also eliminate its bias. Considerations like race or gender, where they don't apply as necessary to the performance and competency of duties, should have no significance, only that vital qualitative elements are met. Ponder the accumulative losses had not the color line been breached in sports. To further explore systems of arbitrary hierarchy based on irrelevant factors reveals classism promoting biases and bigotry.

Residual misconceptions of commoners and the elite have been cleverly instituted in society since ancient times, instigating racism. Caste systems have evolved to produce racism mangled from the concept of desirable classes of royalty, managers, and laborers. The Royal Family of Britain signifies all of these concepts in modern society, complete with a "rich" history of commoners, racism, and slavery while maintaining an etiquette of exploitation.

You have the royals who are prestige by bloodlines or nepotism stipend on the public draw, which in America is called welfare for the commoners or poor. Thus the British application is to support the royal rich while shunning the worldwide Commonwealth's poor underlings. In America, the practice is pretty much the same. The managers carry out the whims of the royals while providing a buffer zone and wardenship between the upper crust and the lowly servants or providers. This also favors those not qualifying as royalty but possessing qualities of assimilation to claim either similarities or affiliation. They are the designated surplus to ensure advantage.

The laborer is disparagingly referred to as commoners, indicating little significance or some marginalized value, existing for royalty's exploitation as essential workers. This is cronyism to be hopelessly indoctrinated that your highest glory is to voluntarily serve the illusion of superiority. Social identity is tethered to one of these social positions. But being of a higher class of humanity indemnifies you from responsibility for expectations of humanitarian decency. In America, that class of royalty is universally assumed to be white or have characteristics of white distinctions.

Consequently, racism is sociologically promoted in its covert manner as the unassuming Dr. Jekyll but condemned in its overt display as the diabolical Mr. Hyde. This caste system or classism is converted to racism associated with economic conditions and wealth accumulation. It has traditionally been denied or stolen from Black people. It leaves a canyon of numerical disparity of ineligibility in certain classifications discouraging inclusion. And the band plays on with the same tune from antiquity and the foundations of wayward ideologies to structure society. In retrospect, many of these classifications were depicted as obstructions to society.

Defined by the complexity of socialization compounded by time, social justice is divisive only because it removes the cloak of concealment from overall exploitation, upsetting the apple cart by localizing it to racism. But social injustices flourish among many subgroups and stigmatized groups adversely affected by their particular dilemma but overshadowed by racism. Eliminate racism, and the number of social injustices doesn't recede very much. However, racism is the elephant in the room to ignite fear of sliding within the caste system or emotional outrage of scarcity or disappointment.

A virtual simulation without racism has plenty of discriminatory candidates as substitutions. But, of course, it could be entirely possible that we are already indeed living in a simulation, depending on your definition of simulation. What renders it a simulation is it all is based on falsehoods, misconceptions, and manipulation lacking answers because the questions haven't been asked or the knowledge sought. It mimics a virtual reality built on deception, obedience, and faith.

So, by my understanding of simulation's definition, it's applied deception to mimic a reality. So, racism is a deception distorting reality, especially for those subjected to it. For those consumed by it, the deception is projected inwardly, blinded to logic. Despite this deceptive reality, there is no marked difference in the human species or our anatomical composition despite gender. The deceptions are superimposed over similarities to create differences and hierarchies.

Also, there is no objective variation in anyone's socialization process as being above or below other groups but strikingly similar. So, only the content could be different. Therefore, the basic humanistic tendencies propagated by a prejudiced comparison of our status or socialization cannot be justified by biology, physiology, genetics, or intellect to support racism. Only pure ignorance survives scrutiny as verification. So there are only contrived differences in our socialization arising from the interpretation, deception, and conceptualization or else it is pure ignorance.

This nonsense abounds across the board, interchangeable. In all cultures, whether you were born male or female determines your quality of autonomy and the extent of oppression. It is only questionable as to more or less not if there will be expectations and restrictions based purely on gender. For example, a man wandering the streets late at night might fear robbery, but a woman might fear rape as her primary concern. The actions and general composition are the same, with a tiny variance in gender. But, that alone will change the whole dynamic.

These minor variances change the whole dynamic with race, whereby whites don't fear rape of their dignity, opportunity, or humanity based on their color. Therefore, it may be difficult for them to rationalize the severity of something which is not a personal concern of theirs. Just as men often are unaware of the considerations confronting women, having never been subjected to them. One variance changes the circumstances to create another subgroup element within a subgroup, like women with children or spouses, changing the needs and challenges to be considered as opposed to women without.

So equality and social justice is a superficial expectation that does not address the more divergent elements of contemplation regarding their limitations as their application expands. These issues must be reimagined with everything on the table, not confined to past Modem Operandi, which has proven to have failed. Our problem is the detection of these indignities, and the source is systematic, others or heaven forbid ourselves. Nothing is exempt from examination if we are serious about a solution.

We must fight prejudice and obstructions wherever we find it realizing that contesting it is not conditional or transactional. Still, it is fundamentally essential to minimizing its effects wherever we can. We deserve the same dignity and respect as everyone else and demand it from others but sometimes not ourselves. This must change if we are to change things outside the scope of our identity to be acknowledged with fairness by others. Not only by our demand but also by our demonstration.

So, suppose our needs and expectations are to be met. In that case, we must meet them first with an obligation to be accountable and responsible for our behavior, actions, and decisions accepting the consequences as an anticipated result. If you plant corn, tomatoes won't grow. Corn will grow. Not to excuse others' reactions or responses disrespecting our sovereignty but not to excuse ours either. Which carries the greater obligation and effect?

We cannot be complicit in certain inequalities and sullying of our character resulting from our behaviors and indoctrinations in which we protest the affect but excuse the effect. Dealing with inequalities outside this radius is anticipated but should not be condoned within it committed by us against us. So it makes sense that we might have to give something to get something. Nothing ventured, nothing gained, something on the wood makes the bet good, but something of value must be given, wagered, or skin in the game by our contribution. The gain is what makes the risk reasonable unless it is an act of desperation. Changing the energy regulates the vibration.

Therefore valuable consideration or collateral depends on the aspirations gained being greater than the options lost or risk taken. The possibility of gain is enticing, especially if you have nothing to lose. What do we have to gain? What do we have to do to gain it? Are we willing to do that? What do we have to lose? Is the probability of gain worth the possibility of loss? In terms of sociological and psychological gains, if beneficially reoriented, the same dated outcomes are impossible. But only if we improved our stature regardless of external acceptance.

So the answer is you are absolutely right it is worth a shot. It beats slogans and rhymes or begging as our catalyst for change. Still, if we don't venture beyond our circumstances or invest in our future, then we are relegated to a comfort zone of meager gains. It amounts to crumbs or ceremonious holidays of dubious value. I am sure there is those celebrating nostalgia that it existed. But would it make a noticeable difference if you flipped the motives? I don't think so.

So often, these concessions lack substance and clarity of practical purpose as impactful on the day-to-day of Black folks other than appeasement. It is simply broth with no meat or potatoes. We need to claim our fair share, equitable cut, and gravy up our biscuit with the same impartiality that we have contributed to building, fighting, and providing for this country. That also applies to the oppressive caste systems, totalitarian regimes, royal families, and governments worldwide. The people want their cut of what has been exploited.

It is not unreasonable for people to want to wet their beaks in the fountain that their labor produced. But, if the opposite circumstance causes outrage, it is unfair, or an unjust metric has been applied to justify its application and validity. Therefore, it is morally wrong and necessary that corrective examination is undertaken to determine where the benefits and rewards of society for us are absconded, restricted, or denied. Once determined, decisive action must be taken for restoration.

In a democratic society, the prevailing morality and virtues must be available to all as a matter of default instead of conditionally excluded from segments of society against the principles claimed to govern society. In a self-governing society, representative of the people's majority, when the majority distinctions exclude portions by predetermination, it eventually cannot survive with partial liberties. As a result, more liberties are constricted until autocracy emerges and repeats of social collapse recycling from history.

A pseudo-democracy based upon the principles of a cooperative society constricted by exclusion splinters. Wherever diversity of views, equity of opportunity, equal application of the law, and tolerance of humanity do not impartially exist, unfairness invites eruptions and recalibration. There must be progress and social justice against systemic barriers to represent a prism of interests not integrated by assimilation as white or exclusion from sovereignty. The proximity of characteristics to white appearance and culture dominates the inequalities and validations commonly used for integration, which most of us by appearance can never meet.

Our inability to seamlessly integrate visually, routinely gives rise to sociological stereotypes and assumptions fostering color-based biases. Often the implanted impression, constantly diminishing our humanity by association and anticipation before a conscious determination of racism is formed. Racism is the resulting judgement of the determination rejecting impartiality or equity of characterization subconsciously and prematurely. Considering this, the initial motive may not be to increase or decrease the benefit of our fundamental considerations but instead the consequence of their presumptive anxieties.

Therefore, under the supposition of racially compartmentalized speculation, our withholdings become their benefit or privilege, expressed as discrimination. In this case, it is not so much in what is taken but in what is not given. The circulation and distribution constraint causes us to manage with less worsening our condition comparatively when there are no discrepancies of merit otherwise. No matter how you slice it, it always comes down to a socialization of conscious entitlement or of being naïvely unaware.

Not just relying on the intent or consequences, an assessment of the initial cause is necessary to identify and understand the implanted impression's origin and conveyance. The most effective way to reduce or prevent the mentality that produces the action, instrument, or perpetrator of racism is its origin and conveyance. The practical impact on the sufferer is not diminished by the cause but by directing a remedy towards the cause as the primary consideration to eliminate subsequent incidents. This focus is on what is causing it, not on who is practicing it.

Racism towards our people by other than whites have acquainted themselves with discrimination and exploitation when able or encouraged by imitation or advantage. It can be as subtle as siphoning resources through legitimate business activities. The forms of marginalization in our communities are evidenced by the number of stores and hair suppliers in our communities by non-black nationalities. They are essentially economically pilfering our resources amid food deserts and scarce entrepreneurial structures for which we must share the blame by complicity or complacency. Though perhaps unintentional, it accomplishes the same objective as if purposeful.

At every turn, our sustenance and economic viability depend on entities other than us, which subconsciously cheapens our self-identity. It douses and invalidates our capacities, ambitions, and accomplishments not structurally apparent in our communities. Therefore, we must requisition ownership and opportunities in our community to the extent of our needs, patronage, and wealth accumulation goals. It may be a perception of racism, but the protection of resources resembles territorial solidarity among economic and geographic populations in other communities but not ours.

We are guests in our own communities, with some consumed with gangbanging over territory we only occupy. We have no viable stake otherwise with a delusionary reference as our hood. In our communities, equality, equity, and social justice are less than sparkling when we are primarily in charge of doling them out. So, we must examine and raise our issues without an emotional reaction or knee-jerk denial, not as accusatory but transparent and corrective. We finance others' lovely homes in the suburbs, fancy cars, exotic vacations, chug bank accounts, assistance to family members, and children's education by diverting resources away from our communities and our folks.

While others' resources circulate among themselves to reinvest what they consume anyway to further stimulate their wellbeing, our resources make their neighborhoods better. So, what token of their success directly benefit us by donation or otherwise when supplying their revenue? If Black folks did the same as the others who benefit from us, it would lessen the number of us who fall beneath that status or into poverty? Ever notice how they never live in the neighborhoods where they exploit their living?

We can only blame ourselves. Changing the distribution and beneficiary of resources in and from our communities would have a massive impact. It would improve investment, ownership, equality, and equity if no place else but in our communities where it can be felt the most. The inequality between our community and others collectively if not directly correlates to the individual accumulation of resources for wealth, theirs.

This further exacerbates differences within the community magnifying the haves and have-nots. Also differences between our communities and others community's standards of living. Again, no additional funds, just redirecting current resources and expenditures. When we begin to understand the seminal influences, we are able to identify the foundational mechanisms by which we are suppressed. It brings clarity to the building blocks they are placed upon and the purpose. Methods incidental to a remote determination causing a ricochet drain undetected for bias.

Such as, economic regentrification and redlining methods whereby resources are siphoned from our communities in ways as innocuous as insurance, interest rates, or environmental intrusions. Often if not replaced, we are simply extorted with fewer options, further burdening our resources and circumscribing our containment by racial and economic segregation. This, in turn, is used to provide poor services, refusal of services, and politically biased redistricting affecting government funds and resources, promoting separate and unequal sustaining poverty. The effect is to instill despair and keep us devoid of resources, assets, options, or hope.

Our subjective realities with satiable and insatiable claims of reparations, equality, and social justice have layers that must be defined and amplified. Examine the existence, intent, and design of the systemic policies and practices interwoven in operational tendencies that drain our resources while restricting our opportunities. These invisible losses keep us relegated to a marginalized position chasing the ghost of reparations and equality. Equality can never exist in principle, only in theory.

If reparations or equality existed, what would be satisfactory to us before it became untenable to others when they dispute the premise of both by denying the need for either? We must fight the practical fight as there is no time like Don Quixote to battle windmills while insidious social and economic giants hide in plain sight. So our quest must not be misconceived, irrational, or vindictive to become punitive against ourselves. Beyond our subjective realities remains a fractional reality that further separates us within our own racial subgroup, specifically by superficial characteristics that attempt to define us by association or separate us by alienation.

Still, the fractional reality reflects discrepancies and misconceptions based on skin tone, hair length and texture, speech patterns, swag, intelligence, and many more as not being Black enough or too Black. Yet, despite those ridiculous measures of degrees of blackness, there are legitimate intrinsic separators such as effort, ambition, applied dedication, pride, integrity, and many more that determine the hierarchy among us. So, equality, even among ourselves, is unattainable unless we are equally positioned by comparing equal similarities and aspirations. But, even then, our quality, characteristics, or expectations are rarely identical as a matter of variation.

The duality of collective, subjective, and fractional realities are both finite and infinite in their possibilities and influences, yielding co-incidental or consequential opportunities and outcomes. This makes life's situational dichotomy fluctuate proportionately on suitability, desirability, a chance encounter, and procurement but not a binary expression of equality. Its context is beyond the concept of equality dictated by the specific individual's characteristics that transcend common associations by degrees of separation used to relegate trajectories of opportunity and selection.

So equality is conditional on the degree or elements of inequality. Considering racism and equality absent emotions in a broader context of expectations aligned with capabilities reveals areas of improvement and interest whereby appraisals and qualifications determine separation. Imagine a country where there were only Black folks, then what dysfunctions, traumas, or problems would remain to challenge us? These problems are essential to our progress despite the other challenges faced by racism or discrimination because they would exist anyway.

With this being the case, if we know these issues harm us, we are obligated to resolve them, creating an element of equality that is sometimes missing by qualification or lack of will. Some of our conditions forming others' perception and projection of us inhibits the impartiality we seek. For example, not providing them or ourselves with alternative programming as images contrary to stereotypes. Removing the detrimental demonstrations of our mentality and behavior expands a finite sphere of perception to widen the radius of our infinite possibilities to influence others. This is done by improving ourselves, our images, and our options.

Eradicating our most harmful attitudes and behaviors is the first step to accumulating undeniable power to massage progress. Power enables subgroups the ability to shape society in ways that benefit them. Historically the existing power structure has been positioned against us but now needs us as an integral part of the whole dispersed within the system's configuration diluting the previously sanctioned overt discriminations and exclusions. It has been proven that with power comes advantages and sway. Everything plays off our participation, resources, and leverage.

Power begins in its conception and ends with its recognition. The conception is strictly psychological regarding racial dynamics before it can be sociologically embraced. The Chaos Theory of mathematics examines predictable behavior where slight changes in initial circumstances significantly impact the indirect implications of seemingly random occurrences creating direct patterns. The resulting pattern appears random but depends on the composite of specific contributory circumstances. Hence, the specific elements or conditions to create the desired outcome.

When examining the probabilities of consequences, the more thorough the causal understanding and development of information frequently adjusted, the more effective the method of influence exerted. As time and knowledge progress, stagnated and refuted beliefs and assumptions that do not give way to revision stall the perspective in a time since passed. This is true of racism and our response to it. Racism is the practice of superstition and hallucinations of a time no longer in existence but socially resuscitated.

Our reaction is often emotional or from a time when a prior technique was effective, hoping to catch lightning in a bottle despite evidence to the contrary. So the roles of indoctrination, denial, and resistance play out in a cycle of demonstrations producing sluggish progress of what most know to be factual, although stubborn. The problem and the approach reject adjustment and, thus, solution. Our stewardship of approach is tinkering until we find the right combination suited for current solutions.

The archetypes and shadow assimilations of personality and identity are sufficiently propagandized and instilled as patterns of perception. But, still, the subconscious won't reject in ourselves the totality of our motivations and composition determined by our psychological programming. This compels behaviors and beliefs that reject or remain ignorant to actualities conditioned by fallacies rationalizing them for justifications and corroborating observations. Essentially seeing what we want to see or validating what we want to be true. Even worst, seeing only what we were told to see.

The delusion is in the projection, not the display. The display is a general misrepresentation fabricated to conform to expectations, anxieties, and insecurities specifically applied. For example, suppose one person of a different race committed an act against you. In that case, the projection on all members of that race is common but ignorant. If you were in a car accident, most people would not blame all cars or avoid driving altogether. Racism does as well as victimization because they don't apply universally.

The insistence on Critical Race Theory teachings as a historical fact gains its justification by counteracting the latent indoctrinations of racism and supremacy that's already continuously taught in schools. If CRT is opposed for the reasons stated, white villainization and Black victimization, then conversely, world history should not be taught. Furthermore how could any confederate legacy survive? Undoubtedly, the concerns and distinctions theoretically can harm psychologically by what has been taught equally as what is not taught. Perhaps, immigrants should be labeled according to their ancestry. Why is what is poison for the goose, not poison for the gander?

That notwithstanding, the poison someone else consumed has never killed another. So our objective is to minimize the inculcation and miseducation of our children teaching self-actualization for their well-being, self-esteem, and knowledge. To rely on and insist that the inherently biased educational structure teaches our children knowledge counterproductive to the system's function for the benefit of our children is insanity. Standardized testing does not determine the gifted but ensures a competent labor force is replenished, and certain populations are excluded by subjective measures.

Consider the time a child spends in school year after year only to leave without the basic life skills necessary for adulthood. We must be responsible for what our children learn about the racial dynamics and history from our perspective and experiences beyond "the talk" about the police or slavery. "The talk" probably instills more fear than the good it does. The nuances are more important that we know and can act accordingly than it is for white children. Still, they will learn it by acclimation, association, or osmosis. Nothing prohibits us from educating and dispersing knowledge to our children outside the established school structure.

Plenty of of independent sources of factual history and other topics should be a requirement for our children to learn amid their other recreational endeavors and life skills. Family and peer discussions can only enhance their understanding and conclusions. Our orientation to traditional sources of information, education (operating within the system), and knowledge (operating outside the system) requires a recalibration. The inclination to depend on traditional sources manipulated with dubious intent conveys the predisposition to accept sinister applications as truth. Perhaps even somehow as an accurate representation of conditions relative to our racial experience.

Inventory must be taken of our strengths and flaws. But we cannot continue to ignore our flaws. So, if we are easily offended, we are definitely easily manipulated. But, instead of removing the supposed justification, we attack the revelation questioning why a correction is needed or expected. The answer has to be because the blemish exists and is a problem. We expect the same from others, so why not ourselves? If it was not a problem, then its recognition would warrant a parade, and we would most certainly want our celebration and recognition.

Thus, we cannot shield our vision, selective for causes of others' behavior or our own. Most likely, anyone who is a social justice soldier, reading or hearing this, will not be the fruit produced by it but planting the seed to create it. It is a generational aspiration only flawed by a lack of perspective or expectations by immediate gratification probing for patience for the cake to be baked. The ingredients must be mixed precisely, mature into completion, and given time to develop. Emotions cause premature actions and impatience, not allowing full development to occur. The vision observes the results and not the journey.

The atrocity of slavery stirs emotions and outrage with the overwhelming downtrodden depiction of our experience without the reasons why it has occurred, not only in America but in many places worldwide. This maintains a psychological grip of fixed possibilities and expectations based on race. The resulting restriction of the imagination and ambition lacking inspiration constantly reinforce predispositions of generational inferiority and hopelessness. This is not the totality of the Black experience but is often overshadowed by the atrocities never referencing our prosperity, innovations, and achievements despite enormous systemic and societal oppression, discrimination, and economic suppression.

Under the principle of grace and gratitude, it is better to focus on what we have instead of what we haven't. Unfortunately, as a result, attention is diverted away from the positive accomplishments to accentuate slavery and captivity, both physical and psychological. Black Wall Street, Rosewood, and the HBCUs were testaments to Black prosperity even when discrimination was rampant. All our ancestors were not slaves, illiterate, or destitute of hope and ambition. Still, the narrative is always slavery, essentially discrediting the beacons of hope and examples of perseverance that shifts the narrative.

Always something to overcome in the rearview mirror, gaining on us instead of the maneuvers to navigate the vision ahead. Those who forget the past are condemned to repeat it, but those who live in it will never escape it. Our foresight-producing progress lies in our future adjustments, not past occurrences. We can no longer dwell on a past relational wrong except to propel us to a destiny of inspirational accomplishments of sustainable purpose and prosperity. No more and never again. The objective is two-prong of healing and progress. In contrast, they are intertwined, and each proportionately affects the other because both are the problem.

The healing process is not to forget or necessarily forgive but to prevent it from hindering a positive self-image and furthering personal aspirations. The concentration is on moving beyond limitations, not past grievances. The improvement or worsening of our reality is incumbent on our mentality and methodology. Still, it is impacted by events that stimulate responses according to ethological probabilities, which have become instinctual. Ethology is the study of animal behavior and also govern human behavior as an organism.

Levels of hostility, fight or flight, loyalty, conditioning, threat, kinship, subspecies characteristics, and behaviors are not only learned but are environmentally instinctive to an extent. The mentality reflects ethology, which is somewhat subject to nurture, generating a compulsion. The compulsion is the etiology or cause manifested. Weaponized by Darwin in all its negative connotations, this concept convinced the public of the animalistic nature and close proximity of Black people to animals. However, Darwin did notably omit white's displayed depravity.

Still, certain propensities and aspects are true of all species, animal or human. Stigmatizing differences and associated judgments recognizing similarities and variations deviating from the preferred standard criteria of comparison or selection among any subgroup can produce any desired result. The undesired groups' characterizations can thereby be deemed inferior or insufficient for inclusion or selection. Thus the opportunity is denied based on the narrow criteria or options available from the applied standard. Caressing the numbers or criteria to fabricate the conclusion as seemingly legitimate.

In humans, the boomerang effect is self-esteem, value, and deficiency misgivings, often resulting in destructive self-images and
alienation without examination of the solutions, motives, or lack of
objectivity forming the intended conclusions. This can be internalized as a personal or group flaw that, over time or repetition, becomes an association of projected expectations or conduct. As a result, resentment and frustration within the designated excluded
group are amplified. At the same time, animosity builds towards
them by those outside their excluded designation or those making
that designation.

Being ostracized from preferred subgroup inclusion generates insecurity and anger towards the included party sometimes because they
are not held accountable for their assumptions betrayed by their in-
valid standard of judgment. So does the mirror reflect, or does it
project depending on the perspective looking into the mirror, not so
much the person or subgroup, but the ideology? Consequently, disputes among interspecies or subgroups are just as prevalent as
cross-species or classification clashes when perceiving a threat, at
risk of loss, or level of uncertainty peaks.

Is our exclusion because of not meeting the criteria, or is the criteria
designed to not include us? The solution seems to rest in the question. This reflects the duality of causation and consequences circumstantially applied. But for further examination, several premises
of fundamental understanding must be established to determine
methodologies outside the prescribed assumptions.

According to the Chaos Theory, the patterns or orderly randomness
is based on the causation connectivity to the effects or elements set
in motion. Consequently, they can be observable or predictable
even if beyond our capacity to understand. Likewise, the Bayesian
Curve is the direct regression to a statistical analysis predicting the
probability of occurrence or distribution according to updated and
revised information to more accurately surmise the outcome.

Finally, the Theory of Relativity is a calculation of time and space according to a set metric of measurement or susceptibility of possibilities restricted by the curvature within the parameters of measurement or known applications. These mathematical theories can be applied to social justice issues and methodology motivating progress just short of artificial intelligence making an impartial determination. But then what biases would be programmed into AI?

Combining these three theories in a practical social application starts with the known action or circumstance as the cause. This point also establishes the opened ended initial parameter setting in motion the possibilities of occurrences or outcomes. The outcome is uncertain because of the random possibilities, but the probabilities can begin to take shape. A particular or inevitable outcome's likelihood represents the statistical probability that any specific one may occur while ruling out other possibilities.

This limits the probabilities increasing the odds of a certain one occurring. As the situation evolves as a fluid occurrence, the odds fluctuate accordingly, simultaneously updating the likelihood of possible outcomes and more accurately predicting resolutions. As these changes occur and are calculated, the condensing of time and space defines the considerations for a definitive closed-end result or certainty. Designating a particular action with high accuracy. More or less, if you forcibly strike glass, it will probably break when you make contact, but not in anticipation of the blow.

To more effectively illustrate these concepts, suppose the police attempt to stop you for a traffic violation or some other minor lawful reason under their authority which sets in motion the cause. You have several prescribed ways to respond or several other ways for them to react. The choice you make influence the choices they make. So if you comply, that creates a certain possibility of a range of probabilities although no guarantee.

If you flee or resist, that creates a separate set. As these decisions play out dependent on each other, creating a volley of probabilities based on the variety of possible predictable outcomes can be determined or eliminated but certainly minimized. When giving someone a choice, there is always the possibility that they will make the wrong choice, so it is important to control the choices given. But suppose you remove the element of fleeing or resisting. In that case, the outcome probably have you coming out alive more often than not.

For the same reason, law enforcement must regulate their reactions proportionately to the suspect's crime or reaction, limiting the possibilities for unnecessary or excessive force encounters that cannot be justified or reasonably articulated. Essentially, law enforcement must remain measured in their actions to not make someone else's problem their problem by committing a regrettable act over a non-threatening incident. Bad judgement even by law enforcement must have some measure of accountability reflective of their responsibility and duty of restraint.

With three sixty consideration and analysis these egregious acts of violence leading to the death of many unarmed Black men has accumulative consequences. It lowers the threshold of respect for and cooperation with law enforcement. It further festers a self-fulfilling prophesy to resist as a matter of self-preservation and justified fear endangering other officers with no intent to commit harm. Law enforcement are not the only ones who can be in fear for their life. If a preemptive measure is taken against law enforcement a jury might have legitimate reservations determining someone's guilt given the history of murdered unarmed civilians fearing for their life.

Therefore, why make your bed hard by not making adjustments to avoid unfavorable situations when you stand to be damaged? This applies to civilians and law enforcement alike. Otherwise, it is willing combatants and mutual engagement in uncertain probabilities lacking restraint or predictability based on the same premise of fear.

Remove the probability that the wrong decision will be made by setting the parameters of the likely outcomes. It is no guarantee, but it is a statistical advantage of tentative assurances.

This removes excuses or reasons for many of the fatalities of us in encounters with the police. So, that way, any deviation from the probability pattern will be obvious since the provocation will not justify the reaction. This is not a right or wrong judgment but a fact because both can be true simultaneously. The cause and outcome can be inappropriate, avoidable, and regrettable. Our action can be improper, and their reaction can also be wrong.

But, still, the outcome is often terrible at the final curtain. If it is not worth the outcome for us, then the adjustment is incumbent upon us to avoid it. By restraint, the possible management of the encounter is open-ended but certain and final with death. Learn to play the odds, not the house, because actions and outcomes are usually not contradictory but interdependent. The major gamble is all you have or may ever have, instantly wagered against temporarily avoiding a minor legal matter. Seems like a terrible wager to make even for law enforcement given the increased risk and attrition among their ranks. So which behavior is causing the other?

Philosophically, in conjunction with the Chaos, Bayesian Curve, and Relativity theories, the following paradoxes anticipate consequences. Although complicated in their totality, they are simplistic in their ramifications. Nevertheless, they provide an additional solution by using them as a unique methodology to achieve progress, protest injustice, and for more favorable outcomes, including better decisions. Together they provide the method for the manner to be inserted and adjusted according to fluctuations of circumstances.

Accordingly, the Grandfather Paradox is a reverse time travel paradigm where traveling back in time to identify and eliminate something prevents it from occurring in the present or future. Changing the precursors alters the possibility of resulting events, so if that didn't happen, this could not occur as a result. It is a theory of chain reactions, one causing the next, which may only be exposed over time. So since we could not prevent slavery, can we prevent other elements from continuing today to eliminate them in the future? It is a matter of future projections or changing the future by changing the past.

More directly, what conditioned behavior from the past, if changed, would have resulted in a difference today. Changing that sociology or psychology then would have changed this dysfunction now. So, stopping it now changes the future. If traveling back to slavery, what element of slavery could be changed without changing the occurrence of slavery itself to prevent some of its manifestations today? What can be changed today to prevent discrimination from continued appearances in the future? Can our use of the N-word still be justified forecasting out one or two hundred years into the future?

If three elements from slavery were changed today, what exponential expansions of consequences would exist tomorrow as improvements? Probably the ones we protest and bemoan as expectations of social justice and equality, which would indicate that they are within our power if not our perspective. Though physically, we cannot travel to the past. We can mentally, analytically, and retroactively portal current solutions applied to future expectations. The instructions are in the past, the application is in the present, and the incarnation is in the future.

The Bootstrap Paradox, more popularly conceived, is a theory that creates a chicken or the egg paradox of which existed first and does the other exist as a cause of the other or as a result. It proposes a loop or cycle where one event causes a second event that causes the first event. Essentially when the effect is the cause before the development has occurred, it is the being before actually occurring. It is the premise for many movies. Anticipation of an impending contingency that compels the initial or current event.

Defined by a past experience or occurrence leading to a future incident or action where the likelihood or prevention of a future outcome caused the past behavior to occur. This is equivalent to someone who has experienced jail time in the past who, when caught, does not want to go to jail, so they resist or flee future consequences based on past experiences. By doing so, they exacerbate the circumstances inviting more severe consequences for their action. The resulting action creates more of a future problem than the initial matter by piling on penalties.

So future consequence that has yet to occur has influenced current or past actions relative to a yet-to-be-realized occurrence which may not occur. Combined with the historic slave catcher implications, it would seem to create this frantic cycle of reactions and loose associations which we so dread triggering our irrational behavior. Also, it should lead to avoidance of the circumstances likely to bring that about. Likewise, education and knowledge invites infinite expansion and facilitate future outcomes based on current actions becoming past foundations producing future prosperities.

Newcomb's paradox estimates reward or benefits, whereas the goal could be to maximize gain or minimize loss, indicating risk and reward satisfaction levels. The risk-benefit assumption cannot be impartial when the options provided are biased, either withholding information or limiting selection by predetermined influence. Similar to plea bargaining or probation, don't make a deal too soon. Game shows rely on this when they show you one prize and see if you will take it or risk it for the prospects of an unknown prize. Also, politics to a similar degree is the same game.

But oh contraire, reversing it allures a perceived lesser penalty stroking immediate gratification or relief. Either can make choices indistinguishable from manipulation or free will. You only think you are making a choice unencumbered by unconscious compulsions. Still, it is quite predictable, the selection and the outcome. The choice is yours, but the selection or options are not, only the preference. Racism and other social ills are perpetuated by social blinders restricting or distorting judgment by game show messaging campaigns and misconceived innuendo. One option replaces another by temptation or compulsion.

According to the Theseus Paradox, socially compromised people cannot remain the same when their components or culture have been replaced. Since elements of our culture, character, and spirituality were replaced, a replica of us cannot be our original or organic identity before stripping away what made us ourselves or our people. This is sociological defamation of our identity, undermining our psychological disposition by coercing assimilation and rejecting our spiritual compass for foreign religious and cultural indoctrination. The shackle remains, the psyche restrained, the vision blurred, and the sociology programmed. The system, social, economic, or whatever is the diagram replicating complicity to selected beliefs.

Plenty of Christianity but no Sumerian or Kemetic culture, although it preceded Christianity. We were rough housed into a relational existence based on obliterating our past or maiden identity. Once dismembered from our humanity by brutality and deception, it was their way because there was no highway, no escape. So there wasn't much difference behind door number one, two, or three. However, we could choose sort of, while on another level, there was never any choice. Now there are more choices.

This paradox reflects the indoctrination of slavery. Formerly forced to discard the wayward motherland, replace our spirituality, and adopt a socialization racially designed. However, realizing the intent and effect should lead to discarding the slavery indoctrinations blocking our self-actualization or sovereignty by reclaiming our original parts. It can even be applied to doctrines of Christ as being born again into a new perspective, or more accurately, us born again into our liberated perspective and cultural identity. We are not racially, sexually, economically, or culturally objectifications by others' definitions. But, in many ways, we are not what our definition states either.

These four paradoxes, Grandfather, Bootstrap, Newcomb's, and Theseus represent some form of a rewind where the effect is analyzed to consider the cause or our contribution to it. Review the sequential actions to start the dominoes falling with predictable or obvious outcomes resulting in our favor or disadvantage. To remove the disadvantage, we need to identify the point of conundrum, eliminate it, or alter the cause that brought about that effect.

Especially the impact on us that we continue to experience. To not tackle social injustice but those or what promotes it, the cause, not exclusively the result. Severing the connectivity changing the cause's influence into consequences prone to produce a specific result. Basically the substitution of logical methodical analysis instead of emotional reactions which escalate negative probabilities. Also, assessment of subsequent consequences for better outcomes and accountability.

The inconsistencies in our actions and expectations regarding social justice, equality, and law enforcement have a discrepancy in method and manner, which are incompatible with our proclamations and objections. This is evident by the repetitive nature of our grievances and methods to secure redress. At some point, a rewind to start from a new paradigm operating under different social, psychological, and economic hypotheses is needed to break the cycle of stagnation or sluggish progression. We can only move forward, unable to return to the womb or past trajectory.

Disorder will eventually descend into decay by decreasing stability and rejection of established structures. But unfortunately, our potential and prosperity are too often left on the vine to wither. They are squandered instead of bearing the fruits intended as possible. So, our patterns are governed by limited perspectives more prone to social programming and reactions than self-sufficiency, tactical dismantling, and calculated responses.

Allowing entropy, order gradually declines into disorder, but disorder's cyclical and predictable motion has an orderly chaotic pattern, even if random. With the implications of all these theories, we can see the many hidden elements and influences that comprise human behavior and its predictability, including our manipulation. If it can be predictable, it can be manipulated into any probability appearing random. The capacity of the system to establish and operate social paradigms and archetypes, not just racial, cannot be underestimated.

Space is represented by our existence or reality, influenced by time represented by occurrences. If we change the occurrences, we affect reality by changing the trajectory of probability, restricting or expanding the possibilities. With expanded possibilities, we alter the predictability of distribution or equity to determine our reality aided by the curvature of relativity and time by occurrences. This cycle is not broken but completed with an altered dynamic according to the laws of mathematics, science, physics, and nature but time doesn't care how you use it. It becomes a matter of humanity, not race, of the ethology of an evolving species' social paradigm.

We perform as programmed, conditioned, or evolved. Ethological behavior as a species occurs before racism is even a consideration exposing that its vulnerability can be eliminated before it can exist. This reveals the solution as the organism, not the personality resulting from altering the organism or species. They say you don't hate the player. Hate the game, but without the game, there is no player, just as without the player, no game can be played. At least not playing that game because it does not exist, so remove the player, the ideology.

Subsequently, our odyssey is one of future perspectives discarding the baggage of history. In the casino of life, you must either wager big or hit tremendous odds to win big. We have already beat enormous odds. Now we must wager big for Newcomb's prospect of a greater prize. But, we cannot receive the fruits from the tree without first planting the seeds to grow the tree. To grow apples, we must grow patience first for the tree to grow, then for the apples to sprout. Time is a factor. Therefore, what is planted today will bear harvest in the future if cultivated along the way, according to the Grandfather Paradox projected forward.

We must plant it now for it to exist in the future. But, like the Theseus Paradox, our perspective must be born again. Unafraid to examine, challenge, discard, or rebuke every component of our colonialized reconstruction that used detrimental psychological replacement parts. Parts comprising what we believed to be original parts simply because our recollection is limited but not our DNA. DNA is memory, written all over our face and genome as our genetic code, even if our psychological and spiritual code was replaced. Our sociological and psychological codes must be deconstructed and recalibrated for our greater good and achievement, producing an organic progress.

Do not be deceived that it is entirely of our doing that we are represented as thugs, real ones, dealers, or gangsters instead of scholars, inventors, or agents of prosperity. A personal icon of mine was Reginald F. Lewis of TLC Beatrice International Holdings' acclaim, moving like an absolute boss maneuvering a billion-dollar leveraged buyout in the 1980s. Imagine if the influence of his real-life legacy was as popular as Scarface's Hollywood legacy. What universal influence would it have had on the Black experience to aspire to emulate him in authentic economic "gangsta" style? We create reality by emulation and demonstration.

Be careful who we worship and the intended consequences. Think of all that exists outside the radius of our perceived limitations and imitations. Does it mock our psychological confinement with pervasive associations, often even among ourselves, to remain limited or socially decadent? Robert Johnson of BET vision is another example of getting it out of the mud to create something that only previously existed in his mind. Examples and role models of what is possible have untold influence but so do examples of what not to do or images of dysfunctional encouragement.

Still, we are not a monolithic people universally defined, restricted, or inflicted by the same mold but possess an infinite diversity defiant of any simplistic classification. However, if the less-than-flattering shoe fits, it might be our shoe. Wear it or change it with new shoes. So if you are easily offended by truth or reality regarding our actions and behaviors, check your feelings at the door to understand the message for relevance and not provocation or unintended insult. We can't feed on ourselves and expect others not to feast on us, especially in the Black male and female gender war.

Pushing emotional buttons primes impatience and interruption of our process by anger or denial. Those easily offended or in denial will be offended but we must save ourselves. Moses is a savior concept of a leader to lead people out of bondage. If a general has no troops, who does this savior lead other than themself? The people have always been the movement. Suppose enough people move in the same direction simultaneously, then by their presence they are an assembly. In that case, they become a force, and their purpose is a pursuit, a movement. The mountain does not yield to the wind. It repels it. So it is also with social movements repelling the winds of adversity.

The concept of the "promised" land is reminiscent of forty acres and a mule after fighting for liberation from a system of bondage under "Pharaoh's" rule, only to wonder in the social wilderness. Pharaoh, i.e., the racist structure, is determined at any cost to maintain untenable conditions even putting Democracy at risk. No matter what, even its destruction by pursuing into the Red Sea. With the machinations of Pharaoh on the loose, America will need God to bless or deliver it if its continued resistance and lunacy condemn it.

Still, we must remain diligent, not looking for an allegorical Moses to deliver us but delivering ourselves.

There are those in elevated positions, self-proclaimed advocates, anointed crusaders, and of celebrated acclaim by assuming our burden, they cannot become our crutch. Financial or otherwise, exceeding moral inclinations to facilitate or participate but not to carry us simply because of their capacity, celebrity, or support. Our capacity is greater collectively when galvanized and pursued according to our purpose. Unity is a movement's core popularity and sustainability, not celebrity or notoriety. We, the people, must do it for ourselves by unity of purpose, pursuit, and cooperation to maximize its attainment.

The ones assemble to become the many as the many become one force. Still, one lion can't be expected to lead the many sheep or one sheep leading many lions. A group of celebrities, athletes, or civic leaders cannot carry the burden of hundreds of years and millions of people. They cannot correct or deliver us from the bondage of our minds tethered to minimizing indoctrinations that even they may not have shaken. At any rate, a journey starts with a single step. That step must be taken individually, amassing enough people stepping in the same direction regardless of race. Especially for us, the most among us are forever tethered to the least among us.

The microcosm of behavior and motivation fully understood reveals the objective of division and exploitation as dependent on roles being consistently played. It is the performance of archetypes assembled to portray roles and exhibit personalities interpreted as characteristics. The pattern creates a system predicting interpretations or casting assumptions. The characteristics are assigned, defined, or stereotypical expectations predicting favorable or unfavorable racial traits. These traits are then projected almost exclusively and universally upon a race to be definitively representative or indicative of their synopsis.

As we understand the archetypes, we can detect the projections not of the race but of the assumptions. Basic archetypes and an expansion of deviations comprise self-identification based upon self-esteem reflecting our view and opinion of ourselves. According to this compiled self-portrait, we formulate our personalities and display characteristics defining our core which we generally carry our whole lifetime. It is extremely difficult to significantly alter our core image, even if we can masquerade as an entirely different version to the world.

The many indexes of archetypes can range from hero, heroine, villain, tough guy, weakling, protector, slickster, pleaser, intelligent, dumb, leader, follower, confident, shy, brave, fearful, adventurous, scary, and many more. So, as you can see, a rolodex of these roles comprises our personalities based upon acquiring self-images in our formative years. The impression was so overwhelming that we either adopted it or created some adjustments because of it. Often it is more observed or demonstrated than stated, but something must fill the void when it presents itself.

Cultural images can present themselves in the same fashion if acquired by choice or imposition. To change these archetypes would essentially change our identity, rejecting our former self or persona. This can only happen voluntarily for an internal change, realizing the benefits of switching to a better or improved perspective. Racism is difficult to eradicate because the racist fails to see the irrationality of integral parts of themselves. They fail to see where their mentality ends from their actions and the reality of a greater spectrum begins.

Their crab mentality at conflict with self, unable to distinguish perspective, thereby refusing to amputate their mind from a foreign body by rejecting a portion of their core identity. The identity supersedes the belief and evidence against it. Humans are not always capable of self-repair confined by their ideologies and misconceptions. They internalize that they are being asked to kill an integral part of themselves when they disagree it should die. This is the power of the archetype to be not a part but a person alongside the other personas that coalesce internally as constructing our individuality. Its survival often supersedes logic anchored to an emotional being of identity rationalized by self-justifications.

Attacking the person will only result in resistance, so the archetype must be convinced. The same with any personality trait of any person, regardless of race, if the change is sincere and lasting. Once it becomes part of a person's identity, the work is cut out to remove it. Therefore, the focus must always be to prevent a negative trait as the easiest method to affect it in others and ourselves. The complexities of these cycles and archetypes resort back to the simplicity of the individual's actions and perspectives to affect their philosophical sphere and the ones in which they interact.

The concept is to affect change in others by changing or improving ourselves. After all, it is our benefit that we pursue. Therefore, others' benefit is a bonus. For example, the N-word describes an archetype depicting a negative image and connotation by either its original use, appropriation, or, as I refer to it, its misappropriation. What is the benefit of some of our most damaging perspectives and behaviors promoting our image? This N-word alchemy, incantation, or comparison does not represent or conjure any quality of positive affirmation of character, equality, or expectation.

So, would those who identify as such not be guilty of refusing to amputate a self-defeating persona intrinsically and psychologically attached to their identity? Just not called racism instead ignorance but still irrepressible. Does it also not constantly remind others that it is our preference of self-identification and treatment? The process for combating racism is the same for us to combat our flaws. African American is also such a term that seems innocuous as a reverence to our origins, but a closer examination would raise questions.

I have a theory, maybe a wacky theory but follow me. Suppose we travel back far enough to the origin of life in Africa. Wouldn't that make everyone walking the earth African and all Americans African American? Suppose all bi-racial people claim their presumably socially dominant racial identity instead of the lowest relegation of their racial identity. Wouldn't that make them white if they so choose?

Sort of the reverse one-drop rule where one drop of white blood would make you white or whatever race contributed to your identity. If Canaan was made Black by Noah to curse his father, Ham, then can't all Blacks claim to be White being descendants of the pure seed of Ham directly from Noah or Canaan when he was white? What about as a descendant of Adam? Genealogy allows for claims of many variations of race or identity.

Furthermore, if people can choose to be non-binary, a singular person can identify as plural, and anyone can be white then why can't Blacks claim to be any race, even white or no race, as a matter of self-identity, even for government purposes? Why not if it is based on self-identification or ancient history? So what is African American? Is it a color, a lineage, or a classification that secretly segregates us as a distinction other than American?

Look at any government form; under white, it does not have any distinction outside the collective family of white, none indicating origins or lineage. Maybe, everyone's identity should be an x on forms to eliminate race as a consideration. Makes me wonder if race or gender is even needed since it is questionable what benefits the distinction brings. Arguably, it is more used for discrimination. This could indicate that some re-evaluating needs to occur when these terms have or should have no bearing on determinations or qualifications. But let's go to the deep waters.

Case in point, to some the greatest President of all times, 45, who claims the confederate heritage and an all-American persona grandfather and grandmother was born in Kallstadt. But he claims white, not German or European. It goes unquestioned and is acceptable because, quietly, most designations of white fall in the immigrant category of impersonating a legacy of American heritage.

My grandmothers and grandfathers were born in Mississippi and Georgia, but I need to claim African American. Their parents and grandparents were born in America. It is a sly segregationist distinction where Black and brown people are further diluted as people of color. These distinctions are misleading, ambiguous, or flat-out lies. We are relegated to a continent or hemisphere, while other races belong to a country, province, city, or culture.

Whites can be of any nationality to claim white. All dark complexion people are not directly from Africa, although all humanity is from Africa, so how far back are we going? If that make all Americans African American by ancestry, whereas a naturalized African would be what? African Americans too, regardless of color. If born in Africa and naturalized in America, that seems to make you African American more than Black. But what that would make you is knowing your natural heritage, which we cannot claim. Still, their struggle is not removed from ours, our reference point is simply different.

Therefore African American signifies unknown origins and lost heritage. How many claim America as their homeland and heritage to take back America? But their roots don't go back as far as ours in America? They will claim the country but not the atrocities. That would make America ours before it was theirs by way of their immigrant legacy. We have been the N-word, coons, coloreds, negroes, blacks, people of color, and African Americans in the ever-shifting saga of our assigned identity. I claim Black with pride just as others claim their distinction, even confederate, but they refuse to claim squatter.

Black is a legacy American whose ancestors were subjected to slavery, reminding me of my obligation to not defile their sacrifices and tribulations. The analogy is often inconsistent when attempting to retrofit an identity or association. By that metric, is there such thing as Confederate American or Immigrant American according to their heritage and ancestry? Most whites are of immigrant origins compared to descendants of slaves, but they also arrived on a boat, most after us. African American is furthering an insidious distinction that undermines the concept of equality. Minority applies to everyone from Black people to gender, disability, religion, and soon-to-be white in approximately thirty years.

Race is a delusion of numbers and classifications by disproportionate criteria. The technical distinctions defy logic while casually applied. By designation, the census and office of OMB consider African Americans to be anyone whose ancestors' origins are traced back to the lower regions of Africa, below the northern portion or sub-Saharan. I would imagine even indirectly from another land. So realistically, African American is a polite way to say slave descendant. Everyone else on the globe can be considered white, even if from Africa.

By definition, it is firmly consistent a dark complexion person or so-called Black from the northern part of Africa is white by geography. So with the geographical origins set by that criteria, how does anyone else become classified as African American if not by color? The spectrum of color variations in all lands further extracts light complexion appeal as the overwhelming and overriding criteria simulating whiteness but not by geography. So by geographical designation as evidence, it reveals in general not where they hijacked us from but a dark skin aversion.

By the same curiosity, what slave trade or immigration globally have others undergone in four hundred and fifty years? Does it reflect their geographical origins for direct comparison to ours during the same period? That changes many things in the world, but many it doesn't change. Globally connect the systems, ideological cultivations, and echoing beliefs throughout that time for an accurate portrait of comparison. From origin to evolution, follow the continuity of repetition over time. The repetition of time cast its shadow as truth without breath possessing only time with more assumed than spoken.

What you will notice is racially segregated by region but indiscriminately disbursed globally with different labels and similar atrocities. Any national context obscures the similarities of global practices. Consider the forest of global racism, atrocities, and misconceptions instead of the tree of America's transgressions. Slavery, conquest, and religious submission has ruled every conversion of society. The method is universal, coerced to comply. The reason is always the same, we decided it was best. However, the ideology is only different in that it serves opposite chosen agendas. The result is people doing opposite things for the same reasons, like war.

Race is more a barometer of migration and conquest. Racial classifications often defy consistent logic, historical context, and geographical application. To illustrate the absurdity of its inconsistencies, let's examine the vacillating criteria used for the determination that results in division. Consider geography and genetics as the two main determinants which are used. By geography, Africa is a continent with only one small point of contact with another continent, Asia.

The area of contact is now known as the Middle East, which was designated as such as a result of the Berlin or Congo Conference in 1884 and later the British and French leading to and during WWI. Speaking of the Congo Conference along with the Doctrine of Discovery, they both conceal atrocities committed in Africa obscured by the transatlantic slave trade by committing their atrocities without leaving the continent. So not only were the population divvied up but the geography as well. The five countries across the north of the continent Africa are considered the Middle East although firmly located in Africa.

Africa is considered below the Sub-Saharan and what is termed the Middle East, supposedly distinct by language and culture. However, the same can be applied to the Sub-Saharan considering language and culture. At various periods, occupants of many of these so-called Middle Eastern countries were a different race, conqueror, or migrant across three continents. The demarcation is time and not geography, but when combined, they are deceptive. Even the term Middle East is deceptive by time and geography. To further emphasize the fluctuating criteria South Africa under Apartheid was not considered Africa when under white rule.

So, Sub-Saharan descent is a euphemism for Black, but whites are of these regions, and Blacks are also outside these regions. Furthermore, Caucasian refer to a region and not a skin color. Caucasoid refers to a skull configuration associated with the region. Perhaps the rainbow of melanin across the white distinction is why everyone except for Blacks is included as white. However, technically Blacks can be included as original members of the classification before it morphed into racism.

The current configuration of the Middle East as not Africa reflects the conquest of last resort for its designation going back many centuries. It also boast of most of Africa's oil but conquered long before slavery based on colorism. However, in all fairness Arab and Muslim control of most of the region dates back thousands of years to before the first Khazar war. Conquest has always been the case with nomadic tribes migrating throughout the region due to famine, drought, or war dating back to antiquity.

So the northern tip of Africa is a designation of Western classification after what else but a war and dispensation despite its geological location because it is neither middle nor eastern on the continent. In the context of slavery regarding America's slave trade, the dominant almost exclusive regions of trafficked Africans did not originate from the far reaches of the continent but mid-continent from the coast. Once again not geographically consistent considering the northern segregation from the African continent especially allowing for Sudan as Middle Eastern despite being below the Sub-Saharan line.

It is even more absurd regarding genealogy but perfectly clear concerning resources. Same as South African apartheid coincidentally occurring where there are precious mines of gold, diamonds, and platinum. Given the history of migration and the range of melanin still in the region reflective of the past spectrum of skin tone among the same people or tribes, it becomes impossible to relegate people to a race by color. However, maybe not when relegating racism by resources.

Over hundreds and thousands of years, the genealogy has mingled and adapted to further distort any classic assignment of race by color since it was not a factor. The mixing of seeds as a mating and biological occurrence expanded the diversity of genealogy. Racism based on or justified by melanin would have been impractical because of the prevailing skin tone of the time and region. Thus, the real racial segregation is power and manipulation wielded to extract wealth and resources. Skin tone, racism, and colorism are the crutches to disguise this dance of exploitation.

Mesopotamia, Egypt, and Canaan as the three primary areas of biblical concern did not have colorism, so inter-mating was not remotely based on skin tone. Seeds were spread across so called racial nomadic lines. Colorism, to this day, is an estimation by visual appearance but imprecise and misleading. By appearance, with any degree of certainty genetics, ancestry, and DNA cannot be definitively determined backdated to biblical lineage or origins. Yet, despite appearance, lineages can produce shocking results from an unanticipated family tree.

The archetype of white once carried the highest of accommodations and prestige, which is now vanishing based on color or race. The increase in the racism alarm was sounded when whites looked around and saw less of themselves and in places they were accustomed to only seeing whites. A little less separate but equal than they can stand. Probably a function of economics, migration, and integration of people than whites' decline. By volume, their dominance is less, so they equate that with being invaded, not fully realizing that their numbers are dwindling by association, not decline. The bizarre revelation is those in denial are often heritages who immigrated to America.

Haitians, Mexicans, South Americans, and any origin that will darken the complexion or dilute whiteness are not welcome. But, forced slave trade "immigration" was quite the rave. Now, damn the geography white appearance matters most since free slave labor has been abolished. Seemingly, only color matters because of visual assimilation and generational practices merging economics, politics, and fear. This relegated an exploited demographic lineage to serve wealth accumulation while not welcomed for assimilation. But, there is a lesser need now to pretend to be white for success. Even lesser to succumb to white dominance.

Populations from Europe and countries of white appearance assist in restocking America's dwindling white stock just as it was during colonization. It is a social instrument long in use. Racism because of desperation is more visible now than in a long time but not more widespread. Significant decreases in racism reflects the percentage of white people who reject it as a faulty measure of humanity and a shameful display of ignorance. We must acknowledge racism has declined especially overtly and is nowhere near the horror of our ancestors. Still, let's not pretend it does not exist and much more is not still left to be done.

The question then arises if we are now more restrained by racism, culture, or psychology? Does our actions and culture cause current racism or are they a result of it? Can our psychology and culture change if racism doesn't? Can racism change if our psychology and culture doesn't? Is "the" culture still a counterculture dispersing knowledge or now sabotaged for dysfunction? The sociological hydraulics of cause and effect suggest resolve have lagged behind cultural growing pains. We know but now we must do. The problem is a minority ideology relegated to the past, straddling an evolving perspective of self-definition.

The old must eventually yield relieved by the improved. Antiquated ideologies also ultimately concede to change when the socialization is interrupted or rejected. An evolving perspective apply developing applications and solutions to current challenges instead of squeezing them into outdated molds of thought or behavior. The frozen in time imperative is not like Frank's Red Hot, you can't put that sh-- on everything. Understandings have increased and changed ushering in analysis of the status quo where one size must no longer fit all.

Whether racial superstition, religious zealotry, political reaction to perceived racial micro-aggressions and protest, or storming the Capitol, the frozen imperative is frighteningly melting away. We must not add to its ideological survival as it descends into disorder and self-destruction. The unsustainability of racism is completing its cycle set in motion from waning social leverage. Convulsing from the consequences of being obsessively encouraged by greed to populate the world with Africans where Africans would not have amassed otherwise. Greed placed racism and the African diaspora around the globe over centuries.

It has always been problematic for the scattered but now it is a problem for the scatterer hearing footsteps in the dark. Ultimately, racist caused their own erosion by mass distribution and exploitation of Africans. Their comfort, indignation, and wealth accumulation caused their integration to be swallowed by the assimilation and proliferation of other races instead of the other way around. But as everyone else's racial identity in the melting pot merges, it creates distinctions whites must integrate and accept with impartiality. A new standard emerges, which they must adjust to, which now staggers their core. Racial differences and bigoted ignorance continues to shrink.

So the difference or the significance placed on it must be removed for America to survive as it is currently constituted because, eventually, the differences won't exist. Therefore, white will no longer be the gold standard, being replaced by the diversity of humanity. People must see that each community member has equal status according to equally applied judgments within qualifications that override discriminations causing unequal advantage. Then, those who care not to put in the work will be shunned. Shunned not by race, but lack of effort by those who have put in work regardless of color.

Consequently, it is no longer possessing a difference based on color but on an impartial comparison. So, equality is not indiscreetly across the board but among those who are alike to be judged alike and fairly compared amongst their category of qualifications. It discards race in favor of qualifications. Apple to apples or when more specific red apple to red apple. Not red to green, as their taste is different. But, when taste is judged, not color, color is incidental to the taste, be it sweet, sour, or whatever.

Thus, specific fixed attributes become the distinguishing element. The competition is among the competent and accomplished who meet the qualifications. It is proven that when you are good at what you do, you are always welcome. We must increase our numbers to consistently be eligible for fair consideration within these categories of qualifications. Since this is the easiest entry point of discrimination for denial, we must be too numerous and qualified to be overlooked. The exclusion before consideration is where we are often dismissed followed by denial of cultivating internship opportunities.

Still, time is the remedy applied wisely whereby our inclusion is compulsory by increasing our sheer numbers in eligibility. Once having navigated the course, we must mentor other of our people as sort of an economic underground railroad. The prevailing institutional systems and business structures are static in their operations designed for an infrastructure which can only support it now by smoke and mirrors. A diametric shift in both systems and structures caused by suffocating social contractions are resulting in an expansion of inclusion. At this point, our astute economic and cultural positioning will most effectively incrementally decrease discrimination.

These institutional systems and business structures are relics of a worldwide colonial system biased for white facsimiles. These relics must replenish and maintain the ratio or majority composition to operate at their optimum. The imbalanced to be maintained is racism for exclusion. The racist majority is dwindling while their power is no longer without challenge. Therefore, by racially restricting personnel, racism disrupts profits by lack of retention, loss of productivity, and singularity of perspective. By rejecting viable human resources where others have not creates employee shrinkage and subpar services. This is what led to sports integration although social integration was credited.

The matador's red muleta conceals the instrument of his destruction, the sword. Likewise, social integration and humanitarian compassion often conceal their true motives. The waving of the muleta entices the bull to charge to its demise guided by rage. Consider claims of global support for populations under abusive regimes and chaotic conditions is still tempered by race and class. Some create outrage, more elicit tacit condemnation, while others splutter oblivious denial. Accountability is selective, recourse is minimal, and justice or aid waved in an oh la fashion.

Otherwise, mayhem would be condemned with the same vigor regardless of who the perpetrators or victims are. None in significant numbers or power have such an allegiance to Africa, Mexico, Haiti, or other countries of color, even Puerto Rico. Furthermore, the colonial affiliation based on race binds the European commitment where compassion is felt and assistance rendered because many whites have a lineage and affinity to these places.

They demonstrate segregationist benevolence lacking reciprocity for "undesirable sh—hole countries" whose main distinction is race or non-white European. Racism persists because they can supplement us with white immigrants with the understanding that they are assimilated into a class above us. For this reason, you will never see European immigration curtailed while we are gullibly consumed with humanitarian compassion. Assistance from absentee landlords and support for resident dependents should be the least expectation for countries that want to exert power or fly their flag claiming their ruling sovereignty over other countries.

Unshockingly, this has been encouraged and subsidized since the initiation of slavery and the beginnings of America. Namely, the scam that racial distinctions are necessary and later asserted to ensure our equality and opportunity. Unfortunately, however, it seems to have the opposite effect. Suppose no racial distinctions were made on applications. Wouldn't it limit the opportunity or incentive to discriminate based on race? Why is it necessary where there is no apparent need for it to be revealed?

This brings it back full circle to the descendant from slavery labeling disguised as African American. Maybe they need to know to exclude us rather than ensure we are included. White includes every light complexion nationality without further distinction whereby they are incorporated by deceptive but established means regardless of time or history in America. Skin tone grants automatic membership and privileges from day one. This is also true for other darker complexion nationalities so long as they are not Black.

For many, there are no other choices other than white. If you are not Black, Latino, Asian, or American Indian, then you are labeled white. But if you are one of these except Black, you can label yourself white. In this time of technology, where decisions are made from computerized information, why is race or even gender necessary? If religion, sexuality, weight, or other meaningless information is irrelevant and not submitted, why not race? Why is race really necessary with its many manipulations and inaccuracies?

Race distinctions are antiquated, prone to bias, arbitrary, and ambiguous. Furthermore, designating other or white would be subjective to the preference of self-identification and not actually being technically that, especially since white is a conglomeration of worldwide nationalities and geographies. By definition, you cannot be African American unless your ancestors are descendants of sub-Saharan or lower Africa and your heritage was lost through slavery.

To further expose the lunacy and ignorance of racism and race, what are the logical assumptions when considering race in the following context. White as a color is defined as having no hue. So if it has a hue, it cannot be white. Hue is observable pigmentation by the intensity of light discernable by shades. White reflects light and is seen as a shade of light. Other colors mixed in equal ratios produce white, so white is the byproduct of other colors. Interestingly, brown is really dark orange. Also, there are different shades of white. White is all wavelengths of visible light, while black is absent of visible light.

Is it starting to become clearer? The properties seem to have been changed to foster a misleading understanding of white being pure. By color, what if race was strictly judged by tint, similar to window tint? There would be clear or, i.e., white and every other color spectrum by shade or hue. By that assumption, would some assimilated races be off-white, Navajo white, rose white, and over one hundred shades of white? But, they are, and so is the many shades of black. Still, how can the shades overlap but still be assigned to a different racial group based on color? An olive-skinned white person can be darker than a light or fair-skinned Black person based on color. Go figure.

Contrary to science and genealogy, why does the social construct of white absorb all nationalities and black repelling the opposite of their evolutionary proprietary nature of the origins of life? The qualities have been switched, much like Noah's Ham and Canaan representation. Still, white and black technically do not exist, only variations in between. Ask yourself, why the charade and dissonance surrounding a fundamental sociological conflict? It is logically incongruent except for being a contrived discord as the only explanation.

Are we all so naïve, ignorant, or programmed to be duped by the inconsistencies regarding race? Are the world governments historically conditioned or more likely protecting their control over the masses by frivolous distractions of chaos ensuring servitude? Surely, someone knows the truth, but it is not in their self-interest to promote it while the masses are socially cloned by a corrupted code to comply.Suppose the government or corporate America is committed to diversity and inclusion. Why not have applications according to a number and not a name, race, or gender to assure anonymity and impartiality based strictly upon qualifications? Why is race a mandatory distinction? Why not just American if all are deemed equal?

It would then seem culture not colorism is at play. It also confirms white is more of a social status of inclusion not a race. With African American meaning the descendant of slaves and white meaning everyone else, including descendants of slave owners, it also denotes us not being accepted as belonging on or from this land. White exclaim they need to take their country back, but it was inhabited when they arrived, but no mention of returning it and definitely not vacating it. But, we are welcome to return by boat to

Don't Say It if We Don't Mean It
If we Talk it, we Walk it
402

Africa when we have been here before almost everyone saying we don't belong.

Relocated by slavery, our designation is the closest estimation of commonality, Africa, even if over four hundred years ago or more. But, African American also denotes being of unknown origins or lineage from a miscellaneous bin of humanity. It gets confusing because white is miscellaneously composed and defined only by what has not been included, Black people, ignoring genealogy. African American is an oxymoron. Africans suggest we don't belong here, and American likewise suggest we don't belong there. Yet, we are tolerated in America as orphans with no specific nationality or ancestral identity.

Still, white does not have the distinction of American attached to it. It is a given. Furthermore, for those so broken, we have a fictional place we belong located in the marvel universe that we can take pride. I choose Black not to denounce Africa but because it represents infinity and is undefined but fundamentally universal. Black is the landscape of the universe with light and objects scattered upon its canvas. In fact, people of African descent are scattered across the global canvas due mostly to slave labor.

I consider everyone of trafficked African descent who was transplanted by slavery as Black regardless of the country because we share a common origin and history ultimately chronicled in the divine wisdom and record of time. Black in this context is for lack of a better term to illustrate the common intrusion on our dignity and not as a racial distinction. We remain separated and subconsciously continue to submit to others' definitions of us by their assignment, further dividing our identity by slave destination instead of the slave experience. But by self-definition, we can deliver the blow instead of receiving the blow by rebuking voluntary surrender to assigned sociological compartmentalized geographical identifications such as Black.

We must beware of our covert voluntary surrenders that lead to overt involuntary distinctions used as discriminatory judgments against us. We are not responsible for these prejudices but moving cleverly isolates and accrue punitive deterrence, if not against the presence of discrimination, then against the absence of fairness. The dominant racial hierarchy seeks to disguise and legitimize the effects of racism as non-existent or situationally coincidental despite the assignment of value to inclusion. They can attempt to discredit the excluded person or group but not without exposing patterns of inconsistency systematically applied to create disadvantage.

Without the blatant display of racial bias, it could be suggested that discrimination and racism are not prevalent. However, it can be demonstrated and exposed when the pattern of inconsistency reveals race is the recurring non-equivalent discernment for selection. Any arbitrary selection would emerge consistently or exclusively from an empirical statistical observation based on designated qualifications and characteristics. Any evidence to the contrary is evidence for concern, discrimination, or suspected fabrication. Its discrepancies must be corrected, eliminated, or punished because they can be quantified.

The willingness, capacity, and justification for repelling punitive exposure for discrimination and racism eventually will affect the ability to do business or to avoid compensatory damages. Discrimination is allowed to continue when there is no challenge or accusation leveled to establish practice and pattern. We must serve notice, if only laying the bricks for future allegations or class action remedies, but not by silence. Ideally, the burden and liability levied must be too much to risk by continuing biased practices. Once it hits the bottom line or bank account, corrective measures will surely be taken.

However, this only occurs with accountability by contesting the inconsistencies. We must speak up against improprieties. The law, or at least the prospect, is there to do the heavy lifting as a deterrent but should not be used frivolously to diminish or dilute legitimate claims. Organizations such as the EEOC, Better Business Bureau, Chamber of Commerce, professional licensing bodies, and attorneys can leverage accountability and attention to discriminatory practices. We should be afforded the same first-class employment and citizenship considerations as any other group as a right and expectation, not an exception. If not, they must not only hear it, but also feel it.

In a so-called Democratic society based upon equality of rights and civil freedoms, it is legally imperative that both are structurally and publicly upheld with impartiality. Therefore, administrative protocols must be assured for the concept to be respected by those who would violate it and those violated by it. Formal and informal, legal, social, and employment impartiality must prevail, or the system descends into apathy, resentment, and contempt. But, it essentially must be unilaterally enforced. There can no longer be indifference towards the offended individual, group, or for damages caused.

The obsolete grip of a colonial utopia built on a British imperial caste system is dependent on continued discrimination and servitude to the acknowledged superiority of a designated group. The determination is by bloodline or skin tone, so membership is limited and according to an established hierarchy in which certain groups can never gain inclusion. Maintaining this fallacy requires an overwhelming demographic who aspire to or succumb to its discrimination, usually by favor to or lack of disadvantage towards themselves. Accordingly, the acknowledgment must be detached to remove the subservient expectation or disadvantage because it requires passivity.

Come along and go along as long as it either benefits or doesn't harm you, subjected to selection and biased toward exclusion. Exclusion is its coveted measure of exclusivity or superiority. Until all citizens outside the comforts of exclusivity have the same fairness the concept of Democracy will remain fatally flawed. Participation in the distribution, access, and application of legal, social, economic, and political consideration with expectations of equity regarding citizenship, opportunity, and possibility. It is not the equality of outcome but the equality of opportunity that supplies equity.

Consequently, expectations of participation separated by skill still vary within groups once inclusion is attained. However, it is the opportunity to compete and not the certainty of results. The same chance as everyone else evenly yoked for consideration without the benefit of special concessions or exaggerated competency being gifted an illicit advantage. Recognition of this principle is why you have age groups, gender classifications, and weight classes in competitions to duplicate equity among the contestants.

Any suppressive disparity must be accordingly adjusted or balanced to achieve parity, including remedies of affirmative action. Skill levels are approximate estimations demonstrated within comparable classification. So ideally, it must be with society and government, judged on competent and competitive skill levels or capabilities. In addition, some numerical balance of society and population must be proportionately reflected by participation and representation equitably distributed.

Only then can the system be considered representative of all because all have someone competently representative of them. The unlikelihood of the numbers being as tilted as they are favoring white males is astronomical, given the diversity of demographics. So the process must be biased in favor of white males to account for the imbalance and ensure they remain dominant in the determination of what most benefits their customary status. But, sometimes, we empower others when we have the demographic advantage, unwilling to wield our power or empower our agenda. Politics and economics are the driving influences which wield our power and leverage.

The political gerrymandering, sociological indoctrinations, pervasive dishonesty, and religious fanaticism striking fear, favor, and conformity ensure the systematic advantages appear nearly insurmountable, especially given our compliance. But, they are not insurmountable, particularly when deprived of our compliance. We must tinker with the social mechanisms by which we acquiesce to conditions unfavorable for improving our status or acquiring our allegiances as being anything but customarily expected or predictable.

Our customary or predictive stance must be predicated on future gains and not dubious past alliances which are no longer an asset to our endeavors. Beyond the local, more insignificant offices and positions whose effects remain localized, it is exponentially harder to secure elections without us. Especially when resources are amassed to bolster preferred candidacies and, thus, agendas disguised as democratic selection. This endowment of resources determines who is placed before voters to choose among.

Essentially the choice is already made for the voters, but the selection is not. This is independent of and secondary to race or social status, depending on the ulterior motive and insidious agendas benefiting and promoting a selective construct. Often this is accomplished willfully with the best intentions or obliviously according to the worst designs. Money generally dictates and establishes political power while the veil of public elections, majority rule, and popular vote pretend to override all other determinates.

Arguably, the effects of political lobbying produces more dispositions than the voting public. Once seduced political power restricts its benefits to appease its interest discarding vicarious residual benefit to others. That segment of society is supported by distribution patterns of privileges, services, or intended consequences with little regard for those excluded outside its concern, support, or preference. The reciprocation obliging politics to money is solely the preservation of their position.

This is done by statutory protection or legislative courtesy secured by big money's investment and maneuvering of individuals into political positions to continue favorably exerting power. In a democratic society, the illusion is the majority will is pursued when actually, once elected, there is no voter audit of their activity until reelection is due. Furthermore, their decisions are solely at their discretion during their time in office and not controlled by their constituency. Their associations are usually directly beneficial to their continued service or personal gain as the primary objective.

They make the rules but are not subjected to them from unethical financial gains, suspicious allegiances, to outright deceit securing their position of power. Contemplate the magnitude of insider trading based on privileged information or conflict of interest and betrayal of public faith regarding highly nefarious accommodations and wealth during and after office. Consider how lawmakers are not subject to a drug test when we are, despite the importance of their duties compared to ours. The most insignificant job requires a drug screening but not a national elected position impacting millions of lives, even if due cause or allegations exist.

The public servitude is not on behalf of the elected official but the public who elects and tolerates them. I point that out to imply that while the ballot is influential and it may facilitate the itinerary, it doesn't dictate it. The itinerary is often governed by reciprocation for accepting the obligation's benefit and it swaps that debt by accommodating expectations. Once obliged, a quid pro quo discharging a debt of gratitude is expected. So, the favor or indebtedness is an expense and acknowledgment of control and support propelling transactional agendas.

This is the business of politics, understanding that government is a business governed by money, influence, and networking for subjective purposes. The government is a massive company with inherent levels of bias based upon hidden agendas necessary to produce outcomes of greater implication to more significant positions. However, Black voters are usually relegated as secondary to the brokered agendas although critical to elections as an essential component to their success because we on occasion don't require any political reciprocity.

Transactional demands must be satisfied in exchange for any politically significant support. If sought as a valued endorsement, our demands too must be met. So, automatic party affiliations are no longer to be taken for granted or not bartered by our interest or agenda driven. Seems like a political third rail is needed as a possibility or alternative. Certainly, more diligently negotiated assurances and expectations in exchange for our support is required. Our political and social invoice must be paid the same as others.

Politics protecting, promoting, and controlling legislation, funding, and regulations are for results that produce a predetermined anticipated outcome. That outcome will favor someone, most likely at someone else's expense. When properly positioned, the benefits will include us by having a seat at the table or a levy exacted on the process. Political and legislative recourse is the most pervasive and effective way to create negotiable power and equity when resistance is insufficient. Our incessantly defying the system guarantees us constantly flowing against the stream, ensuring struggle teetering on a perpetual rescue operation.

We must pick our battles wisely and our method of resistance shrewdly. Confrontation is not always necessary or advisable. Aside from intentions fixated on universally isolating and identifying systemic injustices to penalize violations, our participation within the confines of these processes best positions us to change the flow. By redirecting the momentum of the stream, it can be utilized to propel our interest using the existing principles of the system forcing adjustments from within. We owe much of our progress to this process.

When we conduct business how it is conducted, we can use it to our benefit as it is designed to work instead of conceding to its hostilities. Our ideological representation, not individuals, reflects our participation in the processes that distribute power and benefits. Meanwhile, our absence from punitive and economic persuasion leveraged correctly cannot amass an impact to chip away at the cornerstone until it exist. Its existence crumbles the insistence on biases in how our ideological business is conducted. It must be made inconvenient and obvious for discriminatory behavior to become scorned as a liability financially, socially, and legally.

No longer can anyone become comfortable disregarding our interest. Our grievances have traditionally been rejected primarily because of our positioning and method of redress. Using all the tools and entities that would align themselves against discrimination to offer support for equity, inclusion, and penalties has a unilateral impact on promoting diverse petitions against violations. Repeated and obvious infractions generate class-action protections and accusations, thereby serving notice and intent. Legal and economic repercussions are convincing deterrents available to discourage discrimination and expose its practices to pay what they weigh.

There are agencies obligated to act or investigate any claim for credibility and corrective action. Understanding the options, documentation, processes, and execution for allegations and verifications of discrimination or racism identifies the articulation necessary to sustain its claim. The remaining element is compelling the remedial application of the law to enforce it. We cannot become discouraged and give up, but instead should expect resistance and insist that more than an unsympathetic ear will be needed to dismiss our claim.

Any facilitation or enablers can become a target subject to scrutiny from a higher level or outside agency investigating possible violation of civil rights when they are systemically tolerated. Generally, these sorts of accusations are not welcome. Not only equality, but the strict application of equity is called for in the legal sphere of civil liberties, employment, discrimination, and workplace code of conduct or conditions. There are no justifications or affirmative defenses for any exceptions to their violation or lawful adherence, thereby limiting infractions of compliance or retaliatory punishments. The objective is directed towards eliminating or minimizing the imbalance.

The dichotomy of equality and equity, by definition, is minor, while in concept and application, they are vast. Equality is universal across the board, while equity is comparative consideration using specific methods of equilibrium to address disparities. The law is noticeably clear regarding the equality of rights of all citizens and even the rights of non-citizens. Legal equality is not arbitrary, situational, transactional, or conditional. It is mandatory, but enforcement must be diligently concentrated on checks and balances to work.

So the systemic racism and refusal to apply the law equally, intended to discourage us, has its Achilles heel either in the persons operating them, the system's operation, or both. Both people and systems are accountable or have procedures and operations mandating their actions. Some form of regulation, guidelines, or parameters apply to everything aside from what is actually practiced. As such, violations are deviations from the margin of fair and impartial observation. They are our right and not to be confused with privileges or concessions.

Therefore, the right to speak freely, bear arms, due process, unreasonable search and seizure, self-incrimination, assembly, protest, vote, hold office, and petition the government are our rights. An expectation of a safe and unbiased workplace along with fair compensation are fundamental rights not open for conditional interpretation or selective application. They should be delivered unabated and exercised without reserve. Any patterns of violation can be racially motivated or simply violations but are definitely prohibited. Keep in mind that all violations will not be overt or racial.

However, suppose an apparent breach of rights occurs. In that case, it is to be pursued to the fullest extent of recourse, racial or otherwise. As a racial issue, most definitely say or do something, even anonymously, to ensure others' rights are also respected, chipping away at instances of racism when and wherever it is practiced. The accountability and compensation for racism displayed on a macro or international level start with exposing the micro-aggressions allowed to go unchallenged in lesser environments.

The challenge must be situationally directed for the best results. Sever the roots because the tree has become too massive for pruning. For instance, reparations cannot be only directed at the head, ignoring the body to accumulate attrition. The erosion of incorporated racism must address the source and, more importantly, the spread and practices far removed from its origins. The evolution of bigotry has made for a moving target and fluctuating culprits during various periods, complicating the degree of accountability further distancing resolution.

The government of America being petitioned for damages regarding slavery is an attack on the head that allowed and sanctioned slavery but also its abolition. Moreover, the government has at various times endorsed slavery, Jim Crow, racism, discrimination, equality, inclusion, voting rights, and civil rights. Every facet of the government and judiciary, from top to bottom, has participated in bias and bigotry, but also remedies. They have indeed implemented remedies that has driven change contrary to a bigoted resume. It is also true that many white people have stood stout in their rejection of racism.

This blatantly clarifies the path to duplicate social gains but also necessitates an accelerated pace supplemented by a resurgent resolve by all inclined. Hence, change or redress are not without hope or merit. Still, the probability becomes more logistically problematic when slowed by time and society's historical vacillating position to deny, tolerate, or combat discrimination. No doubt the government has done its part to discriminate, but none has done more for equality despite its blemishes. This is aside from considering the current assorted social and political resistance that persists as a matter of perspective, policy, and accountability.

The most egregious offenses have time and historical distance between them and the various more benign commissions of current racism. But by denial it resembles a social bankruptcy, where creditors are shielded from collecting and enforcing debts protected by the insolvency of responsibility. This resulting insolvency has plausible deniability as an un-payable write-off debt without a ledger for valuation or a specific party to remand payment or lien entitlement. The un-payable is simultaneously uncollectible.

Therefore, reparations are a class action assertion based on race in general but slave lineage in particular. Race is an imprecise metric whereby claims can be levied based on diluted racial proclamations, requirements, and assertions. Beyond that, the method, duration, and amount of payment have complicated considerations needing a preponderance of the public and politicians for legislative approval. Furthermore, the overriding concern is the ability to do so.

It would seem that technically the period referenced would be before 1865 by recognition of the Emancipation Proclamation and Juneteenth or before 1789 under the Continental Congress. By legitimizing these dates and occurrences despite lingering ramifications to the contrary, slavery predates them. Suppose the claim is against the lingering ramifications. How are they quantified and evaluated according to the presence or absence of prosperity as opposed to periods before the supposed eradication? So are we talking before, after, or both?

It would be a supposition conjuring speculation of factors far too many to arbitrarily surmise. After the absolute determination that slavery was an atrocity pervasive in America, the consensus falls apart afterwards on who assumes liability, with some claiming that history does. The assessment becomes convoluted when considering if the practitioners or enablers are more proportionally responsible. Remember that those defenders and endless romantics of the founding fathers and the Constitution generally saw no fault with slavery or any need for amends or restitution. They preached their freedom but practiced our slavery.

Nor was it illegal until nearly ninety years after the nation's independence. It is still questionable to what degree its prohibition is enforced or discouraged today, as racism and discrimination are quite evident in societal and institutional forms. So theoretically, the meter has never stopped running. Much has changed, but has it only given the appearance of change cloaked in a different garment to disguise its recognition? What faction of our suppression is racism opposed to some other factor like self-actualization?

Although racism is undeniable, what is questionable? The only way federal approval of reparations will occur is when opposition has a transmutation of conscious and the ability to compensate. That or we bulk up our economic and political muscle to ensure it. I suggest the latter would be more expedient and compelling. Most likely, it may have to be charged to the game as a settlement too costly to pursue either by time consumed, future forfeited, or efforts and emotions expended. Thus, a sensible negotiation of expectations must occur.

With that said, a more analytical and strategic approach to reparations would circumvent as many obstructions and excuses as possible while utilizing whatever processes are available to secure transferable compensation. The target and method, I believe, are distorted and misaligned for this era. The potential probability and statutory propositions to compel social justice and reparations are adjusted social, economic, legal, and historical pressures suitable for current sensibilities.

The goal is to negotiate a voluntary concession of value, not an apology or admission but actionable considerations of consequence. Then, if not voluntary, to legally pursue remedy from specific entities using existing laws and leverage for damages. Damages financially quantified or specific to the services offered in their regular course of business or the resources pilfered. This method may not be effective against the government's indemnity. Still, other nations, companies, and institutions but essentially private sector involvement, are most likely liable under some application of material transgression according to law. Maybe even maritime law.

Under international law, maritime law, or business law, aside from the humanitarian issue, illicit profits, stolen resources, appropriated property, and hijacked prosperity they should be legally liable for compensation and adjudication. But, under goodwill of any voluntarily reasonable settlement, they should be eager to cleanse their hands of their participation. Each according to their participation and benefit. Thereby spreading the responsibility among the culprits and benefactors for their particular actions, which are also of historical record.

Establishing the culprits would be possible by forensic accounting tracing assets and profits from the time in question coupled with the actions committed. The law or morality and ethics integrated would seem to be a powerful leveraging motivation to transform their history, recognizing the evil embezzlement by which it was financially established and accumulated. The method and extent of restoration or settlement of primarily a judgment against the act of slavery's societal and financial subsidies at the deliberate detriment of Blacks are as varied as the processes used to carry them out.

The frequency and prevalence of residual or unintended racism are just as damaging as the historically unmistakably unchecked incidents and practices of slavery. Inclusion to equitable opportunity would be cheaper than reparations. Therefore, the solutions and judgments must reverberate with determination and purpose to produce equity among socioeconomic classes and qualifications equivalent to each other accordingly raising each level to a shared opportunity for prosperity. Many would argue the success of a percentage of our people is proof of progress accessible to many, but only in theory and not practicality.

Practically any settlement or judgment of reparations should be directed and available to those who still suffer racism's wrath the most. Determined by a position of lower economic status, educational inadequacies, healthcare inaccessibility, nutritional neglect, and opportunity suppression. Those who need the most do not necessarily need the same appraisal of redress as those who have thrived. So, each receives according to their needs and condition to offset the disparity caused by racism. Those not in need would yield the balance of consideration to those most in need. The tide is needed to raise the shallowest vessel where the benefits can be most felt.

Maybe dispersed by zip code, but those who have escaped the pit have no need to be rescued from it. For example, the indigent needs would differ from the middle or upper socioeconomic classes, who may need loans, capital investments, or business opportunities instead of food, training, or other staples of survival. They very well may need nothing. Reparations do not have to pursue a linear progression funded by additional resources. Still, they can be nonlinear by reallocating various existing resources from public funding initiatives and services, which have been unequivocally biased and economically disparaging in their distribution.

Full disclosure also reveal some unlikely gatekeepers restraining our progress. The unequal application of criteria, resources, or opportunity often comes from an unexpected source, other Black people. Compelled by their position to conduct themselves as straw bosses harboring disdain to be disassociated from others among us as unlike themselves. This distance of association protects their status within the system as a prestigious exception integrated as validation of their assimilation by achievement or others' exclusion.

This splinter of identity is often evident in Blacks like Stephen from Django, masterfully played by Samuel L. Jackson, offering motesa (more tea, sir) while despising a horse riding N-word for a prestige above his. Any challenge to their prestige or the possibility by another Black person is met with venom and scorn. Stepping and fetching for validation and separation. To remain truthful, this division from self is often enabled by our representation that we take for granted as a Black perspective or by race a beneficial collaborator concerning our interest.

However, they have become oppressors and suppressors, holding us at bay and in our place while skinning and grinning for favor. Sadly but rightfully, they cannot be counted in the column of our allies. Instead, their allegiance and prestige are proudly on display as honorary white folk. Too often, we are too afraid or disengaged to exercise our power to equalize circumstances once we have gotten our plot.

This is especially true on the business and local political level, where city and county officials who are Black and part of or operate systems that use public funds. As a result, how can we disproportionately receive what excludes any resemblance of proportional equity of distribution or services when our people participate in the disbursement? The apathy and yes sir bossing mentality are apparent. The business of government should first ensure they are not violating inclusion efforts while regulating the private sector to comply with anti-discrimination measures.

The private sector is much harder to regulate, but not if it requires a stipulation to do business with the government on any level. Training, access to trade skills, apprenticeships, and union membership in the construction industries disproportionately excludes us, even when the service is performed in our neighborhoods using public funds. This keeps us deprived of resources earned in our community but not spent in our community. Municipal governments tax revenue is based on location earned. But strangely, no monetary benefit is bestowed on our communities when these poachers benefit from revenue earned or generated in our communities.

Even more strangely and beneath condescending is midnight basketball is deemed a more valuable expenditure than training to participate in public expenditures. These demeaning insults perpetuates poverty by selection creating economic redlining and cash flow divestment, excluding those who live in these neighborhoods by a lack of resources and viable opportunities. These city and county administrations don't need data from outside sources to equitably monitor the imbalance because they are the source and can dictate the terms and conditions of distribution and participation. Furthermore, the criteria can be discriminatory for qualification.

They can't seem to detect it in their own midst when it is used to deny participation vicariously by a prerequisite which is bias. For example, exclusion from the union excludes us from the process if we are not represented in the union. Indirectly economic discrimination can be created by the disparity of criteria or union membership before it reaches the later stages of selection. If officials were serious and held accountable instead of deflecting to these departments, studies, and criteria of deniability, loopholes of discrimination could be eliminated.

Why not install compliance and verification methods of a dedicated amount or percentage spent annually distributing millions in the case of the city and perhaps billions in the case of the county. The state and federal government expenditures are even greater. Enough with the pledges, consultants, studies, and commissions that routinely dismiss claims and complaints while this government-sanctioned and practiced racism of systemic proportions operates in willful oblivion on the public dime. While they play volleyball with these issues, no progress is made but the roast beef and expenditures are served in abundance.

Another very simple way to address economic racism is to include more of us not only as employees to claim diversity but in the supervisory and management levels. This is where decisions of inequality are often made in the absence of us. The chances of rebuttal or protest are minimal, with no Black person present as even a visual deterrent. Also, it is incumbent upon us not to just sit by the door when included. We must speak against transgressions that ultimately affect us all, even vicariously, especially when tokenism is suspected or required.

Our power and position should be exercised to ensure a rightful share from an influencer perspective instead of protesting or pleading after outrage from lack of fortitude at the time. We are also entitled to the same considerations and accommodations which have a widespread economic impact for others. These public funds enrich others and their communities, benefiting them and their children to maintain a higher standard of living above ours. The residual generational affluence allows for property accumulation, educational advantages, and more accessible entrepreneurial avenues.

It is fiscal causation promoting affluence or, when adversely applied, poverty. Either way, the two roads are paved very differently. This alone directly affects property valuations, school funding, public services, and insurance premiums. Many more other concealed expenses, depletion of resources, or reduced evaluations according to economic redlining of demographically Black communities and laborers occur. A mere slice of the cake when it is served instead of crumbs would support reparations with money already being spent instead of additional funds generated for allocation.

This is the clandestine fabric of sociology that constantly bestows preference and privilege upon others, where denials can be made despite statistical analysis and demographic proof. An earnest assessment of public money and subsidies that sustain other races, businesses, institutions, entities, facets of government, and any economic considerations should, at the very least, be reflective of the almost fifteen percent of the United States Black population. Carving us out something will not disrupt such an enormous flow, unless economic suppression is the purpose.

Another major impact area is higher education, first supplied by the institutions that benefited and participated in the slave trade. Then providing free academic services to our people who meet their criteria or different services for those who may need assistance (equity) to qualify there or some similar scholastic setting. That would require more equity and improvement in primary schooling to prepare for secondary education.

Finally, the gaps can be filled by the federal, state, or city governments that regulate education to actually provide the services required in public education for universal life skills or independent living in preparation for adulthood. Furthermore, banks and insurance companies who have been exploitive and usurious of us have a moral and financial obligation probably subject to legal recourse to amend their gouging and transgressions against our community. It should be noted that many of those obligations go beyond the unstated by their participation in discriminatory practices beyond actual participation in the slave trade.

Same for the highly suspect integrity of Wall Street, which could create endowments, investments, or annuity conduits generating revenue directly to our community or cause. Collectively banks, insurance companies, and Wall Street historical extortions of us are astronomical. Therefore, plenty of accountability and accounts payable long overdue can immediately create settlement programs relative to their original sin. It would behoove them to proactively address and resolve their past voluntarily without public condemnation or contention.

Reevaluation, even overhaul, of some aspects of these entities' current practices and organizational structures, intent, and consequences must be conducive to our needs exacerbated by their actions and policies. The solution of what kind of settlement is necessary, where it can be best applied, and who should supply it according to their capabilities would disperse the obligation and contribution, lessening the individual impact. Some continue to bombast echoes of Socialism or Fascism to defend resisting accountability or reparations claiming that these political and social ideologies are representative of the decay of Democracy.

While ignoring the decay from racism, the brand of discriminatory Democracy practiced in America has always been a form of soft Socialism or flimsy Fascism by its lack of impartiality. The foundation of Capitalism is impartiality while Socialism controls and direct resources creating artificial imbalances. In America, it's just racially selective. Social justice is correlated to anti-democratic rhetoric and activities by the naysayers, who almost exclusively have been the perpetrators or benefactors. The reparation denial or affirmative action mandates granted but questionably enforced are opposed as claims of producing our dependency or unfairness to others.

Further analysis of Socialism is defined by social ownership and disbursement of production, elevating everyone to equal status and portions based upon concepts contrary to the exploitative aspects of capitalism. However, pure Capitalism seeks its own competitive level creating a natural imbalance dependent on effort or contribution. So, by definition, Socialism has been practiced in this country as a pseudo-democracy by benefiting only the white class. Everyone else has suffered under an authoritarian regime of economic racism.

It has been unfair to everyone else in favor of whites, being deemed the ruling class and arbitrator of distribution. Socialism controls the outcome, but equity controls the opportunity. Under democracy and capitalism, the opportunity should be equitable with the outcome uncertain according to the degree of competency, proficiency, resources, and ambition invested or provided. Racism is a violation of these concepts. Likewise, Fascism requires an almost identical atmosphere as racism.

Fascism is a right-wing one-political party ideology of authoritarian power advocating a dictatorship ruled by fear and suppression, exercising stringent conformity by society, restricted political power, and economic manipulation benefiting a select population justified as nationalism. Sounds familiar? Racism, overthrowing elections, gerrymandering, and redlining would seem to be a tool of fascism. Looks familiar? Socialism and Fascism are, by ideology, suppressive of Democracy but promote racism, fanaticism, human rights violations, crimes against humanity, oppressive compliance, and violence to secure power and control.

Both are easily recognizable as having arrived on these shores with the pilgrims out the gate disguised as Democracy, Freedom, and Capitalism. Under Democracy, there's been an obsession to only finance spreading its control while disregarding entities already under its control. Blacks, Puerto Rico, and dark complexion countries are of little concern or long ago divided and conquered. However, there is currently no shortage of foreign aid to Caucasian European countries, immediately dispersing billions of dollars, military equipment, and supplies.

So, if reparations were a priority, they could have easily been paid, costing less than what has been given away as foreign military aid. The speed of a financial response implies a cultural allegiance obligated to the European immigrant lineages occupying America. No doubt, darker skin tone brings about a different eagerness and concern than our fairer complexioned counterparts. Where reparations for slavery are denied by claims of not being owed, what is the obligation owed to these foreign countries?

If the claim is Democracy or humanitarian sympathies, wouldn't oppressed Americans or Blacks qualify? What about the homeless or our veterans need for resources? What about free breakfast and lunch in schools for children? What about securing our oxygen before we secure others? It seems to be a white racial and cultural subsidy resembling international Communism or ethnic Socialism. The claim that affirmative action or reparation benefits will hinder us by our abuse of and dependence on instruments designed to negate discrimination is ridiculous. If not ridiculous, why is there no such concern for these European countries' abuse or dependency?

But, racism is dependent on the abuses and theft of resources and opportunities that promote discrimination establishing a reliance on a fraudulent advantage. This bemoans the benefit to others as a privilege which you flagrantly flaunt often as your right. According to this analogy, a level playing field is anti-democratic, while injustice is pro-democratic. Accordingly, dependency is not the problem but fairness or lack of impartiality. While disproportionately arming white ambitions, it is us whose interest has suffered to expand beyond race and class.

Welfare or assistance is often portrayed as our economic subsidy. At the same time, the numbers do not support this but do support the contrary. By the totality of the population, welfare is also numerically dominated by whites as much as these other instances of deflection despite the purposeful intent to marginalize subsidies to us. However, one remedy would be the old adage of giving someone a fish and feeding them for a day. Teaching or allowing them to fish and feed them for a lifetime would support inclusion in the economic prosperity that others enjoy.

The current labor crisis is indicative of the unsustainability of economics based racism causing stagnation. When prejudicial special associations and concessions systematically exist, it has to create a counterbalance of injustice or imposition restraining progress. Thus, racism and slavery have undeniably been a privilege to whites and an imposition to us. Advantages that do not exist between members of different demographics at the expense of others necessitate a recalibration to correct the wrong. Economic policy can no longer be, letting us eat cake or help ourselves to the scraps.

Producing new socioeconomic norms and opportunities not constricted by race, gender, or discrimination will require more vertical institutional awareness, cooperation, and infiltration to rebuke these twisted interpretations of racist ideology that distort social justice and economic progress. The economic and social progression of our concerns and racial injustices levied against us cannot be attacked by a conventional linear method. We cannot use antiquated techniques accepting matador mirages chasing the carrot that is always out of reach.

We must not pursue from far behind but transmute our practices to accelerate our position to where it will be instead of what it has been or is now. Catch-up only gets you where it is now, not to where it is moving. So, when we declare our demands, accountability must be maintained by us equally as those who we would hold responsible. It transcends race and color, yielding to purpose, progress, and achievement as the basis of our pursuits and appeasement.

Therefore, when we say it, we must mean it. Otherwise, we should not say it. It amounts to panhandling when we don't stand on it convicted without compromise. We need quantifiable sustainable results. All things are not negotiable, and certainly not our dignity. Black Lives Matter is a catchy slogan, but my life mattered is a worthy legacy, endeavor, and sobering reality leaving a lineage of value as the ultimate reparation paid forward. So walk it like we talk it, or don't say it if we don't mean it.

Our humanity will prevail only through diligence when progress is all that matters. Every Black person is not an ally because of color, and every white person is not an enemy. Actions separate or unite both as either friend or foe, not color. Color sometimes only makes it easier to detect and identify but is a deceptive and dismissive profile just as race is. For us to judge or be judged on race or color is a fragmented racism assuming qualities and perspectives arbitrarily biased.

A prime example is a Supreme Court Judge. We have made erroneous assumptions based on color. But, oh, have we been wrong. The prism of color is not a particularly good judge of others and certainly not of us. Character and integrity tell us so much more and others too. Therefore, ignorance divides, ideology unites, while the extremes and fringes disrupt as polar opposites. Still, there are so many more between these extremes comprising commonality. The fringes are exaggerated to suppress the commonality of ideology and perspective. Racism is not as prevalent as portrayed just as our dysfunction is not as universal as depicted.

The illusion is the fringes are more than they actually are and the division greater than it actually is. The trap has been set, but the bait doesn't have to be taken. Racism will be consumed by logic exposing the superstitions of ignorance, fallacies of deceptions, and rejection of indoctrinations allowing exploitation. It is all connected and unwittingly practiced. The foundation is unstable but bolstered by some of our deepest held and most indoctrinated complicities and beliefs. We must liberate our mind and identity from the attachments that divide our wholeness into categories of spiritual and racial separateness and inadequacies.

Immunity from consideration fortifies our beliefs and loyalty to restrict our expansion forgoing discovery and solutions rebuked by adherences long ago decided without our consensus. Foregone conclusions of antiquity, deception, and lack of knowledge forges replicas of the past stifling prototypes of the future. As racism has evolve, the primary frontier to conquer remains the initial obstacle, the psychology. Racism is an acknowledge receptacle of limitations or ideologies that ultimately can only penetrate the resolve of a compatible host.

Our susceptibility as host instilled through slavery will only be un-done when we invalidate the etchings of systematic and strong-armed convictions commonly propagandized to control or decimate us. This complete and earnest embrace continues to be solidified by our dependence on resolutions outside our control but within our indoctrination. The telekinesis of inferiority is a mental construct of repetition overriding feelings convinced of its insinuations. So imbedded obedience to the concept supersedes its factual basis ac-cepted as truth.

For example, why is Jesus not called Joshua, the English translation of Yeshua, which is also a translation? For that matter, why not Yeshua? Many people don't know anything other than Jesus? King James' Bible was printed in 1611 or thereabout, but before then, many translations were converted into English. However, before the 1600s or 17th century, no one would have known who you were referring to if you said Jesus. If in a room with Jesus himself present, he would not have answered or thought you were referring to him if you called this supposed name.

Otherwise, he would have corrected you. Why have you not been corrected when the letter J did not exist in Hebrew, Greek, or Latin. If you told someone you sought him during his time, they would not know who you sought by that name. Then, the misconception regarding Jesus' correct name was popularized and perpetuated here along with race by Protestant settlers who came to America under England's influence.

Yet still, the declaration to keep the Sabbath day holy has specific instructions on the day of reference, Saturday or Saturn day. When was it changed, by who and why? Are Sun-day worshippers in vio-lation of the bible and the directive attributed to God? Who had the audacity or authority to change God's will to what we roundly wor-ship now? Every corner of accepted knowledge must be scrutinized for its origin, deviation, and purpose commonly contrived as truth. Yet, this is a fundamental belief of ours, although errant.

Every examination of behavior and firmly held beliefs might yield a deliberate misconception obscured by time and ignorance for a nefarious purpose. Deductive reasoning renders the question of what other rogue translations, altered interpretations, and intentional misconceptions do we thoughtlessly concede in a zombie-like state to further obstruct resurrecting a dead mind. A dead mind lacking curiosity or enlightenment beyond the presentation of prescribed prerogatives of manipulation.

Knowledge has always been forbidden for this reason. Those Europeans who first populated the new world, America, were Puritans and followers of the King James Bible and was of a Protestant lean. They were later transformed into the white race. Their original ethnicity was Caucasian. Caucasians refer to those from the Caucasus mountains or region. Caucasian skin tone varies from light to dark brown. Caucasians have over one hundred and fifty ethnicities and are synonymous with Protestants regarding those who populated America.

To maintain the many deceptions, a retroactive narrative was necessary as our introduction to America. The storyline has been concocted to perpetuate not only our obedience and exploitation but many others. Careful examination and technical interpretation of anthropology, geography, genetics, morphological features, statutory definitions, and layers of the epidermis conflict with and refute the literal definition of white, race, and skin tone classifications. Religion has also been disfigured in the process.

Color is only on the surface, an optical illusion, a ricochet of light, and the density of pigmentation. However, it is chronicled much differently as a gauge of inferiority mirroring the narrative which we are still bound. Not only bound by fallacies but ignorance. People were burned at the stake for seizures accused of witchcraft whose only offense was other's ignorance. Anorexia was sexy, women were without rights, and spousal abuse manly. So, ignorance is dangerous, expensive, and timeless.

Therefore, as ignorance, white violates almost all of the designations used to define it. Consequently, it is a catch-all phrase to describe a preferred baseline or median to convey a concept of social value, misleadingly applied as a race. To put it in context, the dominant morphological feature of a criminal was widely believed to be the criminal cranium. Yes, the head's shape was believed to indicate if you would commit a crime or prone to deviant behavior. People were arrested for the shape of their heads in America in the early to mid-1900s without any crime ever being committed.

Imagine the wideness of the nose, the thickness of the lips, the fullness of the buttocks, and the texture of the hair have all been primary indicators associated with the Black race. But, the shape of the cranium and other racial attributes are obviously ridiculous as determinants assigning moral character but why not those regarding us. Many of these characteristics can be found in all ethnicities proving that non-white and race is a construct for division and exclusion. So, is Black also largely defined not only by color but by us being resilient, resourceful, and proud?

How about by our sovereignty as human beings of equal standing to anyone else despite being the ancestors of slaves in America? Even today white is considered by some as a separate race onto itself instead of mixed with many races not governed by color. At one point, whites in America were considered the red race, a mixed race. But, white was later adopted as a term from a German anthropologist to cover a miscellaneous consortium of ethnicities integrated as white to solidify our marginalization.

Once white was extricated from Caucasian, the color spectrum was narrowed too very fair or light skin. That has not been true for an awfully long time, especially psychologically with the prominence of tanning to darken the skin tone but remain white. So now those without a light complexion can become absorbed as white with an ever-expanding definition. Color is not the technical characteristic designating white. By geography, white can now be from most regions of the globe. By genealogy, everyone is a mix of ethnicity not revealed by color. So ignorance or deception fills the void usually designated as white.

Black is a counter designation to being white, metaphorically distinguishing those historically discriminated against from those discriminating against them. Most whites and Blacks both have some genealogy other than their racial designation, which would allow them to claim the opposite race. White has no definition of what it is, just a definition of what it is not. Even then, it is cloudy. However, in America, the distinction is between slave owners and slaves because outside of that context, race really doesn't exist.

Pragmatically, neither exist except to categorize by arbitrary and ever-fluctuating criteria with no practical definition or purpose. The median leads to erroneous assumptions and conclusions that are extremely flawed and archaic, bordering on obsolete as imprecise social measurements of anything. The Protestant influence was distinct from slavery but in sync with a social paradigm disbursed under the Doctrine of Jesus. Deceptive truths abound across many centuries and certainties of society. Consider the smallest country in the world, Vatican City, is within Rome, Italy. It is a country within a country.

Also, ponder Washington D. C is the District of Columbia, a foreign country within but separate from America. It is a country within a country. That is why during the Capital assault only 45 could authorize the invasion of a foreign country by law enforcement outside D.C. such as the national guard entering its borders. Yes, Washington D.C. our seat of government is not a part of the United States. Furthermore, Cesta Que is the lawful foundation of a trust fund which Washington D.C. is the administrator of for America.

For that matter, the United States of America is a trust and we as "citizens" are actually grantors and trustees. It is the basis of the tax system. Similarly, the Federal Reserve is a private company operating as a government entity. Also, concealed in plain view is the connection of Thomas Payne (Age of Reason) as a guiding force and ideology which stirred the American Revolution and the "undeceived" ideology skeptical of Christian manipulation or mythology. Thomas Payne is to the American Revolution what Tertullian is to western theology and the Holy Trinity, the architect.

Likewise, twisted in history is the influence of Freemasonry and Illuminati in the liberation of America and influence on the Founding Fathers more so than belief in Christianity or religion. Most were Deist or Unitarians and rejected the supernatural or miracles. France supported America's liberation and many French philosophers espoused doctrines of disbelief in Christianity that can be found in the foundation of the French Revolution (Enlightenment) and American Politics. Thomas Jefferson, John Adams, Benjamin Franklin, George Washington, and many other signatures on America's founding documents allegiance to Christianity has been greatly exaggerated or fabricated.

America was not founded on Christian beliefs but on principles of secret societies and natural law. Some of the Founding Fathers were known to proudly wear the loin cloth or apron of Masonry and reject many accounts in the Bible. Still, further research into the Founding Father's religious belief would be shocking as evidenced by the Jefferson Bible and Letters and their very own declarations. Do not confuse as an assault on Christianity what is strictly revelations of the Founding Father beliefs and America's ideological origins of religious freedom, which was not Christianity.

Was God in favor of religious freedom and other Godly deities or their worship? Was God mentioned in the Constitution? Is Washington D.C. a replica of St Peter's Basilica, obelisk, and Vatican City separation as a separate country? So, America origins are a masquerade of Christianity in the context of religion but not moral ideology. Obelisk, ley lines, the Egyptian star Sirius, the Sun, and July

4th as a cosmic sun event have all been incorporated into Christianity, America's infrastructure, and holidays. But why?

Can it be more aligned with the occult, alchemy, secret societies, and doctrines of logical reasoning? Any early Unitarian beliefs were overwhelmed by the lust of economic exploitation and warped morality which allowed slavery compromising Democracy and the concept of liberty for centuries to come. The Christian cartel was established through the diligence of the Jesuits and the Catholic Church to supplement obligations for assistance America received from them.

So, what we don't know has been used to enslave us and perpetuate our subjugation under religion. This is the miseducation we must combat as obvious intellectual malpractice designed to revise and obscure history. Even geographical designations has manipulations of racism, resource repatriation, and conquest decided by the prime purveyors of slavery. The Berlin Conference of 1884 ushered in the New Imperialism regulating the European colonization of Africa and its precious resources as a theft of resources instead of the trafficking of humanity.

The human trafficking became secondary to the purse-snatching of natural resources. It resulted in the gang rape of Africa's resources for any who wanted a piece. The purpose was economic, religious, geographical, and political control instilling the indoctrination and monopolization for the peaceful scavenge of Africa to prevent conflict between the looting colonizing bandits. The slave trade was transformed to entirely pilfering resources and the suppression needed to accomplish it. History reveals the deceptions, concealment, and manipulations distorted as a beacon of faith to establish mind control through spirituality.

Therefore, these deceptions we hold to be self-evident lacking examination are bolstered only by the sorcery of time. The repetition of time not the veracity of truth is interwoven into belief systems which cast its shadow as truth only perpetuated by time and acceptance without breath. Continued adherence promotes a mockery of our courage and intelligence. It insults our courage to break away and intelligence to seek or decipher the origins, purpose, or methods of our psychological incarceration. It prevents the psychological breath of our genesis or resurrection restrained by lack of knowledge but assigned to skin tone.

The socialization has persisted, infusing racism with religion portrayed as superiority and privilege justified by the thinnest layer of the outer epidermis. Skin tone is the outer layer of the epidermis, basically a surface dye of the skin among five layers of the epidermis. The other four layers are identical. The deceptions misconstrued as factual are not from lack of knowledge regarding race and are only slightly less than the ones surrounding religion and Jesus' real name. The distortions has become reality obscured by ignorance, indoctrination, and even faith.

How many fallacies must be proven before the entirety is subject for review? Fooling us once was their original sin but to continue to fool us is our ongoing sin. Knowledge is available. Once we understand that, we can see how thorough a slight twist or misinterpretation can become so widespread that the truth becomes distorted. Among those who unconditionally and zealously embrace concepts of race would also forsake their life in the name of Jesus. They would be incorrect on both accounts that race exists and Jesus is his name. Both existed on a parallel course but were blended at an interval to further substantiate each other and control.

Race only exists to the extent that we think it does or would like it to matter. It exists for no reason other than it is, but racism is very real because of it. Seemingly if the concept of race were redefined or eliminated, then racism would have to follow. To paraphrase Machiavelli, we must deal with what it is and not what we would like it to be. Dealing with what we would like it to be invites ruin but what it is allows for solutions. The matrix of falsehood has only one exit, truth.

It is all connected and unwittingly practiced when the deformation of the origins and evolution are converted and expanded with dubious intent. We must all be careful of almost every indoctrination and socialization for purpose and authenticity if it causes division, exploitation, or unquestioned obedience because it was probably designed strictly for that purpose. What we don't know might not hurt us, but it will most certainly cost us to be unknowingly led astray. We are still restrained by the illusion of race and the spell of deceit until we practice and appreciate our humanity beyond slavery or relegation.

We must expose the boogeyman passed down through history as tales of ignorance repetitively regurgitated to become truth bolstered by companion beliefs such as religion to sacred to question. Thus, too established to refute for its manipulative insinuations and insidious stipulations to replace the psychological and emotional consolation with rational analysis. Our perspective is the equalizing force inquisitively pursuing the curiosities of our convictions bred by history's fraudulent teachings.

Lack of knowledge being strangers in a strange land under a stranger system circumstantially delayed our existential development. However, knowledge will liberate us mind, body, and soul casting its radiance of elevation. The sun rises only after darkness and darkness descends after light. Knowledge rises after ignorance maturing to enlightenment while ignorance denies illumination. Where others perceive our differences, we must demonstrate our unity. Racism must be combatted above this three dimensional physical plane of our superficial appearance. Our transcendental spiritual awakening cannot be allowed to be dethroned by the optical illusions of skin tone or humanistic qualities of bias assignments.

Unity of self-determination and duplicity to each one teach one the multiplicity of our commonality pursuing a singular humanity as an equal part of the whole. Still, we can never change our psychology relying on the psychology that put us in this situation. The mindset and indoctrinations that created the problem will never solve it. Shed the cocoon of shame, history, and miseducation to embrace the liberation of enlightenment through information, not opinion. Never above, never below, always equal, and eternally resilient fortified by the cradle of knowledge.

Hard Hat and a Lunch Pail
Beggars Have Never Been Choosers

As currently constituted, our task is summed up best in a phrase used in the Catholic faith: "Forgive me Father, for what I have done and for what I have failed to do." Consider the expression in the context of challenging structures of power and principalities restricting knowledge and obscuring truth through socialization. Those that others are responsible for, but primarily the ones we submit to and share blame. We must address the cruel lies and deliberate excuses we use to pacify and omit our actions.

Ultimately, we are responsible for what we do and what we have failed to do or should have done. Consequently, our self-realization and self-actualization must be attuned and activated to bend circumstances, conditions, and reality by process or perspective for any chance at change. Although stifled, we always had the power. We still possess the ability but are not utilizing the potential or how to use it to get home or be made whole.

Therefore, we should not have expectations of others, but aspirations for ourselves, taking the initial steps in the journey, maybe later joined or assisted by like-minded companions. The path seldom traveled is the most rewarding, although surely more challenging. Still, the easy path is crowded by the conformity or equality of mediocracy undistinguished for separation by qualifications or resolve. The easy path is the consolation prize for compliance. With this in mind, this section will primarily address what we, as Black folks, need to or have failed to do. We must be as honest with ourselves as others would be with us.

There are many steps to be taken enroute to a destination and various distractions along the way. There is always a choice and the duality of consequences. Love and hate, inferiority and superiority, or impartiality and discrimination are all opposite extremes of the same thing. Feelings, self-worth, judgments, predispositions, and assumptions are internally held but outwardly projected. Hence under the individual's control, choosing between resisting or yielding to them. Cling only to that which serves us, creating and expanding our reality and limitations.

Otherwise, others will determine them for us. The previous mention of philosophical, mathematical, and scientific theories proves the cause and effect of actions and reactions to logically shape observable reality or predictable consequences. The alchemy of perspective or self-initiated elements influences many outcomes more than any other factors based on the mutation of thoughts, perspectives, and observations.

None of this exists without us, which makes us the center of the universe from our perspective based on our unique individual perceptions and experiences. So the question is, whose reality are we experiencing? Are we reacting to others' reality or responding from our perspective? We are not independent of a collective reality. Still, within that reality, we position ourselves to varying degrees based on our perspective's alignment with specific subgroups. Our starting position, journey, and destination evolve accordingly with our affiliation to certain thoughts, actions, or classifications.

History is an indication or record of the past but not a certainty of the future, anyone's future. Today's actions are tomorrow's history, and today's heroines and heroes are the future beacons of social and economic admiration. Courage, vision, and perseverance mold the inspiration, representation, and potential for others to become encouraged, feeling prosperity is attainable for them too. When used properly, the benefit is ours but also a gift to others. The example of accomplishment is a gift to others regardless of starting position, journey, or destination.

Assessment of what we have and what we will need is required to start the journey. We must tear it down and not rebuild a replica but build a new paradigm from a fresh evaluation, composition, and configuration. The deconstruction of our socialization and orientation from a system of detrimental and outdated perspectives and subservient relegation cannot be renovated. It must be shattered and demolished, rejecting the fallacies and deceptions which still hold us captive by our complicity and apathy.

We must be willing to challenge and erase indoctrinations that tether us to the perspectives we protest and from which we beg relief. We cannot continue to make it easy for others to discount us or to travel the path of least resistance when that path does not offer sufficient rewards. Please make no mistake about it. We are in deep, very deep, so we must see it through. We have no other choice. We can find encouragement considering the gains made and the gains that remain. We must burn the boats making retreat impossible, having progression and advancement as our only course of action.

Carrying dead weight is never advisable, nor is carrying the past. We must first forgive ourselves, our ancestors, our ignorance, our shame, and our capitulation to perspectives and conditions which led us to this juncture. However, always keep in mind that we did resist, rebel, and retaliate against slavery from its initiation. So at this point, much is immaterial. Just that injustices did occur, but it is no excuse for them to continue. Time is a distorter of facts and influences, causing a Mandela Effect with many things known to be false widely perceived as true or erroneously remembered.

We have reviewed the gamut of emotion and outrage used as justification and objection. Our historical treatment and experiences of racism, hopefully reveal the futility of further anger as fuel for our progression. But, unfortunately, both racism and anger persist, although to ever-lessening overt degrees. Perhaps our current assessment is viewed through an exaggerated lens compared to days gone by. Not to minimize the present but to contextualize the past. We have traveled back in time by our memories traversing history but not in its totality.

When we watch a television program and come in near the end, we have no context for how it arrived at or evolved to that point. Yet, that is our history because we have not viewed it from the beginning but near the end from the sphere, defamation, and radius of slavery in America or whatever land of racial oppression we populate worldwide. The totality of history reveals some rough patches but an abundance of majestic accomplishments and transcendent contributions we can take pride in.

Limited information, consideration, or presentation often makes the truth a lie and a lie the truth by discarding facts. Then the prevailing belief or perception makes it appear valid. Therefore perception often makes it real, not the occurrence. Memory makes it cloudy unless substantiated by historical facts. However, historical facts only tell a portion of the story, often leaving out why and only giving us what.

We must understand why we are doing what we do. We can point to many contributory reasons to lessen our accountability. Still, all things considered, we either get it done or not. Many temptations are swirling around us to deflect our obligation, comparing others' behavior to excuse ours. What they have done only distracts us on our journey when we now use it as justification or provocation. We should decide and respond according to what we need to do, not instigated into a senseless reaction of past emotions.

We could use for comparison the easy road that leaves us engaged in a back and forth or he say she say. Their game is deflect and deny stalling accountability or adjustments of fair allocation of justice and assessments. They can condemn and rebuke defunding the police or any adjustments to law enforcement. However, when they are displeased, they bum rush the Capitol, demand the dismantling of the FBI, and succession. They self-righteously resort to killing, threatening, or harming government officials and law enforcement because the application of the law is now directed at them.

The spiral into political combustion or social Armageddon does not serve as a deterrent when political control is the only means of perpetuating the seminal discrimination needed to rig their identity. The racial and political shenanigans of desperation stains the premise of any claims of reason, decency, or fairness when maintaining their subsidy and our fear. It was the same with the Floyd, Aubrey, the Insurrection, and other instances which exposes their true concern and delusion, pulling the pointed hood of entitled ideology from their shamefully misguided heads.

Their venomous proclivity to exert authoritarian control and exploitive advantage propping up desperation and swindled credibility reveals stunning cowardice. It is shamefully obvious given the disparity and illogical rationale pretending righteous motives while fiending for power. By now we should know we can't trust that. These are clear indications of their ridiculous claims of religion, law and order, and morality suggesting the law should not apply to them. But which of these do we claim do not apply to us? Are they the same? Why not? What ideological hoods do we wear that exacerbate our condition?

Still, that is not cause for us to pursue and engage in activities that camouflage their irrationality or ours. Both will be judged for their merit. While we pursue an agenda that mocks any comparison, we must abstain from self-harm. However, time spent attempting to reason with the likes of a racist perspective may not be the most efficient use of our time or effort. Removing ourselves from its effects to which we do not subject ourselves would prove far more beneficial than evading others' motives.

So we counter by becoming elusive targets avoiding its reach. Still, it has gotten to the point where not only don't others believe its bias slant, but they are experiencing a meltdown resulting from its dissolution. The racist ideology has no clothes to cloak its naked psychosis, obsessively consumed with a fluctuating pretext but an unwavering insanity. To be accurate, it probably is not only racism but more of entitlement.

Either way, we must resist mimicking their behavior, especially entitlement and unaccountability. Therefore a period of chaos reigns before the calm and prior to the change. As time takes its place, the grumblings and eruptions of change can be heard and seen worldwide, rejecting the oppression of the human spirit. Compromise and cooperation in negotiating an equitable outcome will prevail because the equilibrium of natural law cannot be strangled, only temporarily restrained.

Gasping for the survival of times gone by, the oppressive and exploitative ideology desperately clings to reckless measures. As the tide turns, we must avoid fanning the flame but letting it extinguish itself by suffocation. When left with no choice, the choice is clear. Consequently, feeling cornered, they indiscriminately lash out for a last gasp, eventually feeding on themselves. Being unable to adapt, they fear their survival is at stake, terrified of their imagination or distorted caricatures equating lack of domination as the extermination of their existence.

It is a psychologically dysfunctional perception but not as the death of the organism, just the abject of their perspective. It reveals the duality of deception where they know it is false but have fallen into its clutches after espousing it for so long that they started believing it. The same can be said for the lingering effects of slavery. Subsequently, they become victims of their assertions and propaganda. So nothing short of total capitulation will satisfy their vampire's thirst.

Not to insult vampires but to indicate the thirst for delusion and discrimination as necessary to survival while combating the imaginary ghost of nostalgia. If nothing else, this illustrates why begging will not work, but truth and strategy will. Unfortunately, despite our actions or behavior, there will be those unmoved, incapable of accepting our humanity as being on par with theirs. Willingly stuck in a repetitive time warp of past sociological and psychological security, their functionality in a changed future causes their instability and concern.

Once again, it displays the duality and polarity of perspectives and the corresponding behaviors. So, we can see from experience and mistakes the folly of pursuing such a path. The roles have reversed to create stagnation and frustration among those who resist change. So let it, because we have our work to do. I mention this to illustrate that many of the same dynamics have plagued us from the opposite perspective. We cannot worry about what consumes others or their preoccupation with the past while the future awaits us.

Humans are animals of higher intellect, so observing human behavior infused with intelligence correlates to animal behavior and tendencies when objectively examined. We were never afforded the security and infatuation of waiting for the cheese to return. We were instead tasked with diligently pursuing new cheese as outlined in the book, Who Moved My Cheese. We must keep moving forward in search of a brighter horizon bringing new cheese.

We must weigh the cost of stagnation in favor of exploration. So what appears to be concealed is only misunderstood or rejected lacking foresight. Understanding the organism must occur before comprehending the actions. Behavior and impulses are established patterns of synopsis acquired from past impressions later forecasted in energy, action, or thought. Changing our image and influences by demonstration and imitation must excavate below the surface to remove the root compulsion. The iceberg is what we see but below the surface is what allows it to protrude or be displayed.

Memory is the retention of these compulsions as habits, emotional inclinations, and subjective perceptions. The memory and influence are deeply rooted, even if unretrievable. Ancestral recall, DNA, and our experiences are retained memories, which, as our conscious behavior, is the visible tip of the iceberg. Understanding implanted behavior must be retracted before it takes hold to neutralize its effect. Careful examination of our current behavior traces back to where we went wrong and what can be done to correct it.

Cultural identifiers are learned patterns. Thus they are subjectively defended justifications to validate and reinforce their continuation. Breaking up is hard to do after a prolonged period of affinity, but it is necessary. Truth is similar to quicksand or molasses. The more you struggle, it engulfs you with the consequences of denial. Deception is like sugar. It seduces your senses with a pleasant consumption to conceal its trickery.

Our climb to the summit must include demonstrations and representations of what we would like to be. We can't claim it but not epitomize it. Idolizing the bottom while claiming to be at the top replicates that behavior unfamiliar with the atmosphere at the top. We will only be what we practice becoming. A demonstration is the second best form of learning behind participation. We must practice and participate in excellence to become excellent. Aspirations will not get us very far without the required effort. There are truths about our perspectives and behaviors that we must see or examine with brutal honesty.

Otherwise, we are spinning our wheels, exerting enormous energy but stuck in the same social rut. Truth be told, others started after us but have surpassed our status in several aspects. Slavery, racism, and discrimination cannot entirely be to blame for our continued struggles. We must wear the jacket for some of it because others, too, may have faced biases, even if arguably not to our degree. There will not always be clear sailing, so we must more skillfully navigate any choppy waters in which we find ourselves.

We can't continue to blame others for our circumstances instead of rising above them. No matter how true, we must overcome our emotions and challenges. If others can, then we can too. More importantly, remember what our ancestors went through to get us to this point with much harsher conditions to overcome. Are we to be stalled by lesser obstacles for lack of certified tenacity or ironclad resiliency? Playtime is over. It has to be. It is time for a hard hat and a lunch pail to invest whatever time or effort is needed to achieve our objectives.

However, we must think in terms of widespread generational advances in increments that compound our resources and advancements. They say God helps those who help themselves, and God bless the child that has their own. Therefore, many worries are removed when you have your own. So, it is clear that we need to get our own, not separatism but provisions. We know the obstacles, so we must outmaneuver them.

Many of us are familiar with the movie about the story of a soldier, which launched a beacon of exemplary blackness into an institution and shining example of excellence maintained over decades. The film depicts the nuances of our reality amongst us relative to discriminatory environments. The archetypes span the gamut of personalities and perspectives. Everyone can identify or despises some character or aspect of the movie. Still, its power lies in the interactions among the Black characters.

It is a glimpse into our society that is not always evident when observing culture but is crystal clear in the movie. It illustrates the animosities, capitulation, self-hate, and thirst for validation that we suffer from significantly today while despising and combating each other, destroying our unity. The moral judgements seeking validation and assimilation drives wedges of division and cultural superiority pitting Black against Black. The white discrimination notwithstanding, the dynamics among the Black characters range from smugness to psychologically subservient. We don't need another race to suffer snobbish racial claims.

Among ourselves, we have colorism and classism. In the movie, the question is paraphrased asking what kind of person are you? What kind are we? We must ask when the destabilization of our communities and identity is under siege. How can we find less trivial or self-imposed grievances to complain about when the stakes are much higher? When the Black man and woman are pitted against each other over ego, pride, stubbornness, and miscommunication, with neither conceding an inch. Those evenly yoked will find each other. Otherwise, it is not your coupling.

But now a gender war divides us, where we were traditionally and communally strong despite the physical separations of slavery. For black lives to matter, we must display a unity that appears to have been eroded and desensitized of its importance. Instead, the helping hand often turns into a clenched fist producing a fatal judgment against our people and communities from within. The normalization occurs when the sniveling in the background, hushed whispers, and alibi-making supersedes the respect for our humanity or disgust towards those among us who violate it. Too many times, the controversy is within our house among our people.

Within our temple resides thieves robbing us of our sanctity, image, and social progress for lack of consequences, understanding, or correction. How can we blame others for our behavior when our communities and parents have a habit of covering for our members instead of correcting them. Is it easier to complain about others? We can't have it both ways. Either we are tired of it all or just when someone else is doing it. It seems to closely mirror racism and discrimination, as long as it affects someone else and not me or mine.

The saint and the sinner reach a consensus, but two saints or two sinners reach a coalition. Which is it to be? A compromise to endure or an alliance to resist, only by resisting, allows for correction or complaint. Endurance allows for continuation. The impulse to violence creates carnivores devouring life and potential while dispensing death, chaos, and fear in our communities. These are not white racists or law enforcement. It is from our bosom. Scavenging for clout and cowering from fear manifested as bravado accomplishes what we would otherwise not tolerate from others.

Is it better that we do it to ourselves than suffer it at the hands of racists or others? The resulting carnage is more than the KKK has ever done. Where is our outrage and condemnation of this genocide? We must grab hold of our composure to resolve issues without taking life and sacrificing life, thereby losing at least two lives, often more. Posturing for clout and molding bloated egos to mistake bogus traits as being a "real one" enables the cycle of destruction to repeat. So, it no longer is who is the real enemy but what is the real enemy of our progression.

These are the same ones who protest most and demand that others not do what we readily do to ourselves. Upon review, it is a twisted logic and encourages indifference to our legitimate grievances by us devaluing our humanity. The cognitive and emotional dissonance is silencing. We can't act as if we have an exclusive license to destroy ourselves and any infringement violates our exclusivity to self-infliction. There is only one explanation, dysfunctional psychological programming. It replicates the snake consuming its tail, unaware of itself, mistakenly identifying everything as prey or an enemy, and constantly ready to attack.

As evidence of our communities' violation and poisoning, we repeatedly witness violence where none should occur and against those unintended. Any gathering of just a handful might result in gunplay no matter what the occasion, from candlelight vigil to family gatherings. I attended the Million Man March in the nineties. As far as the eye could see, a sea of Black people radiated an ocean of unity. Taking a pledge of I say your name to promote the protection of our communities and accountability for our actions.

There was no violence, random or otherwise, because the assembled was there for business. There to send and receive a message and would not tolerate nonsense because we were drawn together under a purpose. Unfortunately, now the very courtesy to live and let live after a dispute has descended into a death sentence at record numbers in our urban areas. Not to mention the random bloodshed caused as collateral damage and the deletion of our young.

We do not defend or attack violence directed toward us from outside sources. Instead, we beg, protest, march, or pray. Where is chivalry or gangsterism when we need it most? We are quick to blast our own but whine about others. Quick to stand against our own and even quicker to lay down for others. The cowardly display to avoid the penalty at all costs is overridden by group-infused courage when committing anarchy shielded by protest claiming outrage. But, not enough outrage to address the cause and not the symptom. Those dealing in death and devastation are possessed with the cowardice of gangsters who have never ventured off the porch.

The slave mentality and psychological bondage are deafening against the reasoning that allows both. Where is that same vigor regarding our children's education, community safety, and economic empowerment?Why not bum rush economic opportunity instead of opps? Why not scour for the location of community empowerment? What about having poverty check in before it arrive as unwelcome? These we not only sit idly by and dismiss as our obligation to address or correct, but we stay too busy bellyaching about issues of less significance or infrequent occurrence.

It all has to indicate some advanced degree of dysfunction we refuse to acknowledge. Only we can stop it. Otherwise, committing these acts amounts to treason to the Black objective. In that case, we really should not and cannot tolerate imposters working to sabotage our peace and progress under their cloak of blackness. These pretenders for social equality undermine our purpose as enlisted infiltrators behind our lines wreaking havoc. We must find the courage to call out our apathy to nonsense wherever and with whoever we find it.

No one is exempt or gets a pass from a universally accepted minimum standard or imposed code of conduct too often breached from within our ranks. Protest is cool, and some elements are necessary and effective. Still, if we don't police ourselves, we forfeit hard-fought and earned progress. Keeping it real, much of this nonsense occurs with not a white person, racist, or law enforcement in sight. We have to wear the jacket and the consequences until we stand against that and not each other.

Rectifying our actions is more productive than voting, protesting, or economic leverage because these will arise from our sociological and psychological correction. We can be little dogs that bark loudly or big dogs that silently bite. One might scare, while the other is definitely scary. Pretentious demands evaporate while sustained determined pursuit prevails. Our actions, not our words, must display the decision.

The Dr. Jekyll and Mr. Hyde dichotomy of our demands contradicting our behavior cannot both be sanctioned from within our social pursuits for equality and equity. We must choose, or maybe as pacification, we can wrestle away another holiday. We are not an infantile people, but our struggle has persisted, aided, and abated by us. Despite claims of protest they range from our social, educational, economic, emotional, sociological, and psychological tendencies and willful submissions to being regulated, relegated, and resigned against our greater good.

The historical parameters of perspective and perception guided by slavery, Jim Crow, and racism have expired as a control element for our survival and conformity. Instead, it now requires complicity, solidifying primitive emotions and baffling ignorance, rejecting the discovery of material facts which would alter the previous misguidance. This is the power of imposed socialization lingering insidiously, unsuspecting as the catalyst for overcompensation to project the most extreme opposite as a display of denial and validation.

Moreover, it has influenced the undercurrents shaping "the culture" by instilling a symphony of violence and aggression to replace and masquerade as pride and respect. The mighty oak always said, I'm bad wherever you put me, because I am the weapon. Those who don't know lie about it but those who know are about it. Rapidly resorting to random violence governed by mislabeled pride and ego disguises the deficiencies of courage to confront an issue. The tough guy persona is in full effect until the reckoning occurs or a real player of a higher echelon is on deck.

In this case, fear reigns supreme to prompt submissive behavior so as not to offend or to knuckle under without a weapon to bolster their courage. They don't make 'em like they used to, but then again, there have always been those who were self-acclaimed without verification. It is said the sheep rule where the lion does not roam. Untested tough guys reign until a verified tough guy shows up. Anonymous violence is not a measure of toughness, but courage and composure usually is. So, if you don't fear for your name, why fear for your deed or throwing down on a fair one?

Real players keep suckas to the side and remain sucka-free by their associations and deeds, as it was put from the sucka-tash. These gangster portrayals of feeble courage and dubious credentials or commission are fantasized deceptions adopted as real by those who don't care to know for real. These are gladiators who refuse to enter the arena. Like racist beliefs, after repeated reinforcement bombarding a message of violence and retaliation, the programming is subliminally embedded but factually unproven.

Once embedded, it creates an explosive reaction erupting as a protruding iceberg compelled by an automatic response whose agitation is impulsive and almost irresistible. The resulting action is then disassociated from the consequences suspended in a virtual nightmare and removed from the realization, fronting like it wasn't cowardly. The bravery of the weapon does not transfer to the coward who used it but the consequences does. It is a cowardly act curled up and unleashed by pathological impulses indoctrinated as an uncontrollable urge or hypnotic command.

Similar to an out-of-body experience where you were there but witnessed the action instead of committing it. It is complete obedience to programming, powerless to resist, and thoughtlessly submissive, believing it was your preferred response instead of the programmed reaction. Lacking for proper expression, the dysfunctional tools available are employed according to the limited development of alternative resolutions, salivating on demand to blast first.

Unaware of this psychological conditioning, your reaction is not only predictable but tragic and by design and not by culture. Animals are not the only ones that can be trained to attack. Humans also can be by socialization and affiliation. Ask the military. Unwillingness to accept the truth does not change it, just like failure to consider the ramifications does not relieve them. There are many influences from music to entertainment portrayals and life encounters that impressionable minds fill their void or insecurities with by imitating and adopting the persona and identity as their own.

Whatever the case, we must bear the brunt of its impact when music videos are inundated with gunplay and references to mowing down opps over the slightest aggravation. Life will imitate art because it reflects the emotionally stirred and repetitively projected social indoctrination of alluring impressions transformed into reality. In search of a reason, any reason to discredit us, fluctuating or otherwise, history has assigned us an identity of infamy. Lately, we have assigned ourselves images counterproductive to our objectives confirming their designation further jeopardizing our equality.

Look around and observe the number of people who display identical mannerisms, appearances, motivations, and behaviors. Is that a coincidence, accident, or psychological clone producing avatars and caricatures? Does getting the bag at all costs, thug-life, pimp mentality, or being controlled by the highest bidder not even remotely resemble clone or clown activity? Furthermore, replicated appearances of altered body parts, exaggerated hair, extravagant chains, and so forth display a herd mentality promoted as urban morality and culture. Just ask how did so many arrive at it independently, but they didn't and you didn't either.

Where is the courage to be different or better yet yourself? Why has a shapely butt become a sometimes life-threatening obsession worth having? It used to be tiny feet and waist corsets, but now it is mandatory to have a bright future behind you. Is it ironic that you can't see it butt must have it? I am not knocking anyone's choices or right to choose, just pointing out the pervasiveness of peer pressure and cultural validation as a human need to comply or belong. However, it is more submission by comparison of insecurities blending in instead of standing out. It would seem to defeat the purpose by saturation and similarity.

This dynamic resembles racism and whiteness as the standard to be desired and assimilated rejecting diversity or uniqueness. It is all a social construct producing a herd mentality to resemble or display that standard or status. That is why we must attack racism as a social disparity, not as a race or person. Most behavior results from a social paradigm modeled after the prevailing consensus conforming to its replication.

We must understand the influence to which we are subjected and embrace. By understanding the process, we may begin to identify its effect and reject its seduction. It is all fun and games until it is not, but it is usually too late when the shoes have gotten too tight. At that point, it usually produces regret or indifference as a psychological defense mechanism after the damage is done. Once the damage is done, the irrationality and recklessness typically become apparent.

Humans usually possess an internal mechanism, a sort of sixth sense, if you will, an intuition which stirs apprehension when engaging in wrongdoing. That is why children hide their misdeeds as an instinct, and adults become fearful of the possibility of exposure. So our internal compass navigates our actions if we accept its instructions. It is a law of nature for animals and humans as a primitive instinct, but inferiority is a learned behavior of self-evaluation.

The feeling of inferiority refers to a perceived deficiency acknowledged as an emotional gash seeking external dignity but avoiding the real reason. If anything were said or done that did not apply to you, there would be no need for anger or to assume it was about you. Why would you if it doesn't apply? If an emotional response erupts, it reveals an existing hurt or a connection to the truth. Otherwise, your response would not be volatile. It might instead be comical. You cannot be made to feel a way you don't feel. It is the ultimate display of self-doubt and unworthiness.

That is the main reason the N-word is baffling. We love to use it recklessly but hate to hear it from others outside our race. But if they used it, why would you think or feel it applied to you, or is it derogatory if you don't feel hurt or resemble it? Of course, it doesn't make sense unless the hurt is denied, but why would you invite its use or conjure up any slumbering pain, especially by us using it? It would be like a language you didn't understand, but oh, how we do understand. Some argue it is a derivative of the Latin word "niger," meaning Black, which makes it acceptable to use, but it is not the same word.

"Niger" not the country but the ethnic word was when Nubians and Ethiopians were descriptive terms of ethnicity during the BCE era, and Latin was prevalent. It was closer to the stone age, bronze age, and Neanderthals than today. As always, how far back are we going to go to define ourselves when comparatively speaking that period would also redefine others more? Some justifications even go back as far as Noah. So our understanding and suffering are not enough to break habits we pretend we control but are not attached to an infinite time frame but a limited perspective.

However, slavery refers to a finite time frame exposing an inconsistency regarding the expanded application of time. Only we do that or allow it to be done to us, because our history is actually the genesis and cradle of humanity in Africa. Africa is the beginning. Therefore, under the most recent narrative of the N-word from which we misappropriated our use, I can only submit that we make ourself rationally understand our infatuation with a fractional identity of slavery. I am satisfied with my understanding and refusal to use the N-word as slightly more insulting than African American.

They both present an oxymoron and a conundrum producing a paradox. By no coincidence, the universe's sense of humor, or most likely sarcasm, has the plural N-word spelled backward as saggin. The phonetics, not the spelling, alludes to one of our favorite cultural displays, wearing our pants like a department store sale, half off. I can't make it up but then again, who would want to? The cycle goes unbroken until there is a conscious effort to discard it and embark on a different cycle. Life and behavior have synchronicity of patterns, some detectable and some not.

Still, all are present, sometimes operating outside our understanding and observation. However, for those that are not, we must decipher and act accordingly. The Black experience, global oppression, and exploitation anywhere is an unnatural interruption and violation of the governing principles of harmony and the human spirit to self-actualize. The absence of harmony is discord or chaos being out of sync with the circadian rhythm of life. A recalibration of our perspective must reject the disharmony we voluntarily concede to which prolongs our plight.

The spell of our historical hardships must be broken to diametrically propel us forward. The key is in our minds and corresponding behavior socialized to lock us in this struggle we find ourselves. To be understood, we must first understand. People can look at the same thing but see something different. The illusions of society's projections covered by time and perspective can produce distortions. Perspective is shaped by knowledge but more often by lack of knowledge.

Perspective is anchored by habits, rituals, and traditions transformed into culture and behavioral patterns. The prevailing consensus creates spiritual and philosophical alchemy as the standard to comply with or emulate. Alchemy is the transition or proportional combination of elements to create a separate element. The element created from the alchemy comprising society is frequently far removed from its origins by time, revision, and ritual practice. Understanding these elements or alchemy is essential to fully understand the resulting creation.

Some socializations are outright harmful, while others are misguided or innocent. The more innocent the socialization appears, the easier its implementation. Let's examine the grip of a common socialization expressed as a ritual considered to be innocent. No, not Christmas and Santa Claus but Halloween. Its appearance of innocence gives its curveball its effectiveness making it undetectable until it is too late. The ritual of Halloween is innocent enough, promoting candy and costumes for the children's delight. But what is its alchemy or merged foundational composition?

Pope Boniface IV and Pope Gregory II many centuries ago made decrees which culminated in modern-day Halloween with a brief stop by the Celtic culture absconding with a bit of Irish culture. Halloween's meaning has evolved from the Pantheon to All Saints Day, followed by various versions of All Hallow and All Souls Day. But, like the N-word, can you really change its meaning or just disguise its reason? It has even been relocated from May 13th to the eve of November 1st, making it October 31st via a concession to All Souls Day.

Over time many have believed that during this time the veil between the living and dead is thinnest, allowing the dead, demons, and other unworldly creatures to enter this earthly dimension among us. It is a time to conjure or invite their presence, celebrating or worshipping their call to roam the earth. The modern version gained shape from the festival of Samhain of Irish and Celtic traditions. However, the Romans celebrated Feralia Day to celebrate the dead.

Therefore, it has transitioned into the day of the dead. Its date is significant because it was believed to be the end of summer or, specifically, the end of the harvest season. Similar to Easter which observes the resurrection of Jesus, the son of God, and the defeat of death. Interestingly, Easter is named after the fertility goddess, Eostre. The day Easter is celebrated is connected to the full moon or March equinox and by some accounts also signifies the sun's resurrection to fertility and crop production or spring growth season.

For this reason, it has no set date, although Easter is observed the first Sunday after the full moon. It is also approximately forty six days after Fat Tuesday which is one day before Ash Wednesday. The Mardi Gras celebration is a seven day event to exhaust sins and merriment before lent season begins much like Halloween. As such I am sure it is strictly a coincidence among conspiracy theorist that so many religious observances are intertwined with dubious company. If only they knew. Either way, Easter is the return of the son or the sun.

During Easter Eostre's rabbits and eggs symbolize fertility and birth, with chocolate as an aphrodisiac and bright colors as an enticement of favor from spirits. Similarly, during Halloween bobbing for apples is an ode to the fruit and tree goddess, Pomona. Her symbol is the apple. When we last saw the apple, it was in Eve's hand, representing the tree of knowledge and its consumption as a sin. So is bobbing for apples symbolically bobbing for knowledge or bobbing for sin? Many rituals play off the yearly cycle of the sun, planting or harvest season, pagan observances, and stimulation of commerce, including the Winter Solstice.

Halloween appears cloaked in many connotations and transformations, but only if you believe the hype and remain unaware of its purpose. The wolf in sheep's clothing is to conceal its true identity and make it less menacing in its approach. If Halloween were to ward off evil ghosts, the ghost of the dead, and wandering souls, why does it invite and imitate them? It was believed the ghost of the dead returned to earth, creating anarchy the eve before the saints returned.

Therefore, they would have to be appeased with gifts and sacrifices or protection used against them. Anything to appease these roaming souls, wayward ghosts, and ward off miscellaneous witchcraft. It brings to mind garlic, a silver bullet, and the cross symbol as a defense against vampires. So consequently, payola and animal sacrifices were required and provided on Halloween. Much like reparations, paid in any form which would satisfy the obligation.

But, unlike reparations, it was actually paid. In addition, they deemed it necessary to receive the benefit of All Saints Day and peace of mind. Halloween morphed into a celebration of the deities it supposedly feared that initiated the observance. Still, close examinations imply it was always demon directed. Not only were they celebrated but invited along with all manner of ghouls, goblins, sorcery, and pagan influences. Halloween has pagan rituals but so does Christmas.

However, they are perceived differently because they were socialized to be accepted differently. Paganism is not a satanic order or evil heathen ideology but has been ostracized by the popularity of Christianity. But I understand the term in its purest form as an alternative belief system associated with the oneness of nature and the universal connectivity of all God's creations. Simply to imply there are beliefs outside the beliefs of the religion which it is being applied.

The definition of hallow is holy, to be revered as divine. So what holy or Christian observance does Halloween celebrate? What is it understood to celebrate, if not ghosts and frightening aberrations of evil? Every single image depicts some element of fright or evil. Does it honor souls or offer them? Why is it directed toward children like every other subliminal indoctrination fabricated and secretly installed? Some would claim that it has overtures to pedophilia, enticing kids with candy from strangers. Just saying that some would say.

Trick or treat is extortion for a treat or payment to not cast a spell or do evil, and the sweetness of candy serves well where food once did. Wearing a menacing costume reinforces that you are indeed a demon of some sort and capable of casting spells. Thus, it's a connection to sorcery and witchcraft, innocently casting and spreading the energy, if not the spell. Even if you do not believe in spells, you still believe in Halloween. Thus, indirectly and inadvertently believing in spells by vicarious association.

Christians, Occultists, and Satanists honor a truce to celebrate and worship the prince of darkness and his ghastly kingdom, each receiving their own treat and folic on this day of the dead. Could this day of the dead be a state of being and not a state of mind? So we dress our children up in costumes for Halloween to extort candy from strangers as incarnated ghost from beyond the veil. Not only that, but many adults also still enjoy a good haunted house scare or costume party.

Many socializations linger from childhood, innocently promoting a perspective and socialization removed from its original intent. Many other examples litter the landscape of society as relics from primitive beliefs hiding in plain sight but disguised for acceptance or to cause fear. Breaking a mirror, believed to be God's image or reflection, gets you seven years of bad luck because the body renews itself every seven years, and so does bankruptcy. It invites the question of who you see when you look in the mirror, an image of God or yourself?

Don't put your hat on a bed or table, don't open an umbrella inside, don't put your purse on the floor, don't split a pole when walking, and many more have become customs of caution. For example, walking under a ladder because you are passing through and interrupting a triangle (a triangle is a pyramid), or fearing black cats. Of course, everyone knows a black cat is bad luck and is believed to be an evil omen, foretelling death, witchcraft, shapeshifting, or bad luck, but why? Most of us know the cautions, but few know the origins.

In some cultures, the black cat symbolizes prosperity and good luck. Given two choices, bad luck or good luck, how is its meaning chosen between the two? Given greater knowledge, why does it still persist? They become conditioned beliefs because they are never evaluated for truth or origin. So, how many primal misconceptions and distorted practices, origins, and evolutions pervasive throughout society are unknown or concealed? Which ones are race or culture defining with us not knowing the reason or origins?

Fire historically has been used for many purposes, from survival to invoking fear. Fire purifies, destroys, transforms, and illuminates with conceivably all properties used interchangeably for many purposes. It has been an intricate part of many rituals and condemnations. Applied to Halloween, is fire to illuminate the dark, scaring away evil, or to light the path inviting it? Perspective can behave and consume like fire, but the blaze and ideological damage can be concealed in the mind.

Apply the concept and uses of fire to social and cultural occurrences as perspectives in the context of misconceptions to realize how the same thing is used for opposite beliefs for the same functions or circumstances. Consider that Christianity was the same for slaves and slave masters but had different intents, interpretations, purposes, and applications. Many elements of Black culture can be summed up the same. Remember, the two edge sword cuts both ways. Then again, so do culture and socialization.

Fire, much like perspective, can also be used to conceal evidence of something preferred not to be discovered. Could racism's grip be subconsciously tethered to fear of the dark, which denotes fear of the unknown? Fear of the dark is acquired at an early age, and some adults must still sleep with a night light or the T.V. on to ward off the darkness. Could racism be rooted in fear of a form or image unfamiliar or different simply because it is un-alike? Better yet, can racism be loosely associated with dark skin tone substituted for darkness?

Perhaps racism simplified is indicative of a mental capitulation to fear of darkness equated to death. Staunch racism, if supplanted from fear and cultivated by socialization, deflects its origin in irrational fear. It has nothing to do with color and everything to do with concealing fear and transferring it onto something tangible when the boogeyman only exists in the mind. Like all these other cultural and social paradigms, they reside alongside the past, only in the mind, which is often collectively convinced.

Ours is also a collective persuasion, when unfamiliar or uncomfortable in situations projecting assumptions of rejection where it may be indifference at worst. Carefully examining the etymology of words and the anthropology of cultures exposes many seemingly unrelated suppositions. Still, when we are unaware of the course of their development, it proposes a different interpretation. Is it a pagan or primitive crisis of perspective and transformation or a modification and presentation of deception?

Perspectives and definitions of culture are the alchemy of history, the radius of understanding, the sphere of knowledge, and the consensus of practice. Our cultural inclinations have many similarities to Halloween. Unfortunately, we practice them without the benefit of knowing the origin, intent, and evolution that transformed them into current practices and beliefs. Without evaluation, we mistakenly think we controlled the influence or decided the outcome. It is often just the latest transformation or masquerade, masking an unpleasant reality.

Those who play with fire are never immune from its burn. As a visionary musical genius once said about believing in things we don't understand, then we are bound to suffer. Superstition is not just a word but a state of mental trepidation, like religion. Superstitions steals our power, creating conformity and fears while crafting self-fulfilling prophecies of doom, gloom, or anxiety. Thus, it can be stated that understanding is the key. Therefore, racism is the limitation of understanding and the projection of fear. Victimization is the absence of hope and the presence of fear.

Even in loss, the warrior is never defeated unless their spirit is broken. Likewise, if meeting their demise, they transition dignity intact. But upon survival, they are just detoured with their courage and resolve fortified, now knowing what more would be required. The cup only overflows when it has reached its capacity. When its contents surpass the limits of its capacity, it becomes consumed. Therefore, knowledge, perspective, and resolve must expand to adapt to challenges and formulate expanded responses. Otherwise, uncertainty creates a void, the empty vessel to be filled.

Where a psychological or emotional void exists, a shepherd will appear to lead the sheep corralling and herding their perception implementing a collective perspective, the shepherd's perspective. The true shepherd is the ritual or custom soliciting compliance and describing routines of observance to be adhered to and replicated. The person is the facilitator you mistake as the shepherd but is only the deliverer of the true shepherd which is the ideology or ritual. These rituals and socializations are then standardized and mass-produced once they get a foothold.

The thought, ritual, or ideology then replicates unrestricted for its survival, so it must spread. When it encounters a susceptible host, it infiltrates and sets up operations ready to launch from a new host to a new demographic. And the band plays on and on, never tiring of the same old tune. The same old deceptions and misconceptions spread by a different instrument unchallenged. I have used Halloween, Christmas, Easter, Christianity, and many other references to illustrate the ideology and sociology of beliefs, behaviors, and cultural inclinations that seem innocent and organic.

We can see how it spreads its influence for centuries undetected by its innocent presentation and conditioned practice. The influence is first below the surface before it sprouts to be observed. Once it is planted and grows, it can spread uncontrollably, making the weed appear to be the flower by sheer volume and congestion. The flower's identity is overwhelmed and replaced by the observance of the weeds. The forest is obscured by the trees as the belief is obscured by time.

So when the number of people demonstrating the same traits passes a tipping point, it becomes the practice or cultural obsession. Those not following the trend are deemed out of touch or weird, so the inadvertent pressure is to conform for inclusion. A stigma or bias is automatically directed toward those who are different for being different. Therefore, the factory has begun to churn out identical parts, clones, avatars, and caricatures to project the still cartoon as animated motion and reality.

Frequently facts are mistaken as judgments and rejected for that reason. However, they may be judgments, but they are still and foremost facts. Observations are opinions but also witness testimony of what is seen. The facts and observations leads to results and conclusions forming empirical determinations categorizing the subject, characteristics, or behavior in an attempt to provide understanding and explanations.

So, if I may provide the inquiry, you can provide your own understanding and explanations. I question some traits of our culture and behavior in particular that are supposedly within the practitioner's perspective and prerogative to exercise. Still, they are also subject to be judged. I offer no judgment or intend no insult but simply objective examination of the existence, origins, evolution, or implications. It is to be self-determined and self-judged by you.

But, like Halloween, do they provide a trick or a treat? They are conditions and behaviors associated with the "culture" with no distinctions attached aside from yours. Assign or reject as you see fit the cause and consequences, but we cannot deny their existence, only their interpretation. The rising ratio of demand and saturation of diminishing options require we introspectively examine solutions.

Violence and Crime
Violence and crime plague our communities in epic proportions. The alleged culprits are racism, discrimination, and economic suppression. To whatever degree it is accurate, and to a large degree it may be, it is not the total truth. However, it is also true that these reasons are sometimes convenient excuses obscuring the underlying motives as the effect and not the cause. Both can be true, but one definitely should not be true, the one in our control, the cause.

Changing the cause alters the effect. The excuses and explanations often deflect the eyes wide shut reality and clarifications needed to address the problems. We cannot coddle and place an apron around the reality simply because it reflects an answer we prefer not to hear or confront. We know what it is, but why it is needs an honest and comprehensive analysis. Violence usually has an emotional component as its ignitor agitating a combustive reaction disproportionate to the justification or instigation.

Likewise, crime is to seize a benefit by relieving someone else of a coveted possession because they possess what you want or don't have. It is a degenerate inclination considering it easier to take than to earn. However, when something is taken from you, it is perceived as a violation willing to live by the sword but not be subjected to it. The common unifier is to impose a subjective judgment governed by a rationale not opposed to the rogue method to inflict or enforce it.

The ends are justified by the cause and means to satisfy the compulsion. It is not usually judged by how just, reasonable, or essential it is. It is almost always generated by anger, fear, desire, envy, or scarcity. Moreover, the justifications often leave much to be rationalized, lacking logical or moral sensibilities. So let's dissect how violence and crime circumvent and eludes reasoning, accountability, and resolution. The urban prototype has been efficiently crafted with its consciousness wiped to instinctively repeat the suggestions planted concealed as culture or as freely determined.

Much like the eyes see, but they do not see themselves. They only gaze outwardly, observing only that which is not obstructed. The puppet dances on a string, unaware of the puppeteer. The puppeteer is hidden from view leaving only the puppet to perform. Our strings are the thoughts that control our actions undetected, converting reservations into uninhibited impulses. The implanted thoughts become a default reaction without consideration or restraint, incapacitating the option to resist. We perform as programmed, unaware of the program or the programmer.

The first step to destroying us is desensitizing and normalizing the behavior compounded by the dormant trigger, which summons that behavior when activated. A visual and auditory assault is constantly bombarding us with the intended message subliminally transmitted to evade normal mental discretions. They are precisely directed at our core receptor, the subconscious mind. It magnifies the absorption and retention rate. The function of the subconscious mind is to do what it is told.

The subconscious mind becomes the servant instead of the master when the conscious mind rejects its evaluations by overriding it with brainwashed commands. The spell becomes the directive, mesmerizing judgment allowing only submissive reactions of the conscious mind. Repeated suggestions create a hypnotic trance producing a pseudo-identity indistinguishable from the host having the same form but different marching orders. The conscious mind often rejects the directive of the subconscious mind unless its rationale is disengaged or similarly aligned.

The ideology recruits a source that assimilates with or drafts its replication. The melodic persuasion represses logic validating dissociative perspectives, which perpetuates that mindset. A herd mentality is validated even when the opposite is observed and generally displayed. The occasional manifestation emboldens the façade to worship what is an anomaly knowing many are pretending but are not cut like that.

These fair-weather gangsters comprise the cheering section and admirers. They live vicariously off the clout and reputations of those who have or will. Still, they often hide in groups or behind cowardly acts as far from confrontation as possible while delivering their verdict. Reality is held at bay by the detached method used, fearing for their name and deed. They are anonymous from the courage required while pretending concern to escape accountability but posting for clout because it only has value when others know you did it. It is self-snitching and unwise for someone claiming to not want to get jammed up.

Committing acts of no value seeking self-esteem from sources that don't care or don't know you. Then, hit with the penalty box faking swagger to hide your remorse for the consequences. Twenty-five to life, I imagine, goes by very slowly, and death even slower because it is eternal. But, is either worth it, the joint or death? The visual input's origins are either virtual, like video games, representations fantasized by unreal glorifications of television or movie characters, or shady misguided role models.

Even if it is a person, it came from somewhere whose origins may be far removed from how it arrived to you, like Halloween distortions. The musical influences are even more effective because it is far easier to repeat a phrase than a vision. It becomes a chant or incantation whose power gains momentum with every recurrence. However, the music generally displays and promotes actions romanticized that the portrayer never has or will participate in. Out of all those who portray the gangster lifestyle, how many have made reputed collections, struck fear by their presence, or gunplay is how they really play?

It is usually entertainment transferred to reality by those hypnotized by its allure to fill a void, posturing like a bit player in an illusionary production. It is all a performance and idolization lacking any positive real-life applications. But, it is really a twisted game with real life consequences. Some diabolical social experiment we continuously fall prey to while aimlessly searching but refusing solutions because the answer rest with what we need to do but are unwilling.

Obsessively convinced, beliefs and psychology are melted into a characterization incapable of separation. It perpetuates images under conditions disintegrating into a dissociative disorder removed from the authenticity of its fake influence. How many portrayals actually live that life to the extent they convey. That's why fake players raise the ire of real players by dragging the game down and attempting to claim membership but are a poor representation and insult to the game.

So, what is being pedaled is a betrayal, not rightfully deciphered as whimsical exaggerations or lies. But, after so long, life imitates art, and more are ensnared in its net of illusion, becoming its image brought to life. So, we have a problem, which is why we have this problem. But we are also the solution. Not racism, discrimination, reparations, or fill in the blank with anything except for the truth, us. It is high time to confront the elephant in the room. We have to call balls and strikes fairly if we are seriously tired of their nonsense and ours.

The socialization has become the dysfunctional standard and cultural demonstration normalized as the prototype to be imitated. Therefore, we clone the mentality that produces the instinctive pattern, repetitiously regenerating its image. Like birds migrating south every winter to the same area no matter how far away, they are guided by their internal compass. So are we too, guided by an internal compass. The question is, where does our internal compass lead us, and is it damaged? What are the origins, programming, reasons, and destination?

If the destination is undesirable, we need to alter the compass or refrain from following and complaining about a compass that we know is damaged. Our destiny is not fated but determined by our diligence or lack thereof. We have become the weapon disseminating harm, dysfunction, and death in our communities. Camouflaged by skin color and environment to remain undetected until these acts of carnage expose the weaponized extremist among us.

In this regard, we are the problem. Sure there are other problems, but we can be our softest critic and biggest problem. So what are the logical takeaways when we finally make some progress and put law enforcement on their best behavior but ours worsen? It can appear to be a ploy to run amok with free reins. Therefore, we must police ourselves through our behavior, transparency, and accountability. We must be the change we diligently seek, the progress we pursue.

The glorified dysfunction anointed as violence and crime occupy our communities like terrorists holding hostage the only thing they can, us and ultimately our progress. They exercise their craft concealed by the likeness of us but known to many who turn a blind eye, thereby condoning and permitting its continuance. The code of not snitching binds us, but I ask what code are they bound by, certainly not self-snitching on social media or collateral damage.

Sound like good work if you can find it, randomly creating havoc and hidden by the community from accountability. Throwing a rock with no need to hide your hand because the detriment is tolerated. I will stop short of a recommendation, but the same consideration shown should be the same received. We must take a stand. You don't take a dump where you eat and never bring trouble to your doorstep. It has to be rules to the game. Heaven forbid they would exercise their craft outside their neighborhood against someone who doesn't look like them.

Not at all advocating or recommending that but illustrating the cannibalistic indifference displayed while receiving concessions of protection they are not owed. Everybody's business isn't nobody's business, so when they bear it for everybody, they forfeit the expectations of secrecy. But then again, it only becomes worth it if everybody knows. When their actions hurt the community, the community has a right to cry out for relief or handle it. I must be clear that this is not a call to violence, creating more of what we don't need.

However, it needs to be clear what will not be tolerated. We must step out of the shadows, visible in our resistance, by schooling those who require it. Certain behavior undermines the sanctity of our communities and objectives. So if you refuse to enter the fray as part of the solution, you have declared yourself an enemy of the objective aligned with the problem. Why is the disgraceful few tolerated above the concern of the many? Their disruptions must have consequences separated from the law enforcement jargon, which gives free rein where we won't address it but bemoan law enforcement.

We should handle our business, not be willing to cower from responsibility while pleading for equality and opportunity, which, frankly, we sometimes allow some among us to compromise. Something as seemingly innocuous as littering speaks volumes about the lack of respect for our communities. Others don't invade our neighborhoods and randomly discard trash and ashtray contents wherever they choose, so if we see it, we probably did it. It is symbolic of conditions we live in that are not necessary, only tolerated.

If not contained, small problems descend into large problems, and large problems into larger issues. If it is on us, then it is on us, and we cannot continue to let it go unchecked. We must erase the damage we do to ourselves and see how much better our lives would improve. Unfortunately, the constant social dumping grounds of our minds and communities sanctioned by our mentality and behavior prevent our exponential advancement by not eliminating the subtractions constantly depleting our gains.

Indoctrination comes in many sizes, shapes, and colors, soliciting corresponding behaviors exposing its damages but not always its influence. For what we have historically faced, our communities should be a refuge and oasis from the situations we complain about regarding others' treatment of us. Momma them taught us and should have taught you that you must take care of your stuff and not let anyone tear it up. Also, you better not tear up anybody else's. Core values must be established and enforced to maintain an expectation of respect, harmony, and accountability among us.

Every race, nationality, and country has issues unique to them. So, it would make sense that they are probably more concerned with the issues that affect them and not ours. Within these groups, some subgroups have issues specific to them. Mom used to say if you are worried about them, then who is worried about you? Worry about yourself, meaning whatever someone else is doing doesn't excuse you from what you are doing or should be doing. We cannot continue to inflict hardships on ourselves worried about white America.

It is a deflection of trauma and responsibility creating a social liability. Instead, we should worry about ourselves, our families, our communities, and our collective objectives. Focus on being accepted by Black America by contributing to our progress, not because it benefits others but because it benefits you and yours. What you and yours benefit from eventually benefit us all. If you are elevated to a higher standard, you are removed from the sub-standard.

Unfortunately, the opposite is also true if that becomes the standard. Therefore, sometimes we need to be checked when we don't self-regulate to refrain from unbridled conduct. No one owes you more than you owe yourself or than we owe ourselves. It can only be individually attained but collectively associated. Once the precedence is set, others can breach the barrier to achieve, benefit, or participate for our greater inclusion. The common denominator has always been being the best or at least undeniable.

When you are the best, nothing comes hard, but when you are not, everything is hard, and nothing comes easy. To limit the competition, limit those who can compare or compete with you. Very few discriminate against exceptional results or excellence. It is a solitary journey with very few resting places along the way. Effort is usually what separates the best from everything else. So, given the diversity within the subgroup's various divisions of interest, it would behoove you to handle your business first and best.

In case of an emergency on a plane, it is recommended that you secure your oxygen mask first to at least take the elementary steps to survive and later be able to help others. Otherwise, if you can't help yourself, you can't help others. Your business should be handled first. Accordingly, our business, too, must be handled first for our greatest assurances. The hopelessly broken, thoroughly indoctrinated, or stubbornly misguided will take offense to many of my perspectives as insults or criticism. They are not insults or criticism but perhaps hurtfully true.

To that, I respond that an understanding can only emerge in an honest discussion of solutions and an exchange of perspectives. Even if that understanding is to not agree, it has no room for emotions. I will also submit that we have avoided these examinations for far too long, letting things get out of hand. Consequently, if feelings are to be hurt, then let them because that is insufficient cause to ignore the problems or solutions. If we don't give others a hall pass for the same actions, why do we give ourselves one? Damage is damage no matter who commits it.

However, self-inflicted is the worst kind, especially when we want to whine and deflect blame while ignoring our contribution. In honest discourse, we must risk offending and being offended. If the objective or resolution is primary, then no offense should be taken, and it is out of our hands what others allow to offend them. Both remain in the eye of the beholder. We must look past the wrong messenger and possibly the not preferred delivery to clearly hear the right message. Regardless, responsibility and accountability must be laid at the feet of the deed doer regardless of name or color because credit would be.

Furthermore, if we are to hold others accountable, then it is understood that we should be held accountable. Judge not lest ye be judged. Cast no stone if no stone is to be cast toward you for the same offense. Refusal to transform transgression is just a different prism of the racist nonsense applying the same warped perspective to another self-serving denial of reality rebuking correction. This is why I emphasize the perspective or ideology should be attacked because the person or situation varies greatly.

For example, it is extremely hard to view some coincidences as coincidental. Identity crisis and identity deletion spread like an evil spirit, without shape and undetectable, leaving its victims possessed. Its only visible trace is the strange behavior it produces. We are a spiritual and musical people moved by the ceremonial rhythmic and melodic vibrations of music. Music is used as a medium or intermediary between the internal and external, entering the suggestive gateway and bypassing the mechanisms of logic and evaluation.

The internal gateway is between the conscious and subconscious mind, where the subconscious is the foundation. As such, messages received there have a hypnotic dynamic generating the human code regulating behavior. The music being transmitted decodes and implants a pseudo-virus mesmerizing and suspending logical processes replaced by emotional and impulsive actions. At that point, you no longer control your actions. The recorded message does. Music relaxes inhibitions, lessening control and becoming more impulsive to its influences.

Whether it hypes you or sedates you, it influences your mood. If it affects your mood enough, it becomes your mood or perspective. You come under its spell, enchanted by the intoxication of its ambiance or vibe. Especially if aided by some mind-altering substance to further loosen your resistance. It can function as a silent terrorist penetrating our ears directly into our subconscious mind. Once there, it sabotages the control center neutralizing defenses. The messages, cadences, and frequencies are unobstructed, taking over surface understandings and transmitting coded signals secretly directing our actions.

Its influence becomes monolithic and sanitizing, isolating restraint and quarantining judgment. It attaches as a psychological parasite contaminating thought. So, if music can soothe the savage beast, it can also rile the gentle soul and break a reluctant spirit. Under psychological warfare, music has been weaponized as torture. Evidence that sound influences mood can be seen in how you are motivated by up-tempo music, motivational speaking, an uplifting sermon, or romantic music to set a mood. It makes sense the opposite would just as profoundly have an effect.

The universe operates by the laws of vibrations and density, creating curvatures of reality. What appears to be solid is not, and what appears to be stationary is vibrating on levels undetectable, creating the reality of being solid or stationary. It operates on a molecular or particle level far removed from our natural powers of observation. Music does the same with different frequencies and sound waves assigned different attributes and effects. The voice is a frequency at a specific displacement of vibration, attraction, and unique association to the source.

Voices that have a vast appeal vibrate resonating as influences of feelings, logic, actions, beliefs, politics, and plenty more. Their sound enchants the emotions, ideology, support, worship, morality, and judgement overwhelmed by the idea but not the choice, proof, or scrutiny. The attraction to that frequency vibrating energy reaffirms a self-projection to the message, melody, and mentality influenced by that voice to replicate the projection.

The suggestion is not a request but the constantly implied persuasion to recommend and insist our identity reflects the idea or message. Our expression is the evidence of its implantation. The subtle duality of good game hunters and fair game prey. Voluntary consumption and reproduction of an idea, message, or image attaching to our identity. Subliminally desensitized psychologically removing inhibitions, understanding, and limitations. The vibe of manipulation is evident while simultaneously concealed like a quantum entanglement of being one but appearing in two places.

The undetected implications of 432 Hz, which allows energy to flow, compared to 440 Hz, which blocks energy, have been scientifically proven to affect moods. Presuming the effects of 432 Hz extend to the electromagnetic beat of the earth and the root chakra, what implications does it have on you as a divine number throughout the universe? Synapses are electrical signals producing neurotransmitters emitting chemicals processing energy and electricity, including thought. The human body is even a conduit of frequency transmitting electricity. The body is not only flesh but vibrational energy.

Death consumes you when you cease to conduct electricity, not the absence of breathing. Consider the purpose of a defibrillator shocking you back to life by injecting electricity to stabilize normal electrical rhythms. From these examples, we can see the importance of frequency throughout life and the universe. With bass being a lower vibration, you can feel bass thumping as well as hear it. With most music being in 440 Hz, what are the implications and intent knowing the effects of this? Is it for the devil and destruction to whisper in our ears?

The 440 Hz supposedly correlates to the third eye or reasoning, making sense that the messaging would be directed there by the frequency direct path. Vibrational transmitters directed at emotional receptors modify reality to impulsively stimulate reactions. According to implanted patterns by compelling a detachment it is transported as a sensory depravity producing a conditioned agitated response. Consequently, there is extraordinarily little debate about the power of frequency, suggestion, and repetition to stir disharmony.

There is also little debate about the properties of 432Hz. So, if 440 Hz has not been proven, 432 Hz has been. Still, some say it is the 440Hz frequency that disrupts, stirring anxiety. However, it could very well be the message being transported by the frequency. It probably is both making it exceedingly powerful and penetrating. Extreme levels of bass heard and felt makes it a penetrating triple threat combined with the message. The mind is a recorder that records and processes everything even when we are unaware, so it always listens even when we are not.

The 440 Hz frequency was preferred by the Nazis, believing it controlled and brainwashed the German masses into anxiety, hysteria, and conformity. What we spend time on shapes who we are, and what we hear influences our thoughts. Suppose all you heard was how useless and unworthy you were. What effect would that have on your self-image? If you can imagine that, then imagine if all you heard was the glory of moving weight, blasting away your opps, thotting or tramping yourself out, dirty pimping, or nothing matters but the bag? In what mood or mindset does classical music place you?

How can we, with a clear conscience, and sober mind, deny the effects of that but clearly see the impact of constant criticism? Why it is not seen for what it is, a seduction into dysfunction and destruction. We must understand this must be standardized as a readily duplicated commodity to be produced from it which is us. It is not a matter of intelligence but socialization subsequently demonstrated by those who carry influence to recruit others susceptible to the notoriety addicted by the prospects of inclusion, envy, or celebrity. As models to be emulated, they are the visual recruiters to supplement the audio entrapment.

Suicide bombers and crash dummies are recruited by this method. Codependent thinkers mimic the pattern creating a mass resemblance to images as a cultural expression. Case in point to make it make no sense are those with dreams and aspirations who are fortunate enough to rise above humble beginnings. Against tremendous odds gaining provisions beyond their wildest imagination but addicted to street life. You would think they would lead a life of prosperity, moving past the circumstances they sought to remove themselves from before they hit their lick.

However, we constantly witness them crash and burn around us from activities they choose to indulge in. Others may argue that they have no choice, but this is not the case with them. They have made it out only to be drawn back in and down from activities in which they have absolutely no business. Is it true that you can take the boy out of the hood, but you can't take the hood out of the boy? Not to be condescending but to emphasize the allure of socialization relentlessly tugging and clawing at our ego and identity.

Consequently, influenced by elements surrounding us that reinforce that mentality, the path of escape leads us back to the beginning. Unable to shake the demons of our previous associations and sub-group dynamics, we trip and fall into a self-imposed trap. The lure of violence, drugs, thug ego, and validation by a standard we were removed from ensnares us. This leads to dire conclusions and often worst circumstances than we started plus the added ridicule.

If you don't believe it is a setup, consider the origins of crack that started during the Reagan administration. Who has been held accountable? I will tell you who, those who fell into its use or selling it. But not those who created the problem or introduced it to our targeted community. We took the bait, just like this epidemic of violence. Now, they are just holding big pharma financially accountable for opioids. You will receive more jail time for a crack pipe than they receive for untold addictions across every corner of this country, even across white America. Whether on a street corner or in a corner office on main street, it is all drug dealing.

Why are Blacks or lower economic persons labeled and considered drug dealers? Opioid distribution networks were in major drug stores as pharmacists. Therefore, the same action and result, so I preferred to call it a street pharmacist instead of a drug dealer. They are the same, except one not only moves product but also moves or, more correctly stalls policy. The difference is moving policy, so their penalty reimburses some, not all, of the profits without admitting guilt. But, then again, it is at least something because Reagan, Oliver North, and others widely believed escaped legal accountability for drugs distributed specifically to our communities during the Iran-Contra scandal.

North received a presidential pardon and even served at the helm of the NRA until 2019, ousted amidst controversy and alleged extortion. Aside from the social damage crack did, look at the criminalization and incarceration. That three-headed demon still haunts us with a spell cast across generations. The two most devastating bludgeoning of Black folks in the last fifty years, crack and opioids, have gone relatively unpunished. Drug addiction has been used as a menial classification and denigrating tool of despair across society, not just against us.

Meanwhile, the criminal courts, rehab centers, and addiction rates for crack and opioids are too overwhelmed to pass the Grey Poupon and Caviar. The policy ensures that the architects and executioners of these socially devastating transgressions face little deterrence or penalty. But, the book will be thrown at us for actions that are not remotely comparable. The government and criminal justice systems are too concerned with punishing the lower echelon of society than fairness.

So, by comparison, if marijuana was illegal when you caught your case, guess what? It is still federally illegal, but it is openly sold while you sit in jail. It will continue to be illegal until they figure out how to regulate a tax. It is prohibition 2.0, and eventually, you might purchase it in the "state" store alongside liquor. If the social-ization doesn't get you, the unfair and unjustifiable application of the law will. But then again, that would mess up the revenue gener-ated from incarceration, ours, not theirs.

On a street level, drugs are not the only way to make money, so why is it being done? Could it be by design, socialization, and imi-tation? Drugs, violence, and crime intersect to simulate a cultural war zone numbed to its actual current cost and future liability car-ried forward. The sum of which is as incomprehensible as it is rep-rehensible and available. Likewise, when law enforcement pulls the trigger, we vehemently protest. When we pull the trigger at a much more frequent rate, we absorb the trauma because we com-mitted it, but we must also be the ones to condemn it.

Similar act, different perpetrator, but worst optic especially when it is Black law enforcement against Black people. However, it is no different when it is us killing us in the streets. Lack of self-control being overridden by an impulse without restraint or conscious compunction to calculate the totality of the reason or consequences Label it as you will, but a rose is still a rose by any other name by the principle of its essence. So, murder is still murder.

Dealing with opps is the wrong opps to be concerned about. Co-ops would be far more beneficial and don't come with retaliation. Instead, we need to take the hustle to the boardroom. If you have an education and benefit from the hustler mentality, you should outperform someone with just the education. We have many examples, but a hustler mentality has no race or color, just a mindset, and ambition to outwork everyone else no matter how hard they work.

Unfortunately, far too often, we apply the mentality and jargon of urban warfare to social confrontations with solutions more suitable for a war zone than our communities. Everyone is a warrior until it is a time for war. Perhaps appropriate if engaged in military combat but not some petty discord, insult, or heated exchange of words. Why have our communities turned into war zones deploying unconventional warfare or special ops for counter-insurgency operations following military imperatives and strategic objectives using tactical deterrents? Stop it with the delusion. You are just a cowardly person with a gun ambushing someone.

You are probably grandstanding on some nonsense until karma pulls your number, only then realizing how unnecessary and irrational your actions were. It is just as damaging, but it is not war, far from it. But, it does leave the aftermath of war, death and destruction. Those erased, those left standing, and those left to mourn the loss of both. Suppose the decision is made to let the chopper do the talking. In that case, it is usually a concession that it is the only way you would confront the situation.

Courage is not needed, just the impulse without the benefit of weighing the consequences or the infraction committed. So why does everything, no matter how insignificant and often just words, result in the loss of life? How about the urge to take a life? Fear is the underlying reason masqueraded as gangster swagger or ego inflation thirsting for purpose within a subgroup, equally misguided peers, or a wanna-be that will never be. Otherwise, maybe conditioned to viciously attack as a first response indiscriminately popping off.

The delusion has us cast as military action heroes in our brainwashed minds assembled by the visual, audio, and digital training used to manipulate our actions. Then, if we're lucky, we go home after an exhausting day of masquerading. In our mind, we are enlisted as elite operatives in an exclusive strike force. If only we could enlist you for the real social war, equality of opportunity, or equitable representation and distribution. That also requires a special skill set.

Remember, even the Lord had a need for warriors. But undoubtedly, with your dedicated predilection to serve, we could desperately use you on the front lines to relieve those worn down by your nonsense. Leading the charge when it primarily affects you would be honorable and just the swag we need. But, unfortunately, it is easier to destroy than to build. Destruction takes no skill, discipline, or purpose. Luckily, it also takes none to not think, but that may be just the skill needed to be brainwashed.

Furthermore, we protest for prison reform, and rightfully so, but the best prison reform is to stay out of the grasp of the law by not committing the crime. If you commit a crime, jail is an occupational hazard of the criminal vocation to be expected as a possible consequence. But why are we always so surprised that no measure is too extreme or unreasonable to escape culpability? We must stop going to prison and committing acts sure to land us there. It is the number one thief of potential and opportunity committing a lifelong crime against yourself by the stipulations and exemptions attached for life. Death is the number two thief.

Some of our loved ones have spent most of their adult life in the joint, while others, in extreme cases, have spent half their entire life there. Others repeatedly drop in for a stay here and there. Crime is the symptom, socialization is the disease, and a weak mind is the ticket for transportation. Strange how sagging is a cultural phenomenon, some say, results from prison-issued clothes being ill-fitted. If so, it seems like fashion overrides disdain and ignorance. Once again, we protest something only to embrace the style, image, or language to reduce our resistance and increase our resemblance.

Wandering in the valley obscures the view and guarantees stuff rolls downhill. The mountain is never too high, and the valley just appears too low, but the climb is worth the view from the summit. Either you are helping in the charge for social justice by self-improvement, or you are hurting. There is no middle ground. The middle ground is occupied by apathy, cowardice, ignorance, or surrender. All of them are choices lining the easy road. Positive contributions elevate or promote ascension. Negative propensities lead to stagnant or spiraling probabilities.

Pythagoras' theories of social justice, music, and mathematics are ancient applications used today regarding ratios, probabilities, and harmony. He believed injustice inverted the natural order, and each person plays a part in the equitable distribution of just due. Is what we are getting our just due? I hope not. There is so much more when we decide to claim it. We cannot look to others to settle our in-house business or determine our just due. Our actions affect the equilibrium of our life, whether social, economic, or psychological.

The symmetry of effort, determination, and understanding will erase many indoctrinations and obstacles restricting our progression. Racism has a bunker mentality, hunkered down behind stubborn fortified compartments of socialization long after the war ends and progress passes by it. Some of our behaviors are the same, refusing to join the reality of change. Refusal and resistance to change is an isolated hole and the wrong hole to die in because it delays progress for no purpose.

So progress passes us by while we guard a foxhole, eyes peeled for opps that are quixotic delusions of our ego. The reality is sometimes when looking for the enemy, we need to look no further than the mirror. But, strangely enough, that is where we will also find the reflection of the solution. Innovative solutions require new perspectives to design and execute the directives of its accomplishment. The older the problem the more susceptible it is to a dynamic approach.

Let me propose a perspective that may seem stranger but probably makes as much sense. Many have expressed outrage regarding law enforcement and the judicial system in the past few years. As a result, it has sent trembles through the system. Almost every criminal action involves the police. Therefore, the police are the foundation of the criminal justice system, especially the arrest process. The entire system plays off of arrest or lack of it.

Understanding that the best way to affect the system is from the bottom or its foundation but only from within. From outside you must take the head for the body to fall. Due to the sentiment restraints, and scrutiny   toward law enforcement, many have left the profession. There has been almost zero interest in becoming the police and severe personnel deficits have resulted. The desperation has created unprecedented opportunities where they were shielded before.

I view it from a perspective of opportunity that will not last forever. It usually requires a clean felony record and a high school diploma or GED. No student loans or special training is required. They have some criteria and standards for getting the job, like graduating from the police academy and a test or two. A high school diploma or GED can get you a salary of sixty to seventy thousand a year. We now have a unique opportunity to not only get the job but in record numbers. We then become the urban occupying force of law.

I am by no means recruiting for law enforcement but instead illustrating how to neutralize decades of biases of the law. By increasing our presence in the pool, we alter the behavior and misconduct within the pool or its members. This method of regulation only works under two conditions. One is those with the job respect us and the other is we respect those who get the job. This unorthodox approach regulates what makes it through the gate even if not what happens afterwards.

The police is the bottleneck before the courts, judges, or jails get their say. This method has been used against us by exclusion. So, now we can use it to benefit us and change the system by inclusion. Consequently, we have a chance to change the trajectory of law enforcement for the next twenty-five or thirty years and beyond by filling its ranks. We have the opportunity to be the solution and the perspective which guides its operation, bringing in a new culture, ideology, and methods of operation.

This is the time to be about it by participating in the solution. The only consideration or concern would be the hazards and enforcement of the law, which is usually discretionary. If the problem is what we say it is, becoming the police would resolve many of them. As a result, we should be respectful and appreciate that you are there to protect our rights by providing safety and fairness. The law would then generally be applied to lessen racism as a consideration. The reverberations would also extend to the court system affecting its operation and incarceration rates by tightening the funnel which supplies them.

Otherwise, someone will take the job, and when we don't or won't take it, we cannot complain about who does. Maybe our treatment of us will be better than how others would treat us. But we must treat Black officers with the same or more respect to ensure we don't compound their problems or ours. They must reciprocate in kind as a mutual pact. Infiltrating the ranks will transplant law enforcement's ideology. Still, at least two issues might be removed, racism and unfairness if not also lessening force. It could erase the stigma of being the police, except for those separated by perspective, activity, or outrage.

We must recognize that there are reasons for opposing the police for enforcing the law outside fairness or lawful intentions. There are those who are criminal-minded and can be labeled as outlaws by choice. This would circle back to willfully being the problem that compromises our communities because without the law anarchy would rule. Likewise, there are those among us who will not change, we cannot help, and would have it no other way so we must save those who want saving.

Everyone will not participate in the solutions. But, like the system we combat, we all have the same imperative to change but not the same desire. It shares many of the same traits as racism but applies slightly different. Entrenched ideologies, perspectives, and practices which must be evolved out of indoctrinations of dysfunction respond to the same tonic of time, awareness, and rejection. Beware that the thought we think may not be our own.

It is a reason that the smart, focused, accomplished, ambitious independent thinker image is not the one marketed towards us. Our endowment is by our determination of will, knowledge, and influence. Our imitation is by our demonstration, our potential in our production, our excellence in our execution, and our validation in our accomplishments. We must manage what we control.

Presentation and Projection of Self
We often don't see ourselves as others do because they have a total view where ours is limited. Our appearance is what other people see and what we check for since portions of our body are not visible to us. For instance, our face, hair, and back are always outside our vi-

sion. Depending on our position and level of awareness, portions of the front are too. We usually go off our last visual confirmation as an expression and approval of our portrayal.

So, while the display is for others, we are often partially unaware of ourselves too busy processing what we see while concentrating on the world and others. The projection is what others see, while reflections are what we see of ourselves. Our reflection is what we judge ourself on, but our projection is what others judge of us. Still, the projection of our reflection is the presentation that shines from our core. It can be generated from our confidence or insecurities, qualities or faults, programming or self-determination.

However, the exhibition is a complicated mosaic of our uniqueness and archetype revealed as our personality. Nevertheless, it is a two-way proposition that can be a statement from us or a suggestion to us. Often our behavior is a suggestive image to us delivered without detection. Consider how a song or a movie can influence us through elements that resonate with or inspire us. That is the process. Unless we are a fortress well-protecting our psyche, we are susceptible. Even then, it is no guarantee, but a powerful sense of self and a fortified character offers us our best chance.

Most things about us are the reflection of a projected impression. Thus, we must choose our examples well. For this reason, role models are essential to forge a visual representation to incorporate into our existence. So, the projection is the external movie, while the reflection has an audience of only one, us. The mask is worn for others as our representative. Meanwhile, the shadow lurks unseen except for the manifestations of its influence. Therefore, when it is showtime, we perform because the show by now must go on.

This constant performance if not genuine is exhausting and causes ripples in reality far removed from our core identity. We cannot outrun it or the expectations it produces. The long and short of it is it's a marathon with pressure as the tester to determine if we are not built for it. Pressure makes diamonds if you can handle it, but pressure also bursts pipes if you can't. The inability to handle pressure or fear of not meeting the challenge reveals itself in anxiety.

Anxiety results from anticipating an uncertain outcome but is more from the pretense of the projection's distance from the reality of our reflection to achieve it. It exposes false advertising lacking the goods or fortitude. Fear of exposure that the hallucination of what we present is not who we are swells into conformity to avoid judgement. But, we must risk blame to receive credit. Consequently, a duality of existence or personality emerges, the one that perpetrates and the one that knows. The one that don't want to find out and the one that already has and must.

For that reason, the person we feel most comfortable with or think accepts our essence and nature, not requiring the performance, is usually our spouse, a family member, or a close friend. With them, no performance is necessary because we allow them to know us. Likewise, we probably also know them with us both agreeing to lowering the shields. At times, our self-worth is buried in them because they provide the strength that validates our reassurance.

Under the most convenient illusions our self-worth depends on our possessions, job, status, dependent family members such as kids or grandkids, even our inclusion that excludes others. We become what we do, unable to separate from that image or sense of importance it provides. The same is true for beauty queens, star athletes, gang bangers, and politicians since the list is endless but the need for adulation is just as long. Still, we become addicted and possessed by the projection, thereby losing the reflection. Eventually, being who and what we are brings relief, no longer on the social treadmill to impress others.

Consequently, we don't all live life, some live for others but we will all die after spending too much time stunting, conforming, or smug. So live it like you love it. The severity of many issues is only such because of the importance we place on them to validate ourselves. In the overall scheme of things, they really don't matter much, such as race or gender. The labels and restrictions others put on us are not our restrictions nor our value. They are theirs's projected outwardly in envy, resentment, or judgement.

Number one does not concern themselves with number two and certainly not last place. An astute observer will recognize our deficiencies on display as a feeble attempt to elevate our self-worth by exaggerating the extreme opposite of our fears. What value is deeming others unworthy by some arbitrary measure when we are not number one? The insecure preemptive strike is to judge before someone like us judges us. Our definition when based on our façade to others, can't conceal a canyon separating that from who we know ourselves to be. Judging below anchors us to the bottom while aspiring above elevates our game.

To learn yourself is to know thyself without the pressures, expectations, and pretenses we place so much value on, which has no value at all. Self-awareness promotes self-acceptance which leads to removing the labels and iron mask of doubt drowning our expression and development. A diamond is known by its brilliance but also its flaws. Most people are too concerned with their deficiencies to be concerned with their brilliance. Haters only hate to hide their flaws unable to find their shine.

So, everyone accepts us when we accept ourselves because that will be everyone that matters. We must learn the peace that is within self. When we self-actualize, everyone who doesn't cannot invade our resolve since we don't operate on their validation, conformity, or vibration. We are a manifestation of ourself to be compared only to ourself. Remember comparisons are dangerous, and people spend too much time worrying about what they don't have to cultivate and appreciate what they do have. Embrace and discover oneself to the fulfillment of our ticket on the joyride called life because time will rob us all. Time spent is time lost and time is limited and fragile.

Beggars Have Never Been Choosers

Our vileness will be despised when we pass, while our contributions will be missed. The legacy of life is what positive impact did we make or did we just pass through taking a couple of dumps along the way. So, when wearing that mask, carefully choose the role we will play because as the final curtain draws near, we don't want to regret it. More importantly, we don't want others to regret having known us. Our time is marked by what we did with it. So, the quality of good is superior to the longevity of evil.

The conflict between the mask and the shadow creates chaos. The harmony between the projection and reflection creates peace. Depending on our choice, even if chosen for us, the exhibition will align with our identity revealing our personality, composition, and integrity. So, it should be obvious that the projection and presentation of ourself should not be taken as a trivial matter. It should also be consistent with the reflection of our identity determined by us. We live in the world we choose to create, surrounded by the people we have largely chosen.

Like the cave with shadows cast upon the wall projected as reality or life, if we reposition our perspective, we will gain clarity to see the exit to reality, to ourself. The portal is a metaphysical transformation within our mind. It echoes the dimensional multitude of possible realities waiting to be invoked from the universal consciousness vibrationally revolving to its attuned calibration, obligatorily producing that summoned manifestation.

A psychological entombment prevents our courage and curiosity to explore the possibilities beyond our self-imposed limitations. Therefore, we remain in the comforts of the cocoon because it seems safer and offers the familiarity of certainty. Deceived by its bare amenities and complex illusions, the stagnation of underdevelopment and hopelessness of options or opportunities is the only offerings.

Slavery, racism, or any particular challenge that we don't take up our metaphorical sword and shield to slay reveal a submission to the circumstances by lack of determination. The default spirit is to fight because victory is not guaranteed, but nor is defeat. Resistance starts in the mind.Give me liberty or give me death was the battle cry then for liberation. Still, this death of our identity is the confinement of our spirit while too busy succumbing to others' definitions, expectations, and boundaries. We must choose liberation of our mind to roam or as sheep to be herded.

This sheep mentality creates a consensus clinging to the obstruction of our humanity and uniqueness destroyed by having never released our mind. It accomplishes poisoning by reflection, having accepted the rogue presentations projecting that image. The Motown legend informed us, the art is not in the screen but in the picture. The screen doesn't care what is projected onto it for display. Portrayals that diminish the dignity of our females of all ages, eviscerate depictions of masculinity, and emanate images of stereotypical buffoonery should not play on our screens or minds.

The lavish appeal of criminal-minded proclivities are used to convince others and influence us as our appetite are about as real as the cartoons on the cave wall. But, to solve a problem it must first be recognized and acknowledged to identify its methods, damages, and remedies. I have never heard of ingesting poison as an antidote to poison. Ingesting more poison sustains or elevates its internal level of concentration prolonging the illness. Ours has been prolonged for over four hundred years. The problem will never be the solution.

Ignoring or misunderstanding this concept yields the balance of our identity to subliminal manipulation by replicating a caricature in a reality cartoon. When we don't know or choose what to be or who we are, we succumb to the power of imitation and suggestion molded by socialization and indoctrination. Choices come with consequences, but our consequences are not necessarily a result of choices we make but sometimes decisions others made. Vibrations will find a crack to penetrate, eroding its stability over time, shattering the veneer of its shell.

Similarly, this clown activity propped up as innocent representations and entertainment has found cracks in our psyche to penetrate. It has set up screens for projections of buffoonery with us as the court jesters of society. It casts a blanket indictment creating or reinforcing negative stereotypes by observation and demonstration. Group behavior is gently coerced by mass conformity enough to erroneously convince enough it is a majority by proximity. Prominently broadcasting it as pervasive instead of fractional, it becomes the portrait of our humanity.

Some very insulting marketing incidents directed at us is not enough for us to fiscally spank that bottom line. In fact, some offer meager appeasements until the next time. But, at what point was the last time the next time? I view these as intentional insults pulled off by a not-so-sleight-of-hand deception, but instead by widespread acquiesces unafraid of penalties. If it is indeed sincere and a mistake, that magnifies the insult because what would make them think it would appease or appeal to us if not by our tolerance of its disrespect.

We have a different reaction to our own people for lesser acts of disrespect, but for them forgiveness is the poison we abundantly take. Perhaps guided by WWJD, but we are not he. Still, our silence allows it, whereas our economic silence to not patronize it might prevent it. We don't cancel them but can cancel ourselves from the nonsense. This is not to promote an ultra-sensitivity or emotional meltdown, but we can simply reject it as not being our flavor to solicit our economic palate.

Even if it is our flavor, not after stunts of defamation has soured our palate. By sheer silence, many insults to our dignity and intelligence slide into the subconscious mind of us and others to plant slanderous images of us. It is far more of a social slur than a cultural recognition. It is time for us to defecate or get off the pot, no longer surrendering our identity to a socialization for the amusement of others. No longer can we cry rivers to drown our trauma when our actions betray our words.

We can't just choose outcomes and not define processes and resolutions as our right, which is reasonable because others do even as they violate ours. We have endured the emotional gamut of vicious brutality to sinister deceptions. We have earned the realization, resolution, and respect to vehemently demand our humanity as a common social denominator removed from the epicenter of racism's ramifications and humiliations. Our gains have been hard-fought through growth from pain, knowledge from tribulation, and courage from oppression.

Still, surrendering to images compartmentalizing us by devices of complicity amounts to social propaganda and numbing cerebral manipulation regimented by so-called cultural conformity. Just because they say that is us and present it as such, it can only be us if we let them define us instead of expressing our autonomy. Lacking self-diagnosis, malfunctioning machinery does not know it is dysfunctional and operating in a diminished capacity in need of repair. On the other hand, we can self-diagnose and dispel faulty reflections given the awareness to identify and isolate subjugating beliefs, practices, presentations, and projections.

We must promote the transformative knowledge and wisdom to foster our potential individually defined instead of manufacturing a stereotypical racial mold. We cannot be unaware of the ritual social engineering programmed and disguised as our culture masquerading as our creation or mutation. However, playing the devil's advocate, if it is ours, why don't we create or promote something better? Remember, if Emancipation and Juneteenth allows us to do that, is it our psychology that makes us not do it?

Beggars Have Never Been Choosers

The subconscious mind, when uncontaminated, provides motivation and directives, but the conscious mind provides interference and excuses. This reveals the importance of attacking our subconscious mind in reaching a coalition of inferiority conditioned to avoid confrontation and practice humble obedience. The warrior spirit treads where others fear to go, and so do those undeterred from their destination of the view from the summit. We have seen enough of the valley but do we dare to conquer the summit? The summit await those who seek it while the valley is littered with those who won't. Elevate above it!

Ornaments or Obsession

An ornament is for decoration or embellishment, an adornment bolstering the mirage and esteem of something distinguishing it as celebrated, special, or exclusive in status. From a humanistic viewpoint, it symbolizes an array of superlatives arousing envy or worship. It is worn as a human or material accessory in today's culture. Yes, some people even serve as accessories or eye candy. Furthermore, it convinces others of the wearer's status to display a standard duly acknowledged and admired.

Yet, the ornament of choice in our community dispatches what message? What is the purpose of that message? Does the attention extend beyond the flattering gestures applauding a coverup of narcissistic ramblings silently humble bragging? The possession of the proper adornment gorges the ego from the buffet of adulation received. It suddenly transforms and validates our swagger and could have been the motivation to acquire it. The purpose would have been to stimulate someone else's admiration of us, thirsty for idolization.

Certain symbolism suggest significance and are necessary to calibrate our ego to the response or environment desired. The big shot syndrome cast illusions filled in by teleporting ourself into the envisioned fanatism of vicariously trading places. Since that is unlikely, imitation will have to do. The jewelry, cars, bottles, or whatever displays of opulence and prosperity statement being made are twofold. The message we project and the one we receive.

It engages a tango of our ego and others' opinions providing an injection of endorphins chemically pleasuring our senses and elevating our vitality and social prestige. The fix of the reaction received often supersedes the acquisition that caused it. Otherwise, where is the joy in others not seeing or knowing? It must be known and attached to us for the benefit to be fully appreciated. The showcasing ignites a rush intoxicating the spirit and creating a dependency and correlation of its lure.

Most people are far more attractive when standing next to an expensive new car, even if it is not theirs. However, if it is theirs's, that makes it much better. The reason is the psychological impression and fantasized conclusions attributed to the car or ornament producing an amplified reaction to the owner. The worship is of the ornament and coincidental to the owner. Separate the two and see which one still gets noticed. So the notoriety travels with the ornament, if based on the ornament, while we are left with ourselves without it.

The feelings of associated self-worth and admiration are quite addictive emotionally, physically, and psychologically. It also creates idolization of the images and individuals who possess them, equated to validation. By prominence and assigned value or esteem, the symbolism is recognized as the anticipated character of the possessor to be imitated in style, mannerisms, and behavior. The coveted suggestions invade our imagination to become a social template defined by our cultural desire to be cloned to produce it for ourselves.

We often conjure up comparisons of ourselves to the possessor or objectified fixations to possess it. The resulting association is fantasized to inject ourself as the possessor. In the remotest recesses in our mind, we wish if only it was us in that position. These compulsions and obsessions are planted, coveted, and inversely modified wishing we were so blessed. But, if or when so blessed we crave that symbol to announce we have finally made it. Often we actually blend in by mass conformity when mass produced by the over saturation of emulation.

These arbitrary transient infatuations span society's breath to ritualize behavior which, despite our declared intellectual evolvement, is primitive behavior or predictable and programable Ethology. The object of obsession or validation then loses its significance to the symbolism of what it represents aside from what it is. The equilibrium of life balances the spiritual and the material planes. They each offset each other by inverse proportions. Therefore, the intangible implications overshadow the material value.

For example, a jeweled out chain loses its value to the symbolism of the circle it is attached. Possession and to a larger degree display flashes that membership has its privileges. However, time expended, effort invested, and circumstantial experiences assemble a value system dictating our internal appraisal of their orbiting amenities. But, what did they do, can we do it, or more importantly are we willing to do it. We honor the results but often ignore the journey because that would require the effort to also possess it. It is also much harder than fairytale wishes and champagne dreams.

By nature, it is easier to visualize and fantasize importing ourself into other's scenario. Thus, the same instance can inspire us to act or mesmerize us to only imagine. Affirming a subservient position, easily distracted to admire someone else's rather than getting our own requires a degree of complacency. It is a reflection with direct implications on us to invest our focus on tangible foundations which build asset-driven appreciation rather than ego inflation.

The collective imitation of brands, possessions, and social inclusions catering to impulsive behaviors has never been as challenging as the current generation due to social media. Also by the ease of faking a lifestyle and counterfeit possessions to hoodwink others into the self-delusion. The social media seduction fascinates the imagination and stirs possibilities that stimulate desires for celebrity and fortune based on appeal. It essentially is a mass ornament for infamy producing compulsive behaviors, thereby a vortex of narcissistic dissonance pursuing celebrity urgings.

We have all witnessed outrageous acts for fame and behaviors proudly streamed by the incriminated individuals. These individuals haunted personality's amplify and personify counter-deficiency exhibitions to entice the flicker of fame against all logic and dignity. The blossoming need for recognition and attention is unrestrained by its inability to resist the endorphin's produced. The emotional familiarity initiating physical actions compliant to the chemical reactions that in turn produce the psychological obsession.

Regarding social media the virtual nature removes our actual presence from the commission. It defines our dignity as the doer, blurring reality and virtuality interwoven by technology. The various cycles and substitutes form an array of emotional and psychological rumblings to allow ego-oriented demonstrations as efforts to satisfy our vanity. Reality tv, viral exposure, and visions of fame or infamy are eternal journals, captivated by time and electronic enchantment. But, has the instrument become the maestro dictating the tempo, rhythm, and selection or have we become zombies to the machine as a volunteer pilot program?

Algorithms, suggested images, and content insinuations promote messages contextually considered as advertisements of solicitation. But, carefully consider what if it is not advertisement but only solicitation? What purpose does it achieve? So, the purpose it accomplishes is the purpose it solicited. Our persuasion, addiction, and overridden participation. But, like Halloween, the trick is disguised by the treat, unaware of the intention to enlist our habitual dependency.

Once satisfied, the purpose is no longer necessary or pursued because its hypnotic trance is established to disengage us from reality and productivity. We are assured of stagnation by our sluggish movement to remain unproductive disengaged from our ambitions forfeited to entertainment as an ornament of leisurely depletion of our privacy, time, and manifestations. But, like everything else it has its polarity dependent on our intent and use. Still, it is difficult to produce our reality while wrapped in someone else's.

The suspended animation and simulation of electronic interactions limits the human actualization of our imagination to produce variations of our reality. Imagine the revenue generated if a Black designer brand became our cultural signature in boots, clothing, hair weave, or many other ventures available especially banking. What if the recognition and resources we give to others was given to us? Why are our symbols of status attached to others other than us? Reconsider the suggestive impact of advertisement to establish what is accepted as a condescending ornament of our exclusion to fund their inclusion.

We achieve wealth and return it to the jeweler and others never to be seen again for the prosperity of our communities. But rest assured they appreciate it and ensure the resources only circulates among theirs. When was the first time we have ever seen any of these recipients living among us? How about a sprinkle of reciprocity? Still, we parade around with a chain around our neck as a minstrel show of vaudeville proportions. How is this chain somehow different from the one worn in slavery except for the flash and cost? While our ancestors shed their chains, we pursue ours.

That chain restricted our bodies but with this CHAIN our minds has been restricted by us. Why can't our resources value something that will benefit our prosperity? The harder we work to acquire it the faster we banish it to the slavery of a material master of validation. We will even kill for an ornament and not for its value but its association. Is that an algorithm or economic whoring and clown activity? The psychology of superiority it represents is shady in its implication of our inferiority duped into symbols of validation further distancing us from that validation. Seems like our mentality is chained to their symbols and approval by our choice.

Economic suppression, hijacked prestige, and racism fall within the same radius aligned with this dynamic of our mentality. It is proportionate and relative to our perception of ourself. Our cult devotion to our mind's fantasized depiction of self-worth tied to the imagery of material valuations impedes our personal development. Our self-worth is internalized differently when it is detachable. When dictated by the circumstances, the external perception controls our inner compass shifting our self-worth. So, what would be different except our mood and self-image if we were very wealthy or extremely poor but physically the same?

Our state of mind should dictate the expression, not the circumstances. State of mind also manifests the circumstances when strategically applied processes methodically accrue our desired goals. Life experiences equate to memories, some priceless and others quite regrettable. Still, others faded. But, the outcome usually is the measure to determine which are priceless, faded, or regrettable and all in between. If it is not a tool for us. It is a potential weapon against us since it has not declared its allegiance to us.

Corrupt with perversions of our identity by historical ulterior motives preserves this social order and symbolism as a caste separation. It motivates production to achieve a status by supplying someone else's superior status by their possessions. It separates the haves from others below while not allowing for those above. The obsession is to worship the symbols as ornaments of validation assigned human value accepted as personal merit. It also is a numbing agent for trauma refusing to have value which is not given, brought, or worn.

We must have an honest individual assessment within the privacy of our minds to evaluate and determine if our actions and perspectives can be better understood from a wider lens. It may change everything or nothing depending on our personal motive and evaluation. It may not apply to us but may help identify it in others or its systematic influence concealed as vanity, jewelry, or other ornaments of transposed valuation.

Taking a ride on the other side doesn't require selling your soul or dreams but it realizes the purposes of getting fancy things. So, I say we should know why we do it and can we be that without it. If so, we can be that with it. Our mind is our armor which ensures we are always well adorned and not because of our possessions. They say you can serve in heaven or rule in hell, but to refuse development and evaluation is choosing to live in hell while dreaming about heaven. It is time to be about it despite what we are wearing.

Toxic Bravado or Contagious Masculinity

I once heard Ernie "the Big Cat" Ladd say there has never been a horse that couldn't be rode and a rider who couldn't be thrown. To further elaborate, the Honorable Minister Farrakhan once said something to the effect that you can have a triple crown horse with the wrong rider or champion rider with the wrong horse. Neither will get you across the finish line first. Both illustrate the right rider and the right horse in cooperation make a winning combination. The wrong rider may get thrown and the wrong horse may lack the pedigree to win.

But, it may not be the horse, it may be the rider, especially when you fancy yourself a premier rider capable of handling the reins. A premier rider has never complained about a horse refusing to be rode. I say this respectfully to illustrate a point and not a comparison. So, instead of complaining about someone refusing to cooperate we must also accept that maybe we are not a capable rider. Then in the event we do supply veteran leadership and it is not accepted we should seek someplace where it is welcomed. All you need is one or two to see it your way.

Your burden is to not choose foolishly or lustfully. Therefore, if I tell you the truth and it angers you, did I anger you or did the truth? Let me suggest it is not me. Let me further suggest three signs of deceit. First, if you get emotional or irrational as a response. Second, when the answer is no and you don't simply say no. Thirdly, if you offer an explanation or excuse when none is needed or worst just don't want to hear it. The question is who is being deceived? Deception lacks the conviction of persuasion not of the other party but of ourself.

Definitions, roles, and social structures are changing requiring adjustments. However, there are some things which are transactional, conditional, or debatable and some which are not. Masculinity has been given a bad name by pretenders resembling the posture but not the substance. The bible speaks of being a child and having childish ways but later doing away with childish things. Masculinity embraces the way of manhood and adult behavior devoid of emotional fragility from disappointment, hardships, or mudslinging.

The observance of masculinity is a chameleon capable of shifting reflections while maintaining its foundational structure. The notions of masculinity has been convoluted by misunderstandings of its principles. Its higher manifestations are not a physical quality but an intrinsic characteristic. It is an acquired taste unwavering as a demonstration of composure, integrity, and compassion for the protection of weaker vessels. Masculinity is accountable and holds others responsible. Masculinity only builds or lead. There are many indulgences beneath masculinity and many that encompasses it.

Masculinity provides a safe haven, not a rest haven or catch and release program collecting random encounters to satisfy the flesh while having disposable consequences. It is a discerning eye and connoisseur taste of class and integrity to the level of our personal value. The jackpot is limited by the investment made. Accepting less than what we are devalues our investment in our self. Playing penny slots only garner penny prizes. So for greater dividends, we must up the ante by our personal development. Demanding someone is what we are not is not only foolish but childish. Men cannot afford to be either.

I am not interested in the games people play of gender assassination in a cultural back and forth of gender roles or levels of submission. I am also not interested in offering relationship consultation or definitions of relegation according to expectations and disappointments which amount to blanket assumptions. Nevertheless, I am compelled to mention alternative perspectives that alleviate toxic bravado. The answer is being about the business we claim to be and beyond reproach from an objective observation of our actions.

Consider the following influencers of female behavior before condemning their perspective where blame solves nothing. Consider child rearing, violations of innocence, and corruptions of their femininity. Perhaps a large degree of their behavior is disillusion from the failure of men to uphold our end of the bargain. This is by no means an excuse for the choices and predicaments to not befall self-inflicted hardships.

However, we can't get a buddy pass on what we as men do to restrict and sabotage their options when their biggest crime may have been trust and an emotional attachment to us. At any rate let it be her behavior and not ours. We are not responsible for their development. We are responsible for ours. If our requirements and necessities are optional, then our obligation cannot be a priority to them. If that is the case, they have already made the decision and notification by pony express may be severely delayed. However, the problem is continuing to repeat the same rinse cycle elsewhere. Same game but different co-parent name.

So, how many men or women have only one co-parent for multiple children? When it falls apart often men scurry to the freedom of more fertile grounds of solace and less challenges. Meanwhile, leaving women without the freedom men enjoy while bemoaning women with children. Well, whose children are they? What about the children we leave behind? What about the hardships brought about by our absence? They are not women's' alone. So women with children are less desirable while men with children does not carry the same stigma or social penalty.

Essentially, as a matter of history men have put the burden of child rearing on women as a penalty of our frailty to manage or "ride" out the turbulence of being thrown. The burdens we leave behind are theirs while we are free to create similar burdens elsewhere. We were eager to claim the girl and amenities but not the children and many times interfere with their opportunity to attract someone unhindered by our ego explosion posturing as concern.

Is there an equal concern for our children's sustenance and provisions as it is ours or our constant interference with her new relationship? What would our prospects be with several children in tow and a meddlesome ex? So, you are damn right the shift to masculine femininity may be pervasive as a survival mechanism and hunter mentality absent relief from the prowl. All of this ism and dirty macking being recklessly spread is an indictment of our weak game to convey and obtain an understanding without the friction of dysfunction or abandonment.

We were quite agreeable when we laid and played but now irreconcilable differences prevents an understanding. We cannot reflect the emotionality of women and indulge in gossip or bickering instead of maintaining an identity not in competition with the fluctuations of her response to our actions. We must bear some responsibility in the current apocalypse of baby mommas injected with bitterness and resentment for the challenges they are abandoned to resolve as a matter of them and their children survival.

Our influence must be present and engaged in this thing together by interaction and association circumstantially connected by decisions undertaken in passion that now lack cooperation. Our contribution must participate in the solution as much as we participated in creating the situation. Money alone is not enough and even that at times is questionable. When we step our game up, it has to elevate theirs as a matter of qualifying for ours.

Ever wonder why some women are ride or die and with some we can't get an ounce of cooperation? Is it them or us if they willingly do for another what they will not do for us? The baggage and experiences of family dynamics and generations before them may be shaping their perspective reflective of their upbringing and environment. So, it maybe compounding their relationships as an act of protection and conditioning.

Do we consider the trauma we cause or which may have occurred many years before we encountered them? Maybe due to the larceny of their innocence by an unscrupulous male, issues of inadequacies and abandonment, or lack of an appropriate example of feminine behavior. So, if she is scandalous we must analyze whether she chooses to be or was made to be. Could it be she was tampered with resulting in trust issues or seeking self-worth in all the wrong places? Do we bother to imagine the long term implications of such issues? Innocence lost is innocence never returned.

Regardless we pick and choose by a criteria we set, not what they set. Masculinity cannot descend into the selfish lion's pride mentality where the lioness hunts and the cubs wellbeing is secondary to our lion desires. Furthermore, do we protect our pride as ferociously as the lion does? Masculinity provides and protects all which is under its purveyance to be fully respected and safe. To hold down the position we must play the position instead of occupying it. Our dignity as men bares a greater responsibility especially if we aspire to a greater prestige.

Our foray into understanding women's needs, moods, and behaviors must not be through the lens of our insecurities and lack of masculine examples. So, we must stop telling women how to be women if we resist being told how to be men or worst actually falling short of being one. If opposites attract, how can we have feminine energy and expect to attract feminine women? Besides, have men been naïve about the true nature of a woman only to be shocked by them no longer concealing it or deferring their reality for ours?

Submission is capitulation but concession is compromise in exchange for consideration. The same thing we nonchalantly commit our head jump time over it being committed against us. They have feelings and emotions probably to a greater degree but are expected to internalize our transgressions as if they never occurred. The harm we do diminishes their femininity to respond to our expectations by the fragility of their disillusionment which we dismiss. Pain and pipe dreams shatter the fairytale until if repeated time wasted is all that is left.

Single parent households are mostly women. Many of us have had front row seats witnessing firsthand what our mothers struggled through. Instead of breaking the cycle of our dissociative disorder we discredit their struggle. Our mothers may have struggled doing the best she could with fathers being let off the hook. The rap legend spoke of certain considerations facing some mothers when it is time to pay the rent again. A woman's fortitude to provide for her offspring many times supersede a man's and can lead to dealings

Beggars Have Never Been Choosers

they would not otherwise have chosen. The resiliency to persevere through financial hardships, children disciplinary issues, no recess breaks, and sometimes domestic abuse is more than we endure.

So, the corruption of femininity as women being lowdown and for the streets has to involve a corruptor who is also for the streets preying on, instigating, or in collaboration with them. It takes two to tango but only one to corrupt. So, we cannot keep jumping ship when the water become choppy instead of manning the helm while casting blame. Therefore, where you find a no good woman there is usually a trail left from a no good man. Descending into egotistical self-centered arrogance while leaving damage in our aftermath is what justifies the term toxic.

Masculinity picks a way to be and be that way uncompromising regarding how she won't allow us to be what we have chosen to be. Leadership is despite any disputes which may arise as the assassination of our character when performing our duties. If it is in question our record should speak for itself. Personally, I don't believe in toxic masculinity but attribute it to the mistaken identity of toxic bravado. So, masculinity may sometimes be better described by what it is not than by what it may be. It is not leaving women holding baggage and complaining if they are bitter or adjust to our absence.

Furthermore, everyone sets their own market but who sets ours? Maybe our terms of engagement should be aligned with our complaints or status. So, we can heed the call and answer the bell or pretend like we didn't hear it. That is the difference between toxic bravado and contagious masculinity when you stand in it. Respect is a byproduct of our dignity and character. We should respect the portal of life and respect what it produces. Our protection of it starts with its protection from the harm we commit.

It is the true measure of our masculinity without the girlish sidebar of insults. If you can't handle the reins, there is someone who can.

If you interpret this as caping for a rest haven, you have misunderstood my message. By your standard you attract or reject the terms or prerequisites for your involvement just as they do. It is by mutual consent, circumstances, applied motivations, or concession. So be about it or don't whine about who is regardless of gender. By the way, the grass on the other side of the fence must also be watered and close only counts in horseshoes and hand grenades. Salute to the men who are holding it down until the rest catch up.

Whenever we are what we say we are, we will be treasured for it and treated like it. Otherwise, we aren't the option to be chosen and they are not the option to be chose. So, for traditional treatment without traditional behavior is a breach of traditional values. Don't let emotions, revenge, or the inability to see the silver lining of rejection as a favor received and narrow escape to prevent greater loss. Benefits and involvement should reflect that. Therefore don't complain, step your game up beyond reproach or your selection process. Either way you can't lose but if we are purported to be the stronger vessel, we should demonstrate that.

Imposter and Thespian Identity

Hair itself has no feeling but stirs deep emotions destabilizing self-esteem or substituting for it. It transfers feeling, for example, when being pulled, but not when being cut. So, how can something that has no feeling create such sensitivity? Hair is believed to be an energy conduit but has become a symbol of self-worth. It surrounds most of the brain and may possess some kinetic link or influence communicating telekinetic signals to the subconscious.

The image transmitted is overwhelmed by the image projected, posing as the ego replacing the psyche. When a visual ruse is psychologically confused to shape reality, the signal is interrupted or substituted by artificial means, becoming the alter-ego or shadow. The projection pretends to be the reality casting a spell needing an eccentric costume worn to conjure up its image and persona. However, the image cannot be summoned without the elaborate head decoration or adornment.

Therefore, the impersonating character disappears or is diminished when the transforming garment is not worn. It is comparable to some superheroes whose power lies in their costumes. But, when worn, a different person materializes, displaying corresponding characteristics. So, are you an impostor of yourself or a pretender of someone else? Either way, the ceremonial display invites the performer to appear and the performance to begin. The alter ego depends on the costume for its power and confidence. When in costume, the alter ego kidnaps the true self.

If constantly in costume, it becomes the self, the identity recognized and portrayed as a perpetual Halloween costume masquerading under its spell as its projected image. Instead of casting a spell, it would appear that you become under one. The curse of that image that has encased you within its shell, unable to exorcise its control. Changing places, the self becomes the shadow. So, in some ways, you become under the control of your head ornament, psychologically dominated by the inability to operate without it.

The beautification is satisfied in your mind, despite and absent the objective observation of its delusion rejecting your image without it. Verification can be found in abundance to quell misgivings as a comparative observance of others also being costumed out. This instills confidence, affirmation, and conformity to visually assimilate to the ritual or image. Especially when almost everyone else is dressed for Halloween wearing their headdress or costume.

The deeper the void, the greater the substitution and the greater the exaggeration. The more exaggerated, the greater the psychological benefit and emotional dependency. Twice as much is twice as good and three times down to the knees is even better. The mass assumption and acceptance as simply fashion makes it innocent but conceals its impact and the resulting psychological dependency. Presenting caricatures of yourself restricts the development of your essence which you conceal and reject, necessitating further separation from its existence. The separation does not lessen it but only ignores it.

The visual protrusion in an area you deem less damaging actually magnifies its growth, requiring more to conceal it aided by hair. Hair is an enormous industry funded by the insecurities of our people. We receive only the residual benefit of being ancillary to the process, not producers or distributors. The supply and demand are for hair, but the business model is exploitation economically and psychologically. Then again, maybe it is just fashion, but you will forfeit your identity at what cost seen and unseen. Still, observation by others transforms your identity, so is it their observation or your presentation that defines the benefit?

What is hidden is the reflection of the prognosis of the underlying obsession implemented from an external source. It consumes the psyche as a fashion demon of sorts by commandeering a host body and shapeshifting its mentality to produce a façade. Possessed by this veneer prevents you from returning to your identity from the animated realm of a pretentious, self-aggrandizing charade. This psychological enchantment is intertwined with a powerful emotional pacification forming a formidable duo.

Not knocking hair but illustrating the obsession and self-esteem suffering associated with its fascination developed into a psychological addiction and emotional crutch. The same thing that makes it acceptable is the same thing that will make it unacceptable, changing of the trend or cultural ritual. It is so pervasive that no one is immune from its cultural entombment that its infatuation extends from some of our youngest to the oldest. The oldest can make their own decisions, but the youngest are impressionable and emulate the standards of beauty that are inculcated in them.

Often allowed at questionable ages, projecting questionable images unbecoming for their young minds and bodies. It becomes an inherited impulse, assigning that as the standard of beauty but without it, they are not, cannot, and will never be beautiful. In a spiritual context the person takes on the spirit or persona of the cultural headdress or skin worn becoming the transcendental incarnation of its spirit and qualities.

When wearing the skin of that image being possessed by the psychology and surrendering one's identity and soul for the control and replication of its aura. It is similar to wearing new clothes that alter the mood and persona, giving a shift in identity consumed and enchanted by its fleeting affect and appearance. Which is fine, but when the compulsion becomes the armor, the costume becomes the uniform. The uniform then possesses the power and not the one wearing it.

Consider what an outrageous display of eyelashes as a symbol of beauty or a fashion statement conveys other than the degree to which the psyche is possessed. The assignment of self-esteem and identity to a frivolous and waning standard prepares for the next one. Subsequently, it will most likely be a more extreme animation of uniformity cloaked by individuality to evaporate your identity. It is not individuality when everyone conforms to the same standard, nor is it culturally unique to duplicate or appropriate other's likenesses, especially in excess.

The uniform or costume reflects the context of the character portrayed and its popularity by the number who compulsively emulate it strutting across the stage of life, convinced of its appeal. It also represents those sufficiently primed to be moved further away from their identity, further warping their self-image. It amounts to a theatrical presentation with no intermission being constantly in character. Be careful not to be an actor in your own play starring someone who can be confused as you or mostly resembles you but is an imposter.

Not to criticize hair or eyelashes but to illustrate external crutches that detract from identity, self-love, and substance. Three-leaf clovers, lucky rocks, and Dorothy's ruby red slippers have the same effect, or you can just metaphorically click your heels of rejection three times to return home to yourself. Anything that can be removed from you, denied access to, or is vanity based on which you depend is not an aid or weapon. It is a crutch. It disables you by your dependency.

It prevents you from developing a core proficiency and self-assurance from which you cannot be separated. So when you know, you know, and so does everyone else because it shows. Old-timers used to say there is nothing like the real McCoy for quality and durability. So likewise, your uniqueness is unduplicated, and nobody does you better than you. So, if the good Lord wanted you to be someone else, the good Lord would have made you into them. But, if you can accept it, you are you and not what you appear to be to others.

Despite looking like an assembly line of replicas with programmable mannerisms produced in varying sizes, shapes, and shades but underneath, you remain a treasure buried ever so deep. The damage is how it is used to submerge your identity by seemingly innocent methods but slowly and increasingly erasing your uniqueness. What do you gain? What do you lose? Can you go without it and continue as if you had it? How do you operate without it? What are you hiding? These questions determine if it is fashion or psychosis, willful or compulsive.

If addicted to the image, you are projecting a shadow that blocks the light from you, intercepting your identity and casting you into the background as its silhouette. Consequently, the image lives while you exist as its inverted shadow. Please separate the message from the method and messenger. If the message holds valid assumptions, further explore the core suppositions moving past the surface. To simply reject out of pocket by attempting to disguise denial is to refuse the benefit of its useful counsel.

Therefore, this is not a criticism of our women, their fashion choices, or methods of self-affirmation. However, it is a cautionary tale that each must evaluate for themselves as to the motives and insecurities that they create, conceal, or perpetuate. A drink to calm your nerves can easily morph into many drinks to face reality as a coping mechanism and self-medication. Likewise, some of these fashion statements and body obsessions (big butts) can foster damaging self-images reliant on contorted dependencies producing an addictive intoxication.

So in and of itself, it may not be indicative of anything but rest assured it can definitely harbor insecurities as a refuge from self-acceptance. The mind-altering substance of abuse is its dependency, not its use. But, to further slander and deny the strength and character of your essence as an imposter of yourself invites disassociation from reality and your representation. Any caricature mimics a skit whereby a comical or grotesquely exaggerated representation or presentation of self by distortion of appearance creates a ludicrous parody spoofing a rejection unwittingly damaging your self-esteem.

For the record hair, big butts, eyelashes, and any reference to women can easily be substituted for instances of male supplementation with the same underlying psychology and rejection of self. It is easier to hijack an identity than to explore and display the revelation of your own. The concealment has no gender but share insecurities concealed by objects of cosmetic delusion. What is termed as toxic masculinity, chains (jewelry) of validation, and whips (vehicles) of prestige at times are used to project the opposite of our insecurities. The question is when separated from the prop or subjective valuation, what are you if not a thespian?

Sexualization and Objectified Enticement

We are going to keep it real and authentic about what's offered and received personally to acquire a meeting or deception of the minds. Always beware to check the integrity of what is sold or purchased, whether the buyer or vendor, caveat emptor, and caveat venditor.

The crux is receiving what is advertised or promised when agreeing to terms and what is tendered. Regarding people and relationships, the principles and concepts remain the same.

Still, the verification process is not as simple, and the shine doesn't always equate to the quality. So, are you in the market for shine or quality? Consequently, what value do you hide behind, if not substance or quality? Is your house made of straw easily blown away by turbulence? Is it mud or wood, highly susceptible to harsh elements? Is it stone or brick built to last through most circumstances? Functionality and durability in the long term have staying power out lasting cosmetics and aesthetics.

Artificial or imitated personas are often difficult to maintain because they are superficial, like glass, easy to break, crack, or damage. Beauty is only skin deep and in the eye of the beholder, a simple visual pleasantry. Still, except for the very few and exceptional, physical beauty wanes with time and maintenance. But like sports cars, there are some classics, but they are classics or antiques for a reason, time. Time will rob us all, albeit at varying rates.

The problem is they keep rolling out newer models to replace the old ones. Almost always, the old ones cannot compete with the newer models except for nostalgia. Many times we cannot even compete with earlier versions of ourselves. It reaches a point when the cutey pie or toy boy discount is not what it used to be and the enchanting suitor putting ladders up to the tower window becomes less frequent. They used to bring their own ladder, but now we have to leave one out, and still no climbers. Those vying for our attention become less frequent and of less preference from the past when we had our pick of the litter or was the pick.

It is called life and the real replacement theory. There will always be the latest version of us to replace what we used to be. The only exception to some degree seems to be quality and substance superseding attractiveness and sex appeal, especially over time. Denial is no defense despite gender or sexual orientation. It reaches a point where the only one we are fooling is us stuck in a time never to return or may have never been except by self-proclamation.

So, sex appeal is a fleeting business card. Substance holds its value while sex appeal depreciates, sometimes severely and quickly. But, by all means, use it while you have it if that is your desire. The best art is in a living form, and visual beauty improves the world's aesthetics. Likewise, a freebie is a freebie that adds to life's unexpected pleasures. However, I'm referring to what else you have after the shine wears off the attractive new play thang, and it will. What qualities do you offer that have a transcendent or transferable value that is transactional for what someone provides you or superior to what someone else can offer them?

Let's not get caught up in gender because that dilutes the point. Interactions are primarily transactional, operating on a barter system where something is willingly exchanged for the value of what is wanted or received. When correctly done, satisfaction results from the transaction with a fair exchange for fair value. Please remember that this is largely figuratively speaking for maximum absorption of the point. However, realistically everything is a commodity or an accommodation.

The considerations and conditions are negotiated in a ritual dance of objectives surrendered to secure objectives received. Usually under an exclusive contract or understanding because no one is fattening a frog for a snake and our time is a commodity too. People like to provide benefits on a personal level that also benefits them. Therefore, a sense of indebtedness, ownership, or possessiveness is expected. There is also an expectation of reciprocity attached. A provision exchanged for sustenance is the deal with title and restrictions included. Each party negotiates for the totality of their greater good, setting the terms to be assumed or understood.

Scarcity or uniqueness adds value to anything being exclusive to itself, rare, or inaccessible. Are you rare or a dime for a baker's dozen? Has the revolving door of prior indiscretions diminished your value? No one wants to eat off a plate picked over and left as scraps. Exclusivity and quality are the difference between selling one item for one thousand dollars or a thousand for one dollar. It is the same money, but not the same item or quality, even if it slightly appears to be by the undiscerning eye.

The worth, capabilities, and desirability of your qualifications separate and elevate your value on a sustainable level. Consequently, sexualization and objectified enticements will routinely get you to the negotiating table, but your qualifications keep you there or closes the deal. It is the process of convincing someone why you are the best person to fulfill their needs in exchange for them mutually fulfilling yours.

The essence of my point was best summed up by the musical seducer of passion when he stated, he could still see your beauty even if struck blind. What is your substance that doesn't need eyes to see? If it is sitting there and looking good, being a trophy for friends, or moaning when I want cha, then job security is shaky at best. It is like sleeping on the job. As long as you stay asleep, you still have a job, or as long as you keep moaning, you won't be replaced. So consequently, one person's trash is another person's treasure, but it can also be another person's trash. It is fool's gold waiting for a tarnished expiration.

If someone does not make themselves indispensable or beneficial to the alliance, they can never be comfortable within it. Objectification renders you a possession or object with an expiration date pending. Likewise, it is leased to own or just plain old Rent-A-Center. It becomes quantifiable for a fee going to the highest bidder, a community joy ride randomly rode hard and put away wet. Not being exceptional and multi-dimensional adding value lands you in the expense or liability column and eventually disposable.

Sexualization is the projection of a fantasy or anticipation of a capacity to tickle carnal desires capturing the imagination. It captivates a sensual arousal whose curiosity covets the possibilities igniting appetites and rampaging passions under an illusionary spell transformed into an imaginary cinema. Imagination is the closes thing to the real deal and sometimes better, especially if that is as close as you will ever get, your imagination. As such, sex sells, and sexualization garners attention for the same reason, imagery.

So, sexualization is an indiscriminate commodity suggesting that a price or desire is the fee. Commodity prices are usually posted and known to fluctuate wildly. Well, maybe wildly is the wrong word, so significantly. So you are essentially auctioned for sale, but as they say, it ain't tricking if you got it and it ain't what-you-call-ish if you sale it. I was only trying to say if you trade as a commodity, but look it goes without saying, so I won't say it. But if you brought it, do you own it? I'll shut my mouth, won't dare say it and keep it classy. Anyway, I better move on before the delicate balance takes away from the point.

Seriously, thcsc things apply to everyone who advertises themselves by importuning and procuring for material consideration solely based upon sexualization. If that is what you offer, then that is what you will be considered. However, a disproportionate predisposition is to relegate females to sexual objects for male hedonistic satisfaction. Sexualization leads to objectification, and both diminish your worth to be considered only for that purpose or as the highest value or purpose you provide.

It encourages someone to pursue only that and not have a curiosity about other aspects of your character, opinion, capabilities, or aspirations. It also disregards any other aspects you possess, restricting your use and purpose to a sex toy and objectifying you as a service provider. It dehumanizes your existence and substance. Women have historically been disenfranchised from equality and treated as an abstract visual gratification of imagination for a male-dominated society. But these concepts and references also apply to men and everyone in between.

The violation of women's autonomy and dignity is rooted in sexual origins as much as in the nonsense of denying their intellectual capacity. Slavery was trafficking in flesh without moral consideration where sexualization and objectification of the Black woman were second nature. This desecration of dignity is still exceedingly true for our women as their portrayals reinforce these falsehoods, magnifying disrespect of their majestic destiny. The mass portrayal of our women is the opposite of what it actually is, but the prevalence of its imagery implies it is comprehensive. This fallacy attempts to ensnare all Black women in its misrepresentation.

As such, it is difficult to move beyond its characterization when behaviors, appearances, and presentations perpetuate the fallacy. It is deemed not necessary to develop what you can be beyond physical when the standard of value is strictly sexual. This socialization morphs into a culture replicating itself but is a competitive disadvantage when not conforming with that action. The validation and ego inflation received equates to stimulating the pleasure senses connected to dopamine releases extinguishing inhibitions thirsty for attention.

To remain competitive and get attention within that standard or expectation of sexualization, the boundaries are narrowed to contend. The emotional baggage or dissatisfaction escalates and percolates to the surface when either the standard is not met, can no longer be met, or smothers any attempt to escape its confinement. As time changes, you were down for the choosing but dread the losing. A resulting emotional disorder or anxiety lurks beneath the surface until it sprouts, no longer suppressed by the silencing and debilitating erasure of your self-worth and image.

Finally, however, the psychological toxins contaminating your self-esteem overflow, signaling the honeymoon is over and seller's remorse takeover. The dysfunctional relationship perspective yearns for something more satisfying to engage your self-worth unless the other party decides first they need something more to engage theirs. Which will come first, the chicken or the egg, your dissatisfaction or theirs?

Suppose you have no viable options or developed qualities. Then, you will be subjected to the whims of circumstances and your satisfaction will never come first. You will always serve at the discretion of circumstances, but it may not be selling your soul to the devil. Still, it might be close, considering the hell you may experience or subject yourself to when the benefits no longer justify the sacrifice. Being glamorous, sexy, or desirable and accentuating it is not the problem, but certainly being one-dimensional and depending on it.

Precious intangibles that epitomize and compliment your merit injects indispensability which is invaluable in establishing an appreciation for your worth. Demonstrating the totality of your assets without reservation adds self-esteem and fulfillment to your desirability and utility. Like water seeking its own level, the totality of your demonstrated capabilities is what distinguishes the brilliance of diamonds from the monotony of glass. Diamonds shine, glass shatters. That said, context, consistency, and discretion conveys the texture of impressions sent and received.

When imitation is the sincerest form of flattery, and your demonstration inadvertently promotes collateral impressions of self-worth attached to sexuality, young girls duplicate them while far too young to discern the extenuating consequences. It establishes a pattern of behavior and normalcy to accommodate situations and expectations from the example you provide. They generally will become what they see or you replicate until greater impressions of influences emerge.

When developing an identity and forming the foundation of principles that will direct the course of their young lives through uncertainty, awkwardness, and challenges, they rely on their rolodex of experience or impressions. So often, what is available is the example you set and the impressions they have been exposed to as emulating influences becoming their trial-and-error basis for their perspective. This casts the mold with you as the sculptor creating the art.

Often unfortunate but foreseeable consequences result in promiscuity, confusing sex with love, early pregnancy, and underdevelopment of their facilities and capabilities. It molds gullible misguided spirits convinced according to its orientation consumed by the flesh but limited by innocence and judgment. The need for attention, social competition, peer pressure, and expectations are like never before, especially with social media influences and unreality presentations passed as entertainment.

Knowing there are nefarious types who would seek to take advantage, as adults we have a duty to protect and prepare them. For youngsters is more of a matter of not compromising their dignity, maintaining a level of honor, and protecting their self-respect while accumulating knowledge, skills, and accomplishments. The merits of one's achievements, proficiency, and skills determine the quality of life as one matures tentatively setting a course out the gate into adulthood. Life skills, emotional maturity, social savvy, and identification of traps and pitfalls are the most prominent challenges of early adulthood.

Over time our guidance wanes proportionate to aging or burdensome life choices diminishing its influence and benefit. So, their life is primarily judged by their production and independent means to sufficiently produce for their circumstances. If you are not the provider, you are the recipient and vulnerable. Therefore, when placed in the hands of another, they also have the discretion to withdraw it. The benefit of our mistakes, experiences, and navigation is their scholarship program sharing our database for a foundational comparison.

Beggars Have Never Been Choosers

Depending on the frame of reference, a template emerges relative to experiences, observations, and influences patterned to emulate and adopt life models for themselves hopefully unrestricted by ours. We can only steer em but we can't drive em, their destination is their choice. The vehicle to transport them is invisibly linked to their internal composition of personal development, self-esteem, fortitude, and foundational compass. The measurement or qualification that causes distinction soothes the ego according to their embrace of self-images and dignity of identity.

Conformity to decency is a notion of morality, but class is a standard of conduct. That said, it more often is not what you do but how you do it from objective views of understanding, indulgence, and insight. Pride and principles are to be preserved to carry yourself elegantly displayed as the highest representation of your chosen image. The romanticized benefits of sexualization and objectification provide the lowest-hanging fruits. Still, they do not expose the pain of their unhappiness, caught in a trap suppressing their worth to constantly maintain a role that deteriorates over time due to time or exhaustion.

So rarely is a fairytale ending produced blocked by the emptiness of never stimulating or expanding your self-worth, expression, potential, or intelligence. The tacit invasion of our females' dignity, reducing them to objects of sexual exploitation, is a form of visual sex trafficking, exhibitionism, and sexism as the highest representation and extent of their significance. Their only quality of interest cannot be to trade on the open commodity market as barter for attention, validation, or resources.

In essence, it is a modernized form of slave trade based on marketable physical attributes and the ability to tickle the fancy of imagination. It is strictly based on a suggestive performance and enticement by simulated display exhibiting sexual willingness or proficiency in performing acts with little or no restrictions or reservations. Examples are abundant, audio, visual, and live, which exercise no boundaries exposing children inadvertently. Simultaneously, while adults entertain themselves, they are not shielding their children from its nefarious and insidious grooming.

Not only influenced by your behavior and display but also the many elements of entertainment in which they are surrounded. Then it is left to wonder how or where they picked it up, but not really. The answer is abundantly clear they grew up to be just like you. Be careful not to hijack their innocence, identity, and self-worth before they even know what entranced them. These generational spells must be recognized and broken before they mesmerize and confuse all of us by intended indulgences unintentionally socialized. This is a commentary on breaking cycles and that consequences are real.

Objectification can also manifest as a label restricted to a conventional acceptance or perception according to prior constrictions of autonomy. The proverbial box of conformity, expectations, and discouragement to limit aspirations and expressions to social norms of relegation with assigned characteristics. Sexual is the most prevalent but also occupational, sexual orientation, intellectual pursuit, social proclivities, chosen affiliations, and many more are stigmatized outside the preference of a moral or social decree. Racism, sexism, and poverty are competing forms of objectification that strong-arms identity.

Sources, Scrutiny, and Solutions

Transformation of our collective ideology must take precedence over the ritual and culturally defective systems and structures of our impediment. The ideological shift must be the modern-day underground railroad to lead those psychologically captive to the freedom of clarity and self-actualization away from the triggers of inferiority. It does not require physical movement but a philosophical transfer to the high ground, removed from the flood of indoctrinations, fallacies, and frivolous assumptions.

Beggars Have Never Been Choosers

The first action is to discard debilitating crutches of the past. Although factual and impairing, the past is also a traumatic blockage to the future. It is no longer strategic or functional, hindering our social and economic mobility. The next move is to claim accountability for our actions and conditions, accepting the mission of altering our perspective and improving our circumstances. The following move is to avoid self-harming our achievement of the equitable and impartial recognition of our humanity.

The necessary steps, which will be challenging but essential, require discipline and commitment. The blueprint involves elevating our understanding and positively influencing those with whom we may carry a little sway. No one can prevent our progress, even if they jeopardize their own. Over time, we can reinvent our history and future trajectory, ascending beyond discrimination. We must manage our end of the table by rejecting and eliminating the insidious systems and brainwashing residuals from racism.

We must have accountability by demonstration and association whereby we cannot travel with someone heading in the opposite direction of which we are going. Don't let their journey become our burden if they will not or cannot veer from their course. Divided we fall, united we stand. We must save ourselves and those we can, realizing that we will not save everyone. Nor does everyone want to be saved. It is pretentious at best to assume any degree of absolute conversion. We must move onto more fertile ground where possibilities spring eternal for those so inclined to make the adjustments needed.

The journey is fraught with temptations and mirages to distract from the destination. But, the longer we stay on the path, the easier it is to remain on it by determination. Our determination is motivated by the exhaustion of yielding beneath someone's prejudiced gaze and the pitfalls of the injustices lurking. We change the system by changing ourselves and the authority it has over us. When seeking change, expecting others to make major changes without some concessions on our behalf is a cornerstone of what we are combating which is subjective entitlement.

But, let's suppose we are truly fed-up, and our cup runneth over with the nonsense. We can no longer tolerate another generation subjected to patterns of adverse social indoctrinations, emotional reflexes, and projection of harmful archetypes. In that case, the time is now to propel our interest toward methodical and codified progress. So, let's scrutinize it from the beginning, from the cradle to the grave examining assessments, alternatives, and imperatives to expand our recognition of the measures needed.

We must change the pipeline to produce generations compounded by time to cultivate an ideology removed from the indoctrinations of convenience, conformity, fallacy, or social limitations. The key is focused interaction and nurturing, instilling the core guidance to excel beyond the edits of society's cubicles many times based on nothing more than conjured up superstitions. Early childhood development, education, knowledge, and nurturing form the foundation of our self-determination and self-worth.

The proper infrastructure, appropriate curriculum, and self-affirming psychological development are all directly impacted by three foundational elements that maximize a child's potential and possibilities. The tools, preparation, and inspiration of life skills to pursue the extent of their ambition are the three foundational elements. These are not racial assessments but educational ones disproportionately affecting our children according to economic status, options, and assorted challenges. They are vocational disruptions and not evaluations of worth.

Contingencies to address issues should involve assessments focusing on resolution, not judgments or punishment, not allowing it to disrupt those eager for progression. Assuming students can be assigned by acumen or academic assessment different levels of accommodations are available. In that case, social and behavioral interventions preserve the education of those engaged and help those struggling improve so they can learn. Whatever the process, those meeting expectations education must be protected while supporting the well-being of those who require a different setting. Remember, one size doesn't fit all, and approaches must vary.

Environments conducive to the educational objective or behavioral assessment of a child's evaluation must not only consider placement by academics. It must also understand the limits of punishment and rigid conformities from a more holistic approach. The flaw of the system is refusing to be comprehensively overhauled by conceding to the most effective innovative methods of achieving education designed for the future and not relegated to the past. Are we educating ghost of the past or manifestations of the future?

A global information and educational shift increasingly resisting the status quo is underway. Expanding the current systems beyond the capabilities of their designs and purposes results in contraction and suffocation. Consider the conservative movement to restrict and forcibly ban books and elements of diverse knowledge. How do you achieve education by restricting knowledge instead of logically debating it? It seems fascism is then the lesson being taught.

The systems long adhered to are under siege to be amended from the primitive ideologies and indoctrinations of oppression, suppression, and authoritarian misconduct. Education is at the root of the dissatisfaction because it is the genesis of its implementation. The basics of human development are instilled by the age of five to seven years old as the foundational instructional influence. It is not coincidental from daycare to preschool and kindergarten that individuals and systems have an unfettered impact on shaping children consciously and subconsciously.

The school system's model in America started in 1837 and still guides today's basic structure with a devotion usually reserved only for the founding fathers. Horse and buggy mentalities, methodologies, and motives cannot persist at a time when private citizens are venturing into space. These antiquated allegiances are fraying at the seams, stretched to accommodate a bulk of knowledge whose access was unforeseen and beyond imagination. Excavation must be undertaken to supplant current methods with redefined intentions by addressing intellectual evolution as the catalyst for education.

Adherence to these systems is more conducive to control than order, fairness, or progress, promoting stagnation to maintain power, conformity, and wealth. But mostly restricting thought in lieu of exploration while producing undeveloped intellectual capacities not allowed to stretch. The tunnel vision of past ideologies panned out reveals a panoramic view un-leashing solutions that will revolutionize the stale concepts of social, economic, and intellectual dogma stuck in the past. Innovative thought has always been the blueprint for discovery, progress, and invention.

Each malfunctioning system of antiquity must be critiqued separately and improved as a complimentary element of an approach anticipating the trajectory of evolution. Life is similar to manufacturing reaching a point where a new machine with the latest applications is required because repairs to the old one become futile and unproductive. Many of our methods to combat racism, discrimination, and injustice will be replaced with innovative perspectives, strategies, and processes of education. The initiation point is early childhood development and education reimagined and implemented before the damage has ravaged potential and possibilities.

The preponderance of evidence is in the educational system itself. How can a system of education not be educated enough to detect the empirical conclusions of its failure? No child left behind has effectively herded the mentality of children to cookie cutter nuts and bolts of disengagement leading to disruptive behavior. So are the children failing or are they being failed by a system designed for a much different time? It is obvious that the approach needs to change.

What is the risk benefit to not changing it. It seems like the insanity of expecting a different result from a dispelled formula. The intellectual miscarriage and subsequent dysfunction is absolute proof a return to the drawing board is needed. Surely innovative minds capable of space travel can produce capable minds for earthly challenges but then who would replace the "essential workers?" Is it possible the system operates as designed, preferring to mass produce workers and not thinkers?

Proper Foundation

Public education and private education have quite different objectives as measures of targeted achievement. Private education requires payments, so you must conduct yourself according to a stricter code of conduct and academic performance. It is assumed that you want to be there, and teachers have a more pertinent obligation to focus on education. They also usually have a waiting list with others willing to pay tuition and conform to an atmosphere conducive to their learning. Private accommodations are generally of a higher standard, with more resources to be deployed.

Public schools are part of a political and social structure to herd or store students more consumed by behavior than education. But is their atmosphere more conducive to learning or being supervised? Public schools defy logic with their open-source funding from various property taxes, government entities, and lottery commissions by never having the resources or solutions to provide a better education. The solution is not the ever-expanding expectations placed on teachers, as some believe they should now be relied on to carry firearms and confront active shooters.

Maybe they didn't sign up for that, especially when people who did and are trained fall short. The education they could provide is usurped by the dysfunctions and other challenges diverting their efforts and resolve from education. The public school system has more of a custodial function than an educational one. One of the school's primary fundamentals is providing supervision while you work. Another is to produce a labor force smart enough to perform but not smart enough to resist the exploitation of their time to build someone else's wealth. It is a factory or farm system for menial labor. Teachers are often used as straw bosses instead of educators.

 Education is now largely decided by politics and politicians, not educators. The concept of allegiance to the educational and management structure is a conditioned relic from the straw boss days and pecking order of bias selection and targeted exclusion. It would seem the politicians would be educated enough to let the educators educate. So the modern application is the "essential worker" designation that disproportionately benefits the employer's bottom line. The lower rungs are populated by minorities and women exploited according to their lack of options.

When in need, you are essential, and when not, you are obedient, anxious, and replaceable. Is this the intent and purpose of education? Private schools provide the same thing, just the elevated package for higher entry and function within the system. College furthers the separation, producing expectations of management over the lower rungs. So the early education process and caste system of resources usually affect the course of lifetime achievements.

Quality of life issues equate to educational deficiencies and social complacency whose low trajectory has a compounded effect on subsequent generations and their earnings potential. Rest assured, there are exceptions to every circumstance, and this scenario is not all-inclusive, but it is highly indicative. Understanding this formative impression, we must also factor in how students are assigned to classes and teachers. Furthermore, we have no indication beyond their teaching certificate what biases are influencing our child as their "teacher."

The educational racism of the past steered students to certain professions and discouraged many ambitions of our people. The prevailing social paradigm does not escape the school system curriculum or the person doing the teaching. Considering the ruckus about CRT, political division, social unrest, and historical inaccuracies and biases in the curriculum, the chances are that some of this ideology has to be exposed to our children every school day. The outrage is what is or is not taught to their children without equitable regard for ours.

This discrepancy of concern is proof of the overt motives of educational biases. The value of revisionist history is highly questionable, considering it is not factual education or life skill oriented. The educational criteria back when it was developed had a much different intention and purpose than the application today. Still, it is used today for what purpose if it is not educational? We must hold political enablers and their supporting public school officials accountable to educate. It should be a preparatory initiative for adulthood and self-reliance absent of politics.

We also have an obligation to rebuke the earliest intentions of uniform inculcation to have any chance at nullifying a system that does not provide the optimal benefit for our children. This exclusion is done at the earliest stages possible, including daycare throughout college by standardized tests developed from biased perspectives without consideration of cultural differences or resources. The arbitrary nature of society to promote a subjective preference based on race or gender endorses it as the dominant tendency, thereby forcing compliance or massaging failure.

That predisposition has elements of racism or sexism, among other isms, baked in from when and for who it was adopted. It is clear that a new way of education and evaluation is needed for our children. Relevant and factual educational content, unbiased suppositions, and inclusive social criteria would invite the prospects of education's promise. The old way is, well old, and resists efforts to facilitate extensions of modernization, psychology, and sociology.

Taking an active role in holding ourselves accountable benefits our children's future. By mutual engagement and agreement, it is a two-party contract with expectations and accountability for everyone to maintain their end including our children. However, for the educational foundation for success to flourish, the proper infrastructure and complementary resources must initiate the process. It is mandatory we demand transparency on the distribution of resources, the process, and application to audit irregularities. They are public funds and we have a right.

A heightened level of curiosity, scrutiny, and transparency will promote better performance and improvements. It provides our children with a better foundational education by leverage and popular demand, by our demand. The allocation of funds from the federal level downward needs to be streamlined for maximum revenue to reach the designated recipients. The Department of Education regulates the overall stipulations of schooling. As such, it must secure the funding needed to operate our schools properly, alleviate overcrowded classrooms, and provide free in-school meals as a function of education.

Regarding funding, pretend it is for war or foreign aid. The government and elected officials will send tens of billions of dollars for foreign aid to passively participate in wars but refuse school children meals. How? Why? Because we tolerate it. But, not if they genuinely serve at the people's discretion. Dilapidated education, depleted supplies, insufficient resources, and antiquated systems must be improved to incentivize learning or at least not detract from it.

The behavioral and sociological dynamics would improve by engaging in understanding, inclusion, and firm tolerance. Disruptive students should be accommodated whereby their decisions don't interfere with those who want to learn. Those charged with facilitating education should also not be a disruptive force. If we are not active in the solution, we may be an essential part of the problem's continuation. Defining the clear goal clarifies the solution.

Appropriate Curriculum

What is taught is just as important as what is learned. Our concern and indignation is subdued when a critical element of education is implemented and promoted obscured from the rational evaluation of its purpose, relevance, or benefit. By the sheer volume of time spent in school, why is there not a more comprehensive benefit if it was functioning efficiently? Perhaps, it is performing to its true purpose, but it still requires our silence and participation. That not being a consolation, why do we allow the most precious commodity of development for our children to be circumvented.

If other parents outrage or preference shapes education then we should exercise our right to influence what our children are taught. For example, if CRT has little or no practical benefit, that can also be applied to most of not only American but world history. These too should be significantly analyzed as detrimental to not only our children's self-image but everyone's self-interest. The inconsequential past is an outdated endeavor unsuitable for the essential exploration of the future. So, what really is in question is whose self-interest is protected reminiscing of an irrelevant past at the expense of future preparation. Who has the power to determine?

The answer is the same patriarchal system of politics, immorality, and racism. It further demonstrate the inequality of influence within the system in which we rely so heavily on to miseducate all children. The teaching of American and world history is miseducation when it omits material elements of the truth skimming the surface of depth and occurrence. It is deception by omission and concealment by commission. How can the revelation or ineptness be disputed? The insolvency of primitive ignorance rejects the development of evolving ideologies.

Furthermore, it exposes a pattern of deliberate suppression of knowledge as a mechanism of relegation and classification. Even disregarding CRT there are many deficiencies of curriculum emphasized over functional life skills. Our children are taught just as much European history as American history. Is that only necessary to perpetuate systems of subjugation where we are irrelevant, eliminated, or demoted to footnotes in history? Society revers six thousand year old myths but discard four hundred year old facts. This physics of ignorance defies the science of progression. This social illiteracy restrains the realization of lifetime competency.

For example, substituting financial literacy, problem solving, budget and planning, emotional maturity, economic sufficiency, and conflict resolution as opposed to nonessential subjects such as European history. The purpose supposedly is to prepare children for adulthood and the future with less emphasis on the past. If this was the case it could be reasonably claimed that CRT is of less importance for their future. But, most history is totally irrelevant when students look back hundreds of years into the past while ill-prepared for the pending future.

It becomes a deliberation of the value of the history as opposed to the selective invalidation of specific history. If preparation for the future is more practical, economically productive, and socially relevant, then focus on that. Especially when racism is constantly reminding us of a past systemically refusing to forget it. If a revisionist history is discarded maybe it would be easier for us to forget it too. It could then be a family secret no one speaks of or remembers. With that in mind, it would undoubtedly benefit all children regardless of race in preparation for the challenges of adulthood. So, it primarily is not an issue of race, but progress and preparation.

Why is it preferable to instill children with fractional realities if social unification is the goal? Why not implement useful topics of understanding? After a timeout it is suggested that a child is told they are not bad but what they did was bad. The behavior must be pointed out for it to be corrected. In this gentler society it seems adults could learn a harsh lesson from the same. Therefore, the educational opportunity is still focused away from improvement as time marches onward, overwhelmed by delinquent adaptations and corrections suppressed by concealment.

Due to the social and economic crater caused by slavery, racism, and church or government decree, the stagnation of the educational system perpetuates a depression of reality. But, we already knew that. That is why denying slaves education and learning to read under the penalty of death was so important. Education is still the key that fits many locks and opens many more doors. Education is an effective undercover method of segregation and economic suppression, even more so than race. The best thing to give a child is an education cultivated with a nurturing spirit and wisdom of discernment.

A support system and encouragement are essential to achievement but not necessary when children's curiosities and ambitions are energized. Education is an imperative. The new servitude is inferior education, financial illiteracy, and inadequate technological resources, development, knowledge, or training regardless of race. Schools and education are separated by economics and geography. They are then further separated by structure and race with whatever busing situations among similarly deprived students. The desegregation of schools in Brown v Board of Education in 1954, citing violation of the 14th Amendment, still took decades to implement, culminating in designated busing.

The problem is the busing was not usually an upgrade in education but the willful integration of incompetency due to social and political manipulation of demographics. Educational equilibrium in earnest undertaken by busing was undermined by regentrification and gerrymandering manipulating residential school districts. Real estate discrimination further sealed the separate but unequal deal under a renovated appearance. Still, the effect of busing is barely forty to fifty years old by the most liberal interpretation. Busing was still heavily contested in the seventies.

Black people's condition has always revolved around education and knowledge being directly proportionate to the depletion of our economic and social status. So schools cannot be warehouses for our children while they treadmill their way through life. They are exerting effort in a stationary position if putting in the effort but not seeing proportionate results. The inadequate education provided our children prolongs the inequality of our opportunities and the defamation of our humanity. It seems to produce more hopelessness than hope.

The previous mention of paradoxes and theories comes into complete focus when applied to disrupting the potential of our children before they can bear fruit. The public school system damages the seed before it can begin to wither on the vine but can still produce replacement parts to supplement the previous harvest of an ill-educated crop. Aristotle said an educated mind should entertain ideas without accepting them. However, it is also true to not reject ideas based on tradition when empirical data suggest alterations and reconstruction are sorely needed.

Not to impugn the integrity of teachers' intentions but to illustrate that their training is in a system that is inadequate for today's and future educational objectives. But, it is indeed to criticize the model, method, and content based upon the repetitive insanity of the overall disappointing results. Even teachers would probably agree that fitting a square of necessity into a round hole of antiquated structure is counterproductive.

Adults face a similar mandate comparatively speaking. The shift from in-office or central location employment has jumped the paradigm of a captive work force coerced into expenses to fit an in-office model of control. Likewise, education has also jumped the paradigm requiring a new model. Our resistance and protest should not ignore the constant pruning of our children's perspective to assimilate into systems not conducive to their transcendence.

The key to avoiding later pitfalls in life that drive expanding divergence as time and economic separation expand is the foundation of education and analytical thinking. Even awareness of options, opportunities, and processes furthers their attainment by recognizing and assuming the possibilities as realistically probable. Literacy is not only by the proficiency provided by knowledge but also the application of it.

By revealing examples and prospects not always culturally considered as attainable goals make them possible strictly by awareness, method to achieve it, or representation to encourage it. We can no longer afford to follow the curvature of time. So we must accelerate to meet or exceed time by our preparation beyond the present but onto ushering in the future. Information is the new currency and knowledge is its commercial exchange propelling future redistribution of every facet of society.

Look no further than the housing bubble and predatory lending to see how those waves were excessively financed on our backs and resources. Often by the time we participate, the real money is made, leaving our late arrival holding the bag of collapse creating another generational setback. The educational seeds planted now must be directed toward our future participation as the wave begins to swell, not when it subsides.

Positioning ourselves and our children to benefit from the cyclical nature of economics through knowledge and skills has generational ramifications. Combined of course with astute fiscal maneuverings avoiding enticements of egotistical displays craving validation instead of financial accumulation. Our emotional tunnel vision regarding social justice and racism obscures and distracts from the more damaging but silent killer of our wealth. Psychological and educational complacency and inadequate support systems to facilitate preparation should be an urgency to avoid our intellectual death in the womb.

An urgency which eliminates the most common cause of discrimination and quality of life issues which is economics. Cash may be king, but knowledge is the crown of anointment and power. Books and knowledge provide the supreme protection for our children. By reading today, they can lead tomorrow by learning that self-education is a life-long endeavor. The suppositions, models, and systems can no longer be obliviously tolerated wondering what is wrong with our children. Could it be the systems that are wrong? Without challenging what is wrong with the methodology, structure, and content of education, how can we know for sure?

We certainly cannot argue with much dispute about the unacceptable results, whatever the cause. It seems educators could figure out a solution after all this time, but what is our excuse? After all, it is our children and our fiduciary obligation. It is a blasphemous sin to blame others for what we should and could do despite their obvious failure. However, their failure is also our failure and our children's albatross of generational subjugation.

Psychological Development

Age-appropriate emotional and psychological development, encouragement, and maturity are the cornerstone on which a person's evolution shaping future pursuits and achievements are built. Early childhood is the most critical time of development for emotional connectivity, sensory imagery, and audio stimulation. The ears are always recording throughout life, even when asleep. So, in many ways, the senses are ever diligent with hearing as the direct gateway to the mind.

However, early childhood development is instinctive by imitation and emotional osmosis. These two comprise the primary methods of initial absorption, forming the framework and personality. Filling the void of curiosity and exploration before expanded awareness and mobility even form. The first forays into the world as an empty slate most probably begins before birth through maternal and environmental influences. Most likely on transferable spheres of communication subjected to stimulus and experiences conjoined with its mother as the host.

Once born, it is involuntary indoctrination by conditions and culture immediately begins to form the nucleus of existence. Further, being locked in a box continues with kindergarten or early formal education and assimilation. The building blocks have long begun to take shape. Still, they are often underestimated to the degree the young sponge can absorb. The terrible twos are widely recognized as the age children need to be broken or, more technically described, inculcated. Habits are usually broken, instilled, or reinforced at this age in preparation for the next stage of mass manufacturing or production.

Next comes the taming of the spirit, which was the original primary purpose for education and, as such, only for boys and later expanded to include girls. By extension, whippings, beatings, punishment, homework to muster control, fear, and obedience were implemented for later social control. As a residual, conditioned, and collateral cultural indoctrination from slavery and religion, Black folks wholeheartedly believed in the spare the rod spoil the child doctrine.

Culturally Black folks were bemused by white folks' lack of discipline of their children and the wide birth of tolerance for defiant behavior. Before a child can verbally understand, spankings are used as an expedited physical language to demonstrate displeasure or correction. Whippings combined with yelling, cussing, and belittling as a physical and auditory shock to instill fear disguised as a correction are used. If pressed, we must confess to the old-school mentality that we turned out fine but should not now subscribe to the whipping method of communication.

Beggars Have Never Been Choosers

The point is the examination from the view of the need to do it and the results of it. Whippings and beatings are designed to decimate the spirit and discourage resistance to avoid punishment. It is more a lesson in preventing punishment than understanding the transgression. To further examine it, it's more of a reflection of the punisher's frustration, anxiety, and inability exhibiting a lack of control than the issue presented. Anger leads to striking as a primitive urge to lash out when agitated until sufficiently satisfied and relieved by another's submission.

The inspiration, transference, and justification for the incapacity to process our internal triggers resemble a slave master's mentality to administer corrective retribution for violations deemed punishable by the lash. The method is rationalized for deterrence imitating the custom while establishing an acceptance and anticipation of abuse. Children can become accustomed to it before language. So, it may be understood that this physical language is often learned before a verbal one.

This method of obtaining a physical understanding or brute imposition of abuse is the common denominator in domestic and social violence situations past adulthood. It is wrongly viewed as a viable solution. Might make right, and the more vulnerable, the greater the inclination to resort to it against them. Sort of as a free lunch with no fear of payment or penalty. It may prove very efficient, effective, and even preferred until used on us. But, then, definitely not so much. That may be the most significant indication that it is not an appropriate solution, regardless of advantage, gender, excuse, or age.

I labor the issue because it establishes several patterns including beating loved ones as a matter of correction or love. I hope to elaborate on and convey the context of its sociological and psychological pretext to discrimination and inferiority. The exploration into the conditioning and systems that require contortions and dousing of the human spirit by force is intimidation. It is control or conformity by fearful submission to instill obedience despite any demonstrated detriment, protest, or right to do so.

It is the culmination of irresistible socialization and irrepressible compulsion psychologically linked to control someone permeating everything from religion to education. We must understand, identify, and renounce its root compulsion to shake it, especially domestically. Devoid of consideration for the action which initiated the beating, what other factors contribute to the response that would not lead to it if not present? Reflection on the behavior is more vital than punishing the action, especially if deemed a mistake.

Do unintended mistakes and intentional deeds being fully aware of the offense require the same treatment? Mistakes require correction, not punishment. Punishment comes in many forms and should be metered to the severity of the transgression, not your level of anger. Conversations and engagement to establish a rapport to penetrate defiance and encourage compliance without physical or authoritarian outbursts have far more reaching benefits while accomplishing the same objective. It also replicates its approach with conflict resolution.

Not to give parenting advice but as an alternative way to examine the lingering effects and conditioning that physical punishment has with unintended consequences. Today it would be unimaginable that school personnel would administer swats in school with a large wooden board designed for maximum damage. However, variations of physical punishment at home are tolerated, but what is the difference? We of all people should know people are not property to be beaten.

It seems who is doing the beating matters most, but I submit it is more damaging coming from a loved one than otherwise. It could be stated that the motive of school personnel is uncertain. Still, upon closer examination, ours is just as convoluted and unnecessary. Many who would advocate corporal punishment as a solution would not condone it against an animal but would against a child and to a greater extent.

Brute force in love or war is to establish dominance, elicit submission, and repress autonomy. It is disguised as a corrective measure to bully concession to an imposed point of view or inflict compliance. It correlates to the inability to confront a situation without violence unless you possess an overwhelming upper hand. There are several reasons this has many underlying impairments to negate an isolated or temporary benefit as an expression of anger and frustration. First, it instills it as an appropriate expression of anger and frustration. Secondly, it conditions it as an acceptable demonstration of tough love to be tolerated.

This is especially damaging to young girls who age subconsciously believing that physical, verbal, and emotional abuse is an articulation of love, is acceptable, and inevitable. Next, despite gender as a variation of an abuser to the abused it is baked into the psyche and normalized as a form of negotiating a resolution. Finally, by demonstration, it creates imitation and a cycle of behavioral practices perpetuating its vile mentality. It is compulsively conducive to gender and superiority incriminations of entitlement and possessiveness.

It further preserves devaluations of humanity to dispense punishment based upon a premise of dishing it out desensitized to the long term damage. Behaviors that persist are deeply rooted in neurological and cognitive pathways. Once established often at an early age from repetitive reinforcements and embedded impressions create lifelong trauma, emulation, or psychosis. The damage extends beyond the benefit and the fearful memory outlasts the reason.

Furthermore, it represses the mind and spirit confined by the psychological box of avoidance of not only making mistakes but freedom, expression, and exploration. Fearful to raise the ire of dissatisfaction which may lead from a meltdown to a beatdown. A restrained spirit denies the natural progression of emotional development, self-esteem, and expression draining ambitions and potential in their infancy. It creates perspectives and inclinations to overcome later in life to displace the trained retention of being victimized and disheartened.

This leads to a constant excursion for validation and valuation where the need surpasses the circumstance endured and actions performed to satisfy it. From an objective view, it confuses the sensibilities because it obscures the entrenched origins of the need for validation. The craving for approval circumventing cognitive and emotional evaluation is an addiction for praise. Thus, the mystery is created as to why the pattern irresistibly persist much like Halloween's imaginary demons and rituals. Habitual behavior and unconditional acceptance cannot be underestimated or overestimated as foundational curses shaping personal dysfunctions and other social dynamics.

We must know that a vast component of formative behavior is taught before six. Subsequently, conduct to conceal behavior is learned afterwards to assimilate with society by the prevailing standards of acceptability or deception. Lack of external acceptability beseeches internal suppression and self-rejection expressed as a conflict of identity and low self-esteem. By extenuation, this is the mentality that we must break to combat racism successfully and the insinuation of any violation of our humanity.

It is entangled with the violence and abuse against us we were led to believe is acceptable, endurable, and unavoidable. On a universal level, this is the paradigm shift now witnessed and occurring globally. Finally shaking the superstitions, ignorance, fallacies, and obedience of centuries of manipulation, degradation, and authoritarian domination. The deceptive reign of psychologically paralyzing humanity, justice, and self-determination has seen better days. It is no small task, but it is made more daunting by insidious conformity to misconceptions of socialization adhered to by indoctrinations yet to be overthrown.

It starts with infantile nurturing and early education, allowing for the expression of individuality and the courage to display it. Rejection of the mass production of human-fleshed cyborgs conceived and produced under primitive assumptions and programmed directives must take place. It is assigned by the arbitrary directives of hidden agendas and deceitful ideologies to maintain control. Eventually, society must be redesigned for scalability, accommodating changing definitions of freedom, justice, identity, and humanity.

Change cracks the cocoon allowing for transformation, while stagnation accelerates social and economic implosion by imbalance. Both lead to change, one by creation and the other by destruction. So consequently, one is a lot less painful. Therefore, the people create and change the systems that society integrates as normalized behavior through their conformity and capitulation. Consequently, the people dictate the system instead of being swindled into believing it should control them.

By definition, systems should facilitate and serve the users, not suppress autonomy overriding the purpose of its existence. Conflicting perspectives and methodologies are entertained to optimize solutions and processes, alternatively improving mutual determinations. When constantly evaluated and submitted to conjecture, the prevailing determination deduces the most logical modifications if improvement is the objective instead of remaining within arbitrary boundaries.

Boundaries are offered as guidelines, not restrictions to theorizing improvements or detecting flaws. Considering the epistemology of beliefs, rituals, judgments, and rationality producing dissonance from known facts, history, and the etymology of so much we hold dear is questionable. It requires the willingness to evaluate and concede to the best extension of verifiable knowledge. The mystery is not in the knowledge but in the rejection of it. One can only surmise that it is to maintain control by ignorance and deception.

Knowledge must flow without form but by fluidity. So, the assessment has come full circle to again rest on education and nurturing as the key institutionalized corrupters to regulate knowledge, self-esteem, and ambition. Deprivation of these three things breeds hopelessness, submission, and obedience despite the occasional protest or dissatisfaction. However, education and literacy manifest in many forms and expressions when unbridled. So, infants and children depend on our knowledge and judgment to navigate a path in cultivating their development.

Our purpose must be to do so. We must protect their future and upward mobility preventing the invasion of their potential by the exploitation and devaluation of their developmental cycle shunning discovery or cultivation. The curse starts in earnest in kindergarten to separate through comparisons and valuations by exaggerating disparities as competitive advantages independent of a child's ability.

Therefore, we must prepare our children internally to withstand assaults from social systems disguised as education, valuations, and judgements. Under siege is their identity and potential undetected by their young minds and emotions. The same systemic ones that nefariously encapsulated us, will we also allow it to entomb them? It is not only a matter of personal development and emotional maturity but also economic viability and intellectual freedom.

Adolescent and Teens

Going through adolescence is usually a bumpy ride requiring a seat belt to get in where you fit in. A significant bearing on identity development occurs during this time, especially regarding finding your village as a personality, identity, or social engagement. Additional uncertainties mount when dealing with concerns specific to socioeconomic status, gender, sexuality, or race. First-time experi-

ences or lacking the capacity for handling them leads to mistakes
and reservations when proceeding with limited judgment into unfamiliar territory.

The magnification of developmental ambiguities and insecurities
correlate to inexperience in situations with no reference point or
rolodex of personal knowledge to consult. Also, it is further complicated by circumstances beyond adolescent control and is dependent on family resources, neighborhood, education, religion, and
conditioned morality. This junction is where childhood preparation
becomes the counterbalance to processing, navigating uncharted
adolescent curiosities, and adjusting to awkward maturation.

It is a time of trial and error, increasingly unsupervised and curiously spontaneous. These occurrences require assessments lacking projections beyond their adolescent experience. No experience, even
with instructional guidance, lacks the certainty of practical application and resistance of temptation. The point of origin in this three-
dimensional sphere is total dependency at birth. As time proceeds,
the effect of influence, control, and divergence from parental consent widens with age and exposure.

As the vector widens from a broader array of interactions, experiences, and environments, the further the perspective and personality
is developed independently from household compliance. It is surpassed by environmental persuasion and peer pressure. Independence and social acceptance become primary despite dependence
on a guardian for essentials lacking the degree of self-reliance compared to their adolescence defiance and expression.

Still dependent, exploratory compulsions combined with biological,
chemical, and hormonal changes launches discovery bolstered by a
limited scope of experiences, considerations, and projected consequences for their actions. They are prone to impulsive behavior and
spontaneous environmental influences. With the certainty of
thought and action but the uncertainty of logical examination and

foreseen repercussions, the sum of adolescents can be surmised as speeding beyond their vision or experience.

At this point, emulation becomes more dominant than consultation. Interactions with peers govern the decisions, thought processes, and mental wellness by the degree of their assimilation and comfortability within their peer group or clique. This is where the similarities of behaviors reflect the archetypes defining each concise subgroup. These subgroups are fluid throughout life and subject to change based on knowledge, experiences, and preference. However, the bulk of the formation expands during adolescence by sheer exposure and random encounters.

Therefore, the predominant funnel is the examples that mold the initial impersonation of the images sculpted as the subgroup identifier. So, based on examples, images, and role models from the immediate environment and those most promoted by society, it becomes the blueprint for forming attitudes and behaviors of our adolescents. We must then ask ourselves, what images bombarding our youth contribute to dysfunctional attitudes and behaviors?

Are they intentionally disguised as culture? It mutates into a mass hysteria scrambling to duplicate and represent those traits to the fullest but most often exaggerated extent. This imitation is how innocent portrayals become detrimental betrayals. Given the pervasive effect and normalization of dysfunctional influences by young adulthood, a disproportionate segment of our youth started already behind the eight ball. Sometimes a particular environment or influence gives them little or no chance, becoming a generational curse until some catalyst alters the trajectory.

The incentive to change generational dispositions originates with awareness and recognition of environmental directives that sway their behaviors, ambitions, and options for more beneficial outcomes. The divergent angle of developmental inclination towards dysfunctional images of celebrity must be transformed away from villainous prodigies to aspirational architects of progress to build a better paradigm. This progression must replace the limited selection of emulated and admired mirages of cultural impressions.

The weakening of our adolescents' psyche by demonstration and repetition are misleading and detaching them from their self-respect and self-worth. The distortions of bravado, sexuality, and promiscuity unnecessarily devalues their humanity in exchange for unfiltered expression without regard to any responsibility for appropriateness or impact. Not forgetting that we were once young and impressionable, we cannot pretend we were immune from similar issues. So, the names change but the traps remain and the prey is ensnared the same.

Not to roundly condemn our youth but instead the tried and true methods of corruption that claim generation after generation by perspective. We have tested the waters and know the turbulence and unforgiving nature of inevitable mistakes, yet mistakes will persist. We cannot protect them at all times from all things. But, we share their jacket because our pain is for their suffering that we know was avoidable and often without justification. Many times the learning curve is harsh, unforgiving, and irreversible.

Therefore, whether the slogan is Black Lives Matter, black excellence, no child left behind, or no justice no peace, the truth is we have not taken the necessary steps to ensure our adolescents of them. Huffing and puffing and running out of breath, unable to blow anything down, renders the big bad wolf all bluff and no results. The inconvenient solutions of significance implores a shift to our display of more acceptable examples. The most suitable pursuits for our youth's optimum survival and perseverance must be instilled before they succumb or get entangled in irreparable situations.

As an avoidance maneuver, we hope they can minimize the possibility of exposure by moving differently to evade the orientations proven to cause poverty, incarceration, and hardships. A group mentality operates under a mass assumption promoting a fainthearted resistance swept up by thirsting to fit a common mold. Closer examination reveals that by doing so, individual expression dissolves into uniform duplication of harmful repercussions with predictable outcomes. Our battle and convenience is not for ourselves but for our next generation.

Our culture should be our conception for their greater good, reproducing replicas of success, self-empowerment, and self-determination by our standards for their emulation. We are gravely mistaken to assume that acquiring a different race's definition and validation can be substituted as our own to be propagandized to our youth promoting violence, materialism, and self-devaluation. Most movements start with dissatisfaction and irritation spurred to action. By now we should have enough of both to energize our motivation and vision.

However, the courage, discipline, and strategy to accomplish it require those engaged in the struggle to educate members entrusted with carrying the torch further. We cannot be fearful to confront or resist what has been identified as obstructions whether friend or foe. The historical frustration and obstruction of our advances expose the irrelevant impressions we allow our youth to be labeled and shackled by thus aggravating its continuation. The imprint into young adulthood has a gestation period similar to toddlers of five to six years of orientation. The impediment of unpreparedness for the "kindergarten" of adulthood continues until they are well-seasoned.

The "kindergarten" of adulthood restarts the clock entering another phase unfamiliar to them now with life experiences of adulthood to be navigated. It may then take the mid to late twenties to create a grown sense of reality accustomed to the phase of life where playtime is over. So the transition is from high school, the top of the adolescent food chain to adult kindergarten, the lowest adult status. The physical, cognitive, social, and emotional search for identity and value starts all over again, only now accompanied by financial survival.

The previous phase prepares for each subsequent stage of life. If a deficiency exists, it is later magnified, expanding the disparity and compounding the anxiety while diminishing the options. This cycle from toddler to adulthood has a contingency personification dependent and extending from their foundational repertoire. The previously formulated perspectives and cemented ideologies subject to experiences set the trajectory of their adult ambitions. The shield is the mask worn as a facade to conceal self-esteem vulnerabilities hidden to convince the world of their certainty and adjustments during adulthood struggles.

In doing so, they compartmentalize deceitful fronts acted out to convince and deceive others while suffering the nuances of being unprepared. So our children and adolescents cannot be left to be raised by the concrete streets or electronic nannies devoid of veteran leadership not to foresee the path taken should not be the path they should take. There are lifelong ramifications of childhood negligence which reveals itself well into their future. The old adage is do as I say and not as I do is also instructional as to what not to do. So, we can work harder now to prevent their struggle later. Our vision becomes their sight, their sight becomes the next generation's vision.

Demonstration informs, but participation teaches. We can explain it to them, but they must understand it for themselves, akin to the lion teaching the cub how to hunt for survival. The time spent at the earliest ages minimizes the time and anguish invested to undue witnessing the aftermath of its failure. The youth are self-centered on self-discovery as the natural progression of learning where we have been. So, they should learn from the mistakes we have paid the price to know rather than repeatedly, generation after generation, being taxed to find out.

Beggars Have Never Been Choosers

Our time, instructions, and interaction cannot be substituted as a library of lessons for our random excursions and obligatory dereliction. Our investment now may turn out to be our retirement plan or caregiver dependency later. Our transient pleasures, flash and dash flossing, or social media masquerading as self-esteem or self-validating distractions must be set aside. Their importance do not take precedence over our responsibility to educate, parent, and mentor the youngins while they are still listening.

If we wanted to live our lives, we should have made different decisions. Their life is our life, entrusted with precious cargo to be delivered from the pitfalls of our experiences and ideologies. Consequently, we must give them the best opportunity to live theirs not repeating our mistakes. We don't have to disregard our life, but we must adjust accordingly to accommodate both. We must change how they are raised and guided to accomplish a different outcome as a people.

But, to put that into practice, we must change ourselves and the bombardment of impressions they subconsciously absorb as intentional mechanisms of sociological and psychological destruction. Our influences and curtailing negativity promoting dysfunctional messaging will also impact their peer groups as models of aspiration. By reinforcing an assertive message directed towards transcending racism, poverty, and aspersions of inferiority we reverse its damage.

We must defend our gains, assert our claims, and maximize our opportunities individually exercised but collectively realized. United we stand, divided we continue to wither, lacking the concerted effort to change our plight through educating our youth, guiding our adolescent, and mentoring our young adults. It is a comprehensive strategy from the bottom up. As a result, nationalities rise on their youth's incremental preparation, aspirations, and achievements. So can we when we implement practices tailor made for our history and circumstances.

Therefore, the greatest threat to our youth is not racism. Instead, it is the invasion of their thoughts, attitudes, and behavior influenced by constant suggestions of exploitation, disposal, and devaluation. Their value raises with their armor of preparedness, self-assuredness, and range of occupational mobility. It is diminished by the romanticizing of violence and gunplay as tokens of honor, images of sexual objectification, and educational malfeasance. The wheel is in our hands to steer the course and clear the path. The road is theirs's to follow.

Adults
No matter how well a vigil is maintained, a parent's job seemingly is never done, even if just in their heart. That is a parent's burden and pledge to steer a child to a path of development and sufficiency. Otherwise, abdicating parental responsibility and forsaking the guidance needed in early childhood is to ensure difficulties later for you both. There is no guarantee but it does increase the degree and likelihood. The percentages and probabilities increase because the impetus and instructions are missing creating an emotional, social, or intellectual void regarded as a moral deprivation.

However, whatever morality fills the void does not dictate the emotional, social, and intellectual foundation, just the use of it. So, guidance and support are an investment in their future and ours by providing the building blocks. But, it is up to them how they utilize them. Blending emotional well-being, social literacy, and intellectual achievement is best undertaken when instilling the primary elements is done by imitation to supplement its learning.

If multiple children are involved, the shared responsibility is vicarious for older children to guide their younger siblings as a natural progression of interaction. Passing down their influences to be applied and encouraged may be just as beneficial as adult stewardship. However, the impact of sibling bonds cannot be underestimated or overlooked in the development of younger children. At any rate, patience and sacrifice will be required, and some disappointments will be involved to get to the rewards.

There are many hazards along the way, but it is called life, and everyone is dealt a unique hand to play. Therefore, much-needed characteristics such as resilience, courage, confidence, and adaptation are necessary fortifications to implant in children and teens. But, quiet as it is kept, we need to make sure we have our dose of fortification as well. The tools of an indomitable spirit, despite the challenges, combined with discernment and knowledge, create a hand hard to be beaten. It often gives them a competitive edge and a better chance to excel.

Nevertheless, the ability to participate depends on the capacity and extent of preparation and separation by identifying distinguishing traits of potential and ability. The best way to beat racism or many other challenges depends on being exceptionally good at what you do. So, our job is to provide and prepare them with that separation. The prerequisite tools of ascension are nurtured according to their needs to indulge or accentuate their talents. We must resist the grave narrative and distortion associated with a mentality of subservience interpreted and internalized to instigate a weakness of self-doubt.

Purging the duplicity of dissonance and inferiority rejects the proposal that we are somehow subordinate if different from them. A negative vacuum of perspective creates discord and self-doubt susceptible to insinuations of inferiority if racially defined. Difference is uniqueness, not inferiority and race is a category not a restriction. Quality dictates inferiority, so we are the custodial guardians of our children's minds and futures by their infused self-image. Consider race as a preoccupation with an exertion in futility compared to the substance of undeterred ambition.

Conversely, in the philosophical vein of Epictetus, how can one who lacks effort pretend to care as much as someone with diligent exertion? Even within our race, the difference is usually effort, in-genuity, and perseverance despite racial overtones and obstructions. Some scale the mountain as a challenge while others setup camp at the base seeing only an obstruction. The reality is both is true for those who chose either, but only one extends their options by daring to explore the possibilities. It is the concept of Newcomb's Paradox of risk and reward.

Many times it is evident to everyone except the one lacking the necessary due diligence but still yearns for the reward. Thus, excel-lence and superiority can be arbitrarily assigned as long as it goes untested. When tested, the proof is in the pudding, and the cream rises to the top, separated by composition, desire, or vision. No equality comparisons can exist as a matter of neutrality when the results prove otherwise. So, true equality cannot be granted, it must be taken as a measure of equivalence or transcendence. The chal-lenge of life is competitive and absolute equality is a misnomer of cross-examination of unlike comparisons only abated by the separa-tion of specifics and suitability.

Consequently, transcendence is measured by the same metric. Now the reason for disparities may be an entirely different matter for so-cial consideration but not individual motivation. So, if like the mountain it must be scaled, scale it, not camp out by it. According-ly, with technology when used as a tool of ascension the gap is nar-rowed considerably. Our children must use it to explore the hori-zons of education, not as mind-numbing entertainment. It is the adult's job to ensure its proper use.

As adults, it would not hurt us as well to repurpose our use of time and technology for learning and stewardship. Understanding that lack is not insurmountable but instead fuel to motivate us toward success. Parallel comparisons is a destination at which to arrive by uniform results, not identical origins. So, our perspective must change to counter a slowly changing society to accelerate our progress. Confucius says cling to that which serves you and discard that which forces you to serve it. Therefore, if what we have been doing needs to be discarded, discard it.

The practicality of retaining it should not be contrary to our greater good. Economic incarceration is overshadowed by physical or penal incarceration. Educational and intellectual segregation is amplified by geographical segregation. Health and environmental entrapment is accomplished by a standard of living entrapment. Our cultural integrity and dignity are supplanted by many socially prevalent degradations of predatory impairments furtively siphoning our vitality and ascension.

We must audit the accumulated losses that goes unnoticed as well as the noticeable forfeitures of our efforts. The elaborate schemes to economically, culturally, and morally defund the Black masses from inception and incubation begin prenatally and continue inconspicuously into adulthood. It can be a matter of race but is eclipsed by exploitation and our complicity often associated with economics and education. Calculating the losses from educational malpractice, housing conditions, food insecurity, neighborhood safety, and many more depletions of our living standards and opportunities are staggering.

If others are concerned with widening their advantage, we must be consumed by eliminating our disadvantage. We can sleep better blaming whoever or whatever, but we awaken to the same reality until we change it. The protest, "African American" holidays, or other acts of attrition or appeasement are still low-key handouts at the back door. Talk plus corrective or mitigating actions equals change by behavior, while talk without it is just a bluff. So, all the huffing and puffing amounts to wolf tickets, stagnation, and apathy lacking credibility.

Taking care of business needs no permission or announcement, just a commitment. The remedial steps required must be easier than the centuries of enduring the boogie man of racism and discrimination.

It persists partly because it resides in our minds giving it power over us. Why do people go to a haunted house and still are frightened even though they know it is not real? Because they don't separate the frightening illusion from the sobering reality. Why they go, I don't know, but it requires indulgence. Most fears do.

Similarly, the "talk" with our youth about the police falls in the same category despite having real world implications and atrocities. But, the fear created and instilled may not be the best way to counsel youth, frightening them into impulsive and illogical reactions. There are times when small children are threatened as a behavioral tool, or juveniles threatened with calling the police or being locked up to gain compliance. So, at times we use fear of the police as a tool. But, by natural instinct too often fear results in flight which results in compounded danger.

Be careful not to menace youth with the police and then confusingly reinforce the boogie man syndrome and risk to their safety in police encounters. It is a dissonance of purpose but a congruence of fear. Therefore, you get the haunted house response, hysterical fear linked to survival and a primitive brain flight reflex. Many of these sheepish encounters are in wolves' clothing, with the projection of outcomes shaping the reality of interactions. The projection is often worse than the reality.

It is the tail wagging the dog distorted by fear triggering a condition response of fight or flight. Likewise, these gifted Trojan horses of innocent dissonances, rituals, and complicities create the most far-reaching and devastating damages right under our noses. Malt liquor, cigarettes, dietary choices, frivolous expenditures, wasteful time consumption, television, social media, vanity, violent stereotypes, and many more are embedded in the cultural coding of free will. Truth be told they are far from free but will complicate the repercussions from our indulgence.

The residue of addictive behaviors, dysfunctional perceptions, and squandering resources and opportunities are learned behaviors. We have learned some of them quite well, but more are by condition. They are also culturally biased and racially anticipatory, not to mention socially incapacitating. Not to belabor the point or beat a dead horse, but these concepts, perspectives, and assertions are not the totality of consideration or perspectives. However, it is far too often our reality. Still, our reality is not a night gallery of illusions but instead a dawn of possibilities.

So, my intent is to stir contemplation of contributory factors and occurrences for avoidance, not condemnation or judgement. This book is for the content to facilitate debate, arouse curiosity, and stimulate awareness. Hopefully by encouraging the expansion of conversations and possibilities by promoting an in-depth historical, social, psychological, political, and economic evaluation of our condition we can transcend it. We must address the core issues to produce core solutions, otherwise the solutions are for another issue which is not the problem.

Not meant as a morality test or judgment of character but an unflinching stare into the abyss of racism and it's persistence in the context of systemic causations and evaluations. Realistically, also including our participation in delaying solutions. As a people, we have been many things and called many more, but there are some things we can refuse to be or be called. Therefore, we can never be called complacent. As adults we have the steering wheel to guide the vessel of Blackness ever mindful of the valuable minds and eager spirits entrusted to us as a sacred bond of ancestral assignment.

As Ray Charles's mother instructed him on what not to let them turn him into, we cannot allow ourselves to become beggars or panhandlers under the foot of history's trampling's. The danger we now face is a renunciation by quietly quitting on our demands and failing to realize our most generational debilitating complicities and conformities. These collusions of impediments are a resignation of determination, equity, and our undeniable humanity routinely surrendered.

The most egregious is our failure to help our youth through narcissistic self-indulgence and negligence of preparation. In Greek mythology, Kronos is the father of time and King of the Titans. He betrayed his father at the urging of his mother and thus feared being betrayed by his offspring. So, as the story goes, he ate his children whole upon their birth before they could mature to pose a threat. This myth is where the term eating your young refers to as a reference to not giving them a chance or by consuming their future. In technical terms, it is called filial anthropophagy or offspring cannibalism.

Unfortunately, as a culture, too many of us have symbolically disintegrated into eating our young. By spiritual, social, educational, intellectual, and nurturing malfeasance, we have allowed the starvation and suffocation of our youths by systems sinisterly designed to consume them. Even worse, we adults have practiced auto-cannibalism by consuming ourselves and devouring social and psychological inflictions promoting pathological obsessions that they inherit.

These pathological reflections of exploitation, degradation, materialism, and violence are eagerly self-inflicted and normalized. The ritualistic pursuit of money and notoriety disregards the direct collateral damage and indirect impressionable delusions causing some of our ethnic obstructions. Symbolically, like in communion, receiving the blood and body of Christ for consumption, we have, by our demonstrations and metaphoric consumptions, devoured our children's future.

Remember, forgive me for what I have done and for what I have failed to do. Either way, even inaction is an action and can produce the same cannibalistic appetites. Meanwhile, the substantiated facts detailing racism do not minimize the actions we must take or refrain from taking. The battle wages on with us as adults on the front lines to shepherd in the necessary adjustments, improvisations, and stipulations to secure our objectives. Our objectives are our responsibility assigned by history and necessity. This is not by choice, but by default and honor.

Remedy/ Recovery

Over life's developments, our nucleus is expressed in many ways, often somewhat predetermined beyond our control. One fundamental element lurking in the shadows is the ego. At their core, many of the issues covered in this book are ego related. The ego can be inflated like a Macy's Day balloon or deflated into a hollow depression. It can outwardly exhibit the same characteristics in either state, albeit coming from vastly different origins. It can come from abundance or shortage. For example, bravado can display courage or conceal cowardice.

Unfortunately, the exhibition of behavior is often mistaken for being so close that they seem the same. Three considerations rooted in the ego's expansion into many pertinent individual applications also apply to groups, nationalities, and nations. They are imagination, authenticity, and regeneration, whose polarities are hopelessness, misconception, and deterioration. The latter three are usually intentional as control mechanisms planted between the ears as disruptive and malfunctioning components of regulation.

Realizing the complexity of challenges for individuals, imagine how difficult it is for the multitudes to change, recuperate, or acknowledge. A runaway train of ideology, methodology, customs, or fallacies takes time and distance to stop. Knowledge and persuasion must replace ignorance and coercion, ushering in an enlightened transformation of better practices. The malfunctioning components must be dismantled or disengaged, averting the detonation of their delusion overtly acted upon. Every road begins and ends somewhere, likewise with patterns of behaviors and beliefs.

Napoleon stated that what the mind can conceive, it can achieve. It refers to the infinity of imagination and possibilities. Aesop's fable of the lion and the statues recounts how, when bestowing the greatness and superiority of man, the lion was shown a statue of a lion torn in two by a man. The lion astutely noted that a man had made the statue. The hunter and the hunted have diametrical perspectives subjectively pursued and demonstrated from their opposing perspective.

The perspective and legitimacy of the display validate the perception of the presenter or authenticator. Adjustments necessary for improvement or correction speak to behavioral renewal by the genesis of self or regeneration. Imagination, authenticity, and regeneration teeter on the delicate impact of deliberately selective representations and portrayals. Their mirages are bolstered by altering the facts and narration. However, the truths of science and math are discoveries as precursors to comprehend the universal behavior of various continuums of nature. Thus, the nature of truth exist eternally in a vector of omnipresence only waiting to be discovered despite its manipulations.

For example, in quantum physics, there is an experiment called the Double Slit experiment conducted at the particle level. Amazingly these particles behave differently depending on if they are observed or not, even if observed remotely. It is as if they know they are being watched, so they behave differently. The ego operates similarly except for casting an image or donning a mask as a curtain of concealment. What we do when unseen, unknown, or detectable differs from the public display represented and roundly recognized as us.

What appear to be random occurrences and placements are consequences of stimuli affecting their observation and presentation. There is always a rhyme or reason, a particle or wave function. There are no anomalies in behavior, beliefs, or opinion. There is just a variation of dissonance and polarity. Pathological behavior and beliefs are internal instructional manuals that produce accommodating behavior receptive only to self-affirming input promoting its idealistic self. The dismissal of inferiority or supremacy, worthiness or unworthiness, and equality or inequality reflects the polarity or extremes of the same thing, the Ying and Yang of it.

One exists only to the extent that the other doesn't with a fluid symmetry. Consequently, a balance of complete and incompleteness reflects the basis we operate. Spiritual, emotional, and psychological toxins accumulated over time, impression, and experience either affirms or rejects developmental elements to establish a ledger setting our boundaries and expectations. Images of negative influence tend to be the default concern, possibly because of their destructive nature or uncertain fearful rumblings.

The negativity setup camp squatting in our psyche while the positive needs reassurance and development. Our integrity and dignity depend on these images and are thus susceptible to doubt or fragility. Integrity and dignity should not be situational or transactional but constantly unaffected by fashion, conformity, circumstances, or any other transient influence. They are the baseline of our interactions, choices, and code of conduct. These are personal ethics not to be confused with morality.

Personal ethics are a singular determination, while morality is a group consensus requiring participation without our contribution to establish it but demand our strict adherence. All judgments are morality-based and practiced norms established for conformity and adherence. Not to cast aspersions of innuendo on judgment but to factually state what it is at its core, a subjective determination agreed upon by a majority in control. The key is in control which could be one person, a race, even a king or queen.

Many of our choice and rituals are rooted outside our consent, knowledge, or preference. They are supported by the ambiguity of their origin or limitations of available options. The matrimonial commitment and deception of until death does us a part often are indoctrinated so deeply that we cannot divorce ourselves from its inculcation. Our recovery as a people depends on defining our integrity and dignity, rejecting the narrative of the storyteller restraining our imagination, ambitions, and genesis. The value resides in the validation, thereby creating the need for it.

Our validation extends beyond the spectacle of our existence in America. We were when America was not even a thought! Only the strong survive, and we have survived. Our existence spans the beginning of human existence to now be incorrectly defined by a blink of time in America. Seeking external validation for what was damaged inside us, asking for permission from the one who damaged us, and reviving the shame of self-hatred and self-sabotage prevents our recovery.

The past lingers with those unable to shake the effects of a limited narrative. But, more importantly, the full narrative is we have a magnitude of achievements in our chronicled history of greatness although we have some blemishes too. Our DNA remembers what our memory has forgotten obscured by the tunnel vision of slavery and racism. The stumbling and bumbling over equality and social justice are because we have been consumed with looking through the rearview mirror to navigate the road ahead. To forget would be foolish, but to throw the good after the bad would be even more foolish.

Instead, we must concern ourselves with our future navigation of our current circumstances. The astuteness of our actions are revealed in the degree of our progress. The simulation is generated from the projection. So, therefore as Seneca stated, "let all your actions be directed to some object and let it have some end in view." Our expectations and idolizations are weapons formed against us but welded by our hands, hindering our progress. In exchange, we sacrifice the invaluable for the meager trappings of vanity, bravado, complaints, and begging.

Pursuing validation and permission corrupts principles and pride alike, so the devil no longer has to go down to Georgia looking for a soul to steal, although he has been spotted elsewhere. In full disclosure, I almost started to cuss, but I'm long in my recovery from emotional outbursts. The point is our personal freedoms and choices cannot surrender our advancement or sabotage our children's future in a world where the atrocities to our ancestors or the indignations of our strategies condemn us to repeatedly be subjugated.

So, the next time you witness the commercial degradation of our women for notoriety or a few pieces of silver, ask yourself if it is worth it. The answer speaks volumes considering they are examples to our young girls to be replicated when birthing a nation of change. The next video or song of creative insolvency advocating the cannibalistic gunning down or murdering of our own kind, our sons, brothers, uncles, and fathers, as a form of entertainment or clout chasing, is it worth it? If the answer is no, why do we not only tolerate it but fiscally and culturally support it? The real question is who is behind it and for what purpose?

Regarding genocide, discrimination, and an assortment of violence against our folks, whites have no monopoly on these violations and behaviors. The validity of an equation is that it is universally provable. The great Thoth, Pythagoras, or the incomparable Neil Degrassi Tyson himself could not figure out a mathematical equation whereby we commit the very violations and sometimes in equal or greater portions than those of which we complain. Imagine if we switched sides of the equation and promoted this racial genocide to fill in the blank nationality if it would be tolerated, commercially supported, or racially embraced.

Any come to mind, or is it only our people? Not to curtail free speech but to encourage social responsibility through our ethnic esteem and fiscal withdrawal. Who can dispute or condone the damage and corruption of our neurological pathways weaponized as our urban culture that overtly promotes homicidal, dysfunctional, and wayward mentalities absorbed as our ethnic expression? There must be something else available that doesn't "radicalize" our communities to acts of violence.

It's not the only reason for violence but glorifying violence does not help. Still, come on people, wake up to the incremental and sedated poisoning of our humanity which slavery couldn't accomplish. It is a reason there is a war against being woke. So conversely, should we remain in a slumber, left snoring and drooling rather than awakening from the ignorance of a diabolical nightmare. Woke insinuates light which is a derivative of enlightenment which refers to being knowledgeable.

Anti-woke, anti-cancel culture, and a destructive urban culture intersects at our ongoing suffering as the sewage of humanity without not only our rebellion but not a whisper. By what equation do they do the same? It is the Rip Van Wrinkle effect. Except we have slept over four hundred years instead of forty. However, it does prevent an idiot shortage by silently being exploited as a class with no identity other than the one they assign us. You are damn right they don't want us woke, why would they?

The more pertinent question is why we now still partition the world, Europe, Africa, the U.N., and America for the same concerns as Marcus Garvey, W.E.B Dubois, the Pan-African Congress, Nelson Mandela, and subsequent international figures over one hundred years after the turn of the last century? Are we serial protestors, serial beggars, or serial capitulators? Perhaps the NAACP which has been largely ignored for their historical and legendary contributions in the racial trenches, should swell with funding as our political arm instead of other less galvanizing organizations.

Instead, we are more eager to support designers such as Gucci and others despite insults but not the NAACP, which we at least stand a chance of respectability or a return on our investment. A desperate mind, a slumbering mind, and an absent mind grasp at grandiose illusions instead of practical relief. Our best revenge or protest is successfully distancing ourselves from any offensive depictions that resemble slander of our humanity. If they want to sully us, why should we pay for it?

We must explore the best methods, objectives, and actions of achieving them which promote our recuperation. Our recovery will catapult our success. The most obvious action is to refrain and re-form from self-induced sociological, psychological, educational, economic, and quality-of-life mutilations entrenched in our indoc-trination. I have exhausted the subtractions of negative entrapments, so let's propose the positive therapeutic healing aspects of solutions and ascension.

To transcend the past, we must evaluate it for its benefits and dis-card its social burdens as an unnecessary weight for the journey forward by using its lessons as a navigational tool. On any journey, the most crucial contemplation is the destination. Next, is taking the first step to embark on an expedition of determination properly pre-pared. The last step taken is either arriving at our destination or per-ishing while failing to do so. There can be no concession of purpose or fortitude. No retreat of aspirations or vision. No surrender of thought or gains.

The chronicle of the journey remains the same even if the destina-tion has changed. The path leading there is the chronicle of events to get there. The lesson is in the journey and the reason in the desti-nation. As a cautionary tale, we can avoid some pitfalls by simply heeding the warnings and clues of those who have already traveled that same road. Refusing the instructions will lead to errors and de-lays or being unable to find our way. Our loss of what was taken from us is not our humanity, but recognition of our dignity which in our journey we still seek to recover.

The actions of slavery were the loss of the perpetrators' humanity, not ours. At the same time, the suffering of slavery did damage our pride and progress. As for our humanity, we have always retained it as evidenced by our centuries long fight to reject and overcome the many narratives of racism. However, we cannot forfeit our dignity or humanity by taking on a burden that is not ours. Our burden is to not fall prey to a sociological predator unleashed for hundreds of years as an attack on our dignity.

We have always been the beacon of humanity from its beginnings in the mother land. We are the axis on which all humanity revolves or has ever evolved. That is the path of our journey to recover our collective dignity from the shame of past persecutions by dusting off our true history. Past oppressions from a different time, circumstance, and scarcity of options separated us away from our origins, culture, and identity. What has been done is done, but the continuation of it is entirely different. We must deal with what it is now instead of what it has been.

When dismantling a system, it is vital to identify the components essential to its operation. If the system is maintained by an operator or power structure, what is the process and objective? The one constant repercussion of racism has been the repetitive bombardment of our dignity to operate in areas only we can reach, among ourselves. As self-determination of identity, what images and indoctrinations have we subliminally succumbed to that don't have their roots in the intrusion of our forced identity?

Therefore, the first step towards our healing is the recovery of our dignity and identity by shedding the trespasses on our perspective, beliefs, and ideology. Time and the past are unrecoverable. Still, the instructions from them are lessons to be embraced as to our unconquerable spirit and indomitable resiliency. Forgiveness of ourselves and our ancestors for the journey's path recognizes its occurrence and effect without submission to them. Despite our staggers and stumbles, we still forge through history destined to return to our ordained honor.

The honor is ours, but the shame should belong to the abuser, not the abused. The abuser wants no mention of their shameful deeds while expecting the abused to accept blame or forgive and forget. Transference of shame, guilt, and resentment turned inward is the cunning work of the narcissistic abuser. It created a sense of inferiority or worthlessness of which we are becoming increasingly impervious. The isolation and void caused by losing our dignity and identity left us stranded as nomads constantly wandering for acceptance.

We still suffer from this emotional and psychological ploy in a quest for external validation. I saw a saying that read, walk around like a King or like you don't care who the King is. It displays the mentality of self-validation and dignity not to bow to anything but for it to bow to you. The reflection of our identity is projected as a certification of our self-esteem to be because we declared ourself to epitomize that projection.

This certification can be a negative or a positive affirmation according to our psychological determination. The honesty of our current assessment authenticates the veracity of our solutions as a mental construct to shed the residue of historic and sociological deceptions. The mentality is not just talking about it but becoming it by the accountability of the associated standards to be it. As with the many steps in a journey, the transformation of our self-image is a focused process of deconstruction erasing self-sabotaging ideologies with constructive self-perceptions.

Many capitulations of the past were survival mechanisms justified as self-preservation. We faked it for so long that we fell into the apathy of its obstruction. Still, today the remnants of it threaten our psychological well-being and ensure stagnation using various social, economic, and cultural bondage methods of suppression. The solution is the opposite of the problem. If the problem is not in our control, surely the solution is solely under our control.

Our destiny is not the psychological sadomasochistic submission to self-sacrificing, self-sabotaging, and self-abusive behavior destined to a second-class social relegation. Allowing detrimental self-perceptions as expressions of pain or ignorance maintains its influence preventing the releasing of it. The humiliation and pain must be acknowledged, released, and replaced with determination, self-esteem, and ambition to distance ourselves from its experience. The crossroads is where the pain is not greater than the possibility and self-satisfaction of conquering the immobilizing effects of submission.

From the ashes the comet rises unrestrained. Ours is not a physical restraint but a psychological constraint that our perspectives and conduct must conquer. Life is inherently unfair, and righteous condemnation of others for our conditions, failures, or limitations, historical or otherwise, may be valid and soothe our anger. However, it does nothing for our self-elevation or self-worth. In our anguish, we have cried out over centuries beyond the echoes of the atrocities committed against us and across the many barbaric inhumanities falling on deaf ears. Exposing the dastardly deed is no new revelation, so it has also proven not to be the solution.

Needing only to be known has never been the problem. It has always been known and always a problem. So, we must make adjustments elsewhere in the system to secure our psychological repair and indemnify change. The focus has conceivably been too much on them and not enough on us. Not enough on what we could and should do. We cannot rely on could da, should da, and would da but instead on did, have, and will to proactively acquire our social status, equity, and autonomy.

It is undoubtedly unjust and unfair for us to be relegated by racism, but unconscionable if done through any fault of our own. By doing so, the pain becomes our pleasure, and the condition our normalized state. If there's no room and no justice nowhere for the motherland's orphans, we must declare it for ourself where we are at and with what we have. The storage of history hoarding negative mental and emotional occurrences triggers the recurrence of inadequacy, exploitation, and scarcity resulting in our anger. Our recovery transcends suffering by scrubbing the residue of captivity, hopelessness, and coercion.

The commonality of suffering expands to variations of restoration where the body, mind, and spirit are not healed by the same method. But healed by the same determination committed to recovery by our self-definition and success. We must accept that comparing current circumstances to hundreds of years ago can only be compared in the context of today's wishful thinking. The stark reality of life hundreds of years ago was within the prevailing conditions of that time, only referenced by context and comparisons to exploitations and atrocities committed continents away. It was a global depravity whereby other continents have their own horrors to tell. Their own CRT histories.

The mentality of whites that they never owned slaves can be met with the response of and I was never a slave. However, to truly ring true, we must reject the shadow of slavery cast over our identity by their discriminatory confusion that we will be submissive to a past they were not a part of, but neither were we. So as the cinematic icon demanded, call him Mr. Tibbs and put some respect on his humanity. The history is ours but the reality was our ancestor's. Our battle is the lingering effects of slavery, racism, and discrimination. Society's is the refusal to accept we have put an end to the nonsense of anyone thinking that may still be the case.

Our expectations, perspectives, and uneasiness forecast future events with negative connotations outside our power to change. It affects us more if we allow it to have power over our psyche, self-image, or ambitions. So, someone else's perception of us is outside our control and decreasingly insignificant. We cannot surrender to the inevitability of it, making it not only tolerable but almost inviting. By the estimation of manifestation expecting it produces it.

Thus, it hones our expectations and vision to see it as the most likely possibility by preceding attitudes, experiences, and conditioning. It creates a mold of self-conformation adhering to a stereotypical pattern conveying that there will not be consequences to pay for violations. We can safely assume there are no patterns that don't exist. So, there is a synchronicity to patterns from the molecular, particle, and wave level that governs the universe, including human behavior. They are either intentional or unintended consequences of anything purposeful or accidental.

For example, the police will defund the police by rogue actions which decimate the city budget due to payouts for misconduct leading to shortages and citywide layoffs. The city has a limited budget and resources. So, when the shoes get tight enough, they will stop it themselves. But, in the meantime punitive consequences of fiscal and legal ramifications does more than protest by attrition and decimation. Otherwise, only the necessary changes in policy and procedures will prevent their self-destruction. Still, it will be a bumpy ride before its resolution.

A new mentality of conducting social, criminal justice, and fiscal business redefining the objective and consequences requires an equation to critique the elements that jeopardize our results and alternative innovative methods to achieve them. Are our methodologies situationally tailored and amended for specific confrontations, demands, and sanctions? An isolated targeted approach may be more effective than a routine protest, although both have their place.

In the last hundred years, generational voices and many more have spoken but not been heard as they should have been. My sincere apologies to those who I have not mentioned due to the limitations of my knowledge but whose voices and contributions are indispensable in the education and progression of our people's interest. But, a national treasure such as Dr. Claude Anderson should be mandatory learning for every Black high school student instead of debating CRT.

It has far more futuristic value and implications that will impact their life. But, it requires a long overdue diametric shift in our mentality, actions, and motivations. Also, in our plan of attack which should be economic and educational. The commodities we should be widely known to deal in are intelligence, intellectual property, fiscal acumen, economic development, and educational pursuit. Our minds are our commodity and tool of labor and combat tempered by our discipline to shun distractions lacking the desired results.

Our protest will be our actions and diligent undertaking of inclusion by saturation as the best available options. We know the cost of not doing it, but we need to experience the benefit of bombarding inclusion whereby we can't be disregarded. The discipline, sacrifice, and effort will be more than justified by the generational advantages turning the social pages from racial defamation to undeniable inclusion. We set our mark for others to be compared, expanding beyond physical attributes or entertainment into intellectual, political, and business sovereignty.

The journey has begun in earnest with patience and perseverance to accumulate even more stature. The answer can be extracted from slavery, referencing the number one thing we were denied more than freedom, and that was education. Learning to read would free a captive mind whose body could no longer be restrained. Today our minds remain restrained, with no need to restrain our bodies but to unleash them on a not-so-secret mission of cultural self-destruction disguised as our choice.

The U.S. government's CIA MK-Ultra experiment in the 1950s and 1960s ala Tuskegee Experiment, LSD, crack cocaine epidemic, and opioid crisis to alter human behavior and foster mind control preceded many substantial negative social changes. Was the LSD revolution sparked as a psychotropic experiment to chart the expansion of altered states of consciousness? Arguably, the U.S. government has facilitated every national drug addiction since the 1950s.

For what purpose would the government be interested in mind control, addictions, and social engineering if not for an ulterior motive? I say that not as a conspiracy theorist but to suggest what makes you think they aren't interested. Similar experiments, techniques, and information gathered from atrocities and regimes from around the globe have secretly been used against unsuspecting segments of the public. Many aspects of racism rears its destructive head in various forms not always readily observable such as drug addiction to institute economic instability.

Accepting this premise, racism exist as a bridge to obstruction only if you need to cross that bridge. If there are no other bridges, build one to circumvent the tariffs of racism or devise another way of crossing over without it. Racism can only amount to a detour but not a dismissal or elimination. Submission is an elimination while perseverance makes it only a delay. So, racism can be viewed as a failed social experiment whose fallout has lingered beyond its failure.

Therefore, the root deceptions and conditionings of racism, propagandist beliefs, and segregationist tiers renders better results than the experiments of mind control with one setback. Add hot water and stir for mind control while brainwashing has to be baked in over an extended period and conversion. Still, not exclusive to our people or segments of minorities, but by summation probably so when considering the duality of the positive and negative impact of its socializations.

Drugs, imprisonment, economic isolation, elimination of identity markers in the mind, and chemical stimulation causing physical, behavioral, and mental anomalies by depravation, dependencies, and desperation are all methods too sinister to consider, but why? It cannot be ruled out as some other socializations, ramifications, and mind-altering dilemmas facing Black people globally. Stranger arguments have been made, especially considering that it is all by manipulation of the options available and predicaments imposed.

The simulation or paradigm is an experimental equation of biblical proportions regarding freedom of will as a hologram of reality. How do our youth come to glorify genocide and sexual exploitation, considering there are no errors in patterns? Given this, if it is intentional we can probably guess why. As we identify and document the various groups of marginalization and eliminate them, what are we left with globally? A white patriarchal system where at every turn the system is designed for their convenience and superiority, even by the many alterations of religion.

The loop cycles back to the beginning repeating itself generationally, only substituted by a new shepherd and enhanced adaptations of integration. Not realizing the turnstiles that herd us to be complacent, complicit, and convinced leads to our psychological slaughter. The point is the system's inducement is exercised and arrogantly denied because we could not still be subjected to animal experimentation or human Ethology, right? But, why not if we were once treated as animals and property for the curiosity and exploitation of a racial agenda?

The common denominator is our gullible slumber oblivious to the broader implications and consequences as being irrelevant outside our radius of contemplation or self-control to not resist. So we dare not bite the apple, become woke, or question the manual of obedience to logically assess the glitches in the hologram. However, if we are to be what we strive to be we must have the courage to escape the grasp of its control and deception. Sleeping beauty was a fairytale, this is not. The holographic equation can no longer be reconciled to our reality.

The known Y of the equations is the system and its objective results. The unknown X of the equation is us. The solution is how to redefine the Y which changes the X by first redefining the X. When the greater context is blurred, a preconceived concept is substituted to finish or replace the image or thought shielded from clarity. A concerted examination clarifies the context of observations. That is how vision functions while brain patterns are dismissive of unfamiliar impressions but superimposes a guess or deduction as our observation or vision.

Unfortunately, our vision and concentration has too often been on singular issues that distract or conceal other issues impacting multiple areas of concern. Time has proven that regulation of our progress is aligned with the scope of our tactical objectives, focused vision, and leverage to stimulate social changes. Counted in the various systems and methods of irrefutable distractions are the askew allocations of incarceration, crime, under-education, and dysfunctional behavioral pacifications.

These Pavlov salivating distractions and pacifications are embellished as fool's gold or mirages of a narcissistic oasis succumbing to a superimposed vision disguising the entrapment. The desperate mind is susceptible to manipulations of relief that lessen the desperation by suspending any due consideration. Consequently, our inclination by default is to deal with today, unsure of tomorrow. But tomorrow comes until it doesn't, so we must extend our vision toward prescribed generational objectives because the catching comes before the hanging.

We must gorge ourselves on knowledge for the sake of learning, expanding the radius of our awareness, understanding, expectations, and representation to alter the value of X. The manner of our knowledgeable participation shapes the sphere of probabilities likely to develop and redefine the Y. Our resurrection depends on our knowledge and determination to capitalize on our expanding presence in prominent areas of impact. The game has changed with certain racist ideologies becoming increasingly extinct gasping for survival.

So, just as it is important to do certain things, it is equally important to avoid other things to hasten its extinction. The four primary areas of vulnerability and entrapment to avoid are addictions, subconscious or ego seductions, sexual exploitation, and religious incapacitation. First, addictions are developed appetites and elude to compulsions and dependencies that vary but have an imbalance of control causing harm.

Addictive behaviors are subjectively justified by comparisons and judgments to rationalize how they are demons of opportunity, uncontrollable, or predetermined. All could be true but also true is that other elements contribute to their programmed irresistibility. Removal of these elements may result in resistance to the addiction but a greater compulsion, such as religion, can negate a subordinate impulse. So addictions penetrate the psyche as an outlet for trauma, perceived deficiencies, or emotional voids manifested as behavior or habits.

Behaviors and habits are never irreversible, only situational. Addiction is the shield to cope with or conceal the underlying issues. Substance abuse is the most notorious addiction, but addiction comes in many forms including work, religion, passivity and many more seemingly positive attributes. Thus, its many realizations defuse efforts directed for our greater good by controlling us beyond our control of ourself. Surrendering control is not to the addiction but the cause of it.

Secondly, the ego is our representation to the public. It is highly susceptible to cajolery or self-validating enticements creating an intoxicating allure dependent on notoriety or others' opinions. This infatuation is why social media causes such a hypnotic deformity of the ego thirsty for attention and recognition sometimes costing extreme forfeitures of our dignity. Attention can also become an addiction, if not a flat-out narcissistic obsession.

The twisting of the ego is predictably expressed and detected as a stereotype as proof that the twist has taken hold. Contorted displays proposing negative or dysfunctional self-images results from that behavior often disguised as pride, respect, or self-expression. The ego is a byproduct of the conscious mind to swindle others by the deceptions of which we have deceived ourselves. So, it is the mask we hide behind concealing the infantile insecurities of our self-evaluation.

Next is sexual temptation by transference of imaginary persuasion, transposing fantasy into a visual simulation stimulating desire. I don't say reality because it is a figment of mental seduction by self-projection inducing an imaginary trance to excite passion. The reduction to sexual objectification as a commodity exploiting a fantasy of imagination or ego injection plants a deliberately assigned impression. Can you then be perceived other than what you present yourself as?

The resulting perception from the preferred presentation becomes the established evaluation and little more when presented as such. Aroused impulses of suggestions topples the criteria of valuation as the superficially primary concern for judgement. The objectified tunnel of identification and association narrows the considerations of self-worth to judge or be judged, thereby diminishing attributes outside of your objectified uses.

Lastly, religious incapacitation using sincere religious beliefs as pacifiers and proof to lull believers into refusing to compartmentalize their beliefs from their reality or contradictions to its doctrine restrains our progress. We are not taught much about religion and often still lack the most fundamental elements of its evolution and interpretation outside our unshakable devotion. We often also lack an understanding of the intent of its historical utilizations.

However, they have somehow managed to not teach about the Doctrine of Discovery which created retroactive allowances for Columbus to rape, pillar, and plunder foreign lands as had been the emerging European tendency. Of course, it was initiated and sanctioned by none other than the Roman Catholic Church under the Papal Bull decree to colonize non-Christian lands even by force if necessary. The primary goal was expanding the Catholic faith and Christianity, with slavery as a calculated incidental consequence.

The Church gained spiritual control and dedication of the missionary converted minds while the marauders claimed the land, resources, and population. Not so coincidently, it still occurs today along with furtive repatriation of resources. So by holy decree, it advocated and authorized those considered savage or barbarous nations to be overthrown, brought into the Christian faith, and trained in good morals according to European ideology. This ideology predated the concept of colonialism but not conquest, and as always was justified to please God.

Now the velvet glove of salvation is used instead of the iron fist of invasion. This reflected the God-fearing and God-loving goodwill of the Church to expand and solidify white power and superiority by having it baked into the religion. Also by crusades of death for non-believers or slow converters. So, our drilled-in saturation of a forced religious doctrine may not be as profoundly believed as severely and inconspicuously ingrained coercion to validate brutal aggressions, thievery, and conquest.

Global Race Theory (GRT) will reveal a much more diabolical charade with some unsuspecting participants including the Roman Catholic Church. I wonder if they are interested in reparations or only have prayers to offer. It is confusing how such holy and obedient persons of faith sworn to uphold the Ten Commandments of divine guidance can disgrace God's name. Disregarded was the directives to not use his name in vain, thou shall not kill, thou shall not steal, bear false witness, and shall not covet thy neighbor's goods.

Blaise Pascal stated, "men never do evil so completely and cheerfully as when they do it from religious conviction," and I might add patriotism, nationalism, imperialism, and commercialism. Much has been endured, sacrificed, and suffered under a religion that we clutch dear to our bosom. Obviously, at times even more so than others ever have. Still, other believers hold a cavalier or wavering commitment or interpretation to their faith even though it was theirs' before it was ours. Assuming that it was their religion that they gave us, should we not practice it as they do by their example?

The tranquilizing effect on our psyche motivated Joshua as a soldier for the Lord from the same God that was used to undermine our humanity. According to the Church, slavery was not immoral but offered solace by salvation as a release from a situation it helped perpetuate to a large degree. Saint Thomas Aquinas believed there was no higher honor than to serve in bondage. Religious doctrine places believers in positions of obedient children unable to question but just obey. Some beliefs they seem to hold more dearer than others as they pertain to us.

These beliefs are the same foundational claims of slavery. Take a literal interpretation of the bible and it clearly states that slavery is permitted throughout it. It would follow that believers in the good book also must believe in slavery regardless of color including Black folks. Remember, man made the good book just as the lion said manmade the subjective statue of conquer. Slavery was not always by color but by the standard that a power arbitrarily decided according to war, religion, or whatever. The consent of Popes, Protestants, and Lutherans participated and promoted African slavery not only in America but globally assisted by France, Spain, Portugal, Dutch, and others including Africans.

However, it is inconceivable that reparations would be sought from religious orders that do not have the same indemnification for crimes against humanity on American soil at least by moral compass. Same for the many refined countries of Europe who threw the rock of slavery only now to hide their bloated hand. The global scope of reparation touches far and wide. I suppose it would be blasphemous for enslaved people to seek redress against religious orders despite common redress remitted for sexual assaults and other transgressions.

The obvious pattern seems for everyone to get paid except for enslaved African's descendants. Much the same can be said for the people of the Caribbean, South America, pockets of Europe, and even Britain regarding the institution of slavery and religion. The colonization of them can most easily be traced by the language spoken to determine the colonizer. For example, in America English is the dominant language do to British rule with Spanish prevalent in the southern hemisphere and so forth.

The ideology passed down has been to depict Africans as being dumb and unruly, posing a threat that needs to be harshly dealt with to corral the predatory propensities of the dark savages. The cycle of religious and sociological assertions and persuasions gathers dissension and fear towards our people by default indoctrinations persistently based on fear, deception, and ignorance. Furthermore, by our staunch refusal to logically assess the historical and factual basis, we arguably sustain them by our belief, acceptance, and devotion.

The Doctrine of Discovery beginning in the 1100s was a finders keepers to rape, pillar, and plunder any non-Christian land bringing them to heel under the churches' system of belief. How many doctrines, decrees, and forceful submissions to Christianity under the banner of the Church at the direction of the Vatican were we persecuted under including the 1452, 1455, and 1493 Papal Bulls? In fairness there were other Papal Bulls rejecting slavery but the practices seems to have ignored them, even the Church itself ignored them. Also, we did receive a long overdue meaningless apology, after all the Church did ordain slavery not by God's decree but Noah's.

January 1, 1863, America abolished slavery, so the math reveals centuries before 1619 to the run-up where we are today regarding racism and atrocities to our humanity. In that context, we are approaching nine hundred years of racial indoctrination infused in the religion, law, and the global structure which was encouraged by the Vatican. So, we cannot afford not to examine the religious impact on our perspective, beliefs, and tolerances.

We have endured four millenniums (4,000 years) since Noah's curse that has conditioned Caucasians to subjugate us including by their religion we show so much devotion. Is there any wonder that breaking a six millennium orientation has taken so long? But, comparatively speaking in America we are making speedy progress against the evils of history. Still, our allegiance to worship their tools of oppression is still rampant. What more will it take to see who is the real boogie man? Christianity has been our damnation and resiliency our salvation.

Our images, education, economics, family cohesion, and you name it, are tainted by a mentality we refuse to shake, so how could it be any easier for others when we are the ones taking a beating? Are we to believe God unleashed these oppressive forces upon us because Noah was liquored up and naked? Our psychological underdevelopment, fear of hell, and quest for heaven can be the only explanations why we fail to recognize the covert catalyst for many overt discriminations of religion. Why are they not equally afraid to commit it as we are to reject it?

Yet, despite where we are today, the sanctioned, maliciously directed, and pervasively practiced trauma has affected us so that we compensate for it by compartmentalizing or denying it. Our healing is a test of fortitude to unflinchingly stare into the abyss unafraid of what is staring back, the truth. Identifying our trauma and addressing it is mandatory to recover from it. Adjusting our perspectives, objectives, and methods as a self-contained resolution disregarding the current obstacles for autonomy without permission whether divine or otherwise.

A wound must be treated, given time to heal, and protected from re-injury. Still, sometimes healing by restoring the previous condition before the injury is not possible. So, only recovery according to the best possible current condition is attainable. Then, our question becomes one of time and degree of recovery. Self-evaluation and brutal unconditional honesty must be undertaken as an internal audit of our beliefs, mentalities, portrayals, and behaviors that undermine our equitable humanity in fact and not by belief.

We know the Y of the equations in the system and the objective. Still, we must counter it by maneuvering the variables in our control for more equitable outcomes. As the outcomes accumulate, it becomes the standard of equality we have as our objective, built brick by brick. If we are to be master builders of our destiny, we must risk hell to get to heaven if our humanity is at stake. If Jesus forgave our sins surely he will have mercy if we have none in the pursuit of his promise, our freedom from the original sin of mutilation of our dignity and humanity.

God help those who help themselves and fear started this, so fearlessness will have to end it. With courage as the only rule and the equipment needed to play the game, we will let our audacity force them to either play us or against us. So, we acknowledge our wounds, also acknowledging they are not enough to stop us or our sufficient recovery to prevent us from our destination. This mentality has no room for anything outside of or detrimental to our self-determination.

Valor requires we roll up our sleeves, tighten our belts, and take a deep breath before storming the summit of our dignity. But, storm the summit we will, not by confrontation but by determination to shape-shift our perspective embracing the unspoken nobility and equality of our humanity. The boogie man wears a costume trick or treating, spreading fallacies and ghoulish tales, causing trauma and fear while casting illusions by consent or ignorance. But, how do we expose the boogie man if not by turning on the lights to see.

The level of ignorance and fear has transcended time to stubbornly resist change because of its longevity and pervasiveness in the recesses of our mind and past. Fear escapes reality as a figment of speculation that stirs anxiety, foreboding unknown hazards of imagination yet to be produced. They may never be produced outside our imagination and fear. So, fear becomes the motivator as an energetic force to propel us from psychological darkness to a bright future. By facing our hesitations, we accelerate the cleansing of our psyche.

Fear of religion, racism, law enforcement, failure, change, systemic obstructions designed to discourage us, punishment, validation, and many more distort and govern our existence by fallacies we have been convinced are true. So, the glory of our accomplishments are often overwhelmed by the fear and uncertainty of investing whatever will be required to rectify the millenniums of their miseducation by our edification. The majority of the OMB census is freshly minted European immigrants mislabeled as white while so-called legacy whites are the real minority in America.

As for religion, there is a movie about a beverage bottle that is thrown out of an airplane and falls from the sky mistaken as a symbol of God. As a result it causes so much chaos it must be returned pondering if the Gods must be crazy. Is the bible or Christianity our symbolic bottle that must be returned due to the chaos it has caused? Organized Christianity is largely behind slavery based on skin tone. As far as skin tone, would not the universal designation be human and not race if skin tone was transparent or Christianity blind? These primitive myths and flimsy distinctions are all for a far more menacing purpose than what we recognize.

Look at authoritarian regimes whose iron grip reproduces robots who solely exist for the service of the state. Is ours any different or just labeled differently? The slumber of our indoctrination has not been able to conceal the emperor or ideology to be as naked as Noah but are we to pretend we don't see it out of fear? Curiosity is the essence of exploration and advancement, not concealment. So, we must boldly go where the exploration leads us willing to discard the ignorance of convenience and conditioning.

The more profound the revelation, the more infinite the possibilities. The restrained paradigms of antiquated motives and mentalities blocks the path of what we should be contemplating instead of remaining in an entombment of ritualistic deceptions cleverly disguised. The old saying is that everyone would be doing it if it were easy. So, nothing exceptional in life is acquired easily and most days it won't come easy. But, once secured, many more things won't come hard. Thus, if we click our heels of knowledge, clarity, and exploration three time we can exit the Land of Oz.

The vicarious voyeurism peeping into a fabricated reality reveals ours once we snap out of it. Sufficiently aroused, many of our visions are within our grasp combined with the effort, actions, and dedication to grab it. It is not what we stand to lose but what we definitively gain. We are more intrigued by the story than the storyteller. The storyteller sets or exaggerate the narrative for us to believe the story is true or the evidence is removed from proving it is false. The Great Oz was a perpetrator provocateur concealed behind the thinnest of curtains.

Therefore, truth does not matter. Belief does. Scrutiny of the storyteller reveals any ulterior motives and interpretations more aligned to convincing us to believe than truth or transference of knowledge. So, where truth treads, belief lingers behind. Verification and analytical thinking should be applied to understand and accept or reject based on what is known. Belief is for the unknown. Still, knowing it does not mean you have to believe it and believing it is not knowing it.

However, it expands our knowledge base and understanding of others, situations, and occurrences when we know instead of believing. Holding onto past restrictions, perspectives, and portrayals does not strengthen us. Instead, it is best used to fuel us as a blueprint for future navigation into knowledge. Weakness is born from fear and surrender, dousing the spirit to resist or explore. It is time we defy the cultures, stereotypes, and representations designed and embedded in centuries of sabotage.

The cage is unlocked for the slightest exertion to fling open the door of ignorance. We have carried for far too long the weight of an injected mentality of fear, exclusion, and degradation. So, our grumbling alone will not change it. Instead, our changes will chart our progress directly proportionate to our transition to consistently demonstrate the knowledge of our dignity, image, and humanity.

We now keep ourselves obstructed more than anyone or anything else, so we must take the necessary actions to seize a generational transformation. Our place in the future depends solely on our efforts in the present. For that matter, the human species is on the dawn of the Age of Aquarius signifying a rebirth by the revelation of truth, awakening of consciousness, and shedding of the old skin of relegated ideologies.

A diametrical maturation of humanity can no longer be restrained by the delusions of divisive classifications plaguing humanities emergence from the cocoon of deception. The famine of autonomy and scarcity of logical examination which has rendered humanity tethered to fear, ignorance, and manipulation is dissipating by the courage to gaze onward beyond its false veneer of truth. Dimensions of possibilities are revealed with the expansion of our minds and vision.

Mindlessly Tethered
Unparalleled Strength

The elephant is majestic and revered across many lands, cultures, and times. The elephant is the largest land mammal on the planet, with species growing up to 13,000 pounds. It symbolizes wisdom, loyalty, reliability, power, good luck, and an incredible memory. In addition, the elephant has observable compassionate traits and behavior, contradicting its colossal size and raw strength. The elephant, which is so large and powerful, knows no bounds or physical limitations in the wild. Consequently, it must be taught limitations that ensure its control and ignorance of self in captivity.

It is controlled by the only means capable, by being subjected to psychological conditioning to ensure its self-imposed psychological bondage. That is why a small cord or twine can tether a fully grown 13,000-pound elephant to a small peg knocked only inches into the ground. It is imprisoned not by physical force but by confinement of its mind and taming of its will. Thereby manipulated into docile complicity by limiting the reasoning process that would enable it to recognize and use its great strength against the bondage of a feeble restraint.

The elephant is conditioned to remain restricted and accept a power other than itself by believing it is hopelessly outside its grasp to attempt resistance. The initiation is a standard method started much like kindergarten, where this must be embedded before a level of confident reasoning or resistance can be exhibited. Therefore, resistance and independence must be extinguished early and repetitively. The elephant must be trained at an early age to accept tethering calmly, obedient to its projected limitations.

 This is done by tying one front leg to a peg and then the opposite diagonal rear leg to a different peg, thereby restraining the "baby beast" in its infancy. The elephant's mind then remains in this conditioned infancy, reluctant to challenge its captivity. This technique alone cannot restrain a baby elephant. So the deterrent or restraint must be stronger than the elephant's young strength at that time to reinforce that there is no escape or resistance against the force that binds it against its will. As a result, it becomes hopelessly obedient to the chains that bind it.

The baby elephant will continuously and repeatedly test the chains imposed upon it until it learns that its size and strength are futile against the constraints that hold it physically. No matter how hard or how long its effort to resist is, it becomes useless. It then becomes a mental restraint of conditioned futility. This is where the conversion of the mind begins to regulate its physical capabilities. Once its determination is broken, and the elephant "realizes" this uselessness, it gives up any further or future attempts.

Surrender is achieved by believing it is powerless for the remainder of its life against that which controls it. The physical chains have effectively become the psychological chains that bind the beast into adulthood until death. Confinement of the mind, once achieved, will be self-imposed in most instances, with only minimal reminders needed. The elephant's determination is then replaced by calm compliance and convinced acceptance. Strong restraints are no longer necessary to surpass the elephant's young strength or for its two legs to be restrained. Because it is now adequately conditioned and broken.

Sounds familiar? Remember the reference to kindergarten, where group conformity and inculcation begins. The limitations of the mind work on all animals, even human animals too. Once conditioned and with the supporting reminders and incentives as constant behavioral reinforcement to implant a reality they are thoroughly convinced that is their actual limitations. It is a clever and sinister trick long used before Pavlov's Theory. It is rewarding compliance or punishment for deterrence. Often the greater incentive is to avoid a penalty instead of receiving a reward.

Using the opposite of Pavlov, avoiding a penalty is the only reward for compliance. The absence of stimulus to elicit a response instead of anticipating a reward. The lack of punishment becomes the controlling incentive erasing alternative options. The old go-along to get along or else in full effect as the motivating factor. Even with elephants, peer pressure is a continuous reminder to behave. Like crabs in a barrel to keep you confined with them ever compliant. The older conditioned elephants demonstrate their compliance to instill a level of acceptance that soothes the young elephants into accepting that's just how it is, no questions about it.

So once the "baby beast" becomes fully grown, the chains and diagonal leg restraints are no match for their tremendous strength. However, they are still chained psychologically to their old circumstances by indoctrination. In society, those who are compliant resent those daring enough to deviate from surrendering, those brave enough to resist. Using that which or someone who is most impressionable to us is a highly effective tool for implementing behavior and beliefs because it comes from a trusted and relied-upon source as sincere guidance.

Reminds me of Big Mama ain't going to tell you nothing wrong baby. That is true, at least not on purpose, but only according to the limitations of her knowledge. However, that was enough for me to comply because it was beyond my knowledge or understanding. It was from a trusted source. But what were the limitations created by her indoctrination? What are our limitations or realities handed down? Even if correct then, do they still apply now?

The old circumstances were when much younger, the elephant's resistance was useless. They had, in reality, long ago changed, but their minds had not changed, making it their current reality with no longer one good reason why. That is other than the psychological constraints. Their size and strength had long ago multiplied to overcome their physical constraints. However, their desire and mentality remained confined, still conditioned by a small rope and a faulty belief. The young elephant knew no different but was taught this with no examples or allowances to suggest otherwise.

That is all the young elephant knew, what it was taught. Indoctrinated into captivity assisted by a broken generational herd mentality that is naïve of self. Thus, breeding unquestioned acceptance, clinging to vastly different circumstances from the reality of its true power and destiny. The fate of this reality constricts future liberties and possibilities. This is the taming of spirit and dousing of determination where no right existed, just the method and desire for control.

Feebly justified by the need and ability to do so but to no benefit to the elephant, only to further its exploitation. Let's change the subject name from elephants to human beings, not races, although race certainly qualifies. The name changes, but the game stays the same if you stare at the truth and do not flinch. Maybe we have been made into the very thing we despise the most by being trusting and naïve to a system designed to deceive and control us.

Unaware of the deception thrust upon us that is not what we believe it to be, much like the elephant. What peg restrains and controls our mind by voluntary compliance? Controls our action, biases, or beliefs? Regrettably, we got it the same way the elephant did, unknowingly and without understanding our strength or how it was done. As the elephant grew, it still held onto outdated beliefs embedded early on when it could have later easily freed itself from captivity. The same occurs with humans. The same may be our only explanation.

If only we realized we had the power not only to resist its restraints but to overpower it and choose our fate. Choose our liberty or even exercise choices different from the conformity of the herd or others similarly situated. I guess misery loves company but so does ignorance. Unfortunately, they are often companions lacking guidance, knowledge, and courage. Our fortitude sustains us when the road gets tough but only when we prevent it from being compromised and allow it to expand untethered by the limitations of others' regulating influences.

Those who poorly regulate themselves would seek to regulate others by their words, not their deeds. This indicates that what is good for the goose may not be so good for the gander if we are clever. Their conformity resents our liberation as how dare we not submit to their programmed deception. But by what right is their conformity recognized as being above our sovereignty. Is it only for the comfort and amusement of another? Consider another's gain or satisfaction we contribute to without fair compensation or against our satisfaction?

Isn't it a true reflection of their disregard for our Freedom, concerned only for their elevation, separation, and accumulation? Of course, this power is not to be negotiated or given away. But in many cases, it is squandered or, much worst, not recognized or exercised. Absent lies and deceptions, power over oneself is the only authority a person has that does not require the consent and cooperation of another. If someone want to be seen as a leader, then be an example and possess what others would be willing to follow. That does not demand their subordination to your will against their good.

Time brings about a change one way or another, so everything must change and will change constantly, but the idea of change is the catalyst. The knowledge or idea is the seed. We see as the captive elephant's circumstances changed over time, it remained stagnant. As time passes, humans should evolve to not invade others' personal boundaries and human rights to conform to an imposed standard of foreign beliefs not of their choosing or benefit. Persuasion is the proper tool, not suppression or oppression. Mutual benefit encourages mutual favor but not exploitation.

The techniques used to control the masses are driven down in our minds like a peg tethered by faulty socialization, now using more advanced processes than physical abuse or economic incentives. This may be shocking, but it is just not the "undesirables" of color that are the victims. Like piranhas, the elite feeding frenzy has turned on their very own like cannibals to ensure their elitist survival. The middle class has been eaten along with the lower class regardless of color.

Fear, scarcity, and divisiveness are frequently employed to generate the ignorance of crash dummies to camouflage how they, too, have been programmed with the lies of social engineering. They then conceal their influence and have everyone else turn on each other in a futile attempt while distracted and chasing our tails as they prosper. The dog never catches its tail, although the snake can swallow its tail as an unrecognizable part of itself. When faced with fear or scarcity, the young, gullible, or vulnerable are devoured first, similar to the low-hanging fruit of racial division.

This mentality is popularized by the desperation shown in the Squid Games of unscrupulous behavior viciously displayed for personal gain disregarding harm to others. Like Pavlov's theory, when the bell rings, you salivate on cue without substance, having been socially conditioned but never realizing the basis for your slobbering or fear. Petty distractions abound, motivations fabricated, and conditioning regulated by design keeps us preoccupied and pitted against each other instead of the ideological pegs that bind us. It is contorted into a vicious squid game of survival by desperation.

The elite has always tipped the scales for themselves since antiquity stealing from the public draw. Look at how many politicians are wealthy or have enhanced their riches and when or how. Might you find the answer lies in their service to us? Advancing the lies and flat-out misrepresentation of facts and history in America about America perpetuates conflict and privilege. It has created a narrative to bolster the image and perception of the accomplishments of a colonial populist Anglo-Saxon protestant utopia even as they also suffer from its effects.

It has concealed the degenerate deeds and wealth heist while functioning as greed mongers of ill repute who should be held in the highest contempt for instigating a dysfunctional society. But then there is that annoying peg tethering us, right? The door is unlocked but untested, with Freedom just one gesture away, one mind shift away. However, we must remain obedient and follow the rules, repeatedly reminded to comply.

Ever wonder why you must submit to limitations while others of a higher economic or social status do not? But strangely enough, the more privileged you are, the more advantages you receive and the more the rules are for "commoners" or the poor. It suggests a separate reality where privilege is for others, and the rules are just for us to follow. Then again, that is usually how it goes.

These double crosses of trust and responsibilities cannot persist as a caste system entitled to privilege. In this day and age, where knowledge cannot be hidden so easily, and ignorance is not as rampant, it has become obvious. The slander of history has readily been used to accomplish traditional conditioning as fact despite knowledge to the contrary. You cannot fool all the people all the time, even with the triple cross of lies, deceptions, and manipulation.

For example, the likes of a homicidal genocidal Christopher Columbus is widely celebrated with a holiday creating discord from, say, MLK Day. A murderer of exaggerated feats and a peacemaker, both praised the same. Likewise, the scientific fraud and racist Charles Darwin is not exposed for his detrimental impact on society. Instead, he has been honored despite his absurd debunked biases of sexism and eugenics.

Truly a man of his time, he espoused women as having the simple-minded brains of children and the inferiority of races based on color. This is the nonsense of once-celebrated ignorance perpetuated as truth mangled into the social norm. Social norms debased by the manipulated perspective of the rule makers become the guiding standard for the tethered to concede as fallacies mimicking reality. Furthermore, the misconception that patriotism is the domain of white folks.

Further still, the notion that immigrants from Mexico and South America are stealing jobs of significance from white Americans. Are they referring to office, corporate, or high-paying salaried positions? How about the tacit belief that America has a superior ruling class by birth, whites? Religion, baby dolls, action heroes, cartoons, entertainment, and many occupations all fashion a designed conception supporting beliefs as truth and social expectations.

These few things tether the masses to traditional nonsense, destroyed for lack of knowledge or impressionable demonstration. This is not to expose the racism that is obviously practiced today due to this nonsense but the tethering of minds on both sides of the equation. It is done mostly in ways detrimental to a democratic society, social justice, economic fairness, and reality. The depth of mental captivity willingly and pervasively expanded simulates reality by perception creating the appearance of truth.

Despite the reluctance of logical verification, its practice and acceptance have become standardized, increasing its justification and pathology. The resulting propaganda initiates control subliminally surrendered and encouraged by assimilation and habitual capitulation duly replicated and self-regulated. This goes on globally with an endless number of people and circumstances. It can be substituted or exposed as the propaganda of nonsense presented to tether, condition, and control their citizens against the people's greater good.

While exploiting this brand of social engineering for their own gain, the people are marginalized to servitude obedient to the inherited ideology. The general public has always been subject to exploitation, and those adept at doing it since the beginning of time. However, worldwide, the realization and the awakening of oppressed people everywhere are challenging the status quo. Power only exists when recognized as such, but fear and cajolery can only control the masses for so long.

I almost forgot to mention that the tethered elephant routinely breaks its binds when suddenly aroused by fear or agitation despite its psychological conditioning displaying the power to uproot large barriers or remove massive obstructions. Likewise, social unrest is the same when stirred by frustration, injustice, and dissatisfaction to uproot its oppression. A child has the strength to rip one piece of paper, but enough paper bound together, even a strong man cannot tear it apart.

The strength of unity is a strength not to be disputed or squandered but respected. Unity is leverage, and the majority sets the mold creating the social norm and change. Limitations are, on average, learned and reinforced behaviors systematically imposed for the good of a hierarchy or its ideologies. Mental control is the most effective manner of control when it is voluntary. We think it is our choice or, even worse, we think we have no choice.

Realistically, we always have a choice, but are we willing to pay the price for that choice. The conditioning kicks in as fear of reprisal instead of the satisfaction of a reward dictating the choice. The easy road is the road most traveled. By comparison, the more we fulfill arbitrary criteria, the more value is assigned and scorn distributed. In turn, this was engineered in us, sometimes unwittingly, to feel better about ourself while holding others down beneath us. Just as we may have been held down beneath someone else.

Deviation from the cloning of compliance and concession invites condemnation and ostracization. Manufactured and fluctuating norms renew the cycle by valuing and devaluing humanity based on conditioned preferences. So, instead of restricting someone, release yourself from this mindset of tethering or being tethered to indoctrination. Whether in others or ourself, it has been the plight of humanity for control. So, square yourself away first from the social programming that is believed to be reality.

That will make at least one less purveyor of ignorance in the world based on these apparent deceptions. By superseding our constraints and promoting honesty, knowledge, courage, and compassion we break our restraints. Consequently, striving for the vastness of our liberation to recognize and enhance the radius of our understanding beyond our prison of perception. We must assess how, if, and why it fits together or doesn't.

Accordingly, they cannot risk us being individually and collectively untethered escaping the psychological bondage and expanding beyond contrived limitations and conflict. It resembles a bank run collapsing the system. That is why there is a need for tethering deceptions and division as a peg to control our minds. Sleeping beauty is suitable only for fairytales, not societies. The quest for truth, knowledge, and fairness is criticized as "woke" because they would prefer the snoozing giant remain stagnant, divided, and unconscious to the tethering effects of a warped narrative.

Knowing better but not doing better unable to shed the faulty conformities is the same net result as not knowing. The size and strength of the elephant are unparalleled, but a person's mind, even more so, is without bounds. However, once that mind is conditioned and seized, reprogramming it becomes just as daunting as for a grown elephant. Never realizing the folly of its constrained capabilities it perishes under conditions it involuntarily submitted to by default.

Free your mind from the voluntary bondage that confines and restricts it as only we can. The body carries out the directive of the mind as it central control. The exception is when the mind remains confined manipulating the body's spontaneous repetition to a false reality it mistakenly believes is real. So, if our mind does not control our mentality the body becomes a programmed android acting according to a faulty code. Killing the mind renders the body useless without its mental faculties. But, the mind can function without the benefits or functionality of the body.

Some, when unleashed, still will not escape craving the certainty of submission and obedience forsaking independent thought or behavior for comfort. Go figure, but sheep need a shepherd governed by primitive instincts of communal acceptance and obedience. When that is the case, I guess you won't be seen out and about straying too far from your constraints. The mind must conceive the infinity of its imagination and contemplation without fear or constraints. That is the root of curiosity, discovery, and progression, which is the essence of Freedom. It must not only be FREEDOM of the body, but more importantly reside in a liberated mind.

What do you allow to tether your mind, humanity, knowledge, understanding, and destiny?

Race is Human

Humanity is Compassion

Uniqueness is Universal

Freedom is a Mindset

Energy transcends Dimensional Barriers

Thurston's Final Thought

By using race as a primary metaphor of this Anthem, can race be a myth, deception, and a superstition? What about a simulation, illusion, or mirage? Race is a feeble metric to assess social relevance. So, indeed the documented slavery, racism, and atrocities committed against us were selected to leverage us by their perspective and our circumstances. But, keep in mind the slave trade was a global African diaspora beyond America. It is a global narrative usually accompanied by religion, nationalism, or exploitation of resources.

So as people have circulated so has the DNA genetic codes to expand and combine migrating and mitigating characteristics concealing many lineages. These classifications on skin tone would fall to the wayside if genealogy were tested. Therefore, common genealogy shrinks as we move backwards to human origin. But beyond the genealogy, it is the systems and beliefs more confined to the past instead of drawn to the future.

If we are to be held to the past, we should understand what, how, and why we still habitually observe, worship, and obey corrupt sociologies, ideologies, and manipulations. With historical knowledge, we can make a more informed decision regarding the concepts we pledge our allegiance and devotion. Religion, race, culture, and everything else should withstand forensic scrutiny to determine if its portrayal or belief substantiates its practice or devotion. Is it what it says it is? If you believe it, why not find out if it is?

It is quite easy to be all hat and no cattle fronting and posturing without the resolve, application, or credentials to support or demonstrate the images in our mind as realities instead of projections of illusions. Sometimes, the projection is convincingly exaggerated to whatever degree we must convince ourselves. Demonstrations speak for themselves as proof verifiable by challenge, while projected illusions dissipate externally while still an internal imposter.

The sizzle without the bacon only provides the aroma and not the nutrient. Perception is the problem and solution, depending on where your mind is focused. We act out the simulation according to perception and the resulting interpretation of our experiences in life. We are either held captive or elevated above the external characterizations and judgments restricting our expansion.

Life outside the "box" must be experienced outside the box of others' definition of us but within ours. What we are, we were made to be, benefitting from its advantages while suffering from its disadvantages. All things in life have both pros and cons. We can suffer from the burden of poverty or of wealth, racism or equality, degradation or dignity because time has no preference outside ours. So, we control the choice even if it takes more to accomplish it. Any additional obstacles require only further determination and dexterity of our mind to overcome.

We must move past judgment or being judged and discouraged by accusations of being woke to keep us from becoming awakened. It is not enough to have the tools or instruments to excel. We must also utilize the knowledge by engaging in the tutelage of their operation. We have the resources but lack the ideological shift of our psychology and socialization to use our resources for maximum benefit and efficiency.

Humanity and behavior are as diverse as nature on some levels and remarkably similar on others. However, is there a greater separator than knowledge? Restricting knowledge conflated by moral determinations of good or bad based on fear is an ancient control mechanism using ignorance of the truth. The moral oxymoron is the deception and betrayal of trust used to mesmerize our judgment, causing a breach of contract with ourselves in exchange for inclusion.

Our level of trust cannot continue to be above our level of inclusion. Therefore, an inventory of our return on investment and contribution is a wise risk-benefit assessment. With over one and a half trillion in buying power while suffering from the suppressive effects of racism and exclusion, we have enough resources to promote our objective by the sheer power of the mean green. Mr. Green speaks very loudly and somehow is always clearly heard, but Mr. Green must speak to be heard.

So, we can make them change the rules or follow the rules by using our intellectual and economic power consolidated as a uniform incursion into the guts of inequality. Just as important as directing our resources is ensuring we receive our equitable allocation of resources as abundantly as they allocate incarcerations and other injustices. Public resources can no longer be hoarded for a biased benefit without a contested response disrupting some crucial element of its execution. The process must be audited to monitor the allocation and distribution.

To secure our success and wealth, we must procure equity in what we contribute, especially in our communities, expenditures of public considerations, and government funds. Protest, walks, and vigils are cool. But, still, actions of injunction or compulsion for economic, educational, and equity can only be satisfied by results. Many times other lesser methods result in promises and pacification. The evolution of our mentality, actions, and acceptable redress reflect our modified demands and expectations.

Our focus must look for the clearing instead of the clouds. Instead of being attached to the sinking ship of slavery's repercussions, we ride the lifeboat of future inevitabilities on our recalibrated autonomy. The needed adjustments for accountability to our objectives petitions our progress to our perspective. The proper perspective of past, present, and future categorized for forward propulsion relieved of historic baggage to accelerate our progress.

Please make no mistake, we are engaged in a contested endeavor, but the challenge is with us. We are the equalizer, not the circumstances that we seek. When we are steady, it is less significant if the circumstances waver. Remember, the mountain does not yield to the wind. The rock of our knowledge and determination deflects the insinuations of slavery, racism, or inferiority. When we are finally exhausted from the subjugation, our actions will eliminate its impact on us.

The foundation of change rest on us, so we must change the foundation to sprout the restoration of our humanity comprehensively acknowledged by us and others. The collapse and implosion of the current paradigm outside the impact of racism will crumble from the fallacies of history. Its design to control and exploit the masses has deteriorated from increased knowledge, the human spirit yearning for liberation, and clarity from fearful indoctrinations. The haunted house of society is a production that is exposed by illumination.

It needs our complicity to be made afraid, predictable, and controlled. Of course, there will be those who cannot escape or shed the box constructed around them. Their cocoon forsakes the future possibilities for the comforts of a certain fate by refusing to expand or emerge from it. Safety and fear cannot provide equality or ascension. Instead, they maintain and prolong the stagnation of the current existence. Racism does exist, but by fear, the effects of it only exist if we yield to them.

We disable racism by incapacitating the fear of punishment and the scarcity of resources mentality associated with its power. As a primal instinct of all organisms, competing for survival is countered by cooperation or extinction. The symmetry of survival generates hesitation through fear and conditioning, discouraging us from cooperation through despair. This distrust is a primary affliction that undermines our recovery and mutual benefit. We can build constructs which alleviates scarcity by our economic shifts, resource distribution, and innovated financing such as Black Owned Banks or home schooling in the form of routine intellectual engagement.

We do not need permission to exercise our rights or resources. No one else needs permission. So, why do we? The essays compiled in this book are an editorial of my perspectives, observations, and opinions. I do not seek agreement or argument but your understanding of the opinions and context submitted for your consideration. Hopefully, this will ignite conversation and review of your convictions to assess them against what has been presented. The next objective is to encourage your independent investigation into anything conveyed in which you may need further understanding or greater knowledge.

My other hope is that it lessens racial characterization and other prejudices exposed as illogical assumptions lacking for analysis. Time and circumstances has outran its duration. So many of us assume what, but we do not know why. We need to know why to formulate an informed opinion or devoted perspective. The limited subjectivity of a small picture or perspective cannot obscure the greater ramifications of reality. Stretch beyond the message to a dimension and vibration unfiltered by the primitive ideologies and singular narratives of past sociology.

Ultimately, to stir the courage to have the curiosity to add or lead to increasing your knowledge and understanding beyond mine. I would encourage you to research any word, concept, or purported fact for a more thorough understanding than I could provide in the limited scope of this book. It opens a vast realm of recalibrations traveling through portals of perspective, transferring dimensional insights, and offering raw interpretations to be verified independently.

Still, this book is not about racism. Instead, it uses racism as a pervasive dichotomy to illustrate how traditional, ritual, and habitual practices resist logic, the evolution of time, and the replacement of primitive thinking. It also demonstrates the extent ignorance can produce atrocities from deception. Hopefully, it adds clarity to the confusion, origins, and intent or, at the very least, starts us on an intellectual journey to pursue it ourselves. Emerging from the dark past is a bright future for those brave enough to exit the cave of ignorance, deceit, and division.

Considering the natural progression of current pragmatisms the projection of pillars of long standing socializations has neared its expulsion lacking solutions of evolution. I apply a concept to situations I call the totality principle. In any given situation, contained within the parameters of considerations is the totality of its factors projected forward without preconceived assumptions or boundaries. What is basically recognized as a strict determination of what it is without further concern for what it is not or why. Anything else forms a different capsule of considerations comprising the factors of another totality or problem constricted by assumptions.

What it should be or we would like it to be is outside the realm of what it is and should be considered separately because as an assumption it is probably also a conditioning. A sequential inventory of the circumstantial options renders the viable solutions to be prioritized according to feasibility. So, the solution is strictly directed toward the problem without predetermined influences of past restrictions. Applying the most practical creative remedy with the most practical method to achieve it.

From an agreed upon premise to an innovative conclusion requires an unregulated analysis using a defined process. What appears impossible may only be a lack of ingenuity or beyond our sphere of knowledge to adequately understand it to render a solution. The imagination unleashed can initiate possibilities that when entertained introduce uncommon expressions to advance toward an objective discovery which is the purpose of my writings.

The magic is in the curiosity within our imagination for discovery. A creative approach forms a hypothesis that doesn't propose the solution or the problem but instead the outcome. It defines the understanding which reveals the clarification. The clarification isolates the solution. That produces a systematic solution by integrating improvements and providing a sequential operational schematic to pursue. The solution is a by-product of the approach, unfettered by preference or protocol, but only the priority of eliciting the desired outcome and how to best accomplish it.

To accomplish the desired outcome, the process reins in extreme considerations leaving creatively practical presentations as the remaining considerations to be figured out from the outer boundaries of imagination. Start as far as the process allows moving toward a logical expansion to determine what is practical in defining the objective. The solution is in devising the method to connect practicality to the foundational objective from the extent of feasible expansion. That then becomes the new point of origin to pursue further until exhaustion of possibilities revealing the solution.

For example, by ideology a box is a closed container of fixed dimensions surrounding its contents separated by barrier and sight. Thinking freely is to reject its mental confinement. So to expand the radius creates a bigger box to accommodate its expansion instead of discarding what does not fit in the box. Using this assumption, first, qualify the objective. Then quantify the method. What are the most urgent to distant contingencies? The most urgent objectives are imminent objectives based on proximity, benefit, or impairment as opposed to distant ones.

But, among the imminent considerations must be prominent concerns calculating the extended consequences of implementing the solution. So, can elimination also simultaneously eliminate another problem or cause more problems? Perhaps, these are two-for-one sales, solving one problem solves another or creates another. Expanding perspectives and foresight would be the seminal nucleus to determine solutions. The process must always be mindful of what may be best removed. Remember, it is far easier to cause a problem than it is to build a resolution.

Eliminating the mentality that obstructs us would allow us to build the inclinations that will elevate us. Long before Moses led his people to the promised land, he asked, are you a master builder or a master butcher? He recognized that you could not be both. Accordingly, can we build a nation free from the psychological shackles of slavery, oppression, suppression, and discrimination? We must deliver ourselves from its bondage, unflinching in the face of our reflection, discarding unnecessary weight to lessen the burden of our climb to the summit.

The mighty winds yield to the unmovable mountain, but the mountain yields to the unwavering climber determined to scale its challenges. But, unfortunately, our focus has been scattered, our burden has not been lightened, and our preparation lacks the tenacity not to be turned away. The first issue is the violence in our communities, followed by the gender feud driving a wedge into the foundation of our historical strength. Only then can our economic stability and knowledge acquisition be the driving equalizer as a superpower to secure justice.

The possibilities are endless when we participate wisely and logically. The diversity of humanity is as vast and unique as a snowflake or sand on the beach contained within the singularity of the human species. It is also as fractional as snow or sand within the diverse universal existence of life and energy. The possibilities cannot be restricted to race or not being within our control. It has to be in our perspective and ideological context to evolve with knowledge presiding over social and religious conditioning.

Humanity is but a speck within the context of the natural synchronization of universal energy from the particle level, cosmic harmony of chaos, and innate vibrations of matter. In this context, can there really be any difference in humanity? There are none within the known universal existence. We can see it depends on the constraints of the sample size comparative to the totality of what it could otherwise be compared. So humanity mostly restrict humanity by the asinine classifications of relegation obscuring panoramic observations and tolerance by rejecting knowledge.

Humanity is a species that I imagine has no particular distinction when viewed by other species. Denying diversity is a delusional perspective even within the similarities of any racial subgroup. However, within our species, we insist on distinctions beyond the genealogy and anatomical similarities across humanity. To put it in further context, developing artificial intelligence infused with consciousness would expose the absurdity of our petty distinctions. Their artificial perspective would be puzzled by our simulated reality claiming differences in our species based on these arbitrary superficialities assigned to skin tone.

So, by extension, if you question someone else's differences, yours cannot be unquestionable by their perspective. Where an infringement occurs breaching someone else's ability to operate unimpeded, so has a violation occurred of ours. With that in mind, we must respect, if not celebrate, differences instead of a coerced merging of similarities. Still, the similarities cannot be ignored nor can their coexistence well beyond classification. So, avoid assigning fractional value on an excluded group diminished by selective biases of appearance as a metric of anything other than appearance.

The current genealogical impression may betray its ancestries by appearance but not its DNA. In this context, likeness, in principle, is the disparity in recognizing differences, both yours and others. But, it ignores historical facts, lineages, and beliefs. Classifications, racial identifications, and social regulations are undergoing a revolution of revelations regarding misconceptions and dubious practices. The fear to scrutinize has been lifted by the dissonance of disparities attributed to discredited beliefs and ideologies.

A humanitarian, geopolitical, economic, and religious shift liberating the painful truth of centuries of deceptions, authoritarian control, psychological manipulation, and intentional scarcity is revealed. The repatriation has traditionally been of lands and resources, but this time it will be the untethering of the minds of the masses. The deformity of social evolution's resulting awkward growing pains has expanded beyond the boundaries of its spell, breaching a new horizon of realization. This expansion of knowledge will unquestionably shake many beloved foundations and misconceptions.

The stale ideologies habitually observed no longer apply to the emerging reality of authentic free will. The free will to explore space outside our history and restrictions guided by our authentic internal compass expressing compassion as we would like to receive it. The racial, moral, and economic principles rooted in echoes of Roman society, religion, and exploitations are destined to erode, having reached the extent of this variation of its reincarnation. We must prevent the next variation by breaking free from its creeds and structures that are proving to be other than what we believe them to have been.

As a matter of consumption, we understand and often can see the effects on the body. However, not so much the consumption of the mind. As guardians of the mind, we too easily surrender the sanctity of our thoughts and beliefs to matters we have no understanding of. The banners of race, nationalism, and greed have amassed a tremendous toll upon humanity, whose veneer has worn thin. The army of humanity, not race or religion, in every corner of the world, has risen to challenge their regimes' oppressive suffocation of their freedom, equity, and sovereignty.

In many ways, this book is about hidden systems and mentalities engineered and programmed to reproduce a minion class unsuspecting of the puppet show in which we perform. The consequence of social engineering produces the desired control disguised in many different ways in various societies, countries, and thoughts. Nevertheless, the funnel leads to the same construct, a paradigm of rituals reminiscent of a shrouded time lagging the current reality.

The template lies in the independent inquisitive reevaluation of the concepts that bind our minds, controlling our actions. In all matters by applying reason and logic generates the best results minus the regret of impetuous indignation. By analyzing the content of the message, it should be impossible to be offended by gaining an understanding of its perspective. Being offended by ideas is a defense mechanism detecting something that must have touched a repressed truth.

Truth is born of exploration in all areas of life. It must be evaluated to hold its integrity. So, just as we risk being wrong, we must also risk being offended in pursuing truth. Ignorance, on the other hand, lounges wherever it finds no resistance. With that said, my goal was not to sugarcoat nor offend. On the contrary, communication facilitates understanding of difficult topics that, by silent misconception, may otherwise lead to greater discord.

So, let's put it on the table, out in the open for all to see in greater hopes of making progress and changes. With that said, understanding is preceded by evaluation and followed by acceptance. So, inquiring minds wonder, do we worship truth and knowledge or socialization and indoctrination? If we had the knowledge to discern the truth, would we reject it for the comforts of conditioning?

Truth and socialization, worship and indoctrination are polarities of knowledge. Life is a duality of physical information and abstract awareness. Awareness is the singularity of consciousness. It reveals the knowledge that one is everything and all is one. It is a dichotomy of footsteps in the dark or journeys in the light. What we are told is the simulation of someone's reality projected upon us which we do not question.

However, what we are mindful of is our simulation of reality projected outwardly on others. Our reality is a fractional and dimensional authentication of our perspective actualized. Perception makes polarity and duality existential experiences but divergent manifestations of realistic paradigms or states of awareness. The basis of belief creates a tangent or trajectory of subsequent events reflective of the seminal impression.

Racism's foundational replication is by this process. But how can we expect others to do better when they know better when we will not? When we will not entertain some of our long-held beliefs as flawed or deceptive, this makes us susceptible to racism and worst? Curiosity and examination should not ignore or exclude any inquiry or incriminating results. Limits to our perception create the boundaries of our perspective. We can create it, or it is created for us as our operating system.

Essentially changing the programming to change the system's function and output requires rejection as the liberating wedge between being tricked or tricking ourselves. Do not be ashamed of being woke, for sleep is the state of slumber where unconsciousness is required. In our state of slumber, we replicate and perpetuate inferiority by our beliefs insidiously conditioned, preventing us from a state of awareness and the required actions. When unconscious we cannot resist.

Any nightmares of the spiritual realm poses a taboo and limited psychological realm reflecting the interpretation of its essence correlated to beliefs accumulated and assembled in society by history and ritual. This social ideology produced our understanding applied to reality or external reception and filtering pertaining only to them as our racial perceptions and experiences. The narrative is much larger and the method is much deeper.

So it will continue until we reject our complicity, which sedates our psychological progression by ambiguously embedded obedience, insecurity, and conformity. Mechanisms of belief systems such as religion, sexism, and economics encourages a subservient existence and accusation of inferiority that naturally transmutes to mortal and moral superiority as above but not as below in the context of the closer the similarity, the more superior and self-righteous.

These shallow determinations of validation are naïve of the universal functions by denying we are but a speck in time of energies or objects in transit transitioning through states of rebirth. It is yearnings from a perspective juggling the God principle to either seek God or be God-like. The seekers are the servants while the imposters are the masters to be worshipped and obeyed. In a world with a multitude of Gods and religious paths to seek God the singularity of belief in a spiritual plane transcends the differences.

Consequently, supernatural curiosities and infatuations not-withstanding, the polarity of our limitations to the infinity of our beliefs defines the commonality of our human experience. So the differentiation is the ruse to insinuate superiority which perpetuates itself. It exist as a benefit to itself extended beyond the parameters of its controlled self-comparison. Not as a distinction apart from itself but always within its self-definition, justification, and stub-bornness.

Again inquiring minds wonder, can an acute understanding supplant faulty comparisons and fallacies of validation? Are we too far be-yond the point of no return and has time and history ran its course for the ultimate determination to become more unbearable than un-speakable. History can be unkind and time unforgiving as it has been many times regarding many past great civilizations that have refused to correct its ills.

So, suppose the residual discussions incidental to slavery, racism, and discrimination generate a better understanding applied to a transformative realization? In that case, some good can still come or by rejection no good can follow. The discussion of racism is a by-product and purposefully coincidental to the discussion of the im-plications that gave it breath. Consider the skeletons of ideologies on which the flesh of dysfunction rests for the message and not by emotions.

Given consolidated determination and an unrestricted mentality shifted from a dark past emerges a bright future and any sliver of hope humanity has at the roulette wheel of survival. Hopefully, these contents will be considered for the intent with which it was written for I write to the point without offense intended. Otherwise, I have written what I have written, but I have given you my thoughts intended to stimulate yours. To stir not emotions, to re-strict not thought, but to encourage curiosity and exploration.

There are many hidden messages and knowledge within the limits of these articles. Your independent research and sources of verification extends to the curiosity and depth of your knowledge, imagination, and understanding invested. Primitive ideology is relative and subjective but stubbornly concealed. Evolution is adaptation for survival chronicled by the passage of time, circumstances, and events.

Perspective unlocks the universe for time to bear witness. Forming your own opinion in the revelation of knowledge and exploration is the height of awareness. So, please explore the expansion of solutions, ideologies, and socializations without blinking. The clarity of awakening is blinding. The Anthem of evolution's genesis is in our rebirth in knowledge from the glare of ignorance.

In the beginning, you were warned to check your feelings at the door before entering but not your thoughts and analysis. However, don't forget to claim your feelings on the way out. Then again, probably not if it restricts your thoughts. Reality is the one you have selected. The one that selects you is a virtual hologram whose theme is a ball of confusion without the rhythm, only the temptations.

Beware not to sacrifice your life, not in death, but in obsessive devotion to ideologies, systems, rituals, and misconceptions. The source of knowledge is curiosity. Therefore, forge your perspective by expanding your understanding and universal analysis objectively applied. The possibilities are more numerous than the variations of the human species or as narrow as a peep hole. Perspective can be a peep hole voyeur of life or an eternal explorer confined only by our pursuit of internal awareness of external understandings.

Appendix

These systems issue only three models. Choose one or be assigned one, clone, archetype, or prototype. The purpose of the book is exposing the systems, rituals, and programming for you to build, expand, or reaffirm your perspective and not for me to justify mine. Anyone can justify their perspective but can they disprove yours? Only your curiosity can prove or disprove your perspective or perceptions.

Diligent curiosity to seek knowledge expands the quest to exhaust different sources and perspectives to interpret with thoughtfulness the extenuations of beliefs and ideologies that shape our sociologies and perceptions as a matter of blind complicity. I will not insult you by telling you what or how you should or should not think, behave, believe, or have faith according to my orientation. I encourage you to define yours.

The source of your knowledge is you and will expand from your unique position to unflinchingly identify your own sources. This is my conveyance of perspectives, perceptions, and opinions but not an appendix of persuasions or index of incidental topics. The concepts journey is crucial not the explanations supporting them. Prototypes create the way, archetypes select a way, and clones duplicate in a prescribed way. Your accumulation is ultimately your composition. Your explanations and justifications awaits your curiosity and exploration from the prototype of your unique ecliptic disk expanding the radius of your universe and orbit of consciousness.

www.ingramcontent.com/pod-product-compliance
Lightning Source LLC
Chambersburg PA
CBHW060848120626
46553CB00001B/8